LEVINAS'S RHETORICAL DEMAND

D1714402

RONALD C. ARNETT
Foreword by Algis Mickunas

LEVINAS'S RHETORICAL DEMAND

The Unending Obligation of
Communication Ethics

SOUTHERN ILLINOIS UNIVERSITY PRESS   CARBONDALE

Southern Illinois University Press
www.siupress.com

Copyright © 2017 by Ronald C. Arnett
All rights reserved
Printed in the United States of America

20 19 18 17   4 3 2 1

Cover illustration: drawing of Emmanuel Levinas by David
Deluliis; used with permission of the artist.

Library of Congress Cataloging-in-Publication Data

Names: Arnett, Ronald C., 1952– author.
Title: Levinas's rhetorical demand : the unending obligation
    of communication ethics / Ronald C. Arnett ; foreword by
    Algis Mickunas.
Description: Carbondale : Southern Illinois University Press,
    [2017] | Includes bibliographical references and index.
Identifiers: LCCN 2016031744 | ISBN 9780809335695
    (paperback) | ISBN 9780809335701 (e-book)
Subjects: LCSH: Lévinas, Emmanuel. | Communication—
    Moral and ethical aspects. | BISAC: LANGUAGE ARTS &
    DISCIPLINES / Rhetoric. | LANGUAGE ARTS & DISCIPLINES /
    Communication Studies. | PHILOSOPHY / Ethics & Moral
    Philosophy.
Classification: LCC B2430.L484 A76 2017 | DDC 194—dc23 LC
    record available at https://lccn.loc.gov/2016031744

Printed on recycled paper. ♻

Contents

Foreword

Algis Mickunas
OHIO UNIVERSITY AND VILNIUS UNIVERSITY

This text is filling a "credibility gap" in communication that, in the main, is left unattended. To the credit of the author, Professor Arnett, the choice for this filling is the ethical principle of Levinas. The term *principle* does not suggest a specific dogma but instead a disclosure of a domain overlooked by most ethical theories. To explicate this domain, the author asks the reader to follow Levinas as he debates and counters major modern thinkers concerning human encounters. The reader should not look for an account of the nature of reality or, for that matter, the cosmos; rather, the concern is with human life, the ways of human relationships, and human "duty" and "responsibility" with respect to each other. In the text Professor Arnett mentions various phases of the life of Levinas, including his interest in Russian literature, phenomenology, and, above all, biblical studies. While biblical studies is constantly present throughout the text, a brief introduction to the main trends in Russian literature and aspects of phenomenology, relevant to understanding Levinas's encounter with "the other," is in order. In order, too, is touching on the great debate that seemingly disclosed the very foundations of Western philosophy, the philosophy of Being explicated by Heidegger. This kind of introduction is in the spirit of the author, who introduces literary texts to make the case for Levinas.

Not all traditions are philosophical in the Socratic mode—stating a position, arguing for it and allowing counterarguments to contest such a position, and having that lead to further contestations and proposals of other positions. In some traditions, main concerns are explicated in stories either by writers or by oral transmission. Russian thinking was hardly a matter of professional philosophers but is best expressed in Russian literature, which deals with profound metaphysical, social, economic, and moral issues. The term *literature* is, accordingly, not restricted to stories and novels but extends to essays on topics ranging from metaphysics to revolution. Given such an understanding, it is possible to trace an invariant in Russian literature that was available to Levinas and is still available to us. The invariant is understood to be transcendental, calling for a fulfillment in the Russian lifeworld, extending from the eighteenth to the twentieth centuries. The struggle constituting this calling was and is between the immediately lived, but not thematized, intentionality toward *intrinsic human worth*, expressed in sacral and secular modes of writing and the world of traditional and Westernizing *values*. To understand this intentionality it is necessary to make a phenomenological distinction between constitution and construction. Constitutive intentionality opens up or discloses an awareness that either can or cannot be fulfilled in a given lifeworld. The latter is a significant interconnection of all events and objectivities, including a self-interpretation of the subject as being in this lifeworld. It is given as self-evident and taken for granted that all events and objectivities in it are realities in their own right. For example, in the West and East it is granted that we live in an economic world where things, processes, and people have economic value. Whether we like it or not, we understand this world as our reality and cannot see any reason to doubt it—despite our complaints that this reality is unfair to some or even that it should be arranged differently. Even our scientific and technical achievements have the same value. What is crucial is the recognition of "value" as an invariant in this type of lifeworld.

The great Russian literatures faced this Westernization and "modernization" and hence were written between two lifeworlds: one that was maintained as an established tradition, the other as a construct of scientific and political enlightenments of the West. The former, the feudal-aristocratic, was deemed to be decadent, corrupt by some, and by others as spiritually superior although in need of revisions, specifically its serfdom. The latter, the Western, while partially unknown and alien, was regarded as the bearer of ideas that would transform Russia and bring it into its proper place as a European nation. While numerous texts categorize Russian writers in terms of Slavophiles and Westernizers, idealistic and materialistic, theocentric and secular, our task is to disclose the lived awareness that comprises invariants that are not posited as objects of reflection. Rather, they involve a tacit awareness in terms of which all judgments are made, whether such judgments are phrased theologically, politically, ethically, socially, or economically. In this sense, the appearance in Russia of Western enlightenments brought in various systems, from romanticism through idealism to materialism, but the invariant of such systems is what has to be understood in order to disclose the Russian challenge to the European Enlightenment and its own tradition. A point worth emphasizing is this: *Russian writers occupy a point of crisis between two worlds, such that the crisis transcends both and is a critique from a transcendental position.* But to understand these literatures it is necessary to offer a brief sketch of one basic level of enlightenment. This level is accepted by all major figures of the twentieth century, even if not explicitly noted. Thus Heidegger's temporal horizon of the possibilities of Being belongs to the modern lifeworld and assumes the priority of the will, as articulated in his rector's speech.

While the process of valuating events in favor of human "needs" was briefly indicated—that is, various reductionisms of the human to biochemistry, genetics, and mechanics—the lived awareness subtending this process intends an objectivity that is unique to enlightenment. One level of this objectivity is designed to be accessible to quantification, and hence it has to be measurable homogeneous matter. This design, of course, is meant by a specific exclusion of the entire perceived world and hence is in no wise accessible to experience. Yet covered by this homogeneous materiality as an intentional object is another intended objectivity: *temporal possibility.* The lived awareness that intends such an objectivity is an empty will, prior to the question of its being free or determined. It is to be noted that the term *temporal* does not suggest "being in time" but rather an open horizon without any specific ontological locus. Hence any temporal location would have to be established within such a horizon. If we attend to the language of enlightenment to date, we shall note that, subtending the question of "reality," there is a prior discourse concerning the "conditions for the possibility of reality." Such discourse is premised on the first lived intentionality of empty temporal possibility. It opens a horizon of possible intentions and their fulfillment, requiring a second constitution of objectivities: possible valuations of what the will intends as valuable for us. This is the enlightenment's alpha and omega: empty temporal possibility and its temporal fulfillment by all that we value as our mode of final being. Both Marxism and capitalism offer the same intentionality. The intentionality of fulfillment of possible valuations as temporal does not lead to perceptual awareness, since the latter, in its naturalistic mode, is quite limited and merely qualitative. Hence the fulfillment requires a constructive intentionality that can establish possible conditions for possible reality. One minor aspect for this establishment is the shift of reason to instrumental rationality whose task is to calculate what reality is valuable for us and then calculate the conditions for how such reality shall be achieved. Values, in this sense, are calculations of possible results realized solely as material. To achieve any value, the human has to be reduced to a system of interests, needs, desires, power, and all must act aggressively against others to fulfill such wants. Indeed, language itself is split into numerous technical discourses. No doubt, the Russian Westernizers took this type of instrumental intentionality for granted but also recognized that *values signify a field of instrumental connections and are not ends in themselves.*

The issue of temporal value possibilities is the driving force of enlightenment at this level. Transcendent or eternal possibility is abolished; hence temporality is the pressure that demands a prolongation of our temporal existence. There is no other option; being temporal, we want to live as long as possible and hence the frantic rush for the latest technologies that promise to protract our lives. Such technologies have become equivalent to the value of life and death. The public domain is an arena for the struggle for life itself, and any means can be used, whether lying, killing, or wars; all will do as well, as long as they promise to keep us safe to ensure our continuity at any price. All the changing technical inventions promote other inventions as values of life: we want to go on. Thus the political shift to dramatic conservativism. The latter is a promise, by whatever means, to guarantee our security, safety, protection, and continuity, as long as we surrender our freedoms to participate in the public domain and to engage in public dialogue. In other words, the public domain, as the condition for other democratic institutions, is no longer maintained, despite all the rhetoric about democracy and its "values." We are closer to a Hobbesian world than to that of Locke and above all Kant. The intentionality of enlightenment has worked itself out to reveal its truth two centuries later. Indeed, we are living this intentionality as an awareness of our lifeworld in such a way that while speaking of democracy, rights, equality, and freedoms, we intend such a world as a struggle for temporal and technical continuity. Thus all is valuable that enhances this continuity—and purely materially. *The lifeworld of the Enlightenment that Russia encountered consisted of possible construction of iron, coal, cement, chemistry, biology, and physiology.* The human acquired a material value as producer, maker, a *Homo laborans*, a man of science and ultimately a technocratic functionary in a system of conditions and results that became the Soviet model.

The interpretation of the world in terms of value did not escape Russian thinkers. Realizing the vast sweep of scientific reification of all spheres of life, including, according to Khomyakov, Hegelian idealism, Russia is in a position to offer spiritual values. While the latter may stem from theological understanding, they are primarily found, according to Kireyevsky, in the primacy of a community of the faithful whose tacit and intuitive awareness subtends the Western rationalistic abstractions. It is this constant reappearance of the background intuition that escapes value construction and that demands—without becoming thematic—an evaluation of all values, whether they are rationalistic or materialistic. Indeed, there is a lived awareness that intends a given, although not directly articulated, presence expressed in terms of Russian superiority in morality and spirituality and is offered as a salvation for the decadent, juridical, bourgeois, materialist West. As we shall see, this "superiority" is not offered only by Slavophiles but also by modernizing Westernizers. Tacitly lived, this presence is central to the Russian crisis and offers a transcendental awareness that is in a position of illuminating and questioning the legitimation of two possible lifeworlds. An immediate difference between values and the tacit intuition of this presence is that the former are constructs while the latter is regarded as given, although covered over by faulty social, political, metaphysical, and even scientific preconceptions.

Values and valuations have to be evaluated, not by their own self-proliferating constructions, but by a discovery of a constitutive awareness that is correlated to a tacitly lived presence offering the possibility of performing a suspension of commitment to a given lifeworld. Instead of constructed values, this presence can be called *intrinsic human worth*. As we shall see in Russian literature, such worth cannot be constructed, and it appears in the background of all values and valuations. It also provides a background on which every lifeworld can be regarded in its essential morphology and questioned concerning its legitimacy.

This is to say that a given lifeworld's limits are exhibited from a transcendental lived awareness that demands "more" and does so on the basis of discovering what this more is. The constitution of this more—*intrinsic human worth*—is not a construction but a disclosure of an intentionality whose meant "objectivity" as *human worth* is present as absolute. We should not despair while using the term *absolute*; after all, in all awareness there are such terms denoting a pregiven *arche* whose denial is its unavoidable inclusion. This is to say, to attempt to negate an arche is to include it in the very negation and hence to comprise its absolute affirmation. We shall call this the *principle of self-inclusion* and venture a claim that only transcendental phenomenology is in a position to function within this principle.

A Crisis of a Lifeworld

Confronted with the inadequacy of feudalism and aristocratic rule and the emergent *iron age*, Russian writers, beginning with figures such as Turgieniev and Chernichievski, moving through Kineyevsky, Belinsky, Herzen, Bakunin, Lavrov, Mikhailovsky, Tolstoy and Dostoievski, Berdyaev, Shestov, Lossky, and all the way to Gogol, had no choice but to place themselves *between the two lifeworlds—the old and the new—and thus to locate their writing at a point of crisis*. There must be a unique situation that allows us to extricate ourselves from our lifeworld and to raise the question of its legitimacy. That such a question can arise means that we rise to lived awareness, which no longer belongs to a lifeworld in which we live. The fulfillment of our taken-for-granted intentions and the categories to which they correlate—including the numerous value gradations, the epistemic understanding—leave out the legitimating question given in lived awareness that something is not fulfilled, something that no value can account for: *intrinsic human worth*. To reach the latter, the lived awareness must suspend the lifeworld and explicate the access to the transcendental lived awareness that correlates to intrinsic human worth and demands legitimation of the lifeworld in which one has so far lived in full belief and affirmation. The lived awareness and its intention toward human worth asks whether the lifeworld offers any fulfillment and confirmation of this intention. At this level of awareness the categorical and epistemic understanding fails, and an existential question of action becomes preeminent: can I act as I have always acted and fulfill the intention of intrinsic human worth? The question embodies such requirements as honor, honesty, dignity, the other; and through the other, self-respect and justice. If honor, honesty, dignity, and respect cannot be fulfilled in human activities, then the legitimacy of this lifeworld is placed in absolute question, revealing at the same time the awareness of *absolute human worth*. It is at this juncture that the transcendental lived awareness in Russian literature recognizes that the world of values, constructed by the Enlightenment and by the world of decadent aristocracy, requires evaluation as to the adequacy of the values for human worth. Such a question is one of principle that required an essential delimitation of the constructs of both worlds and whether they could be adjusted, discarded, or become open to the absolute requirement of transcendental awareness of human worth. We are in a position now to attempt our venture into lived awareness that is led by the intention correlated to human worth and place ourselves at the point of crisis.

Dostoievski gives back the key to paradise because the ruler of paradise values equally an innocent child and a decadent master. For the master, a favorite dog is more valuable than a child, and in the lifeworld of feudal lords this is an acceptable standard. Dostoievski's rejection is an affirmation of human worth for its own sake. He will accept eternal damnation but will not accept a lifeworld in which crimes against children are permitted. He raises an absolute question: is life worth living in a world where such a degradation of human worth is a standard, sanctioned and accepted even by the highest authority? Indeed, the entire corpus of Dostoievski's writings is a striving to disclose this awareness. In *The Brothers Karamazov*, the main figure, Karamazov Dimitri, insults and degrades an impoverished elderly captain who no longer has any social value; yet toward the end of the story, Dimitri attempts to apologize by offering the captain money. Impoverished as he is, the captain refuses to be bought and thus degraded again. He reveals his human worth as being above any price, above any social value, and "compels" Dimitri to recognize his own human worth in the face of the other and his nobility, dignity, and honor. In short, it is "illegitimate" to attempt to place a monetary value on human worth. It is telling that Dimitri recognizes his own degraded state by first recognizing the other's human worth in the presence of the captain, who, while having no social value, is acting honorably, nobly, and truthfully, revealing as the other to Dimitry that he too must accept his own human worth. Across Russian literature appears something given to awareness that is akin to Kant's *thing in itself that possesses no purpose and no value but is to be respected unconditionally*. While enlightenment opened up an entire level of constructs called values and announced that the thing in itself is unknowable, Russian literature is intent on showing that any question of legitimation of a given lifeworld discloses a transcendental constitution of human worth as *the thing in itself.*

This is where the initial formation of Levinas's communicative ethics, based on the presence of the other, found a first encounter. For Russian writers, all the social degradations imposed by serfdom as a traditional value gradation reveal the common Russian acceptance of the absolute human worth. After all, it would be impossible to degrade others without recognizing the other as a possessor of intrinsic human worth. We cannot degrade a creature who, in its lifeworld, does not recognize a need to justify its deeds, to make a choice between two lifeworlds; in short, to call a dog *dog* is neither a degradation nor a negation of intrinsic worth. Only another person can be degraded on the basis of recognition of her human worth. This is to say, degradation, reduction, insult are possible only when we recognize her, and through her our own, worth, honor, and dignity. The degrading of others in an effort to elevate oneself is an indication of the worth of others, an indication of our anxiety in the face of the other's intrinsic human worth, her unavoidable height. Unable to withstand the other's human worth, we condemn her to death and thus prove that we are unwilling to admit our own self-degradation, our own crisis, and cannot withstand the dignity of the intrinsic human worth of another. The outcasts, the exiles to Siberia who have lost all social value, still strive to exhibit dignity, honor, respect and thus reveal the final human position for its own sake that cannot be abolished even when threatened by death. This is the Russian positive negativity: *even at the pain of death I shall say no to a lifeworld that does not allow human worth to be fulfilled*. This merely discloses the constitution of human worth as a *transcendental given that is beyond life and death*. This appears in extreme cases where the guards who manage prisons or concentration camps immediately condemn to death anyone who shows the other respect, dignity, and honor. Here is a recognition and a lack of honor and dignity in the guards who function as valuable servants of the state. This logic calls to the others to recognize the crisis in their lives, to legitimate the lifeworld in which they live, and to ask whether such a lifeworld fulfills their lived awareness of their intrinsic worth. This is to say, the very presence of the other who is aware of her intrinsic worth performs a tacit phenomenological bracketing and hence challenges a blindness inherent in this lifeworld. One can then raise a question whether such a lifeworld is worthy of one's intrinsic worth. In the case of Levinas, it is somewhat unsettling that he looked favorably on the Marxist revolution in Russia, which brought mass murder, not only in Russia but everywhere it spread, and the entire degradation of human life to "labor value."

Phenomenological Issues

Phenomenological arguments disclosed that despite metaphysical dualisms of all sorts, such as inner/outer or mind/body, which are still in vogue, the encountered other in direct awareness is given as "expressive." The other is present as sad, joyful, passionate, challenging, proud, defenseless, and erotic, but not as a physiological or empirical entity. Although expression is a self-presentation of corporeity, the expression is not locked within the limits of a physiological body. Every corporeal gesture, every movement forms a continuity, producing a variant of itself and prolonging itself into a schema. An adjustment to one expressive configuration is an adjustment to a series of like configurations where expressed desire can be desire expressed by anyone and in anything. If her expressed desire is a variant among other possible expressions of desire, then it is equivalent to and interchangeable with them. The particular expressions pass, but in passing they create a schema for continuation, proliferation, and repetition.

While inhering in individual gesture, a display of active corporeity, expression transcends the boundaries of anatomical individuality and captures others in its mood. This being captured by, being moved by, expression is well depicted in such phenomena as desire and eroticism, where one is transfigured, elevated, ennobled, and, at times, degraded. One basic way that the social communicative power of expression is depicted "in enlarged images" can be gleaned from myths. While all humans engage in rituals that appeal to all sorts of unseen powers, these are ineffective if they be no more than merely ideological constructs. Rather, they are an intensive concentration of expressive characteristics: they love, they hate, threaten with horrible punishments, and demand our passionate commitments and our bodily gestures of self-effacement and subjection. Mythological figures are depictions of expressive communication that goes beyond the location of such figures. Expressivity in myths pervades the universe. There is no dry, geometric space in bodily experience and communication; this aspect is seen in the depiction of mythical figures. When one is confronted by the expressive characterizations describing, for example, Aphrodite, one finds a description of bodily moods across all events and things. It is the tenderness of everything calling to enchantment, to embrace, and to sweet and breathtaking flow of all into all. It is an expression manifest across all things as attractive and harmonious. And she is contrasted to Artemis, the feminine. This goddess is the soul, the expression of wildness with its heights and depths, with her animals and tormenting beauty, with her rejecting look and maternal care, and her blood-lusting drive to hunt, her playfulness, tenderness, bright glory, inaccessibility, and horror—expressive characteristics.

What the mythical figures suggest is the generality and at the same time the individuality of expressive body. Its generality proliferates and can inhabit anything, can be manifest across the face of all events without being reducible to such events. Hence the mythical figures are depicted as transcending the characterization of things in their anatomical properties; yet as manifestations of expressivity, the figures are inner-worldly. In this sense, they are a way of capturing the expressive corporeal process without any reduction to anatomy or physiology. Such a process can appear everywhere: in the faces of statues, where the great utopian dreams of days to come are inscribed in the uplifted postures of the "revolutionary" classes; the victories shine from canvasses, tensed with fierce steeds and proud warriors, while the defeats are spread across the canvas in prostrate bodies—all corporeal expressions.

Corporeal expressivity, in brief, can assume any "embodiment," since it is not something called "interior" or subjective but rather directly present, inner-worldly, and yet transcendent of materiality. This transcendence is precisely what is capable of affecting us, although the expressive dimension is primarily the direct dynamics of an active, corporeal being. The affectivity is not an intentional act stemming from an interiority of a subject but a movement of expressivity that comprises the very sense of gestures and is transmitted through gestures, postures, and mobile face and limbs. This means that the immediacy of expression is not so much faced or confronted as participated in and lived through. It is like the "lively" tune that sends our limbs into a frenzy, or the Dionysian tragedy sending horror across the faces of the audience. The horror is a spontaneous expression of being moved, being gripped by a presence where what does the gripping and the being gripped are one. This response suggests that we are in constant communication with each other and with the world through direct participation in the excessive sensuality of ourselves and worldly events. These considerations prepared the ground for fuller understanding of erotic expressivity in social communication. These dimensions of expressivity are the first level of analyses of communicative participation with others so well articulated by the author's reading of Levinas wherein one faces the other and is immediately "called upon" to engage with and be for the other.

Levinas has argued that our primary interaction is not a transmission of information—with a sender, message, and receiver engaged in codification-decodification—but is contestation, disruption, irruption, surprise, aggravation, and pacification. The understanding of this interaction presupposes a difference between the ego that encounters the world in terms of possession, appropriation, and enjoyment, prescribed and limited by linguistic forms, and the self that is facing another human being. In facing the other, one encounters something in the world that one cannot appropriate, cannot make into an object, cannot reduce to some prescribed linguistic designation. The face of the other, its *epiphany*, resists any objectification and even subjectification. It is not the resistance of a solidity that would provoke my abilities but rather the diminishment of such abilities. It invites me to relate without evoking any power. The endlessness that speaks from the face of the other diminishes my power not because of, but despite, its defenselessness. For Levinas the unique power of the other unfolds precisely when, speaking objectively, the other is defenseless.

The presence of the other is a presence in communication, in saying. The saying contains the very force of the speaker who is the announcement, the *kerygma*. The saying is addressed to the other, not as a well-coded truth-functional proposition to be decoded, but as a proposal, as an opening of options for the other. In addressing the other, I am ready to be exposed, to be vulnerable. In this sense communication does not consist solely of the content to be communicated. It is possible only by an exposition of oneself and the other, with all the hesitations, bluster, and weaknesses. For the other I am to be read directly, full of risks, and for all to see and hear. This suggests one's carnality, one's affectivity and vulnerability. Carnality, at the outset, is directed toward the other, endures the other, and in being next to the other must bear a unique responsibility toward the other. This is what makes my singularity. The singular offers himself to the other in total vulnerability and without any guarantee of what results such an offer will yield. Such an offer is possible only if life is patient, a positivity that, despite breaks, resumes and insists. My response is an expression of my stance, packed with my perspective, attunement, and world. In the face of the other I become equally vulnerable, and this vulnerability extends to the carnal body, transforming the latter into sensuous, erotic solicitation. In the face of the erotic, the carnal does not hold its form; it is not an attitude taken toward some objective correlate to be appropriated for practical manipulation; rather, the corporeal posture "shifts" and becomes laden with ambivalences.

Yet erotic nudity does not interrogate, contest, or elucidate anything; it has no signifying power; it can uncover without disclosure. It pulsates with shifting allusions, teasings, direct solicitations, offering no lacks, no negativity as sources of signification in the face of absences. It is suggestive, in the face of which one's responsibility collapses, and the mobile face shifts to ardor, clouds over with ambivalences. It becomes uninformative and yet excessive. The communication is scattered in debris, fragments; words and signifying gestures turn to laughter, nonsense. This is not to say that for Levinas it is nothing but sweet tenderness; it is equally profaning. It finds itself faced by a presence that is exhibitionist, inciting, and amoral. Such erotic tenderness is rash, shameless, uncovering, and exposed without anything being comprehended. It is a secrecy that is violated without revelation. The carnal touch is without a will, a project, or a preestablished pattern. If there is an anxiety, it is not willed but vulnerable to every carnal shift. This is precisely the locus of pleasure, sensuality that is full of itself, and yet it is never content and constantly augments itself, not by its own interiority but by the pleasure and sensuality of the other. The profaning tenderness moves with the shifts of the other, by exposing to exposure for more without horizons, without past or future, with only the insatiable presence. While circulating surfaces, it is more intimate than any significant discourse, than any frankness can ever accomplish. It is a complicity that even misunderstandings do not abolish, since it was not established by significant understanding. Thus one cannot expect any information from this "language."

For Levinas, then, communication with another in a face-to-face encounter is an interruption of the continuity of phenomena, their mutual significative differential, a disturbance of a given order. In this sense, the totality of natural order, the sequence of infinite continuity, does not support the other. Alterity is a trace of disruption, of irruption into the presumably normal order of phenomena, and it is by virtue of alterity that this order cannot achieve closure, cannot become a system of univocal terms. And eroticism, for Levinas, is the very substance of another, where the erotic receptivity subtends the receptivity of singular, and field, sense data communicating vectors of significance; it is a carnal receptivity that pulsates with the pulse of radical alterity. Yet it is still a movement toward radical alterity even in the face of it being incomprehensible. In this, Levinas reaches the limit of intentionality and the languages that it supports. As Professor Arnett constantly points out, ethical communication for Levinas does not follow categorical imperatives but addresses us in a silent listening and hearing—adhering, and ad-hearing, us to an immemorial call of our responsibility.

Acknowledgments

I offer my thanks and gratitude to Duquesne University, the Spiritan community, my colleagues in the Department of Communication & Rhetorical Studies, and to Rita McCaffrey, who, as our administrative assistant, lends creative genius to the running of a department defined by otherwise than convention. I am deeply thankful to Susan Mancino, senior graduate research assistant, for her outstanding work on this project and numerous other works. This is the fifth book project that Susan has assisted. I will be forever grateful. Additionally, I am appreciative of Hannah Karolak for her research assistance as well as of my colleague Janie M. Harden Fritz for her thoughtful comments and generous use of her time in a careful reading of the manuscript. I am thankful that my professional colleague Michael Hyde has continued to nourish Levinas scholarship within the field of communication. I am honored that my former professor who introduced me to phenomenology, Algis Mickunas, wrote the foreword to this work. As a scholar and as a teacher, he inspires and brings light. Additionally, I offer thanks to Karl Kageff, editor in chief at Southern Illinois University Press; I rely on his love of ideas. SIU Press continues to be the publishing house that maintains a large number of my scholarly works. I am deeply appreciative. I offer thanks to our retiring president, Dr. Charles J. Dougherty, who made scholarly activity on this campus an expected norm, and for the heart of kindness and faithfulness manifested by our dean of the McAnulty College of Liberal Arts, Dr. James Swindal. I am thankful for the gracious scholarly support from Patricia Doherty Yoder and Ronald Wolfe. This book is one of a number of projects made possible by the Patricia Doherty Yoder and Ronald Wolfe Endowed Chair in Communication Ethics.

I conclude with my thanks to my student and colleague David DeIuliis, an outstanding student and an incredible artist, who provided the sketch of Levinas for the cover of this work.

I dedicate this work to John E. Murray Jr. (1932–2015), former president and chancellor of Duquesne University and a glorious jazz musician. As always, I dedicate this work to my family: my wife, Millie; my son, Adam, and his family, Karen and Kellan; and my daughter, Aimee, and her family, David, Alexa, Ava, and Aria.

LEVINAS'S RHETORICAL DEMAND

Introduction: Emmanuel Levinas and Communication Ethics— Origins and Traces

[T]he disturbance of the Same by the Other who is not absorbed into the Same—and who does not hide himself from the other— describes the awakening, beyond knowledge to an insomnia or watchfulness (*Wachen*) of which knowledge is but one modality.
—Emmanuel Levinas, *Entre Nous*

The other or the master whose own presence teaches the idea of transcendence is not "a midwife of minds." The other's teaching does not consist in making the ego rediscover the truths that are immanent to itself, which are inscribed within it for all eternity, and then only have to be contemplated with complete peace of mind. The hearing of the other's speech leads beyond the world to which vision limited me.
—Joëlle Hansel, "Ethics as Teaching: The Figure of the Master in *Totality and Infinity*"

Levinas's Rhetorical Demand: The Unending Obligation of Communication Ethics begins and concludes with one basic assumption—our responsibility to and for the Other has no demarcation or conclusion. Levinas offers a contentious response to rhetoric in *Totality and Infinity*.[1] His rejection of rhetoric, however, spurns an "originative I," or what has been termed an imperial, sovereign, or hateful self, that begins and ends with concern for and about oneself.[2] In contrast to such a self-focused perspective, one must respond to the rhetorical demands of the face of the Other that transports one from a visual ethic to an audio ethic of "I am my brother's keeper." Such an orientation with ethics results in an ultimate return to an obligation to a particular Other. Rhetorical demands commence in three separate and related origins: the face of the Other, an immemorial audio ethic, and the unique historical, social, and personal requirements inherent in one's unique response to another. These origins shape ethical identity by framing a communicative agent as a "derivative I."[3] Communication ethics, as outlined in this work, pivots on a rejoinder of responsibility to three rhetorical demands emanating from a human face, an immemorial ethical echo, and the historicity of a given moment. Together, these rhetorical demands shape a distinctive communication ethic responsive to the particulars of a person and situation.

Introduction

The "derivative I" is responsive to the Other, to an archaic audio ethic, and to the particularity of replies that address a given historical moment. Each answer transpires without the assistance of process, procedure, or rule book. These rhetorical demands comprise no single reaction; they reside within an anarchy of responses with no template for correctness or assurance of ethical action. The linking of ethics and anarchy announces the fulcrum concern of Levinas's project: "ethics as first philosophy" is a counter to self-righteousness, which finds excessive confidence in ideas imposed on another person. Levinas's ethics dwells in trembling actions as one attempts to act responsibly; such ethical deeds do not fuel the confidence of self-righteous assurance. Out of not knowing the correct behavior, Levinas's ethics assumes a basic existential face; one must act in obligation and responsibility to and for the Other with full recognition that ethics is an unending commitment devoid of perfection and a priori assurance. Levinas's project is theoretically challenging to everyday self-centered assumptions, while being simultaneously practical—communication ethics from a Levinasian perspective admits the challenge, ambiguity, and necessity of learning in the performative enactment of responsibility.

This entire project, *Levinas's Rhetorical Demand: The Unending Obligation of Communication Ethics*, is an interpretive turning to Levinas in order to discern ethical direction in rejoinder to particular stories and events. I explore a social artifact with communicative entanglements in each chapter that invites examination for its ethical implications from the corpus of Levinas's work. This interpretive exercise provides an example of a Levinasian perspective on communication ethics in responsive action. I chose the specific artifacts for investigation featured in each chapter due to their ethical ambiguity, which invites Levinasian insights.

I introduce this project with a section that emphasizes "Ethical Praxis," the doing of Levinas's mission of "ethics as first philosophy." The next section examines "The Rhetorical Demands of Imperfection," which acknowledges Levinas's disdain for rhetoric and explains why the term *rhetoric* is actually applicable to his otherwise than conventional perspective on human agency, described in this project as a "derivative I." I conclude this introductory chapter with "The Saying and the Said in Communication Ethics: A Relentless Responsibility," which frames a rationale for ending each chapter with a discussion of Saying (the revelatory insights of an ethical spiritual awakening) and Said (the temporally solidified insights from community and education that assist in the doing of ethics). The Saying announces a call. I am personally called forth. I am personally charged with responsibility that has no final clarity of template. The Said provides clarity and prescriptive description. Throughout Levinas's work, the Saying is interrupted by the Said and the Said interrupts Saying. Life, ethical life, a just life, requires the building of structures known as the Said and the responding to the unexpected through the Saying. Indeed, the Saying informs the Said, and the Said informs the Saying, each through temporal acts of disruption.

Levinas, from the vantage point of this author, is essential for those interested in communication ethics absent a code or metaphysical assertion. His ethical project is a unity of contraries[4] that debunks two contrasting and equally problematic perspectives on human responsibility. He counters the assumption that we must abandon ethics in a moment defined by continual disagreement about the nature of the Good. Additionally, Levinas rejects efforts to impose a single ethical template on persons and situations. From a Levinasian perspective, communication ethics is an existential burden enacted each day, by each person, and responsive to each moment through one's own uniqueness of responsibility to and for the Other.

Ethical Praxis

Levinas's ethics understands *communicative praxis*; this term, popularized by Calvin O. Schrag, outlines communicative action and decision making in the midst of everyday life.[5] Schrag lends insight into communication that is active and alive in social life between and among persons. Levinas provides a similar contribution; his ethic dwells within the ongoing fabric of social life with ethical direction and answers found in meeting the particularity of a given moment and person. This ethical perspective on the human condition addresses the uniqueness of persons and situations in the enactment of theory-informed action that continually propels a communicative agent intimately involved in the depths of human learning. In the case of Levinas, this perspective on ethics commences with the rhetorical demands of a human face, an immemorial ethical echo, and the distinctiveness of a historical moment that claims unique reactions from "me."

The practical application of Levinas's work is the trundle upon which this project rotates in explicating communication ethics as an unending obligation. This interpretive work on communication ethics proposes no answers; my task is to offer a performative illustration of Levinas's "ethics as first philosophy" in communicative praxis. Levinas suggests a communication ethic that advises without providing the false assurance of an a priori metaphysical diatribe on ethics. Communication ethics, understood within the genre of praxis, embraces responsibility without an ironclad blueprint for discerning truthful/ethical action.

To employ insights of Levinas, one must apply ideas about communication ethics without the assistance of a code or template; such is the reason this book does not conclude with a summary chapter. The interpretive focus of this venture is communication ethics discernment in interpretive response to Levinas's "ethics as first philosophy" and, as such, is intentionally void of final answers. Application, judgment, and uncertain conviction guide this endeavor—illustrating a communication ethic in action responsive to the praxis of responsibility inherent in Levinas's "ethics as first philosophy."

Levinas's project is an essential theoretical read that renders practical insight into this epoch of ethics in contention. His project navigates a world constituted by ethical ambiguity within an era delineated by narrative and virtue contention.[6] In this historical moment, in which ethical straight lines no longer subsist, if indeed they ever did, one must discern what it means to be responsible in particular situations and with particular persons without the succor of predetermined answers. The assertion of this endeavor is that this historical moment demands understanding ethics as fundamentally a communication activity in which there is no one answer. Responding to the face of the Other, listening to an immemorial ethical echo, and attending to the unique demands of a given historical moment are key communication ethics coordinates that announce the rhetorical demands of Levinas's corpus of concern about an awakened sense of responsibility for the Other.

Attending, listening, and responding to rhetorical demands for responsibility require engaging all means available to us in discerning communication ethics action. This sensitivity to figuring out an ethical direction demands a comprehensive liberal arts education. What one learns and understands affects ethical decision making. As stressed throughout this interpretive communication ethics project, Levinas's mission is far afield from a mystical, nonintellectual account of communication ethics. The defining characteristic of Levinas's work on responsibility lives in the praxis of meeting and responding to the particularity of ethical responsibility.

Levinas's work has practical application when met as an awakening guide about responsibility that refuses to shelter "me" from accountability in my actions to and for the Other. Throughout this interpretive description of communication ethics, I repeatedly stress Levinas's use of the term *awakening*.[7] Levinas's use of this term reflects the unique character of his story about the immemorial nature of ethics. The face of the Other awakens a person to this ancient ethical echo; this awakening is precognitive.[8] Levinas's conception of awakening remains in contrast to Kant's famous awakening from "dogmatic slumber" inspired by David Hume (1711–1776).[9] Obviously, Kant's understanding of awakening is not precognitive.[10] Levinas's conception of ethics as first principle pivots on this originative understanding of the awakening of responsibility.

Aristotle defined rhetoric as "the power of discovering all means of persuading by speech."[11] This work understands communication ethics from a Levinasian perspective with a similar commitment—an obligation to discover multiple means of understanding and ratifying communication ethics action in the depths of attentiveness to uniqueness and particularity. Education, community, family, friends, and institutions all lend stories and narratives that affect ethical decisions; they assist in discerning responsible action in the particularity of everyday life.

Levinas frames an understanding of ethics that is rhetorically dependent on exteriority. One learns from the rhetorical demands of the Other, an immemorial ethical echo, and the requirements of the historical moment. Additionally, exteriority guides learning from educational places and writings. All of the aforementioned forms of exteriority inform one's interiority of responsibility to and for the Other in a specific situation. Exteriority commences a "spiritual awakening" as one attends to the face of the Other.[12] This awakening shifts attention to a second stirring—to an audio immemorial ethical echo of "I am my brother's keeper." The third awakening from exteriority begins with the assumption of responsibility in responding to the particularity of a given moment and person without predetermined ethical presuppositions. Throughout this process of ethical attentiveness, there is the exteriority of learning; for Levinas, education is central to ethical action.

Levinas contends that the doing of ethics necessitates constant learning. The ideas and practices we bring in response to a particular ethical dilemma are the obligatory acts of responsibility that one must bring to a given person in a particular place. Levinas's project is not another form of mysticism; one can understand his project better as an ethical midrash composed of response to multiple voices.[13]

Claire Elise Katz articulates this perspective cogently in an essay titled "Levinas—Between Philosophy and Rhetoric: The 'Teaching' of Levinas's Scriptural References":

> When Levinas inserts a phrase from Isaiah or a reference to Cain, he has exposed us to his reading, a *midrashic* or rabbinic reading, of the Bible. He does not simply insert a phrase, but does so strategically. He places the reference where it fits with his description of the ethical relation and the call to human fraternity. Since the meaning of his references is not obvious, the reader needs to attend to the text and the reference to understand why he placed this particular reference within the context of a philosophical discussion.[14]

The midrash is a form of biblical interpretation fundamental in the Jewish biblical commentaries. These interpretations contrast; they do not "involve the privileged pairing of a signifier with a specific set of signifieds."[15] Levinas found philosophical, practical, and religious attraction to the interplay of ethics and ambiguity in ethical interpretation and action.

Levinas's project announces interaction between East and West with a spiritual awakening and an immemorial ethical echo implemented by education, community, and temporal rational decisions. His scholarly mission suggests a communication ethic that addresses a world of ethical ambiguity and a reality of constant strife in a postmodern world defined by narrative and virtue contention.[16] Levinas's ethical corpus is a Said of rhetorical demands that never silences the Saying of ethics within the particular. In his books, one does not discover well-defined answers; instead, Levinas describes the process of ethical awakening that demands paying attention to a call of responsibility; his position is contrary to an age that pursues reassurance in process, procedure, and consistency.

The power of Levinas's insights lives in ethical praxis that is rhetorically otherwise than convention. His understanding of ethics embraces the imperfection of the human condition and meets this reality with responsible communicative action and decision. The notion of imperfection is essential for understanding Levinas's rejection of self-righteousness. For Levinas, a communication ethic is not a code to follow or a structure to impose but rather a commitment to a relentless responsibility to learn and apply ethical learning amid a particularity of historical demands.

The Rhetorical Demands of Imperfection

Robert John Scheffler Manning, in a splendid interpretation of Levinas's ethics, repeatedly used the phrase "otherwise than convention."[17] There is little about Levinas's overall scholarly mission that fails to fall under this rubric. Levinas's disdain for rhetoric[18] ironically has rhetorical power. His "otherwise than convention" posture informs a creative and persuasive perspective in contrast to Being as first philosophy; Levinas offers an ethics that works rhetorically to demand responsibility from each one of us. The quality of meeting and response to the human condition hinges on answering a call to act responsibly. Each unique ethical reaction emerges without concrete assurance of the correct form of responsible action.

Throughout this project, I attend to Levinas's mission as a conceptual house for ethics with the following coordinates: the human face; a voice that is immemorial; attentiveness to the historical moment; and intellectual practices of formal and communal education that assist in ethical implementation. As stated previously, these coordinates are rhetorical demands that initiate human awakening to responsibility. Each coordinate gathers unique attention from a "trace" that calls "me" into inimitable responsibility.[19] I do not muster the courage to be responsible; the Other calls me. Ethical action demanded of each person in particular moments within existence defines communication ethics in action. An ethical trace represents a call to responsibility within an acknowledged realm of imperfection. The full-blown metaphysic of ethical behavior and action is absent. An ethical trace is more akin to a nagging sense that something requires my calculated attention and action, yet I am not sure of the correct ethical response. Imperfection constitutes an unending obligation that commences ever anew with a trace refusing sharpness of perception. An ethical trace resides in ambiguous responsibility that repudiates ease of interpretation or obligation.

The coordinates of an ethical dwelling inspired by Levinas's project tender no fundamental answers; the communication ethics building blocks are, however, clear—a continuing obligation to read, listen, and attend to responsibilities to and for others. Levinas suggests that communication ethics in action is discerned in the midst of life with a knowing refusal of imposition. If one demands a communication ethic in hopes of foisting answers upon persons and situations, then Levinas's "otherwise than convention" orientation provides no resolution. Communication ethics in action is fundamentally a social task. It is a performative enactment of the trace of the sacred that commences with the face of the Other. It is rhetoric otherwise than presupposed ethical correctness. Rhetoric refuses public adoption of a singular code.

The doing of communication ethics does not begin with the concrete face of a friend but rather with the impersonal face of another; such an understanding of communication ethics is stronger and far more fundamental than liking or familial association. The conception of communication ethics as a rhetoric of demands dwells not in a place or in a person but in the performative doing of responsibility. The contribution of Levinas to the study of communication ethics is not mystical or a corrective template of suitable behavior; it is recognition of the enactment of responsibility in everyday life, which eschews the temptation of an ideological warrant. Levinas's ethics rests in ambiguity of action and unending ethical obligation. Despite my own inadequacy, it is ultimately a "derivative I" called into responsibility without clarity of direction.

Perhaps the clearest approach to Levinas's undertaking is reflection upon situations where one feels keenly responsible without clarity of correctness or direction. In such moments one is responsible for another without conviction about proper action. Consider a friend who requires help, with you feeling inadequate to the task. Consider a young parent called into responsibility with no answers about how to assist. Consider the obligations of a teacher, religious leader, or business owner responsible for others, with each having a nagging recognition that "I" am not up to this task. Yet, in each case, the person moves forward in responsibility without prior promise of outcome. Such a conception of communication ethics requires a continual commitment to learning in order to assist another ethically; ethical behavior from this standpoint does not rest within self-righteousness; it seeks guidance in the midst of trembling recognition that one is responsible. Without efforts to discern temporally correct ethical actions, others will suffer. When one enacts ethics without guarantee of the acceptability of one's decision and with the press of troublesome reality, unexpected consequences are inevitable. One must answer a basic rhetorical demand generated from the view of communication ethics, "if not me, then whom?" Without the assumption that "I" am responsible, such a perspective cannot respond in a chaos absent of direction. Communication ethics from a Levinasian framework begins with ambiguity and concludes without complete assurance; this perspective on communication ethics is an ongoing enactment of human responsibility without an assertion of righteousness.

Levinas's rhetoric of imperfection assumes that answers dwell in an ambiguity of ethical directions; one must discern ethical action within the mud of everyday life. A person who identifies with

Levinas's "ethics as first philosophy" finds a sense of fuzzy direction through an unstoppable trace of ethics in the face of the Other that requires attentiveness to an immemorial ethical echo. The trace of ethics reminds one of a personal and unceasing responsibility and obligation. One cannot embrace clarity of conviction about action and outcome; obligation of responsibility centers on response to an ethical trace that demands that one read, study, listen, and attend to all that is around us in order to respond in assistance to another. When Thomas Merton was asked if he wanted to be a saint, he responded, "No."[20] I would have liked to talk to him about such an answer from a Levinasian perspective. Merton understood the connection between imperfection and spiritual awakening. Such an insight drives Levinas's project. This conception of communication ethics must forgo the expectation of exactness and clarity of conclusions because such behavior reifies ethics and dishonors the task of genuine responsibility. For Levinas, there is one penultimate rhetorical demand—to ready oneself for ethical action and application in response to the particular. Levinas paints a picture of a person doing communication ethics who has the conviction of responsibility intertwined with a refusal to embrace self-righteous or self-appointed saintliness. Such ethical action dwells within the tension of the Said of responsibility and the Saying of revelatory discernment that is ongoing and unending.

This communication ethics endeavor rotates around the unity of contraries—the Saying and the Said. Imperfection and indeterminacy are natural consequences of the Saying and the Said interrupting one another. This unity of contraries does not permit complete reliance on the solidified or on the revelatory. The face is a Saying. The immemorial echo is a Saying. The demands of a given historical moment and the Other function as a Saying. All of the knowledge we bring to a given event in response to the Saying dwells within the Said of what we have learned and all that which shapes the environment. We ascertain knowledge in order to respond in our distinct manner of helpfulness and inadequacy. Ethical action morphs into the Said of performance, which gives way once again to the power of Saying, which becomes the clarity of Said. A thoughtful colleague of mine in theater questioned the use of the term *performative* tied to Levinas's ethics, stating that theatrical performance should remain invisible. My response was that ethical action is a unity of Saying and Said.

It is performative (visible within the realm of the Said) in that we take public responsibility for the consequences and, in addition, the behavior requires intellectual consideration in order to address the unique rhetorical demands of a given historical moment (a creative retort derived within the revelatory power of Saying). For Levinas, this combination of Saying and Said moves ethics far afield from a mystical discernment.

Levinas's ethics embodies a lack of assurance that renders an ironical form of guarantee—I am responsible, which requires learning and preparation for ethical responses with no end to obligation. For example, when I spoke with a student who was fearful of taking initiative due to concern about making mistakes, I used Levinas's conception of Saying and Said in a discussion of learning and the risk of existential tests of action. The student, in the beginning of a venture, constantly heard the Saying of another activity. The new undertaking encouraged walking away from the first task without completion; the student wanted to live within the revelatory power of Saying, which makes constant shifting of attention mandatory. To follow the call of Saying alone makes it impossible to set one's feet on real ground and respond to what is before us. The student repeatedly stated to himself, "What if I make a mistake? I refuse to commit myself to one project; it may go haywire." In response to my student, I stated that mistakes require completion in order to discover that they are wrong. A mistake given the opportunity to mature into a Said offers the possibility of examination and learning, which gives rise to further revelatory insights of Saying. No one can learn if avoidance of completion makes testing of ideas and directions impossible. Levinas's ethics does not repose on the whim of perfection; it flourishes in the enactment of thoughtful action that requires public accountability. Life enjoyed, not feared, permits completing mistakes (the Said), which lends insight into ethical shifts and change of revelatory Saying. Such a perspective on communication ethics is void of neurotic guilt and requires continual discernment within social existence[21]—ethics without risk is an ironical totalization of Saying that refuses to take a stand.

Think of a person who demands human perfection and rebuffs acknowledgment of mistakes. Such a person demands life within the Saying of revelatory abstraction; this perspective declines permission to plant one's feet in a single location and make decisions that must bear public testing. One must articulate the Said of completion inclusive of potential mistakes in order to figure out what is temporally suitable or otherwise. Mistakes complete the Said by offering a trace of a revelatory Saying that suggests a path "not yet" followed. When asked to identify the most important element of a life of faith in the church, Dietrich Bonhoeffer responded with a public admission: recognition of sin within the church is necessary as one finds a reason for the importance of faith as a narrative form of guidance.[22] Bonhoeffer's comment suggests that communication ethics is not a home of perfection; it is better understood as a responsive dwelling from which mistakes occur that unleash a trace of insight that propels novel Sayings of innovative directions.

Increasingly we reside in a world that wishes to eliminate risk, chastising those who make a temporal choice of an erroneous path. For Levinas, mistakes and responsive decisions house the insights of the revelatory/the Saying. Completed mistakes permit a trace of the Saying to move one differently. I conclude this emphasis on the interplay of Said and Saying related to imperfection with a retelling of a favorite story associated with then president and later chancellor of Duquesne University, John E. Murray Jr.

Early in my career at Duquesne University, a departmental mistake arose. I no longer remember what the gaffe was, but the president brought me into his office and asked, "How much money do you need?" I said, "Money for what? Money cannot fix this." He then explained that the only time to have a party is when a mistake arises. The president was a glorious jazz musician and successful attorney who understood the power of mistakes displayed via attentiveness to the Said, which simultaneously houses new insights within a trace, insights that energize the Saying of novel comprehensions.

In the performative act of the Saying, Levinas discovers a communicative reminder. There is something more powerful than mistakes or even death; it is the face of the Other. The Saying of communication ethics is more formidable than human error—the trace of an ethical Saying reconfigures a person's responses. Perhaps willingness to grasp mistakes most often illuminates a trace of the Saying. How else is one to explain Levinas's lifelong commitment to ethics? He lost all but his immediate family to the atrocities of the Holocaust, and then he stressed the face of the Other as the original site of ethics. He responded to Martin Heidegger's emphasis on tool with a contrary emphasis on enjoyment.[23] Levinas reminds us that, in the face of mistakes, conceptual and tragic, meeting life with joy in our learning is an existential and ethical mandate. Even in the heart of horrors and barbarities, one finds traces of a revelatory Saying that transform a community and the world—such is the power of Levinas's insights understood as a communication ethic.

The Saying and the Said in Communication Ethics: A Relentless Responsibility

In this interpretive and responsive project, I offer the reader a brief outline of the chapters that compose *Levinas's Rhetorical Demand: The Unending Obligation of Communication Ethics.* In each chapter I frame a communicative artifact that announces ethical quandaries and issues. I ask the reader to follow my particular attending to each artifact with the goal of explicating the applicability of Levinas's scholarly mission about ethics. After establishing the event under analysis, I turn to Levinas's corpus, sometimes doing an examination of a given idea responsive to his major works, other times turning to a series of articles or a book from Levinas's productive labor in order to uncover points of ethical application and insight. The goal of this enterprise is to expound Levinas's ethical undertaking, openly admitting the brilliance of his understanding of "ethics as first philosophy." I conclude each application chapter with interpretive suggestions for communication ethics centered on the theme of the unity of contraries—the Saying and the Said. Some of the examined events emerge directly from Levinas's life, while others are events of ethical ambiguity for which I contend Levinas offers ethical understanding.

The following chapter titles disclose the scope of the social artifacts that guide this project. Chapter 1, "Primordial Gesture: The Difficult Freedom of Communication Ethics," outlines the originative nature of communication ethics and the manner in which communication scholarship gestures toward this primordial phenomenon of responsibility. Chapter 2, "Footprints and Echoes: Emmanuel Levinas," details interpersonal footprints within the events of Levinas's life. Chapter 3, "The Commencement of Responsibility: The Enigma of the Face," discusses the face of the Other as a primal site of ethics.

Chapter 4, "Proper Names: Saying, Said, and the Trace," explores the interplay of these central terms in Levinas's *Proper Names*. Chapter 5, "The Impersonal and the Sacred: Igniting Personal Responsibility," considers the intimate linkage between the impersonal and the sacred. Chapter 6, "Imperfection: Ethics Disrupted by Justice—*The Name of the Rose*," explains justice as explicated in Umberto Eco's *The Name of the Rose*. Chapter 7, "Possession and Burden: Otherwise Than Murdoch's Information Acquisition," details the problematic of information acquisition in the case of Rupert Murdoch and the *News of the World*. Chapter 8, "The Ethical Parvenu: Unremitting Accountability," examines the famous Davos debate between Martin Heidegger (1889–1976) and Ernst Cassirer (1874–1945), with attention to a lasting lament expressed by Levinas as a result of the conference. Chapter 9, "Heidegger's Rectorate Address: Being as Mistaken Direction," expounds Heidegger's rector address at the University of Freiburg, which announces a "why" for the necessity of Levinas's project. Chapter 10, "Adieu to Levinas: The Unending Rhetoric of the Face," details the metaphor of the French *adieu*, which unites welcome and goodbye, announcing the power of the face of the Other over death. Communication ethics from the standpoint of Levinas is unending and unstoppable, refusing totalization.

Levinas's Rhetorical Demand: The Unending Obligation of Communication Ethics is a celebration of human responsibility and the admission of its unceasing ethical burden. This perspective on communication ethics counters perfection, self-righteousness, fascination with process and procedure, and the assurance of universal truth that beckons our implementation alone. This orientation to communication ethics is attentive to a unity of contraries, never landing on one standpoint without awareness of interruption emerging from another direction. The trace of ethics resides in a human face (an ethical optic) accompanied by an immemorial ethical echo (an audio ethic). Communication ethics is a tension of constant interruption of the Said by the Saying and the Saying by the Said. Disruption of confidence arises in the contentious interplay of ethics and justice, East and West, an "originative I" and "derivative I," and a certainty of obligation challenged by the uncertainty of ethical action. A Levinasian understanding of communication ethics is an invitation into an ethical anarchy that responds to the before, the beyond, and the "not yet" call of responsibility to and for the Other. Communication ethics is an unending obligation to respond to rhetorical demands of the face, an ancient ethical voice, and the historical moment, ever attempting to learn by acting responsibly to and for the Other. Levinas is known for this commitment; however, his project cannot be explicated as an ethical template. The Other is the site for ethics, and justice always includes those not central to a given conversation—they cannot be forgotten. Justice does not permit one's own life to be forgotten in the midst of this ethical obligation.

CHAPTER I

Primordial Gesture: The Difficult Freedom of Communication Ethics

As if we should present a front against this Third World ravaged by hunger; as if the entire spirituality on earth did not reside in the act of nourishing; as if we need to salvage from a dilapidated world any other treasure than the gift of suffering through the hunger of the Other, a gift it none the less received. "Of great importance is the mouthful of food" says Rabbi Johanan in the name of Rabbi Jose b. Kisma (Sanhedrin 103b). The Other's hunger—be it of the flesh, or of bread—is sacred; only the hunger of the third party limits its rights; there is no bad materialism other than our own. This first inequality perhaps defines Judaism. A difficult condition.
—Emmanuel Levinas, *Difficult Freedom: Essays on Judaism*

In moments of awe, things "speak" in mysterious ways. The experience is humbling. It is a time of wonder. What does this mystery mean? What should one do? For the religious Jew, wonder "is the state of our being asked," the state where one . . . is acknowledged.
—Michael J. Hyde, *The Call of Conscience: Heidegger and Levinas, Rhetoric and the Euthanasia Debate*

Emmanuel Levinas's project of "ethics as first philosophy" evokes a communication ethic that embraces a "difficult freedom" of ethical demand without accompanying assurance of a stipulated program of action.[1] For instance, Levinas repeatedly stresses the "nonreciprocal"[2] nature of human meeting and responsibility, which gives performative life to the difficult freedom of communication ethics carried forth without reward of mutual benefit. I contend that Levinas's project describes the originative form of communication ethics communicated through an archaic ethical voice that echoes before and beyond time with the task of charging my present situation with the demand of responsibility for a particular Other. Communication ethics commences with an immemorial ethical echo promoted by a primordial gesture that initiates within the human face. Communication ethics is a primordial gesture to and in response to the Other.

Introduction

Levinas's project of "ethics as first philosophy" is an ongoing response to three commands: (1) attentiveness to the face of the Other, which propels one to a (2) commanding immemorial ethical echo, "I am my brother's keeper," which then (3) returns one to a particular Other with a charge of responsibility that is void of ethical formula and any sense of self-righteous assurance. Levinas's project embraces the proximity of the face that transports one from a visual ethic to an audio ethical echo that articulates an immemorial ethical obligation of responsibility, demanding engagement in discerning appropriate behavior via reasoning, thinking, and reflective action. Levinas's project moves from an ethic of optics (the face of the Other) to an audio ethic (an archaic commanding charge) and then returns one to a particular Other with an obligation without assurance of righteousness of decision and action.

This chapter pivots on the notion of primordial gesture, an ethical sign that is before and beyond time. My contention is that Levinas's phenomenology begins with attentiveness to primordial gestures that are both optic (the face) and audio (an ethical echo). In this chapter I explore ethics as a communicative first gesture, briefly examining the profundity of gesture for understanding sociality; this perspective recounts George Herbert Mead's (1863–1931) conception of gesture and its primal social implications. In the first section, "Communication Ethics as Primordial First Gesture," this material functions as a segue into Levinas's conception of the face as an originative primordial gesticulation. In the next section, "In Response," I examine work in communication ethics responsive to Levinas's insights. Finally, in "The Saying and the Said in Communication Ethics: A Difficult Freedom," I discuss Levinas's work as a gesture toward a primordial ethical call that generates response within ongoing communication scholarship. I summarize this scholarship by emphasizing six major points, which I elaborate and explicate with the aid of Levinas's *Difficult Freedom: Essays on Judaism.* The goal of this chapter is to frame the uniqueness of the ethical terrain covered by Levinas and outline its compatibility with ongoing insights in communication ethics.

Levinas's undertaking pivots on a difficult freedom of ethical responsibility without assurance of correct conduct. His position assumes these elements: (1) a spiritual awakening, (2) the interplay of a visual and audio ethic, (3) responsiveness to the particular in response to a universal ethical command, and (4) a demand for responsible action without an accompanying sense of self-righteous assurance. Levinas does not offer ethical answers; he highlights a primordial gesture that calls one into responsibility within the uniqueness of a given moment and place. At such an instant, one utters, "here I am," with recognition that clarity of action must be discerned in the meeting of the particular. Levinas's version of communication ethics, as framed by this author, outlines a difficult freedom of responsibility without assurance. The performative definition of this communication ethic commences when one acts under a fundamental acknowledgment called forth by the Other—"if not me, then whom?"

Communication Ethics as Primordial First Gesture

Levinas is attentive to an originative communication ethic, a performative first gesture that moves us toward and beyond. Gestures signal ethical implications that define and shape identity. For instance, we often discern the presence of a friend from a distance as we attend to distinctive kinesthetic gestures that permit recognition of the friend's familiar rhythm of movement.

Edward T. Hall, Ray L. Birdwhistell, and, more recently, Adam Kendon register the importance of gesture in everyday communicative life.[3] For the purpose of this chapter, I turn to the insights of Mead, one of the founders of symbolic interactionism, who frames communicative gesture as a fundamental prereflective dimension of human sociality.[4] Scholarship on gesture illuminates signification enacted in prereflective performative action. As a musician friend indicates, it is possible to be both technically competent and counter to a performance of distinction; prereflective performative meaning moves the technically competent into excellence.[5]

Accuracy in performance, whether musical, theatrical, or athletic, announces the necessity of excellence within the prereflective undertaking of communicative gestures. Knowledge of an artistic craft enhanced by the inimitability of communicative gestures transports a presentation from technical competence into a realm of the artistically memorable. Communicative gestures influence social worlds, as detailed by Mead's interest in the practical import of gesture. Mead emphasized that human beings engage in the sociality of adjustment via response to gestures. Human sociality begins with prereflective responses to human gestures.[6]

Mead describes gestures as arising from nondeliberative engagement. He exemplifies gesture through a sketch of an athlete boxing and/or fencing: "If the individual is successful a great deal of his attack and defense must be not considered, it must take place immediately. He must adjust himself 'instinctively' to the attitude of the other individual . . . a great deal has to be without deliberation" (Mead, *Mind, Self, and Society*, 43). Mead articulates two major assumptions: adjustment occurs unreflectively, and adjustments have social implications—we adapt to one another.

Mead links gesture to Charles Darwin's (1809–1882) emphasis on presymbolic language that evolves into social agreement (15–18). The prereflective understanding of gestures requires adjustments to the Other, who witnesses to a primal source of human meaning (75). Gesture is the first "social act" that requires alterations in relation to another (80). Mead describes a "triadic relation" of "gesture," "response/adjustment," and "social engagement" (80). Gestures are an initial welcome into the human community that is before symbols. Gestures are "conscious" without clarity of self-reflective appraisal (81). Mead's understanding of gesture is akin to the manner in which "intentionality" is understood phenomenologically within human interaction; gestures generated are adjustments prior to reflection that initiate human sociality.[7]

Mead understood consciousness as operating at both prereflective and reflective levels of awareness. Consciousness in phenomenology is "consciousness of"[8] without an overt reflective consideration, which lends insight into consciousness of gestures that requires meaningful adjustment and particularity of response. Mead's triadic relation of gesture, response/adjustment, and sociality structures the communicative value of his conception of prereflective consciousness. This chapter emphasizes the sociality of Levinas's project within a scholarly community attending to human communication between persons. Levinas's ethical corpus functions as a gesture of responsibility that requires response/adjustment. The following provides an impressionistic rendering of Levinas's originative ethical gesture and ongoing responses and adjustments to his work.

In Response

Amit Pinchevski reminds us of Levinas's assertion that communication is a gesture toward the Other, which contends that communication is not merely a rational process of detailed information but is more akin to love that reaches toward the Other. The act of communicating is a gesturing with attentive care to and for the Other.[9] As Mead stated, a gesture requires response and announces the sociality of the human condition. Levinas's project is a primordial ethical gesture that invites response and adjustment, which constitute the beginnings of human sociality. This section explicates a public trace, with Levinas's project functioning as a vital conceptual gesture—the particularity of the call to responsibility matters; it shapes human identity. I offer a description of work within the field of communication that has pointed to such a trace, listing ten gestures that highlight Levinas's project of responsibility in action.

THE GESTURE OF FACE AND CALL

Levinas's ethics as first philosophy can be understood as a scholarly gesture that challenges the "originative I" of modernity and of the West.[10] Before attending to a select number of overview essays on Levinas, I first underscore several important works that introduced Levinas to the communication field. Michael Hyde's *The Call of Conscience: Heidegger and Levinas, Rhetoric and the Euthanasia Debate* and Pinchevski's *By Way of Interruption: Levinas and Ethics of Communication* provide an insightful understanding of Levinas through the lens of communication ethics.[11] This chapter recognizes the scholarly efforts of Pinchevski and Hyde in their uniting of theory and application in the study of Levinas's impact on the field of communication. I turn to select journal articles that frame Levinas's ongoing contribution to communicative engagement, which display the importance of his scholarly corpus in announcing the signifying gesture of the human face, which connects us to an immemorial call for responsibility.

Communication scholarship as gesture acknowledges the ethical dimension of the face of the Other, which places demands on me to assist without imposing on the Other. The distinctiveness of Levinas's ethics project takes us to the proximity of the face that redirects me to an immemorial ethical echo; this gesture both changes and charges my own identity in the performative act of responsibility. The Other demands with a rhetoric that instructs me, which calls forth a response contrary to my impulse to impose or tell. Katz, in "Emmanuel Levinas: The Rhetoric of Ethics," suggests that Levinas has "transformed the landscape of ethical theory"[12] by turning upside down our conventional understanding of rhetorical responsibility. Our obligation to the Other is not chosen—it is an obligation demanded of us by the face of the Other.

THE GESTURE OF TRACE

Laurie Johnson, in "Face-Interface or the Prospect of a Virtual Ethics," connects Levinas's ethical mandate to cyberspace.[13] She illuminates the difference between an empirical and a phenomenological understanding of the face, with the latter requiring imagination that foregrounds the face of the Other in both cyberspace and face-to-face meetings. Johnson suggests that we do not meet an empirical person; we encounter a phenomenological face that transports us to an ethical demand, enactment of a responsibility present long before the actual firsthand meeting of persons. Johnson's attentiveness to cyberspace does not limit the face to the empirical; the face is a phenomenological imagination[14] that calls each person to responsibility. Johnson's work responds to Levinas with recognition of the power of social media. Pinchevski, in an article from *Philosophy & Rhetoric*, gestures in a similar fashion. He takes Levinas into the world of media[15] as he suggests that the bedrock of ethics is a call of responsibility that shapes human action.

Spoma Jovanovic and Roy V. Wood, in "Speaking from the Bedrock of Ethics," examine the tragic collapse of the Twin Towers on September 11, 2001. They paint a picture of alterity and ethics in action, reminding us of the interplay of trace, Saying, and Said that permits ethics to testify, as was displayed in the stairwell of the Twin Towers: "'If you had seen what it was like in that stairway, you'd be proud,' . . . 'There was no gender, no race, no religion. It was everyone, unequivocally, helping each other' (Walsh 2001). Ethics, communicated in simple gestures, words of encouragement, and displays of care, guarantees that our lives have meaning. The trace we leave behind when we are gone from sight or from life on earth is something not to miss but instead to cherish as a model of human decency."[16] Jovanovic and Wood detail the power of ethical interruption within moments of the unexpected; in darkness, the voice of ethics can guide with genuine light that resists those seeking to extinguish the good. Jovanovic, in another essay, "Difficult Conversations as Moral Imperatives: Negotiating Ethnic Identities during War," continues to explicate this ethical posture with an ethnographic explication of why she rejects the *moral imperative* of war, particularly in Yugoslavia; her examination emerges from the eyes of a person of Serbian descent. She responds to "descriptions of savagery and barbarism"[17] and rejects the assumption that there are neutral stories; however, there is an ethical a priori that is before Being that calls us into a personal and unique responsibility for the Other. Ethics is a voice more ancient than Being and is otherwise than the urge to impose on another.

THE GESTURE AS PARTICULARITY

Imposition is enacted in raw and primitive fashion through "violence," as understood in Kenneth Cmiel's examination of the manner in which Hannah Arendt (1906–1975) and Levinas discard expectations of modernity, which are central to violence and, according to Cmiel, fundamental to an emerging communication discipline. In this examination, "On Cynicism, Evil, and the Discovery of Communication in the 1940s," Cmiel emphasizes imposition as a form of violence that eclipses the hope of getting "beyond ourselves."[18] Cmiel critiques the notion of a "communication breakdown" (101). Citing Levinas, Cmiel states that a communication breakdown is a disruption of expectations that can transform the banality of hegemonic routine. Learning from difference requires attentiveness to moments of disruption that invite a communicative anarchy attentive to particularity that is in contrast to violence.

David A. Frank continues the discussion of particularity in "The Jewish Countermodel: Talmudic Argumentation, the New Rhetoric Project, and the Classical Tradition of Rhetoric," where he details an alternative to Western presuppositions about argumentation.[19] Frank states that both Chaïm Perelman and Levinas situate their philosophies within the particularity of Judaism. Such a perspective on argument does not arise in discourse alone, but rather in response to a guiding story of a people. A story suggests without dictating or imposing. Angela Cooke-Jackson and Elizabeth K. Hansen in "Appalachian Culture and Reality TV: The Ethical Dilemma of Stereotyping Others" contend that an epiphany happens as one resists imposition of a definition that embraces the "unethical."[20] Resistance to definition rejects the imposition of image and stereotype. Ethics fuels resistance that counters the eclipse of difference and strangeness.

THE GESTURE DEVOID OF AN IMPOSING GRASP

Gerrie Snyman's "Rhetoric and Ethics: Looking at the Marks of Our Reading/Speaking in Society" agrees with the necessity of resistance and denounces cultural stereotyping. Snyman states, "Levinas intends to keep the 'Other' in its strangeness, individuality, and otherness. By ignoring these characteristics, the 'Other' is reduced to that what the self wants them to be—constructions of his or her own likeness."[21] Imposing on the Other misses the call of the Other. Imposition gathers negative energy. Rochelle M. Green, Bonnie Mann, and Amy E. Story articulate this point in "Care, Domination, and Representation."[22] They remind us that efforts to hurt, dominate, and oppress have one common theme—attempting to secure energy from acts of imposition that dismiss difference.

The face of the Other resists imposition and interrupts daily attempts to possess and discount, as outlined by Michael Hyde and Kenneth Rufo in the "The Call of Conscience, Rhetorical Interruptions, and the Euthanasia Controversy." The face of the Other is an ethical interruption without prescription, which led Levinas to avoid framing a single theory about ethics. Hyde and Rufo contend that Levinas outlines three basic coordinates that arise from interruption:

(1) "Where art thou?" and (2) my unique particularity of response that then gives rise to (3) "Here I am!"[23] Interruptions from the face of the Other resist and restrain the impulse to impose an answer that will endure throughout time; an immemorial ethical saying interrupts the Said. Stephen Coleman, in "New Mediation and Direct Representation: Reconceptualizing Representation in the Digital Age," contends that the Said of culture, society, and environment holds within it a trace of Saying.[24] Within the Said dwells a trace of Saying that, after a given duration, resides within the Said once again. The intimacy of Saying and Said framed by Sean Cubitt in "Immersed in Time" argues that Levinas's project is a unity of contraries that leans toward infinity without forsaking the necessity of totality. Cubitt stresses that contemplation is totality disrupted by action, which offers a temporal glimpse of the infinite.[25] Additionally, frenzied action becomes a totality necessarily interrupted by contemplation. Cubitt asserts that mutual interruption disrupts the abyss of totality.

THE GESTURE OF THE UNKNOWN AND UNSEEN

Prophetic Saying erupts and transforms; it reveals scholarship attentive to visual communication and the human face, which is exemplified by Stephanie Houston Grey's essay "Exhibitions in Life and Death: The Photography of Lucinda Devlin, Gunther von Hagens' *Body Worlds*, and the Disassembly of Scientific Progress." Houston Grey states that visual scholarship "assesses damage that these exhibitions render to modern rationality."[26] Their critical visual perspective portrays the manner in which the human face affects an audience and calls forth an ethical commitment more foundational than the rational materialism of scientific progress. The human face moves one to ethical responsibility without clarity of answer or response. This theme continues in Gary McCarron's "Undecided Stories: Alfred Hitchcock's *Blackmail* and the Problem of Moral Agency," where he cites Levinas's work as important in understanding endings without clarity.[27] McCarron emphasizes meeting uncertainty void of rule and standard as akin to Levinas's witnessing to a spiritual awakening that calls us into personal responsibility.

The face is not an abstraction; it requires attentiveness to a concrete Other. Boris Gubman, in "Jacques Derrida on Philosophy, Language, and Power in the Age of Globalization," suggests that the revelatory character of the Other is the fulcrum of democracy and undergirds the messianic promise of welcome for the unseen and unknown Other. Acknowledging revelatory action recognizes novel insights that emerge through ideas and persons. Revelatory insights are so powerfully unexpected that "no one can see . . . [them] coming, and [no one can] see how [they] should come, or have [a] forewarning of [them]."[28] It is in the welcome of the Other that we find the unpredictable as a needed promise that arises within a given temporal moment. The unpredictable lives within the face of another charged by an ethics that dwells before and beyond time.

Susan Petrilli's "Semiotic Phenomenology of Predicative Judgment" underscores the Levinasian truism of countering both the ontology of Being and the primacy of metaphysics with an ethics that functions "otherwise than being." The otherness of otherwise than being has its origin within the ethical, not the cognitive or rational. This precognitive call of ethics "exists, flourishes, intrigues, preoccupies, makes responsible, but not to the end of determining being."[29] Ethics exists long before the discourse begins. Petrilli continues this perspective in "On Communication: Contributions to the Human Sciences and to Humanism from Semiotics Understood as Semioethics"[30]; she clarifies semioethics as a sign within the face of a particular Other that moves one to an ethical echo that demands responsibility without the benefit of technique or code.

One hears this call in the proximity of a face-to-face encounter that constitutes alterity that is beyond the immediate personality of the person. The human being, from a Levinasian perspective, desires Otherness. The desire for alterity goes unquenched; it makes the welcome of infinity possible. In "Working with Interpreters of the 'Meaning of Meaning': International Trends among 20th-Century Sign Theorists," Petrilli outlines relationships among alterity, desire for Otherness, and infinity, all of which give rise to hospitality and responsibility.[31] Petrilli continues to outline semioethics in "Iconicity in Translation: On Similarity, Alterity, and Dialogism in the Relation among Signs," where she differentiates two forms of logic: an assemblative logic that classifies objects by gathering them in accordance with genres such as race, ethnicity, group, class, and any form of supposed similarity; and iconicity, or agapastic logic, which attends to absolute Otherness of difference, singularity, and uniqueness.[32] It is iconicity, or agapastic logic, that is the generative source of creativity within Levinas's project.

THE GESTURE AND THE UNENDING
REACH OF THE OTHER

Difference and alterity permit Jonathan Corpus Ong, in "The Cosmopolitan Continuum: Locating Cosmopolitanism in Media and Cultural Studies," to offer a textured view of cosmopolitanism responsive to the Other and distance. Levinas's understanding of the Other presupposes distance; it infuses a "distanciated identity."[33] Levinas's prescriptive attending to the Other commences without noting the color of another's eyes; he rejects a "moral maximalism" with the disruptive nature of alterity, which respects and learns from radical difference (Ong, 462). Ong turns to Levinas as a principal voice for a discussion of pragmatic alternatives to hegemonic locality of control—the Other is a disruptive and creative force. The prerogative of distance and acknowledgment of radical alterity in the Other makes "welcome" possible.

Engaging an ethnographic emphasis on a story of unexpected welcome, Christopher N. Poulos, in "Accidental Dialogue," sketches discontinuity between hospitality and prescription. Without openness to the Other, hospitality fails to greet the unexpected—accidental dialogues cannot be forced, only appreciated. Such a dialogue is akin to a communicative spirit of "holy sparks"[34] that emerges from a dwelling that welcomes within a spirit of hospitality that is open to accidental dialogues.[35] The dwelling of *bienvenue* transforms the stranger into a guest, who unknowingly demands a response from me that invites an accidental dialogue capable of transforming human identity.

THE GESTURE AS WELCOME

Emphasis on welcome is at the heart of Hyde's explication of acknowledgment.[36] Hyde underscores the welcoming power of a call that moves one to responsibility for another.[37] Jeffrey Murray emphasizes acknowledgment of the face as a rhetoric that originates from the Other as the face disrupts my sense of routine.[38] Murray announces the reality of disruptive rhetoric from the Other that "leads you beyond" the moment and the self.[39] Murray salutes Levinas's criticism of rhetoric while emphasizing a rhetoric that is otherwise than speech grounded in telling. For Levinas, rhetoric within the West preaches from a self-described text that encourages a failing to attend, listen, and respond to an ethical echo that charges and transforms one with responsibility. Murray concurs with Levinas's rejection of discourse that imposes on the Other rather than being transformed in ethical response to the Other.

The disruptive force of the Other is the resultant consequence of a Levinasian "welcome."[40] D. Diane Davis, in "Finitude's Clamor; or, Notes toward a Communitarian Literacy," states that Levinas's understanding of welcome includes a demand from alterity that carries a surplus of meaning and responsibility. Davis underscores exposition and alterity, as opposed to assertion of imposition.[41] Davis's essay registers Levinas's commitment to the social; Levinas understands dialogue as a meeting of differences dissimilar to a medieval act of disputation. The social frames the power of listening, as opposed to hearing, with the former tied to identity transformation. Levinas's project commences with attending and listening and eschews the impulse of telling.

Lisbeth Lipari, in "Listening for the Other: Ethical Implications of the Buber-Levinas Encounter," details the difference between hearing and listening, with the latter carrying forth responsibility for the Other.[42] It is in listening that one assumes responsibility for a given action, as one answers a call that continues to shape one's identity. Identity seeks me; I am called forth in response and the performative action of responsibility. Responding to a call as one meets the Other shapes identity through performative responsibility.

THE GESTURE AS THE ANARCHY OF ETHICS

In "An Other Ethics for Kenneth Burke," Murray brings Levinas into conversation with Burkean scholarship, stressing how the communicative agent is called forth by the Other. In this case the Other's face initiates a calling that inaugurates a human drama of responsibility. Murray explicates the unpredictable anarchy of the human face. He emphasizes a basic Levinasian assumption—when the face of the Other is eclipsed, a communicative agent cannot be called forth into responsibility. Instead, communication becomes an act of "annihilative propaganda."[43] In another essay, "Kenneth Burke: A Dialogue of Motives," Murray states that Levinas's "ethics cannot be an evaluative scheme or conception of the good."[44] Levinas's notion of the good is void of a conceptual structure and tied to anarchy of responsibility, not to a coordinated program of ethical codes. For Levinas, the notion of anarchy announces revelatory responsibility. The face of the Other begins a recognition of responsibility without dictating a programmatic or ideological response. Levinas unites anarchy and ethics under the guise of responsibility without predetermined actions.

Anarchy of ethics invites a revelatory conception of identity that is beyond technique and control; this position frames Pinchevski's "Ethics on the Line," which examines computer-mediated communication and the limits of chat room "control."[45] Someone or something undermines control in the chat room; interruption welcomes a continual shaping of identity. The meeting of alterity disrupts routine and ideological rigidity while working to counter domination and hegemony. The key to Levinas's ethics is interruption, not dominance of form. Pinchevski emphasizes the necessity of avoiding oral scripts in chat rooms. He reminds the reader that written speech takes time and invites distance—speed does not necessarily drive good discourse, but neither does the impulse to control the discourse of the Other (160–63).

Murray, in "The Paradox of Emmanuel Levinas: Knowledge of the Absolute Other," challenges Manning, Jacques Derrida (1930–2004), and Richard J. Bernstein, who argue that Levinas's project is rhetorically hyperbolic and requires an epistemological reading.[46] Murray argues that such an interpretation of Levinas misses the reality of a basic paradox of the "infinitely Other" and the "absolutely Other."[47] Murray states that he wants to correct this conceptual misreading of Levinas, which he asserts falls into a theoretical abyss of totalization. It is the paradox of the uniqueness of the Other (absolutely Other) and the beyondness of the Other (infinitely Other) that propels a Levinasian understanding of and engagement with the Other. Murray offers an important reminder: forgetting the paradox of an absolute Other and an infinite Other moves us foolishly to the search for easy ethical answers or formulas.

THE GESTURE OF DISRUPTION

Michael J. Salvo's insights emphasize a unity-of-contraries perspective that shapes Levinas's project in a different genre of scholarship. In

"Ethics of Engagement: User-Centered Design and Rhetorical Methodology," Salvo stresses the importance of Levinasian "identity" as both infinite and absolute.[48] Salvo suggests that design begins with a paradox that lives between expectation *and* the unexpected. Salvo submits that design reposes within the paradox of the absolute and the infinite, within the demands of what must be and a continuing hint of the unanticipated. Salvo connects Levinas to a conception of design that is creatively responsive to the anticipated and the unexpected.

Katz offers a related reading of Levinas, as does Diane Perpich; they both suggest that Levinas's ethics is an "undermining of system."[49] Levinas's conception of ethics falls outside the realm of totalizing—justice and concern for the unknown neighbor disrupt ethics. In Murray's essay "The Dialogical Prioritization of Calls: Toward a Communicative Model of Justice," he further clarifies how justice disrupts ethics and vice versa. Levinas linked religion and justice for the Other; to omit this relationship misses the ethical call of God (*Difficult Freedom*, 219). The interplay of ethics and justice is exemplary of the disruptive interaction of finitude and infinity. Ethics disturbs justice, and justice unsettles ethics. Murray states that ethics and justice are in tension, yielding the necessity of public dialogue: "[Making a] vigilant public dialogue is required of us, in perpetuity."[50] The proximity of the face of the Other produces ethics and a phenomenological attentiveness to those not at the immediate table of conversation, which constructs the realm of justice.

The relationship between ethics and justice undergirds the work of Pat Gehrke in "Being for the Other-to-the-Other: Justice and Communication in Levinasian Ethics," where he details the tension between Levinas's view of ethics and justice—the "Other-to-the-other."[51] Gehrke states the nature of obligation beyond the proximate Other that extends to the unseen Other. Gehrke reads Levinas as a "philosophy of the Other" with a "unidirectional obligation" to the proximate Other and simultaneously to the distant and unknown Other.[52] The demands of justice, as framed by Oona Eisenstadt in "Levinas versus Levinas: Hebrew, Greek, and Linguistic Justice," describe the tensions of a Levinasian view toward universality that is "Greekjew" and "Jewgreek," with each emphasizing particularity and difference but with contrasting emphasis.[53] Eisenstadt asserts that there is no unitary voice in Levinas; instead, there is a unity of contraries.

THE GESTURE AND THE "DERIVATIVE I"

Levinas's perspective on communication ethics is otherwise than convention in that a "derivative I" is called forth by the Other in contrast to an "originative I" of self-assertion characteristic of the West.[54] The importance of this perspective emerges in the work of a number of authors in the field of communication who emphasize communicative agency and identity discovered in response. Variations of this insight guide the projects of Hyde, Gehrke, Lipari, and Pinchevski.[55] To conclude this section, I turn to an essay by Stanley Deetz that argues for the importance of ethical content over valuation of the communicative agent alone. In his 1990 essay, "Reclaiming the Subject Matter as a Guide to Mutual Understanding: Effectiveness and Ethics in Interpersonal Interaction," Deetz offers a preamble to why Levinas is essential.[56] Deetz's essay is a counter to the Western obsession with an originative communicative subject, a fundamental Levinasian theme. Deetz reintroduces the importance of subject matter as ethical content, reminding us that a content path must trump attentiveness to the immediate relational process. Deetz challenges a therapeutic sense of openness and process in communication; he understands ethics as content.

Deetz outlines a schema of communication without freezing participants into an ism or technique, ideology, or procedure. He underscores the prominence of subject matter shaped by ethical content while detailing ethical content propelled by anarchy of outcome, accompanied by a prescriptive demand to take seriously ethical implications for each communicative encounter. Deetz concludes his essay with a discussion of fostering conversations that disrupt dominance and invite a communicative anarchy that acknowledges the content implications of ethics. Deetz's perspective is consistent with Levinas's work in that outcome/ethical mandate cannot be possessed or controlled. Deetz's essay yields insight into the fundamental nature of ethical content as composed of the interplay of the prescriptive (ethical weight that guides conversation) and the descriptive (the communicative task engaged in the particular interaction).

Deetz's essay opens the door to Levinas's unity of ethical demand and anarchy of responsible outcome. In *Difficult Freedom* Levinas contends, "The romanticism of the heroic stance, and the self-sufficient purity of feeling, must once more be substituted. This substitute must be given its proper place and be put first. It is the contemplation of ideas, something which makes republics possible. These republics crumble when one no longer fights for something [ethics that matter] but for someone" (150). Ethics is composed of ambiguous content discerned in responsible action. Levinas's project is a difficult freedom composed of two elements: a clarion call to responsibility and the doing of ethics without a script. Ethical judgment is not mystical; it arises from education, thinking, and reason that engage discernment in enacting the particularity of obligation toward another.

The Saying and the Said in Communication Ethics: A Difficult Freedom

A growing communication response to Levinas's gesture points toward the primordial call of ethics. His ethics suggests a difficult freedom; we are ethically obligated to and for the Other. We must respond to the immemorial demand of responsibility without the clarity of implementation tactics. Difficult freedom embraces a unity of contraries: universal and particular, infinite and finite, Said and Saying, ethics and justice, ethical optics and ethical echo, Jew and Greek, and the passive-I propelled by a tenacious-I in ethical response. Communication ethics understood as a difficult freedom turns on the revelatory power of an ethical awakening and the Said of education and institutions. Levinas's *Difficult Freedom* is an appropriate action metaphor for detailing such a conception of communication ethics.

THE FACE IGNITES PHENOMENOLOGICAL MEMORY AND IMAGINATION

Levinas's communication ethic is again "otherwise" as he explicates the interplay of the human face (an ethics of optics) and an immemorial ethical echo (an audio ethics), which gives rise to a "derivative I" called into responsibility with an obligation to learn from the rhetorical demands of the historical moment and the person to whom one is ethically directed. Responding to the face of the Other requires phenomenological attentiveness to a human face, alerting one to an ethical echo of debt and necessitating an intellectual life of ideas that offers ethical guidance without totality of assurance.

A disruptive welcome opens the door to a communicative action of ethical direction that is present in the rawness of the human face. It is the face of the Other, not "enrootedness" in a sense of place, that permits Levinas to be less wary of technology than of love of a given location (*Difficult Freedom*, 232–34). Uprootedness, for Levinas, is more sacred than pagan worship of a particular habitation. Levinas's recognition of the disruptive nature of the face renders uprootedness a greater ethical encouragement than unquestioning assurance associated with both infinite and absolute mirages of provincial clarity. He writes,

> The fact that the vision of the face is not an *experience*, but a moving out of oneself, a contact with another being and not simply a sensation of self, is attested to by the "purely moral" character of this impossibility. . . . The commerce with beings which begins with "You shall not kill" does not conform to the scheme of our normal relations with the words, in which the subject knows or absorbs its object like a nourishment, the satisfaction of a need. It does not return to its point of departure to become self-contentment, self-enjoyment, or self-knowledge. It [an ethical call] inaugurates the spiritual journey of man. A religion, for us, can follow no other path. (10)

Communication ethics is a *difficult freedom* that discovers direction in a face without false assurance of *the* correct action and direction.

As Levinas suggested, there is a difficult freedom that acknowledges the power of ambiguity tied to responsibility to and for the human face. Levinas stated a demand for Jewish patience that makes the continual waiting for the Messiah possible (202). This patience finds support in the meeting of the face of the Other—with the face being "an optics of the Divine" (159). Genuine responsibility requires meeting the face of another, which demands responsibility enacted within the uniqueness of a given moment. The call of responsibility from each face insists on an action and a specific response that is personally and contextually unique. Meeting the face of the Other and being called to responsibility are infinite tasks and cannot be defined by the totality of happy endings. Unclear moments are to be expected and require vigilant responsiveness to the face of the Other as one is called into responsibility without assurance of rightful action or outcome.

ETHICS AS INTERRUPTION,
RESPONSIBILITY, AND WONDER

A difficult freedom calls one into unique responsibility without the clarity of an answer; instead, an immemorial burden demands that one search for genuine light. Levinas describes a lack of schemata of assurance in discussing Franz Rosenzweig's (1886–1929) work *The Star of Redemption* and the importance of Jewish community dwelling within the "eternal," played out within the particularity of a human person—the singular of the person as "ipseity" (*Difficult Freedom*, 190, 195). This dialectic of an eternal community and a single person, the universal and the particular, disallowed Rosenzweig from endorsing "historical necessity" (201). An immemorial communication ethic is a difficult freedom that rejects the impulse to reify answers and control one's own identity. This view of relational engagement never "reach[es] a conclusion, but constitutes the very life of truth [found in discourse together]" (163). Such obligation pivots on a radical uniqueness of responsibility and distinctiveness ushered forth by the ipseity of identity.

For Levinas, history offers no permanent criteria for judgment; history is but one major reminder that the light of miracles is forever dependent on the wonder of darkness (230). Levinas's project offers hope as the intellect responds to an ethical mandate of concern for the Other, interrupted by the disquiet of justice for the unseen and unknown neighbor: "The third party is other than the neighbor but also another neighbor, and also a neighbor of the other, and not simply their fellow."[57] Levinas recognizes that the fundamental problem of human life is attentiveness to the Other with responsibility and concern for a person far beyond emotional and/or physical proximity. Communication ethics is a difficult freedom of discerning genuine light via interruption of the proximate Other through the distance of an unknown neighbor and the wonder of darkness.

ETHICS AS ANARCHIC AND REVELATORY

Levinas's project announces a realm of communicative ethics contrary to normative conventions centered on "telling" and blind adherence to prescriptive directives from authorities (*Totality*, 65). Additionally, Levinas casts off a communicative agent composed of self-righteous regard for one's own identity. Levinas's orientation illuminates an ethics "otherwise than being"[58] that is contrary to Heidegger's project and the Western fascination with an imperial self. In Western ethics, the imperial or sovereign self embodies decision making by personal preference, "emotivism," aptly defined by Alasdair MacIntyre.[59] Levinas's project avoids emotivism by rejecting the purity of objective codes of ethics that enact imposition. Levinas's understanding of ethics leans toward an unending obligation without aligning with the assurance of either totality or infinity. Levinas's communication ethic begins with a voice that is before time and tied to an everlasting ethical echo. The origin of ethics is outside me, and the responsibility for a performative depiction of ethics resides with "me" alone. For Levinas, there is no ethical template to which to adhere; responsibility in ethics is creatively responsive to changing demands, which he details in the shift from Judaism of prayer to Judaism that privileges reason in the search for a temporally correct ethical response (*Difficult Freedom*, 271). Indeed, for Levinas, ethics has no singular script. Ethics occurs as anarchy; its priority commences without recourse to principles, without vision, in the irrecuperable shock of being-for-the-other-person before being-for-oneself, or being-with-others, or being-in-the-world—to name some of the contemporary philosophical formulas of postmetaphysical thought. Ethical priority, according to Levinas, occurs when the moral height of the other person demands from me action that shapes my identity and principles (*Ethics and Infinity*, 10). The unpredictable nature of an ethical action functions as ironic bedrock in the call to responsibility.

Ethics does not abide in programs and personal sentiments but in responsibility that attends to the revelatory, to an ethical awakening that embraces no answers other than a responsibility to engage all insights from education, judgment, and action. Communication ethics is a difficult freedom of obligation enacted in a responsibility of constant judgment that involves the revelatory and ongoing learning.

Levinas gestures toward an alternative to the desire to possess the Other; his project is ever responsive to an ethical echo that alerts one to the revelatory meeting of particularity in a given historical moment. Communication ethics resists framing within a code or script; the call begins with responsibility, not assurance. Communication ethics commences with a spiritual awakening of my unique responsibility.

FROM ETHICAL CALL TO INTELLECT TO
PARTICULAR RESPONSIBILITY

Levinas asserts that the intellectual task is central to ethics. Such was the reason that King Josiah established a kingdom around a lost and rediscovered book—*The Book of the Torah*—in 622 B.C.E. (*Difficult Freedom*, 53). Ethical responsibility requires attentiveness to an ethical call engaged with reason within a community of interpretation. Human responsibility is ultimately personal in action—guided by education, interpretation, and responsibility in the particularity of action. The hearing and doing of ethics is a difficult freedom.

Levinas's ethics functions in a manner that is otherwise than convention; he challenges the social expectation of reciprocity. Levinas's emphasis on nonreciprocity of ethical obligation required him to reject Paul Claudel's (1868–1955) emphasis on "interested" love; unlike Claudel, Levinas highlighted noninterested love that attends to the face of the Other without the goal of facilitating one's own demands as a prerequisite of assistance (125–26). Noninterested love/caring leans toward the Other, following the mandate of an ethical echo that calls one into personal responsibility and then returns one to engagement with a particular Other without an ethical formula.[60] This return to the Other follows a phenomenological call of ethics that resists undue "enthusiasm." Levinas contends in *Difficult Freedom* that "[t]he sublime forms of the human are no longer full of pathos" (28–29). Ethics is not something to be "be possessed . . . [ethics demands that one] be responsible" (54). A "spiritual awakening" acknowledges the face of the Other, who transports me to an ethical echo, an ethical command—"I am my brother's keeper." One returns ethically to a particular person, informed by intellect, ideas, and reason in performative responsibility to and for a particular Other. Levinas's ethics embraces an intellectual life that is not "ashamed of contemplation" (155); discernment functions as a necessary crucial step in moving an immemorial ethical echo into a particularity of responsibility.

In *Difficult Freedom* Levinas explains that intellectual argumentation does not begin with the communicator but with responsive engagement that originates with the particular, grounded in monotheism, which assumes that the power of language and speech is originative with a creator—not with a communicative agent (178–80). It is in the particular that one invites creativity and justice; "history offer[s] no criteria to judgment" (227). For Levinas, "divisive beliefs . . . are indispensable to human harmony" (276). The connection of argument to particularity rejects imposition on the communicative context. Difference and the Other are central to the intellect and to learning.

Levinas witnesses to the importance of reason in a faithful life within the Jewish faith; one must consider intellectual commitments that can put a life of faith at risk. Such a demanding intellectual commitment is a risk, appropriately characterized by the title *Difficult Freedom*. Communication ethics is a difficult freedom dwelling within an ancient demand for personal responsibility. This responsibility is not mystical; it relies on a commitment to learning and reason. Levinas reminds us that to be a chosen people does not mean having "exceptional rights, but [rather] . . . exceptional duties" (176). One must answer the call of interruption with clarity of responsibility, not assurance; to fail to do so effaces the face of the Other.

Avoiding the call of the Other eradicates responsibility to and for the Other by a refusal to attend to the interruption of responsibility. Restraining oneself from imposing on another does not originate with me but rather with a primordial gesture of the human face. As Levinas stated in *Difficult Freedom*, if there is any form of humanism that is not deformed by arrogance of individualistic domination, it is "[t]he humanism of the suffering servant" (171), where imposition demands that I assist the Other, not out of mysticism or willingness to follow an ethical program, but through a call of responsibility enacted and assisted by an active intellectual life: "Pure piety is no longer enough. We can still pull off a pedagogy of exaltation, enthusiastically admit propositions that demand adherence to a reason at the expense of a total effort; but pure feelings which, even when they are pure feelings or hothouse feelings, pass for ideas, have no future. Nothing is really vital, we have to say, unless it bears the mark of intellect. No cheap acquiescence!" (268). Levinas understood the intellect as a manner of restraint and public contribution, which counters self-righteous emotivistic assurance. A difficult freedom offers no easy answers, just the demand to respond to a call of interruption with intellectual discernment.

UNITY OF CONTRARIES

Levinas did not embrace Enlightenment rationality; his commitment was to contemplation that casts off "formula" and responds to "revelation" (214). Difficult freedom emphasizes infinity in opposition to totality, while simultaneously recognizing that totality is necessary for the "extra-historical temporality" of the "beautiful" (222). Levinas emphasized Said and Saying with recognition of the power of infinity in Saying that lives as a trace within the totality of a given Said. The interplay of Saying and Said witnesses through the Said of culture that preserves a trace of Saying, which suggests Cassirer's commitment to culture in contrast to Heidegger's increasing turn to a poetic and local sense of Saying. Interestingly, the Said of Cassirer affected Levinas, keeping the performative responsibility of ethics before him. Understanding culture as the interplay of Said and Saying balances the oxymoronic relationship of the absolute/totality with the infinite of the Saying that sparks a prophetic word. On the one hand, "By being coherent [the Said], speech has lost its speech [the Saying]. From this point on, there is no longer any word that has the authority necessary to announce to the world the end of its own decline" (207). On the other hand, to embrace Saying alone puts at risk the continuing power of the Said, which houses a trace of a Saying that can be unleashed in unexpected moments in a life. The immemorial voice of ethics charges one with responsibility and continually relies on contemplation, thinking, and reflection to determine appropriate action.

To understand ethically requires a rich intellectual life of a unity of contraries that yields differentiation in the command of ethical obligation in action. Levinas stated that arduous thought must be connected to "great books of Judaism" that are "the principal condition for the survival of the Jews in the Diaspora" (258). Levinas transports us into a world of ethical obligation and responsibility enriched, textured, and shaped by intellectual engagement without totality of prescription. His ethic begins with a prescriptive announcement of an ethical echo uniquely and particularly implemented for another. He then describes how implementation emerges from stories that pronounce ethical action. Within the contraries of prescription and description dwells responsibility for the uniqueness of ethical deeds enacted with the knowledge of "if not me, then whom?" What initiates the need for ethical discernment and intellectual energy is the charge to be ethically "upright," which performs an unending obligation of responsibility (*Ethics and Infinity*, 86).

For Levinas, an upright Jewish consciousness requires texture and differentiation: "The difference between nation and religion, universal and particular, public and private, political life and inner life, places within its just limits the Jewish destiny and stems the potential overflowing of the Jewish soul" (*Difficult Freedom*, 245). Levinas emphasized the importance of tradition as a gesture that points through "the tradition of Jewish exegesis or the return to the original text" (119). In making the case for the importance of considering the originative power of the original text, Levinas referenced the work of Claudel, a Christian he considered too free in his interpretation of the Old Testament. Levinas wanted closer concentration on the original text to avoid the danger of a telling impulse, which misses the unique gesture of a given tradition by relying on a form of colonial imposition.

Levinas's view of the Messiah speaks of the importance of a bodily gesture that implies what might or should be, without falling prey to normative assumptions. Levinas does not equate tradition with a normative hegemony of conventional assertion: "One has failed to say anything about the Messiah if one represents him as a person who comes to put a miraculous end to the violence in the world, the injustice and contradictions which destroy humanity but have their source in the nature of humanity, and simply in Nature" (59). The Messiah is a gesture toward humanity with thinking and reasoning about a story of the faith that gives meaning. The embodied idea of a Messiah testifies to the power of a gesture that leans toward the Other. The contention of this project, *Levinas's Rhetorical Demand: The Unending Obligation of Communication Ethics*, is that the human being is defined by ethics, not as a first philosophy, but via a communicative first gesture of responsibility toward and with another. Ethics is a communicative gesture leaning toward the Other in responsibility within a unity of contraries of a universal mandate ignited and implemented in the particular.

COMMUNICATION ETHICS AS PRIMORDIAL GESTURE

The ability to read ethical signs that are "not yet" and/or those that never will become symbols permits communication grounded in silence to welcome one into a social world rich in contextual, relational, and social meaning. One reads the "not yet" as symbols representative of a Levinasian emphasis on Saying. A primordial ethical gesture is a sign that speaks, requiring the Other to respond or adjust. The Saying of a gesture demands response/adjustment; it connects one to a world of sociality initiated through prereflective responses.

From a Levinasian perspective, ethics as first philosophy begins with the power and demand of the communicative gesture of the human face, which returns one to an oral ethical origin. Gestures beckon; they involve us in social leaning toward the Other. Particularity of gesture permits one to touch the universal temporally. As Levinas stated, "[T]he Divine is absolutely universal, and this is why it can be served in purity only through the particularity of each people, a particularity named enrootedness" (136). The primordial ethic awakens via the particularity of a human face that renders access to an ethical origin that is proximate to the universal. Levinas assumes a prereflective responsiveness to the face of the Other that invites a sociality of ethics and demands attending to an audio ethical call. The gesture of the face dwells in an immemorial echo, which is composed of an embodied oral tradition of responsibility. The gesture of the face begins with the "moral height" of the Other (*Ethics and Infinity*, 10). Levinas understood ethics as an archaic demand acknowledging the Other's moral height over me as a communicator.

The communicative gesture of the face of the Other returns me to an immemorial ethical echo, "I am my brother's keeper," which demands a response from *me* of "here I am." The Other calls for my unique rejoinder of responsibility. Ethics is a rhetorical welcome that ultimately burdens me in responsibility while shaping my identity, discovered through the meeting of exteriority and sociality. The proximate face demands attentiveness to the unseen and unknown neighbor; ethics is a first philosophy that justice interrupts. We are demanded by the face of the Other to focus on the Saying of an ethical echo without ignoring the insights of education, justice, and institutions that preserve the Said that houses traces of Saying. Ethics and justice dwell within the paradox of infinity and the absoluteness of finitude. Neither ethics nor justice renders final answers; both dwell in temporal response without final assurance.

Response to an immemorial gesture is not personal but is tied to impersonal caring that announces ethical obligation as social creatures. Unreflective responses to primordial gestures of the face are consistent with an impersonal immemorial ethical mantra—"I am my brother's keeper." The impersonal nature of an initial gesture of the face is the primordial gesture that asserts a communication ethic guided by an ancient ethical echo that demands my unique and particular responsibility.

Primordial ethical gestures are prereflective communicative commands that originate from the Other. The response may not be quiet or gentle. Ethics performed within a tradition of difficult freedom does not adhere to the necessity of a gentle figure guiding Jewish ethical thought in action. Levinas exemplifies gruffness through the ethical action of Elijah, "the prophet without pardon, the prophet of anger and punishment, a suckling of crows, inhabiting deserts, without kindness, without happiness, without peace."[61] The archetypal Jewish model of an ethical prophet functions otherwise than a quiet and calm sage. Responsibility that gestures toward an ethical direction announces performative conviction. In reading Levinas, some have contended that his ethic dwells within God alone; others have called his project agnostic.[62] As for the corpus of his work, the answer resides in the interplay of these perspectives, a unity of contraries. Faith, for Levinas, is played out in responsibility in which an oral echo rests in an ancient voice; in order to respond with one's own unique obligation, all conception of God fades and one's personal responsibility remains—knowing full well that the call of humanness is housed in one basic ethical demand: if not me, then whom. Communication ethics is a primordial gesture that ignites a series of ethical events performed within a difficult freedom, a world without assurance or clarity of formulas that demands urgency of response from no one but me.

CHAPTER 2
Footprints and Echoes: Emmanuel Levinas

The Bible—or if you prefer, the Judeo-Christian source of our culture—means the affirmation of a primordial bond of responsibility
"for the other," such that, in an apparently paradoxical way, caring
for others can precede caring for oneself, saintliness representing
the irreducible possibility of the human and God, of being called
by man. An original ethical event that is also primary theology.
There, ethics is no longer a simple moralism of rules decreed by
the virtuous. It is the original awakening of an "I" responsible for
others, the accession of my person to the uniqueness of the "I"
called and elected to responsibility for others. The human "I" is not
a self-enclosed unit like the unit of the atom; it is an opening, the
opening of responsibility that is the true beginning of the human
and of spirituality. In the appeal that the face of the other man addresses to me, I grasp directly the graces of love: spirituality, the
experience of authentic humanity.

—Emmanuel Levinas, *Unforeseen History*

[T]he ideals and interdicts of this identity—what it casts in relief
and what it casts in shadow—shape our philosophical thought,
our epistemology and our philosophy of language, largely without
our awareness.　　　　—Charles Taylor, *Sources of the Self:
The Making of the Modern Mind*

Biography finds vivacity through footprints and echoes of a life, inter-
preted in the interplay of actor and spectator. Both Kant and Arendt

outlined the conceptual movement from behavior to meaningfully understood action as the product of interaction between actor and spectator.[1] A spectator's interpretation transforms human conduct into meaningful public action, registering the behavior of an actor within a background story context. With the assistance of a biography, interviews with Emmanuel Levinas, and a short autobiographical statement, I offer a story about persons and events concerning a scholarly figure that made manifest the fundamental importance of "ethics as first philosophy."[2]

Introduction

Philippe Nemo (born 1949) wrote the foreword to Salomon Malka's biography on Levinas. In six pages Nemo proposes a rough outline of key events that shaped Levinas's life. From Levinas's Lithuanian birth to his French citizenship and patriotic loyalty, his study of the Torah, and his engagement with Western philosophy, we witness a man immersed in the relationship of cosmopolitan and provincial ethical commitments. Levinas's life was one of conviction, manifested by loyalty to family and friends and his more than thirty years as director at the École Normale Israélite Orientale.[3] Nemo's foreword cites the preface to Malka's biography on Levinas, which claimed that one must understand Levinas's project from the vantage point of a "hidden referent, the Shoah," the Holocaust.[4] Levinas's undertaking of ethics begins with recognition of the human face as the first interruption manifested as a call to responsibility. The face moves us to an ethical echo uttered long before an immediate interpersonal meeting. The hearing of an immemorial ethical whisper connects us to witnesses and testimonies that are not yet and no longer at the immediate table of conversation.

This chapter turns to footprints and echoes related to Levinas's life and ethics project. The first section, "Malka on Levinas," relies on a biography of Levinas centered on places, faces, and acknowledgment. The second section, "Conversations with Philippe Nemo," recounts interviews between Levinas and Nemo recorded in *Ethics and Infinity*. The third section, "Levinas's Signature," responds to Levinas's autobiographical statement in the concluding chapter of *Difficult Freedom: Essays on Judaism*. The final section, "The Saying and the Said in Communication Ethics: Origins and Echoes," announces communication ethics connections tied to the Said of footprints and the trace of Saying within an echo that calls one to responsibility. Our lives are shaped by spiritual awakenings that commence with the Other and shift us to an ethical echo, charging us with responsibility in the return to a particular Other propelled by an unending burden of responsibility. Levinas's conception of humanity begins with responsibility originating in an ongoing ethical echo tempered and interrupted by requirements for justice, a demand for attentive concern with and for the unknown, forgotten, and ignored.

Levinas wrote about the immemorial power of ethics, offering a prophetic reminder of our responsibility to the Other. He renewed ethics as vital to a world capable of executing his parents, two brothers, and six million others during the Nazi reign of terror.[5] His project is one of courage and insight that displays the fundamental difference between optimism and tenacious hope.[6] Levinas grounds responsibility in an ethical call composed of footprints and echoes that point to an archaic Saying of ethics without forgoing the importance of institutions that solidify the Said of justice that propels concern for the widow, the destitute, and the forgotten. His story, thoughtfully framed by Malka, is at the heart of this rendering of an introduction to Levinas's life and historical circumstances.

Malka on Levinas

Malka's 2006 biography, *Emmanuel Levinas: His Life and Legacy*, focused on three major themes: (1) places, (2) faces, and (3) acknowledgment of responsibility, which witnesses to a disruptive relationship between ethics and justice. Levinas's project is otherwise than convention; it testifies against the normality of violence and hatred perpetuated by an "originative I."[7] Malka's biography offers comprehension of the power of ethics as a prophetic hope, particularly against the backdrop of Nazi action and legacy. Malka begins telling his story about Levinas by underscoring significant places that shaped Levinas personally and professionally.

PLACES

The camps of World War II propel the "*aletheia* of ethics."[8] Levinas witnesses firsthand the reality of unspeakable suffering as he offers

43

a remarkable alternative—enjoyment in response to the meeting of human existence in all its variants. Malka suggests that enjoyment begins with Levinas's childhood, a time marked by his relationship with his wife-to-be, Raïssa Lévy, the granddaughter of Chaim Volpa (her grandfather) and Chaya-Lina (her grandmother), who owned the Levinas family's residence. They grew up together, drifted apart, and then found one another once again in Paris. Raïssa lived next door to the Levinas family in Kaunas, Lithuania, before Levinas left in 1914, the year of the declaration of World War I. After becoming a French citizen, Levinas returned to Lithuania in 1932 to betroth Raïssa. As stated earlier, the two had known each another since childhood and, after losing touch for some time, met again while Raïssa was studying music under Lazare Lévy (1882–1964) at the Paris Conservatory. Raïssa was an accomplished musician "with a wonderful voice."[9] She was also very interested in literature; while in France, she discovered the musical works of Claude Debussy (1862–1918). There was an intellectual alliance between Raïssa and Emmanuel in addition to their commitment to each other. When asked if their meeting was by chance, Levinas responded, "How so by chance? We were bound" (Malka, *Emmanuel Levinas*, xxxvii). They were married sixty-three years and had two children and four grandchildren (241).

Levinas's birthplace in Kaunas is "at the border of Latvia and Russia . . . once known as 'Jerusalem of the East'" (3). Before the war Levinas's father, Yekhiel, ran a stationery shop and bookstore. The Levinas family—Yekhiel; Emmanuel's mother, Dvora; brothers, Boris and Aminadab; and Emmanuel—lived a short distance from the shop on Kalejimo Street on the edge of the Neman River. Levinas was born on December 30, 1905, according to the Russian Julian calendar (January 12, 1906, according to the Gregorian calendar) (6). Both his mother and father took great interest in education, as his father's shop supplied materials to local schools and his mother encouraged his interest in literature. Beginning at a young age, Emmanuel and his brothers were taught by a private Hebrew tutor in their home. The Levinas family was Orthodox and observed religious practices of kosher dietary laws, synagogue attendance, and Sabbath observation. At home his family spoke Russian; for Levinas, Russia had a "sacred mission" of bringing religious insight into philosophy through authors such as Fyodor Dostoyevsky (1821–1881) (9). Levinas grew up with awareness of both Hasidism and the Musar movement, which are quite distinct but bound by a common agreement—the importance of ethics in everyday life.[10]

With the declaration of war in 1914, the family immigrated to Russia before settling in Ukraine, where Levinas was one of five Jewish students permitted to attend the state high school in Kharkov. In 1920 his family returned to Lithuania, which had been declared an independent state by the Lithuanian Council in 1918. After the family's return to Kaunas, Levinas entered his final year of high school at the same time his father regained his stationery shop (Malka, 8–9).

Levinas then traveled to France; at Strasbourg, in 1923, he initiated his university studies, where he sought to perfect his French. Additionally, his attraction to philosophy seemed natural, coming from his interest in the Russian literature of Aleksandr Pushkin (1799–1837), Mikhail Lermontov (1814–1841), Leo Tolstoy (1828–1910), and Dostoyevsky. At the University of Strasbourg, Levinas encountered the work of Henri Bergson (1859–1941), Jacques Maritain (1882–1973), and Étienne Gilson (1884–1978). Levinas also encountered the work of Edmund Husserl (1859–1938), the founder of phenomenology and a Jew who had converted to Protestantism in 1886. One of Levinas's fellow classmates who had a significant impact on him and his family was Maurice Blanchot (1907–2003).[11] Blanchot was a French novelist and critic; the two met in Strasbourg in 1926 and became lifelong friends. Levinas obtained his bachelor's degree in 1927 and defended his doctoral thesis in 1930; he then left for Paris, while Blanchot moved in more right-wing, perhaps even fascist, political directions. In contrast to his friend, Levinas wrote critical pieces on the political climate such as "Some Reflections on the Philosophy of Hitlerism" for the journal *Esprit*. The caring camaraderie between Blanchot and Levinas, however, exemplified "victory of friendship over the ideologies of the age" (Malka, 28–30); it was Blanchot who cared for Levinas's wife and daughter[12] after Levinas became a prisoner of war in a camp near Hanover, Germany, from 1940 until 1945.

Between 1928 and 1929, Levinas studied at Freiburg University. At that time Husserl, a Jew by birth, had yet to be run out of the university, and Heidegger was several years away from delivering his famous *Rektorat* address.[13] In 1930 Levinas completed his thesis on Husserl, titled "The Theory of Intuition in the Phenomenology of Husserl." An interesting statement occurred in an exchange with former Husserl student Jean Hering, a professor of theology at Strasbourg who offered the young Levinas a copy of Heidegger's *Being and Time*. Levinas responded, "But there's no Husserl in it!," to which Hering replied, "This one goes further than Husserl" (Malka, 36–37). Levinas was highly supportive of Heidegger's creative insights.

In 1929, after hearing Husserl deliver his original material on the *Cartesian Meditations*, Levinas continued to be impressed with Husserl's writings and was influential in bringing the *Meditations* to French soil. Of course, at the University of Freiburg, Levinas met with Husserl's disciple, Heidegger, who had come from Marburg University, the place of Heidegger's first professorship. Heidegger's roots rested in traditional German Catholicism; he devoted his first thesis to Duns Scotus (1266–1308), a medieval Franciscan thinker on infinity. This Catholic sensibility, however, did not continue to propel Heidegger's work; as stated by Malka, "Heidegger burned his bridges" (41), following his own originative path.

For Levinas, the experience at Freiburg centered on the work of Husserl and Heidegger. Remarkably, he did not encounter Rosenzweig's scholarship at that time, "but his [Rosenzweig's] shadow hovered over the city and showed itself to be just as decisive for him" (42). Rosenzweig's work, particularly *The Star of Redemption* (published in 1921), was crucially important to Levinas. Interestingly, Rosenzweig flirted with Christianity only to reconnect with Judaism at the last minute, answering the call of responsibility to his original faith after a period of inactivity.

One of the renowned experiences in Levinas's intellectual career was at a conference in Davos, Switzerland. The conference ran as a colloquium for three weeks from March 7 until April 6, 1929. There were two celebrated speakers: Cassirer and Heidegger. Cassirer was a neo-Kantian philosopher and one of the few Jews to hold a major academic post in Germany; he was rector at the University of Hamburg (1929–1930). The highlight of the conference was a debate between Cassirer and Heidegger. Levinas found himself more impressed with the insights of Heidegger than those of Cassirer. Heidegger was already involved in fascism—a fact unknown to Levinas at that time. Many in the audience felt more in common with Cassirer than with Heidegger; however, Heidegger was a "great curiosity" (51). Levinas was intensely fascinated with Heidegger at that time; this fact left him with considerable sadness later in life. Levinas had no way of knowing that Heidegger would accept in 1933 "the rectorship at Freiburg and deliver a discourse of servitude to the Nazi powers" (51). Reflecting on that historic moment in his young scholarly life, Levinas felt "tears of grief" (52).

During the years between the conclusion of the Great War and the commencement of another one (1918–1939), France was a model of emancipation and integration; it provided a "safe haven for the economic, political and intellectual refugees who were streaming in from the rest of Europe" (53). Levinas became a naturalized French citizen on April 8, 1931, establishing roots as a Frenchman and as a Jew in France (66). The Third Republic in France had made it difficult to become a French citizen; one had to be recommended by the Bureau of Seals. Levinas, however, passed scrutiny with the head officer of the bureau, who provided a note of admiration about his understanding of French history.

As a French citizen, Levinas fulfilled his military duties and was officially discharged as a chief master sergeant in 1934, eleven years after he arrived in France to study at the University of Strasbourg. Levinas then became an assistant in the education department at the Alliance Israélite Universelle.[14] In 1938 Levinas devoted an article to Maritain, stating that both Christianity and Judaism were at risk under the rule of Hitler. Levinas admired the existential work of Maritain, a Catholic convert, while demonstrating an increasing interest in the work of Rosenzweig, whose philosophical explorations were inspirationally important to his own work.

Six years after Levinas arrived in Paris, he continued to function as a noncommissioned officer in the reserves; in 1939 he was part of the mobilization to the front lines of battle in France. At that time the famous German general Erwin Rommel (1891–1944) was in Rouen from June 5 to June 15, 1940. The Tenth Army to which Sergeant Levinas belonged surrendered on June 18, 1940. Levinas found himself in Stalag XIB, a prisoner of war camp in Hanover, Germany. His wife, Raïssa, on October 24, 1940, wrote a note to the president of the Commission of Revisions of Naturalizations,[15] stressing the naturalization of Levinas as a French citizen. She sought to protect him with an emphasis on his citizenship overriding the fact that he was a Jew. Levinas never lost his French citizenship, even though denaturalization was common after 1927; Levinas was exempt from this action due to his prisoner of war experience (Malka, 66). He was in captivity for five years, during which he wrote the legendary description of a dog (Bobby), penning the famous line, "Dogs may be German, but not Nazi" (71). Levinas also paid homage to a Catholic priest, Father Pierre, the counselor of the camp, and Father Chesnet, the chaplain of the camp, who assisted Jews in the camp and prayed at Jewish gravesites (72). Additionally, when Levinas found small amounts of light at night, he read Georg Wilhelm Friedrich Hegel (1770–1831), Marcel Proust (1871–1922), Denis Diderot (1713–1784), and Jean-Jacques Rousseau (1712–1778) while others played cards. When reflecting on his time in the camp, Levinas emphasized the face of evil. He replied that the menace of evil is that "[e]vil has no face" (75). During the five years Levinas was incarcerated as a prisoner of war, Raïssa and their daughter, Simone (prior to the birth of their daughter Andree Eliane and son, Michael), remained in Paris in hiding. The family found support and protection from Blanchot and the Poirier family, who worked as pharmacists and assisted the Levinas family when they moved to Rouen. Upon his release from the camps, Levinas learned that his parents and siblings perished during the war (165, 236). Levinas never spoke of his family's execution, offering only a few lines of dedication in *Otherwise than Being*, which did not appear until 1974 (80). In this dedication Levinas also acknowledged his mother-in-law and father-in-law, who were murdered around the same time (267).

Levinas's first book, *Existence and Existents*, partially written during his imprisonment at Stalag XIB, reflects on his experience in the camp. Levinas stated that one must always have "access to the Jewish texts . . . [, which] give new priority to the inner life" (82). Levinas often summoned the notion of "trace" with the idea of a face, suggesting that powerful works of literature and philosophy evoke a trace of what it is to be human.

In 1947, when Levinas returned to civilian French life, he became the director of École Normale Israélite Orientale, a branch of the Alliance Israélite Universelle that trained Jewish students to become teachers, serving there until his retirement in 1979.[16] Levinas, the philosopher and educator, was an administrator for much of his professional life. He dreaded the possibility of student rebellions and understood that people can be tasteless. Malka stated, "He [Levinas] often lacked self-restraint, was easily irritated" (90). Levinas maintained a certain distance from people, while working to gather the best teachers and encouraging the study of languages. Levinas did not function primarily as a philosophy professor; his first occupation was that of principal and director. From 1953 to 1961, Levinas was, however, the only philosophy professor and the only teacher engaging in Jewish studies. After he completed his oral exam for his thesis, "The Theory of Intuition in the Phenomenology of Husserl," in 1961, he began to teach at the University of Poitiers (1963–1967) while continuing as principal of École Normale Israélite Orientale. Levinas resigned the directorship of the school in 1979; many considered Levinas intellectually oversized for that institution. Without a full-time university appointment, he left behind few disciples.

During these years Levinas rejuvenated interpretive exegesis as he examined the work of Rashi, an acronym for Rabbi Shlomo ben Yitzhak (1040–1105), "the illustrious biblical and talmudic scholar from medieval Champagne" (107). Levinas offered two courses on Saturday, one on Rashi and a second on Russian authors. Levinas spent mornings introducing people to the importance of daily interpretive practice with the Torah. One of the dramatic components of Levinas's working with Rashi was the ever-important statement of "here I am," which announces both modesty and personal availability in a responsive commitment to the faith (109). Rashi stressed the importance of living within reality and meeting human sickness, "[b]ecause it is not good to die without warning" (114). "Ritual, commandment, liturgy, rejoices the philosopher—look for their signs in the appearance of a face in the light of day" (119). Much emerges in the language of the face of the Other, which offers an invitation to genuine light. This light is, however, "never a mystical adhesion" (121). Just as one cannot possess God, one must be careful of mere "chatter" about God (123). Rashi commented on the descendants of both Moses and Aaron in the Torah, where only the progeny of Aaron are mentioned, not those of Moses. Rashi's comment was that the vitality of faith does not abide with descendants of pure lineage but with those who assume the responsibility of "here I am."

Levinas's approach to the Talmud was akin to a "phenomenological midrash" (125). In engaging these readings, Levinas attended to a trace, an impression left behind—similar to the approach of the great master that he often referred to, Chouchani, Levinas's Talmudic teacher from 1947 until 1951.[17] Levinas "was not preoccupied with the viewpoint of historians or philologists" (Malka, 130). He was interested in the phenomenological implications for living life as a Jew. Levinas turned to the Talmud because "[p]hilosophy can lead us only to the threshold of mystery, into which it cannot enter" (136). When philosophy finds the impenetrable, one embraces the faith's call to action and responsibility.

FACES

Levinas unearthed inspiration from the lives and works of Jean Wahl (1888–1974), a French metaphysician, philosopher, and professor at the Sorbonne, and the Talmudist Mordechai Chouchani. Wahl invited Levinas to deliver lectures at the Collège Philosophique, a French philosophical society, shortly after the publication of *Existence and Existents*. Levinas also attended Friday soirées hosted by the Catholic phenomenologist Gabriel Marcel (1889–1973). At meetings of the Collège Philosophique, multiple people presented; each speaker appeared at the invitation of Wahl, including Marcel, Jean-Paul Sartre (1905–1980), and Jacques Lacan (1901–1981). Levinas stood on the margins, not having university status like another one of his friends, Blanchot. Levinas's book *Totality and Infinity*, dedicated to Marcel and Wahl, recognized their central leadership in the group.[18]

Wahl died in 1974; he let himself go by refusing a cardiac operation and lived his last few years in his room wrapped in a robe. Wahl's last request was to have a priest, a pastor, and a rabbi present at his funeral. There was no rabbi, but there was Levinas, who spoke at the graveside of his friend. In addition to Wahl, perhaps the one who had the most fundamental impact on Levinas was Chouchani. Information about Chouchani is ambiguous and minimal. He lived his whole life as a Talmudic "tramp" (156). Disciples surrounded Chouchani everywhere he went, among them a future Nobel Peace Prize laureate named Elie Wiesel (1928–2016). Chouchani was an enigma who left significant traces on Levinas's life and scholarship. With Wahl as the poet and academic and Chouchani as the prophet and traveler, Levinas benefited. Wahl was at the origin of Levinas's university career, and Chouchani modified and renewed Levinas's perspective on the Judaic sources. Between the philosopher and the Talmudist, Levinas infused his own path with double inspiration (160). Levinas's life rests between the extremes of an academic and his traveling Talmudic teacher, Chouchani.

Levinas's association with the celebrated Chouchani and Wahl is legendary; in addition, his profound friendship with Dr. Henri Nerson, a gynecologist whom Levinas met after the war, influenced him greatly. Levinas wrote the dedication to *Difficult Freedom* in Nerson's honor.[19] Their friendship was meaningful—many of Levinas's former students compared their friendship to that of French writer Michel de Montaigne (1533–1592) and the humanist scholar and writer Étienne de la Boétie (1530–1563), who were public servants for the Parliament of Bordeaux. Dr. Nerson's daughter often spoke about her memories of Levinas and Chouchani. Nerson and Chouchani had a significant influence on Levinas as he listened to their stories and their passionate engagement with ideas. Levinas referred to Nerson as a man of prodigious "moral elevation" (253). Persons of deep insight and love of ideas and the arts assisted Levinas's scholarly corpus. Levinas was incredibly precise as a writer. When he found himself in the midst of writer's block and unable to uncover the proper phrase, he habitually listened to music, which reopened the door to his scholarly writing.

Precision and creativity of thinking attracted Levinas to Heidegger. Levinas both admired Heidegger's work and engaged it in a contrarian fashion. There are many questions about Heidegger's membership in the Nazi Party, his "moments of folly," his very short time as rector at the University of Freiburg (1933–1934), and his life after his resignation (161). Heidegger's reception in France and throughout the world met with challenge as his involvement in the National Socialist Party became public. Levinas asserted that "Heidegger's commitment to Nazism had not been a circumstantial adherence, and his resignation was not followed by protest. His [Heidegger's] attachment to National Socialism began long before" (162). In many ways Levinas brought phenomenology to France, but his work was not equated with Heidegger's; Levinas's labor was understood as otherwise than Heidegger's. Interestingly, Levinas's anger toward Heidegger's participation in the Nazi Party was seldom stated; however, William J. Richardson (born 1920), at an international colloquium at Loyola University (May 20–23, 1993), recalled his first meeting with Levinas in 1963, as Richardson was about to publish a book on Heidegger.[20]

Richardson had extended his hand to Levinas, who did not accept the gesture. Levinas contended that Richardson's book celebrated 1943 as a prolific year for Heidegger—the same year Levinas's parents suffered in one concentration camp while Levinas was in a prisoner of war camp in Hanover, Germany—Stalag XIB. "Levinas [then] turned on his heel and disappeared," writes Malka (165). Levinas introduced Heidegger to France and admired the work of *Being and Time*, but he never forgot the mistakes of the man—stating, "[P]hilosophy . . . does not always guarantee wisdom" (168). One of the major points of separation between Heidegger and Levinas was that Levinas rejected the assumption that death has the final word—a difference articulated by Derrida, who was instrumental in publicly highlighting Levinas's scholarship.[21]

In 1964 Derrida published an article that would eventually be called "Violence and Metaphysics: An Essay on the Thought of Emmanuel Levinas."[22] Levinas was impressed with Derrida's work on Husserl and referred to Derrida's scholarship as representing the insights of an "abstract painter" (Malka, 183). Conversations with Derrida in response to *Totality and Infinity* influenced *Otherwise than Being*, published in 1973, twelve years after the publication of the former text. The exchanges between the two men continued, displayed eloquently in Derrida's eulogy, *Adieu to Emmanuel Levinas*. Derrida expressed deep affection and respect for Levinas upon Levinas's death on December 25, 1995.

One earlier moment of respect between Levinas and Derrida emerged during the Beaufret affair. An effort to publish a collection of essays in honor of Jean Beaufret (1907–1982)[23] incorporated a large number of major French philosophical luminaries, including Derrida, Roger Laporte (1925–2001), Michel Deguy (born 1930), René Char (1907–1988), and Blanchot. Derrida learned that Beaufret had made an anti-Semitic remark "in reference to the nomination of a professor at Clermont-Ferrand" (Malka, 179). The professor happened to be Emmanuel Levinas. With that news, Derrida immediately withdrew from membership in the Beaufret tribute; he considered Beaufret "[a] sycophant of Heidegger, moreover his constant advocate and apologist, his interlocutor—to whom the *Letter on Humanism* is addressed" (179). Heidegger's statement, titled "Letter on Humanism,"[24] was addressed to Beaufret, whose most significant work, *Dialogues avec Martin Heidegger*, had no mention of the Jewish question; this fact was an additional reason for Derrida to decline participation in the volume. The book on Beaufret,[25] when it finally appeared, had an essay by Blanchot, who stated the following: "For Emmanuel Levinas, with whom, for forty years, I had been bound by a friendship that is closer to me than my own self: in a rapport of indivisibility with Judaism" (Malka, 180). Blanchot and Levinas maintained a friendship that trumped political differences, attending to the face of the Other that directed each to an ethical echo of unending responsibility. A similar admiration guided the relationship of Derrida and Levinas.

Derrida displayed respect for Levinas in yet another incident, the Boutang episode, in which the university directors of the Sorbonne nominated philosopher Pierre Boutang (1916–1998) to become the chair of the metaphysics department and to succeed Levinas. Many were outraged that when Boutang was a young man, he had written "abhorrent things" (180). He was a follower of Charles Maurras (1868–1952), a French writer and political theorist whose nationalist ideas anticipated fascism. Levinas's refusal to be a part of a petition against Boutang surprised Derrida; Levinas forgave Boutang due to the fact that during the war he helped his friend Wahl. Levinas did not pardon the actions of Heidegger, but in the Boutang case, respect for an opponent permitted him to forgive another with whom he deeply disagreed.

Levinas's respect also extended to the Protestant world of scholarship, exemplified, in particular, by Paul Ricoeur (1913–2005), with whom Levinas had a long and significant relationship.[26] In *Proper Names* Levinas paid tribute to Ricoeur, who joined the Friday seminars held in the home of Marcel (Malka, 188). Ricoeur, unlike Marcel, embraced a clear Protestant perspective. Much like Wahl before him, this Protestant philosopher "assumed the role of intermediary between the world of the university and Levinas" (192). When Ricoeur later heard of Levinas's death (December 25, 1995), he was deeply saddened, accentuating Levinas's philosophical engagement with "exaggeration and excess" and his deep love of Russian literature (194). Ricoeur refused to describe Levinas as a Jewish philosopher but rather as a scholar who "has the Judaism of a philosopher" (197).

Additionally, Levinas's work attracted attention from Catholic scholars. In 1972 Levinas received an honorary doctorate from the Catholic University of Louvain, situated in the Flemish part of Belgium. From that time onward, he regularly returned to the university.

It would be fair to say that the University of Louvain deeply admired Levinas's work. "He once said, 'I feel at home here,'" writes Malka (203), who considers Louvain "a center of Levinasism" (205). Louvain, as a Catholic university, represented the positive Catholic reception to Levinas's work.

Levinas was party to a number of conferences set up by Enrico Castelli (1900–1977), a philosopher very close to Pope Paul VI (1897–1978). During a visit to France, Pope John Paul II stated the following: "'You have the good fortune here in France to have someone like Emmanuel Levinas. How is it that he is not here?' Alain de Rothschild, president of the Central Consistory, Émile Touati, president of the Paris Consistory, and the chief rabbi were left dumbfounded" (225). In 1977 Cardinal Karol Wojtyła visited Paris and spoke admiringly about Levinas's work as he praised the insights of Ricoeur.[27] Wojtyła became Pope John Paul II the following year.

Levinas was a frequent guest of Pope John Paul II; Levinas deeply appreciated his philosophical connection with the Holy Father and his friendship with a number of Catholics who connected him with this phenomenological pope. While in Chicago, Levinas spent time with Adriaan Peperzak, a former Franciscan, who was teaching at the Jesuit Loyola University, which was facilitating ongoing connections with Pope John Paul II. Peperzak, along with Alphonso Lingis (born 1933), who translated *Totality and Infinity* and *Otherwise than Being*, introduced Levinas to the United States. However, it was Derrida, whom Malka calls "the pope of continental philosophy in America," who brought international credibility to Levinas's work by continually citing its importance (207).

One might imagine that Levinas and Arendt, both working within the Jewish intellectual tradition, might find much common ground; however, in 1979, when in Chicago, Levinas met Arendt; they did not seem to be "on the same wavelength" (208). They did not embrace the same Jewish directions. Additionally, Levinas rejected another perspective—that of the Hasidic movement; he was wary of excessive enthusiasm in religion. As relayed by Bernard Dupuy, a Dominican priest responsible for Jewish relations: "If you had set him down in a Hassidic community for five minutes . . . you would see him tremble with fury. It was unbelievable" (213). As stated earlier, Levinas was attracted to the work of Rosenzweig's magnum opus *The Star of Redemption*, which enacted "dialogical thinking" that embraced intellectual responsibility within the faith—a position contra Hasidism (217).

Levinas displayed sensitivities for the political in his response to Germany in 1983, when he received the Karl Jaspers Prize from the University of Heidelberg. His son, Michael, stood in for him as the recipient. Whenever Levinas had responsibility and work in Germany, Michael assumed the responsibilities. Levinas vowed "to never return to Germany, where he had endured five years of captivity during the war" (261). Levinas contended that he had been saved by the French uniform and being in the French army. Such a position only furthered his love of France; his commitment as a patriot actually made him a Gaullist, according to his son. Michael referred to his father as a "philosopher of cracks," in which he unmasked fissures within the Western tradition (262–63). The care for Levinas's work continues with his grandson-in-law; David displays profound commitment to Levinas's legacy and an "astonishing capacity for work" (244), which includes coordinating international conferences on his grandfather's scholarship. David's wife and Emmanuel's granddaughter, Jöelle, is a scholar continuing the tradition of Levinas's commitment to ethics as first philosophy. Jöelle is the founder of the Raïssa and Emmanuel Levinas Center in Jerusalem. She has organized international conferences on Levinas at the Hebrew University and has edited multiple books on Levinas, including *Levinas in Jerusalem: Phenomenology, Ethics, Politics, Aesthetics*.[28]

ACKNOWLEDGMENT

Levinas was unswerving in his commitment to ideas and books without confusing their proper place in the hierarchy of existence—responsibility for the Other is primary. Love of life brought Levinas to music, a sense of humor, and eventual recognition as a major philosopher, which was slow to emerge. Levinas, acknowledged for his significant work after his retirement and departure from the Sorbonne in 1976, did not inaugurate his university life until he was already in his fifties (Malka, 274–75)[29]; he was a solitary thinker who had spent much of his time working with young people at École Normale Israélite Orientale. He was a "philosopher of anti-ideology" who was critical of ideology (278); Levinas acknowledged the importance of rationality in discerning direction and proper implementation of ideas. Malka states that few rabbis today cite Levinas; many consider his work un-inhabitable. Yet, in 1980, major scholars, such as Blanchot, Derrida, Jeanne Delhomme (1911–1983), Mickel Dufrenne (1910–1995), Jean Halpérin (1921–2012), Edmond Jabès (1912–1991), François Laruelle (born 1937), Jean-François Lyotard (1924–1998), André Neher (1914–1988), Edith Wyschograd (1930–2009), and Peperzak, composed a volume that detailed the profundity of his contribution.[30]

In 2002 the international congress at Hebrew University of Jerusalem was devoted to Levinas's insights, which are "impossible to confine to one category" (Malka, 288)—the name of the conference was Philosophical Interpretations and Religious Perspectives. Distinguished scholars attended, giving talks in English, French, and Hebrew. Levinas had more kinship with the "diaspora thinkers" than he did with the Jewish state (288). However, this man who had been born in Lithuania and adopted France as his own country "never ceased, throughout his life, to declare a visceral, carnal attachment to the Jewish state, to its rebirth, to its right to be, to its safety" (291). Ultimately, Levinas's loyalty to human dwellings trumped all other considerations. Levinas had difficulty with French government pronouncements, such as the decision to place an embargo on Israel during the 1967 Six-Day War. He had a similar reaction in 1973 during the Yom Kippur War, in which "[t]he Egyptian army crossed the Suez Canal on the most sacred day of the Jewish calendar" (293). To Levinas, the meeting place between Jewish and universal thought is the very habitation that tears us away from every home that is easily established: "the face of the Other carries upon it the imprint [and demand] of the Creator" (299). It is the face of the Other that calls forth concrete decisions and responsibility, defining our humanness. I now turn to the famous interview with Levinas conducted by Nemo, which provides an interactive view of Levinas's recollections that supports Malka's journalistic portrait of Levinas.

Conversations with Philippe Nemo

Nemo's interviews with Levinas, broadcast on Radio France-Culture in February and March of 1981, compose *Ethics and Infinity: Conversations with Philippe Nemo*. The interviews afford a glimpse of Levinas's insights. The conversations allowed listeners and readers to engage "the *saying* of the living author [that] authenticates the *said* of the deposited work."[31] Nemo, a French philosopher and professor at ESCP-EAP European School of Management, understood Levinas's philosophical and pragmatic sense of home in France as nurtured by "an unwavering rational and spiritual decision" (Nemo, preface, vii). Levinas was outgoing and, at times, "effusive" (viii). He was part of the intellectual milieu of Paris, engrossed in intellectual, artistic, and political life. Nemo lived only one hundred meters from Levinas, but many facts about Levinas's life were unknown to him. Nemo rebuts a common misunderstanding of Levinas as among "sleepwalking disciples" without their own critical perspectives (ix, xii); Levinas's work is, indeed, prophetic. This assessment is akin to that of Richard A. Cohen, who authored "Better than Being," the introduction to *Ethics and Infinity*, and translated the interviews.[32] The title of Cohen's introduction denotes Levinas's creative and critical response to Heidegger's ontological understanding of historical revelation. Levinas's rejoinder to Heidegger was a profound countermove of "ethics as first philosophy," as prior to Being.

In *Ethics and Infinity*, Levinas takes us into an ethical world *immemorial*, existing long before the stress on Being, a world that demands space for an ethical utterance: "I am my brother's keeper." Levinas rejected the Shakespearean conundrum of "to be or not to be"[33]; instead, he underlined the importance of the human face as a call of ethical height answered with the exclamation "here I am" (Cohen, introduction, 11). Responsibility trumps Being. To illustrate this point, Cohen references Gandhi in the late 1930s during India's striving for independence from British rule. Gandhi knew the British would eventually leave, because "[m]oral force is a scandal for ontological thinking" (13). Moral force, demand, and responsiveness center Levinas's work, which reminds us of "an infinite responsibility before others" (15). Levinas's scholarship prompts listening to an archaic ethical echo that appeals to moral uprightness as one attends to the face of the Other.

Early in the interview, Nemo asked a fundamental question: "How have you harmonized these two modes of thought, the Biblical and philosophical?" (23). Levinas's response specified that they do not need harmonization; however, it was out of his religious tradition that Levinas learned the importance of books from which the study of ideas naturally emerges. Husserl's work returned him to an ancient biblical heritage with an ethical call that commenced infinitely earlier than Being.[34] Husserl's insights harmonized with a biblical demand that humans function as responsible participants in the meeting of existence. This decentering of the self continues in the scholarship of Heidegger and in Levinas's project, with ethics functioning as the fulcrum of human existence.

In *Ethics and Infinity* Levinas stated that Heidegger had written "one of the finest books in the history of philosophy" (37), *Being and Time*. Heidegger took philosophy to existence, engaging seminal issues that outline human experience through descriptions of anxiety, questions of nothingness, and existence itself. Heidegger vacated the realm of "absolute thought" exemplified by the works of Hegel and his phenomenology of existence (43). The ethical separates Levinas's project from Heidegger's ontological project. The prominence of an immemorial ethic underscores Levinas's project with a human face beckoning one back to an ancient call of responsibility that is prior to existence itself.

Levinas attends to the "there is," a dwelling in the emptiness and silence before all creation (48–49). The "there is" is as impersonally and existentially fundamental as the phrase "it rains" (48). It is in revelatory encounter with the face of the Other that one finds "deliverance from the 'there is'" (52). Liberation from the "there is" comes from a "dis-inter-ested[ness]" that moves from the demand of possession related to the self to ethical action in response to the demand of the Other (52).

The rejection of possession recognizes the necessity of uniqueness, separation, and difference. Impersonal enactment of responsibility permits the reality of the "there is" to fade; the person, the face, the event, the object discloses itself in an existential reality, a solitude of being. The notion of solitude is a central theme in existentialism, announced by Heidegger, Sartre, and Maurice Merleau-Ponty (1908–1961). Solitude stresses the "transitive" and elusive. For Levinas, "solitude" as isolation is contrary to his project; solitude of ethical action emerges in response to the call of the Other and is central to Levinas's understanding of the "here I am," the "if not me, then whom" sociality of his work (57–58). Levinas describes a sociality that engages in an impersonal ethic authorized by "me" when the solitude of existential life requires the enactment of my responsibility.

Levinas defines "filiality" as a relationship with an Other, as a parent attentive to the alterity of the child and wary of the impulse to possess. The alterity of a son or daughter commences with "I am." The renewal of the parent via the offspring represents complete exteriority of comprehensive alterity, which displays a "pluralist existing" (71–72). Responsiveness to renewal and all-inclusive difference discards the compulsion of possession and totality.

Levinas's first encounter with the critique of totality emanated from Rosenzweig's rejection of Hegel's system of absolute thought. Rejection of totality and the absolute makes ethics as first philosophy a responsive freedom lived out in matchless accountability for the Other cared for in response to a call of "absolute individuation" of the ethical that originates with attentiveness to the face of the Other (81).

The phenomenology of the face articulated in *Ethics and Infinity* argues for an impersonal encounter with the Other beyond familiarity where "[t]he best way of encountering the Other is not even to notice the color of his eyes!" (85). Caring is impersonal, begun in the face of the Other, and commanded by an ethical echo prior to a particular encounter. The face points us to a sense of "uprightness," giving rise to an ethical mandate of responsibility to and for the Other (86). The mandate of the face signifies, in an impersonal fashion, without context, a demand to attend to responsibility for the Other. The face is the original site of an originative trace of the Saying of ethics. For Levinas, justice demands a limit on ethics for the Other, as attention is turned to responsibility for those not present in face-to-face discourse—the unseen, the unnoticed, and the unheard demand justice. Additionally, ethics disrupts justice, with the face of the Other pointing to an infinite call of responsibility; recognition of the face is impersonal and moves justice as a necessary interruption for those not proximate, which interrupts ethical attentiveness focused on a given person.

Levinasian ethics involves "responsibility as responsibility for the Other" (95). We are literally tied to the Other. For Levinas, we are responsible, guilty, and held hostage to and for one another: "My responsibility is untransferable, no one could replace me" (100). We are hostage to a universal ethical echo: "I am my brother's keeper." One then discerns the particular requirements of response to and for another. It is in reply that we discover who we are, ascertaining ourselves in acts of ethical responsibility that offer testimony to a timeworn ethical echo.

The glory of this ethical testimony begins with the historical utterance—"here I am!" In such a moment Saying enters the public arena as Said. It is in such a moment that an ethically charged witness stands out, responding to existence and life, uttering from an interior voice that is exteriorly propelled. In the midst of the "crooked road" of life, a witness stands upright as an ethical typology in the midst of existence (109–10). For Levinas, an ethical witness nurtures a philosophical and religious life.

Prophetic witnessing is at the heart of revelation. The prophetic mode reposes within the Bible, its "literary origin" (115). However, religion is not identical to philosophy. The task of religion is to prophesy and console. Philosophy seeks to know. Religion ultimately connects one with meaning through God. Knowledge is not the fulcrum upon which religion rests; the center is faith. To be truly human moves toward both knowledge (philosophy) and faith (religion) in response to a creation larger than oneself, while demanding ethical action and responsibility: "Every accusation and persecution, as all interpersonal praise, recompense, and punishment presuppose the subjectivity of the ego, substitution, the possibility of putting oneself in the place of the other, which refers to the transference from the 'by the other' into a 'for the other'" (117–18). As stated, Levinas's project gathers around one major assertion—the ongoing and unending enactment of a phenomenological ethical reality: "I am my brother's keeper." The final section of this sketch of footprints emerges from Levinas's own signature, which further underscores responsibility as impersonal and without completion.

Levinas's Signature

The "Signature" included at the end of *Difficult Freedom* was initially published in 1963 when Levinas was fifty-seven years old. Some of the material below is redundant with the discussions from Malka and Nemo. I decided to leave the information as stated in order to offer the reader an appreciation of what Levinas himself wanted to record. "Signature" functions as an autobiographical statement, opening with recognition of the importance of the Hebrew Bible, a reminder of Levinas's birth in Lithuania, his love of Pushkin and Tolstoy, and the Russian Revolution of 1917, which he experienced at the age of eleven while living in Ukraine (291). From 1923 on, he was at the University of Strasbourg, where his friendship with Blanchot began. His teachers were Frenchmen who were adolescents at the time of the Dreyfus affair.[35] Levinas, as a newcomer to France, developed deep roots and love for the country and its culture.

From 1928 until 1929, Levinas was in Freiburg. Husserl and Heidegger "signified" the University of Freiburg. While in Freiburg, Levinas discovered phenomenology. It was not until six years later in France that Marcus Cohen recommended the reading of *Der Stern von Erlösung* to Levinas.[36] Levinas's "Signature," in *Difficult Freedom*, explains that Rosenzweig's writings on Jewish identity allowed Levinas to understand Judaism as "a path of truth" (44). After the war Levinas became the director of the École Normale Israélite Orientale, a school with a one-hundred-year tradition, where frequent visits from Chouchani were of importance. He also completed his doctorate of letters in 1961 and then secured "[p]rofessorships at the University of Poitiers, from 1967 on at the University of Paris-Nanterre, and since 1973 at the Sorbonne" (291). Levinas refers to this short inventory as a biography driven by the memory of the Nazis and his deep appreciation for Husserl's contribution to philosophy. At the Sorbonne, where he taught from 1973 until 1976, Levinas was a frequent participant at the soirées offered by Marcel. Levinas emphasized his friendship with Wahl, who was long in captivity in Germany. Their friendship was highly significant to Levinas, as were the regular conferences that Wahl inspired at the Collège Philosophique.

At the conferences and with his friends steeped in phenomenology, Levinas articulated his appreciation of Husserl and the questioning of Platonic privilege: "In spite of his intellectualism and his conviction about the excellence of the West, Husserl has thus brought into question the Platonic privilege, until then uncontested, of a continent which believes it has the right to colonize the world" (292). Levinas refers to Heidegger and his work on the "Being of being" as "the disappearance of every existent" (292). Levinas points to a world of "existence without existents," which is contrary to the Enlightenment hope of existents rising up and controlling existence or the "there is." Levinas lamented about the Western impulse to impose on existence and the Other. He rejected both Hegel's world of absolute thought and the Heideggerian view of Being. Levinas turned, contrarily, to a primordial understanding of human proximity of one to another in order to reclaim the impersonal call of ethics: "The disproportion between the Other and the self is precisely moral consciousness" (293). It is the ethical, not Being, that is the first call to the human.

In *Totality and Infinity* Levinas warned of the danger of reducing the Other, *l'Autre*, to the Same. The effort to move the Other to the Same invites violence, whether in war, bureaucracy, or in searching for metaphysical principles or laws that level difference. Contrary to René Descartes (1596–1650), who placed the "I" within *cogito*, Levinas enlisted the notion of an "I" called forth in response to the meeting of responsibility for the Other. The "I" discussed by Levinas, unlike the Cartesian "I," is propelled by a desire of responsibility that can never be quenched. It is "[t]he privilege of the Other" that calls forth the "moral consciousness" of an "I" (*Difficult Freedom*, 294). It is the face of the Other that functions as an epiphany that calls out self-knowledge previously unknown. Such a transactional call defines Levinas's understanding of an "ethical consciousness." Ethical consciousness responds to "the highness of the Other" with an attentiveness that necessitates differentiation and separateness. The "I" called forth by the infinite refuses to control the Other or to govern the "there is" of existence. The "I" called forth by the Other is responsible, not dominant or imposing. In such moments of responsiveness, human transcendence happens and identity shifts and changes, not from strategic calculation, but from genuine receptiveness to the Other. As Levinas suggests, the Other holds the "I" "hostage" in a manner that demands acknowledgment of and responsibility for the Other, which as a by-product calls forth my own life of "uprightness" (294–95).

Levinas manifested genuine respect for Husserl's last work, *The Crisis of European Sciences and Transcendental Phenomenology*.[37] In this scholarly missive, Husserl takes phenomenology into the world of origins with his suggestion of "genetic phenomenology."[38] Husserl understood the layered nature of existence and our need to discover such realities without falling prey to reductionism. Husserl returns us to a world of multiplicity that is better understood as an infinite onion with layer after layer of significance and meaning. One can observe the beginning signs of Ricoeur's emphasis on "emplotment" and Hans-Georg Gadamer's (1900–2002) stress on "horizon."[39] The interplay between the particular and the universal is central to Judaism (*Difficult*

Freedom, 136); it is essential in navigating the unique and many-sided understandings of origins that guide genetic phenomenology.

For Levinas, there is a constant attentiveness to particulars, which is the sole form of access to the universal. The face of the Other is a call for attending to a universal ethical echo: "I am my brother's keeper." However, this universal call plays out in the particular, not the abstract. What it means to be my brother's keeper has a singular answer: one must turn to the particular and answer each question uniquely. Repeatedly, a person must stand before God and existence with a single communicative gesture of "here I am."

In the preceding biographical and brief autobiographical fragments, we find that Levinas emphasizes creative origins that commence with his daily work with the Talmud. His attentiveness to origins attracted him to phenomenology, "the things themselves," to responsiveness to the human face, to attentiveness to an immemorial ethical echo. Levinas understands the complexity of responsiveness to origins and answers that do not rest in extremes of codes or subjectivism; ethical applications and origins dwell in the unique relationship between the particular and the universal. It is in such moments that one stands before God's world saying, "here I am," not in self-righteousness, but within a prayerful sense of uprightness. Ethics is a never-ending task of discerning human responsibility in a unique given moment in time that nourishes an ethical call older than Adam and Eve.

The Saying and the Said in Communication Ethics: Origins and Echoes

Levinas's "ethics as first philosophy" pivots on ethics, justice, the meeting of difference and opposition, traces, and the everyday. His life and philosophy embrace origins of difference. Multiple languages, places of engagement, and commitments of faith and intellect yield traces of Saying within the Said of new directions and places of study and practice of ethics. Levinas's origins of difference yield insights that are otherwise than convention. For instance, Levinas is known for his commitment to ethics that cannot be reified into a programmatic metaphysical plan. Ethics engages the proximate, those before us, and our response and obligation are disrupted continually by justice. The demands of justice require consideration of those not part of our immediate ethical proximate obligation; those not at the table of immediate conversation must be considered. Justice, in the development of institutional obligations that attend to those out of immediate sight, must also be interrupted by ethics; at times, the immediate ethical obligations to a given person trump the demands for justice. Levinas's interplay of ethics and justice refuses reification, solidification, and codification.

Ethics.—Levinas's project begins with the face of the Other and moves one to an ethical echo that infuses one with a charge of responsibility to return to the Other in the uniqueness and particularity of obligation. The face of the Other is the originative point of ethical awakening. When one is inattentive to the face of the Other, the commencement of ethics finds no movement into responsible action to and for the Other.

Justice.—Levinasian justice disrupts ethics, reminding us that obligation does not rest with the proximate Other alone but must attend to those not present who demand our attentive concern. Ethics without program and metaphysical assurance finds disruption in uncertainty and its limits. Justice announces the boundary limit of ethics, demanding concern for those not proximal to our immediate attention and care.

Interplay.—Levinas's project turns on engagement with the particular and universal, totality and infinity, ethics and justice, Saying and Said, and an ethical echo culminating in the response of "here I am." Ethics emerges from response and within a unity of interruptions that curtails confidence in my action. I am responsible, not self-righteously assured.

Ethical traces.—From the face of the Other, the Talmud, and the joy of existence, ethical traces of Saying emerge. The face of the Other meets me in ambiguity, not familiarity. The notion of trace is central to the abstruseness of the face of the Other. The Other moves me to an immemorial echo reminding me of ongoing responsibility.

Everyday work and uniqueness of call.—Levinas was a magnificent philosopher who, as a director of École Normale Israélite Orientale, grounded his life in Others in everyday practical activities. Communication ethics dwells in the height and depth of the routine of concrete life, not in the clarity of abstract theory.

This chapter, working under the metaphors of footprints and echoes, reminds us of the importance of concrete experiences in conjunction with ideas of weight and height that infuse time before time with ethical import. Footprints are visual, a potential ethical optic. Echoes are audio, a prospective/ancient command of responsibility. Together, footprints and echoes suggest that all of existence matters, as we follow an ethical obligation that demands that we witness to and testify for an immemorial voice beckoning us from the wilderness into a call of unending responsibility. Communication ethics is housed in the Said of life, the footprints we leave behind; such marks are our traces of the Saying of ethics that transform "me" as I attend to the demands of the face of the Other.

CHAPTER 3

The Commencement of Responsibility: The Enigma of the Face

The thought awakened to the face of the other man is not a thought of . . . a representation, but from the start a thought for . . . a non-indifference for the other, breaking the equilibrium of the even and impassive soul of pure knowledge, an awakening to the other man in his uniqueness indiscernible for knowledge, an approach to the first one to come along in his proximity as neighbour and unique one.

—Emmanuel Levinas, *Alterity and Transcendence*

Whether it is our face (Brown & Levinson 1987; Goffman 1967), our thirst for justice, the person we love, or a simple artifact, they are experiences and/or presented as what we are attached to, what counts, what matters.

—François Cooren, *Action and Agency in Dialogue: Passion, Incarnation and Ventriloquism*

The face of the Other cannot be claimed or possessed. Such is the reason Levinas equated particularity of ethical responsibility with attentiveness irrespective of the color of another's eyes.[1] It is not our relationship with another but our responsibility to and for another that shapes ethical obligation and ultimately our identity. Levinas's teacher, Shushani/Chouchani, announces the actuality of such a perspective.[2] Despite the centrality of Chouchani to major scholars such as Levinas and Wiesel, we know little about this famous teacher of the Talmud. I turn to Wiesel's and Levinas's discussions of their relationships with Chouchani in order to understand the power of the human face as an enigma that commences with a spiritual awakening of responsibility. The task of this chapter is to explicate the enigma and the ambiguity of the face and its initial call for responsibility. Levinas does not simply discuss the face as the primordial call that initiates responsibility. He does not invade the privacy of another life. This chapter exemplifies a pragmatic care for another's uniqueness that resists the practical, philosophical, and/or psychological unmasking of the Other.

Introduction

Levinas often described the significance of the nudity of the face as the primordial origin of alertness to responsibility. The face is the initiation of a spiritual awakening that turns one to an ethical echo that calls forth an enactment of unique and personal responsibility. This chapter outlines an important character in Levinas's personal and scholarly life, Chouchani, announcing the face as an enigma that calls forth personal responsibility, the heart of communication ethics.

The emphasis on face and responsibility begins with "Wiesel's Recounting" about the impact of Chouchani on his life. The chapter then turns to Levinas's text, in *"Alterity and Transcendence,"* in which he united the face of the Other and transcendence. Finally, the chapter examines the "The Saying and the Said in Communication Ethics: Chouchani and the Face," with recognition that the face is the origin of Levinas's ethics project. Without attending to the face of another, recognition of an immemorial guiding ethical echo of responsibility goes unheeded.

The face is an enigma on two counts. First, as one encounters the face of the Other, the meeting is impersonal, not personal. Second, as one returns to the face of the Other after attending to an ethical echo, there is no template for the manner and substance of ethical responsibility. Such a task necessitates the discerning of the ethical charge of being human. I offer Chouchani as an example of this enigmatic beginning of responsibility via Wiesel's discussion of his relationship with Chouchani, which underscores the notion of ambiguity related to this itinerant scholar.

Wiesel's Recounting

Wiesel was a Romanian-born Holocaust survivor, the recipient of the 1986 Nobel Peace Prize, the author of eleven books, and a writer responsive to the Holocaust experience.[3] Wiesel recounted his experiences with Chouchani in a memoir, *All Rivers Run to the Sea*, and in a chapter in *Legends of Our Time*, lending insight into his meeting of the itinerant scholar Chouchani.[4] Wiesel's reflections begin with the assertion that no one actually knew this man's (Chouchani) real name. This nomadic teacher was a "Wandering Jew" who labored to obscure clarity and "destroy what seemed secure" (*Legends*, 87). The identity of Chouchani was unknown; the more one asked about him, the greater the confusion. One of the reasons for the perplexity was that Chouchani consistently remade his past; he dismissively responded to probing questions about his background. Chouchani fabricated one birthplace after another. "The vastness of his exaggerations exceeded the level of falsehood," which led people, at times, to question whether his voyages were real or just imagined (88).

Chouchani had the habit of appearing suddenly without notification. Each appearance seemed to materialize from nowhere. He would interact with people/students for a while and then abruptly depart. Chouchani was so strange and inaccessible that he actually generated fear in many of his students. Wiesel recounts the story of one of his meetings with Chouchani. Wiesel writes that this mysterious teacher approached him unannounced while Wiesel was riding a train on his way to give a talk on the Book of Job. After questioning his knowledge on the Book of Job and asserting that Wiesel "understood nothing" about the book, Chouchani invited himself to Wiesel's Shabbat talk (*All Rivers*, 122–23). Wiesel recalled, "That Shabbat is engraved in my memory like a punishment. No one had invited Shushani, and I wondered whether the sole purpose of his gate-crashing was to ruin my talk. That was his method. He liked to demolish before rebuilding, to abase before offering recompense" (122). This itinerant teacher came without introduction and without a hint of conventional politeness.

Chouchani supposedly traveled the world numerous times, without out a passport or any obvious income source. He was the master of thirty languages; people attested to this fact, stating that "[h]is French was pure, his English perfect, and his Yiddish harmonized with the accent of whatever person he was speaking with" (*Legends*, 88–89). Chouchani's attire did not match the eloquence of his linguistic diversity, however. He was dirty to the point of startling the onlooker, who would quickly step aside when Chouchani moved forward.

For three years Wiesel was Chouchani's disciple in Paris. Wiesel first met him in Paris after a religious service concluded; Wiesel witnessed Chouchani standing outside the synagogue, conversing with a group of the members. When Chouchani noticed Wiesel, Chouchani interrupted his own fast-paced speech and stared directly at him. This first meeting involved a series of questions that put Wiesel on the spot; Chouchani ridiculed Wiesel's choice of philosophy as a subject for study. Wiesel asserted that Chouchani learned with a singular purpose—to answer questions and to question others. Chouchani was intensely committed to learning and expected the same from others. Chouchani repeatedly asked Wiesel to probe him with questions; Chouchani modeled the importance of supplying answers and used such moments to draw forth insights from his rich knowledge base. When Chouchani stated that Wiesel's coming to France was for one purpose only, to meet him, Wiesel became scared, with his heart beating ever so rapidly.

In Wiesel's first meeting with Chouchani, this wandering teacher queried Wiesel and offered responses; Wiesel told Chouchani that his comments were beautiful, which sent Chouchani into a rage. Chouchani argued against the term *beautiful*; he stated that a human being finds definition by what enrages him. This seventy-plus-year-old man seemed ageless and adhered to no authority; he lived without any obvious sense of place. Mystery defined the man. Not surprisingly, a number of persons stated that Chouchani enjoyed ridiculing people—he had a manic and compulsive need to deride at least one person a day. He was able to accomplish this task with his knowledge base; he seemed to know everything. Chouchani was a man who conscientiously worked within the shadows; ambiguity was a defining characteristic. The mixed reaction to him resulted in some calling him a saint and others referring to him as Satan (*Legends*, 89–94).

Stories about Chouchani were legendarily grand. For example, one tale has Chouchani caught by a Gestapo agent, whereupon Chouchani informed his captor that he was an Aryan professor of mathematics. The Gestapo agent, who also served as a professor of mathematics, called him a liar. At that juncture Chouchani proposed that if he gave his capturer an unsolvable math problem, the agent would be required to free him without further questioning. However, if the Gestapo agent could solve the math question, then the Gestapo agent could shoot Chouchani without any protest. As the account goes, on the next day, Chouchani secured his freedom. Evidently, the Gestapo agent failed to answer the problem or Chouchani's actions convinced him of his uniqueness, saving his life. After the encounter, Chouchani went to Switzerland (*All Rivers*, 127).

Wiesel stated that from his first encounter with Chouchani and upon hearing others offer stories about the man, he was often so troubled that sleep eluded him. Nevertheless, Wiesel knew that Chouchani had something of importance to teach him; he sought out Chouchani the next day, sensing that there was something vital about this unconventional character. Then, abruptly, Chouchani was no longer in France; he had left, perhaps gone on one of his tours that would take him around the world.

Months later, Wiesel was on a train to Taverny, and he saw Chouchani, who asked if he could sit next to him. Wiesel acquiesced to Chouchani's request, although he felt embarrassed by his proximity to such an unkempt creature. The two men arrived at Taverny, and to Wiesel's surprise, Chouchani got off the train with him. Chouchani followed Wiesel, inquiring about Wiesel, his academic area, and his work with students. Wiesel then described his lecture that centered on Job, only to have Chouchani state that Job had suffered much and continued to suffer from Wiesel's lecture. Chouchani stayed and worked with a number of Wiesel's students; when he was about to leave, a student inquired about his next destination. His response was curt—it was no one's business but his own.

Wiesel recounts his association with Chouchani in a succinct fashion in *Legends of Our Time*. Wiesel argued with him, with the objective, no less, of asking Chouchani to be his teacher! As a teacher, Chouchani followed his own pattern:

> He came back twice a week, never the same day, never the same hour. Sometimes he came early in the morning, while the city was still sleeping; at other times, he seemed to draw the twilight in behind him. He stayed three hours, four, five, six. A day, a century, for him it was all the same: he denied time. As soon as

he arrived he began to speak on whatever subject preoccupied him that day. And each time I felt the same sense of amazement.

Later I learned that during this same period he had other disciples (Emmanuel Levinas was one), and that he devoted as many hours to them as to me. (*Legends*, 103)

After being Chouchani's disciple for three years, Wiesel indicated that he did not know him any better than he did after their first meeting. Chouchani refused to let anyone "imitate" him; he refused to respond to any requests that required him to justify himself and his origins. Chouchani did not permit anyone to reify him by taking away his "future" as they attempted to "possess" knowledge of him (105–6). Then one day in 1948, without saying goodbye, Chouchani left. He did not return. Upon Chouchani's departure, Wiesel traveled to Israel, only to learn that Chouchani had journeyed there after leaving France. Neither man stayed very long in the Holy Land. Wiesel learned a short time later that Chouchani was living in Montevideo, Uruguay, "leading the same life there as in France" (108). Wiesel often considered boarding the first plane to Montevideo to find his teacher, but resisted. For many years Wiesel met people from all over the world who had known him. Wiesel wanted to find Chouchani one more time, even though he feared this man who condemned him to "doubt." It seemed as if Chouchani had an odd form of "immortality" (109).

In *All Rivers Run to the Sea*, Wiesel referred to Chouchani as the "mysterious Talmudic scholar" with an aggressive communicative style; Chouchani also intimidated with his slovenly appearance (121). This brilliant man permitted his students to lose face to the point that they wanted to escape. Additionally, Chouchani worked with Levinas and others who supposedly paid him "fabulous fees" (124). Chouchani functioned as an enigma to those he taught; he intentionally kept his life a mystery from others:

Everything about him was a mystery. Where had he come from? Philosophy, Marx said, has no history, but what about philosophers? Don't they have a history? This one seemed not to, or else he meant to keep it secret.

No one knew his real name, his origin, or his age. What kind of family did he come from? (124)

Chouchani would take questions on any topic from the midrash, the Torah, politics, history, and even detective novels. He responded to all questions with one exception—those centered on himself. In fact, personal questions made him angry. Chouchani's attention was on ideas and events, historical and contemporary. His objective was to call into question "established truths" (126). Wiesel sometimes wondered about the legitimacy of Chouchani's being a Talmud reciter and scholar for hire as he acted as a "sage" or as a "beadle" while giving lectures on the Talmud (129). Through the insights of Malka, there are similar assessments of Chouchani.

Malka's biography intentionally kept the enigma of Chouchani alive; Malka only disclosed three major personal points about him.[5] First, Chouchani was born in Lithuania as Mordechai Rosenbaum. Second, he had a photographic memory, which permitted him to sell his textual services to others. Third, Malka disclosed the nature of Chouchani's death. One day, in the middle of his speaking, Chouchani's head fell softly on a female student's shoulder; he died in 1965, in Montevideo, Uruguay. Wiesel offers a reflective account of Chouchani's death:

> In Jewish tradition such a death is considered a *mitat neshika*, or gentle death: The angel comes, embraces the chosen one as one would a friend, and takes him away, sparing him every trace of agony and suffering. He was in full possession of his faculties. Since an essay I had written on his teachings was found in his pocket, I was asked to compose the Hebrew inscription for his tombstone: "The rabbi and sage Mordechai Shushani, blessed be his memory. His birth and his life are bound and sealed in enigma. Died the sixth day of the week, Erev Shabbat Kodesh, 26 Tevet 5726." (*All Rivers*, 129)

Wiesel's account of this influential enigmatic face provides an entrance into this question: how does one person fundamentally transform and alter the life of another?

The corpus of Levinas's project provides no direct answer to this question but announces insights that recalibrate a life, displayed in *Alterity and Transcendence*. It is the Other who alters one's life; the profundity of the human face transforms. The face refuses possession; Chouchani is an exemplar of protected identity grounded in ambiguity and lack of precision. Vagueness associated with Chouchani's identity, not clarity of historical description, guides discussion of his importance. Levinas offers a description of alterity and transcendence that dwells within a world unclaimed by undue lucidity.

Alterity and Transcendence

Levinas wrote the essays that constitute *Alterity and Transcendence* between 1967 and 1989.[6] The book "leads us directly to the idea that transcendence is 'alive in the relation to the other man.'"[7] Transcendence is a "going beyond," an act that permits recognition of the separate and distant that resists amalgamation of the Same and the Other (Hayat, 9). Transcendence permits one to discover oneself beyond oneself, altering identity through the meeting of alterity and difference. Through alertness to alterity, identity formation is a by-product that emerges from performative acts of response. Transcendence, for Levinas, materializes from exteriority, not from originative interiority imposed on another. The face of the Other functions as an original dwelling, a primal home for the possibility of transcendence.

Transcendence infuses the vitality of infinity and totality, the Saying and the Said. Without transcendence, the notions of totality and the Said reify insight, lessening the ability to apprehend the "beyond," the "not yet." In each of the essays in this collection, Levinas examines an expression of transcendence that arises via a responsive encounter with a human face that initiates transcendence within ethics as first philosophy.

Transcendence, for Levinas, is an original awakening of thought that requires attentiveness to alterity and subsequent unique responses. Recognition of difference requires distance and consideration that permits one to respond to the distinctiveness of the Other. The original locus of transcendence is the human face, which resists precision of definition: "The best way of encountering the Other is not even to notice the color of his eyes!"[8] Levinas stated that Plotinus provides one of the first introductions to transcendence, stressing a totally transcendent "One" that has no multiplicity, materiality, or division.[9] All of life and creation begins from the One. Plotinus, founder of the Neoplatonic school, initiated the concept of happiness, *eudaimonia*—a union with the One, with happiness functioning as a flight from existence. Plotinus wrote in the mid-third century, with Levinas returning to the insights of Plotinus in order to articulate a "why" for philosophy's dissatisfaction with philosophy; discontent emanates from an aspiration to seek union with the One—such a drive, according to Levinas, is at the heart of the "demigod" (*Alterity*, 10).

Monotheism also manifests the ambition to connect with the One. Additionally, a pure rationality yields a similar expectation of union with the One and absolute knowledge framed by Hegel. For Levinas, philosophy was a move counter to the One and questions of immanence and the One sought by both Hegel and Husserl. Levinas uses the Husserlian view of "intentionality" without assuming a sense of union (16–17); Levinas understands separation and distance as fundamental conceptual keys. Levinas offers a "double intentionality" that consists of the following relations: consciousness of and consciousness for. The former connects one to alterity, the "thing itself," with the latter assuming responsibility for the Other (26). By attending to the face of the Other, one is spiritually awakened to an ethical echo that commands acts of responsibility. This awakening leads one back to the Other with conscious responsibility for the Other implemented within a particular place and relationship. Levinas rejects transcendence that advocates union with the One. Levinas describes a conceptual shift toward transcendence of an "I" called into responsibility for another. This responsibility rejects union, accentuating separation and distance. This ethical call transports us to a response chosen from manifold options that unite transcendence with multiplicity.

For Levinas, in *Alterity and Transcendence*, ethics and transcendence call into question the essence of a routine human identity, providing reminders about the reality of a "surplus of signification" (27). "Bad conscience" emerges when the "I" unites with the Other; only distance and separation permit consciousness of responsibility for another (21). Bad conscience unites with the sovereign or "hateful I," refusing to respond to the possibility of transcendence (28). Good conscience engages alterity, which distinguishes one person from another, one form of responsibility from another, and one concept or idea from another—rejecting the impulse to confuse "this" with "that." The "secret of sociality" dwells in the vigor of distance and separation (30). Only in such an exceptional view of sociality is a person called into the performative testimony of "here I am." The "I" that answers emerges unique, unattached, and formed by and within a sociality shaped by separation and distance.

Levinas emphasized that the notion of transcendence stipulated by Plato relies upon a "theory of reminiscence" (31). Ethics, as understood by Levinas, connects one to both an immemorial past and a situated rationality that is necessary in discerning a proper response. Plato connects reason and *logos*, with the latter assuming access to the animation of time before time. This is an alive past that "regards me," according to Levinas. This sense of the before and the beyond accounts for a surplus of meaning that cannot and should not be totally represented. Levinas stated that the ethical resides in an immemorial "voice" that moves the human being from "for-itself" to "for-the-Other." Levinas termed this transformation the "transcendence of inspiration." The immemorial past appeals to a person transformed via ethical responsibility and action; Levinas describes this momentary access to an immemorial past as a "heteronomy of ethical obedience" (31–35). This external demand originates with the face of the Other and shifts attention to an immemorial call for ethical action that gives rise to a "derivative I" constituted by responsibility for the Other.

One of the significant directives suggested by Levinas is that the carrying out of an ethical change is not personal. In fact, such action necessitates an impersonal portrayal of responsibility enacted with disinterestedness that guides responsibility to and for the Other, "disinterestedness of a responsibility for the other and for his *past*—a past that for me is immemorial" (37). Responsibility hinges on responsiveness to a universal call that dwells within the immemorial, which returns one to a particular face with the obligation to the Other, an ethics of optics transformed by an audio ethic that eventuates in the returning of one to a "derivative I" without predisposed assurance. Levinas's description of ethics resists totalization of ethical expectation and procedure—the loss of differentiation and difference.

Levinas counters amalgamation. He contends that universal belief in rationality is yet another form of totalization; it imposes and reifies meaning. Levinas argued that from Aristotle to Husserl, meaning resides within a whole or a unit, which permits one to discern "a characteristic property of natural things," thereby ordaining the power to confer meaning on things in the natural world (43). Husserl, as understood by Levinas, sought to intuit the whole—the gestalt of meaning. On the other hand, Kant's theory of schematism[10] dismantled totality; it revealed meaning as partially displayed in a temporal moment. Kant's position "destabilized" the totality of rationality without eliminating rationality per se. This position is imperative to Levinas's critique of Being, which understands totality as both a reality and fiction. Totality as reality is the whole from which parts emerge. Totality as a fiction recognizes the power of parts in the constitution of a temporal whole—hence the interplay of part and whole (*Alterity*, 49–50). Totality, as both true and fictional, permits new insights to emerge as one pushes off the previously known, such as institutionalized comprehensions. Totality is an impossibility that is simultaneously a vital space or collection of the whole that provides a space from which innovative particular discernments emerge. Levinas reminds us that many wish for totalization of ideas and positions; however, peace among persons is "otherwise than in the totality" (51). Just as totality is understood within the dialectic of truth and fiction, Levinas offers an otherwise than conventional casting of infinity.

Levinas states that exodus from the "originative I" with recognition of the limitation of the "I" alone is a central philosophical pursuit and objective of Marcel, Merleau-Ponty, Ludwig Feuerbach (1804–1872), and Martin Buber (1878–1965). Each of these authors framed the inescapable interplay of the "I" with sociality; this communicative engagement with another produces, shifts, and changes human identity. Levinas argued that the infinite is a contrived form of "irrational hiddenness of matter," which makes the infinite a fixed conception. This "bad infinite" assumes that we are forever discerning and uncovering convention alone (59). Kant's categorical imperative requires self-imposed restraint on the individual decision maker. In this case there is a totalization of the infinite. "But is not the bad infinity at the bottom of all the triumphant infinites?" writes Levinas (74). His connection of infinity to ethics assumes that infinity cannot be "reduced" or sorted into some form of unlimited possibilities (75).

Infinity accepts a unique response to alterity that invites particularity of insights. One has access to the infinite only in response to alterity, not within the universal. The call of responsibility is never the same, engaged ever anew. Repeatedly, the unique face of the Other turns the "I" to a call that demands responsibility that cannot be discerned in advance of meeting a particular person. The infinite dwells within the reality of a recognized temporal totality of the particular. The infinite resides in a place "beyond dialogue," in a space inclusive of those present and those not part of a given encounter. The proximity of the face understood within a context considers those not present and never forgets that justice inhabits an area beyond the particularity of a given face and a specified moment. The inability to specify a given location or place of ethics and justice is central to Levinas's critique of Buber's I-Thou relation[11]; Levinas refuses to give ethics a rarified location.

Levinas illustrates his refusal to reify ethics in his discussion of the ten points declared at Seelisberg, Switzerland, during the International Council of Christians and Jews Emergency Conference on Anti-Semitism, July 1947 (*Alterity*, 79–80). In response Levinas wrote an essay, "Beyond Dialogue," on the twentieth anniversary of the conference. He reflected on its twenty-year history as akin to something eaten and digested by Saint-Exupéry's boa described in *The Little Prince*—the boa had swallowed the elephant without chewing; it was "already digesting it" (85). The events of that time required digestion and reflection on events forgotten and/or ignored. Long-term consideration is necessary when ideas fail.

The act of long-term consideration is akin to a slow swallowing of historical events; such action permits the seemingly forgotten to call us beyond dialogue. Such a request begins with "maturity" and "patience" that replaces the immediacy of optimism that abides within dialogue (87). One cannot forget those not at the event of dialogue; beyond dialogue dwells the hope of justice. *The Little Prince* grapples with a seeming impossibility of correct discernment as he discovers that none of his drawings of the sheep assist. It is not until the sheep is drawn/sketched lying asleep within the confines of a parallelogram that Levinas asserts an image offering a "cradle of our hopes" (89).

Dialogue is sometimes premature; instead we must attend to an existential demand for patience and waiting. One must wait for an answer that is not present while living in an awakened past. At some juncture, good ideas cradled in silence awaken, permitting them to speak once again. Historicity permits conversation to reach across generations as we attend to questions similar to our own and learn from distant eras and their responses. Rejoinders from the past rest cradled in a parallelogram, awaiting awakening. Existence resides within the interplay of historical consumption and the silence of ideas that sleep until aroused. The responsibility of the "derivative I" is to discern action after awakened to ethical responsibility. In each historical moment, there is the interplay of questions, responses, and the responsibility of a "responsive I." Sometimes, however, there is a call to wait for an awakening of an insight long forgotten.

Levinas states that *il y a*, or "there is," represents the realm of the "impersonal." In this realm there are two potential paths: one, a movement back to the self, an egoism that seeks to protect oneself from the realm of *il y a*; and, two, a meeting of the Other, driven by exteriority and desire for sociality. Levinas visits the I-You construct of Buber with its stress on mutual benefit[12]; he counters with an emphasis on the impersonal that attends to proximity guided by distance between persons that eschew reciprocity in ethics. Without distance, imposition shapes the demand of reciprocity. Justice emerges from an initial human spark of ethical engagement with the Other, giving rise to institutions and laws that protect those not immediately part of a given action or decision. Within impersonal ethical action, the faith of saintliness lives and acts without reciprocity and possession. However, within the realm of justice, the third (unknown persons) requires reciprocity in order to render necessary assurance for all.

Levinas suggests that in the realm of science, we discern with a pure "originative I" that controls with reason and public experimentation. Life is a laboratory within existence that dwells within the daily testing of moral reasoning. The realm of everyday living does not belong to a sovereign "I"; the laboratory of existence is a social space. Levinas rejected reciprocity while admiring Buber's fundamental contribution—the importance of the "you"—the social "you" of persons in interaction with one another. Wahl called this form of "dialogical philosophy" the "movement 'toward the concrete'" (*Alterity*, 93). The "I" and the "you" in dialogic engagement prompt us to acknowledge human faces as the primary place of Saying.

While Buber forged his dialogic contribution, parallel writings on dialogue arose with Marcel's emphasis on the relational nature of human life. Additionally, both scholars pointed to an "extra-ordinary relation" (94). Within the dialogic encounter, there is something "beyond," a disinterested God who offers the possibility of a communicative background for Others. Levinas repeatedly underscores the importance of disinterestedness as a profound form of concern that invites dialogue that cannot fade into the I-It. A background of disinterest permits meaningful encounter; perhaps dialogue works best when support remains quiet, shaped by lack of personal recognition.

Levinas emphasized contributions from both Buber and Marcel to an extrarelational connection; each committed to a "you" that emerges from a spiritual intersubjective tradition. The love of the neighbor, the second commandment, constitutes a particular path of engagement with the Other.[13] This commitment is the first commandment—to have no other gods before God. The commitment to God is the extrarelation, propelling me into an encounter with and responsibility to and for another with the "you" of relation. Levinas framed his ethics within the proximity of the Other that initiates attentiveness to an immemorial ethical echo uttered long before a given meeting.

This distinction between Buber and Levinas fades when Levinas moves from ethics to justice. Justice incorporates those not present at the table of conversation with commitments of public reciprocal assistance. Justice obliges institutional agreements that require reciprocity between persons and unite Buber and Levinas on the theme of reciprocity.[14] Levinas writes, "I now pass from the relation without reciprocity to a relation in which there is reciprocity, equality, between the members of a society. My search for justice presupposes just such a new relation, in which all the excess of generosity that I must have toward the other is subordinated to a question of justice. In justice there is comparison, and the other has no privilege with respect to me" (102). In contrast to Levinas's view of justice, which incorporates reciprocity, ethics involves one's being held hostage by the Other, an obligation *sans* reciprocity. Reciprocity in ethics opens the door to imposition of behavior on the Other. Levinas continues his contention with Buber's positions on the subjects of utopia and socialism.

Buber asserts that utopianism is the only avenue to a wholly other new society after the loss of an eschatological sense eclipsed by the Enlightenment and the French Revolution. Political danger begins when the nation-state initiates efforts that trump the role of civic society. In such a moment, the social dimension of human life is lost to the realm of domination and rules. Civic society carries a common life between persons; the state cannot provide this essential realm of meaning. Buber contends with Hegel's conception of the state, which united universality of thought, will, and freedom in subordination to institutional space (112–13).

Buber's view of socialism assumes the necessity of regenerating social "cells" that nourish human connections between and among persons (114). He resisted the utopian expectation associated with state structures. Buber envisioned a socialist explication of philosophical anthropology that embraced I-Thou relations within and throughout civic society. Levinas contended with the I-Thou space while agreeing that all institutional structures must ultimately depend upon reciprocity. In a public setting, the lack of reciprocity relegates persons to dimensioned positions where they suffer from domination. Institutional life requires reciprocity without eschewing the temptations of individualism and ideal representations of self.

Levinas contends that the Jewish tradition opposes images of representation. The biblical rejection of representational images garners mistrust and prohibition of reified icons. Representation banishes uniqueness and eclipses one's ability to recognize alterity—failing to understand the importance of difference. Images have mutability manifested before us without smell, taste, and touch. Images are representations, which are dependent on a party line or a subjective reading of what they imply. Only in the meeting of the unique face of the Other does the possibility for transcendence of meaning emerge. Alterity transforms, unlike representations that impose a given set of implications and meanings.

The unique face of another calls forth "gratuitous responsibility." Levinas's position does not begin or end with guilt; it commences with genuine response to the face of the Other. Representation, on the other hand, is a form of "primitive mentality" that functions as a false substitute for particularity and uniqueness of otherness. The human face defies reification of the image. No image assumes a position between us; one adopts a "non-transferable" sense of responsibility. Accountability, which belongs only to me, connects *moi* to "meaningfulness" that is immemorial and prior to representation. Levinas differentiates the rights of an individual from my responsibility for another. He secures the rights of the Other, not the rights of *moi-même*. Levinas questioned the "rights of man" as reification of the Other's obligation to me, not my obligation to another (121–30).

Levinas responded to the formal characteristics of the rights of man articulated during the French Revolution with the *Declaration of the Rights of Man and of the Citizen*. The French National Assembly adopted this representative document between August 20 and August 26, 1789, which consisted of seventeen articles.[15] Levinas resisted formal representation and advocacy of rights. He stressed the connection of rights of free will with the invitation to a "war of each against all" that fails to take into account different psychological, cultural, and social dimensions of human association (*Alterity*, 146–47). Levinas cited Kant's suggestion that we must engage in "free limitation" of our own rights with an emphasis on the categorical imperative and practical reason.

Levinas asserted that the only way to curtail the rights of *moi* and the rights of the Other is for attentiveness to alterity to trump egoism: "That the Rights of Man are originally the rights of the other man . . . the *for-the-other* of the social, of the for-the-stranger—such appears to me to be the meaning of their novelty" (149). Levinas's understanding of rights begins with the Other without forgetting those who are not immediately part of the conversation. Ethics and justice trump the rights of man.

Levinas wrote that the two world wars of the West shattered human ties in Europe. The great wars of the twentieth century were "fratricidal struggles" propelled by imperialism and desire for expansion that continues without satiation (132). This reality of the human condition contributed to the "shattering of the universality of theoretical reason" in the West. Levinas equated imperialism with the imposition of what one claims to be an undisputable truth. The shattering of this dream came from two grand wars that were extensions of earlier efforts to augment colonial expansion. The conclusion of war often reveals the problematic nature of peace. Promising peace assumes that one can envision a future that is identical to a demanded conception of the world. This promise is a form of "bad conscience," which assumes a false optimism of eradicating suffering and death. Such optimism bypasses one's own unique responsibility. Levinas was leery of efforts contrived in hopes of generating a "unity of one" that does not recognize the reality of "multiplicity" and the danger of sociality that results from "absorption." Peace limited to a "common genus" misses the importance of difference and alterity (132–38). Recognition of uniqueness and difference makes the notion of "proximity" dangerous when attributed to peace. Peace necessitates reliance on impersonal concern for the third party and concern for and about the one not in proximity of the conversation and decision making. Proximity, for Levinas, does not live within geographical closeness; responsibility for Others is performed without regard for familiarity. In acts of justice and peace, attentiveness to those not near or known dictates the necessity of reciprocity: "Consciousness is born as the presence of the third party in the proximity of the one to the other, and thus it is to the extent that it proceeds from it that it can become dis-interestedness. The foundation of consciousness is justice" (144). Active concern for the unseen Other invites a phenomenological proximity that Levinas equates with justice that emerges from impersonal responsibility and reciprocal obligation. Justice via institutions permits commitments to continue after death.

Death is an unknown, a dwelling mystery; it is an inexorable defining characteristic of being human. Death is the ultimate interruption that disturbs and disrupts totality. Death is the significant unknown that remains at the center of philosophical thinking: "Spinoza will say, as you know, that philosophers should think of nothing less than death. Heidegger, by contrast, is the one who pursued philosophical thought's reference to death the farthest. The philosopher's morality marks his thought as it does his existence. A finite existence" (155). Heidegger's *Dasein* pursued death through the individual self, announcing the reality of finitude in the most personal of fashions. The anthropology of being human necessitates the meeting of death, both in sorrow and in person. In death the call to responsibility, for me, continues to speak from the Other, demanding response, even in my loneliness for the Other; responsibility continues after another's death.

Marcel stated that love for another requires acknowledgment that death is not possible for that person. Love has phenomenological roots and reaches beyond the empirical reality. Death of another calls for unique response from me, perhaps the most powerful of utterances— "here I am." As one stands offering such a proclamation, responsibility follows. "Bad conscience" emerges when response to the death of another lacks or rejects acts of responsibility (167). Human anthropology resides in the reality of death with the call of ethics continuing long after the empirical presence of the Other is no more. The face moves one from an ethics of optics to a phenomenological attending to an ethical call of responsibility. The face of the Other is a beckoning to an immemorial voice of God.

Levinas commences a discussion of the *parole* of God with an ethical fact: the voice of God originates with a glimpse of the face of the Other that invites transcendence, not immanence; the latter summons violence in the reification of the face. The image of the Other, like the image of God, does not emerge with clarity; to seek possession of the face moves one to a position contrary to ethics. The face of the Other cannot be possessed or controlled; it demands my responsibility and resists ownership. The vocation of humanness as understood by Levinas necessitates a disinterested responsibility for the Other that begins with attentiveness to the uniqueness of a human face.

The first ethical obligation acknowledges the face of the Other, which moves one to an ethical echo and then back to care for a particular Other; this gesture of ethics keeps the rationality of justice from dominating, disassociating it from totalitarianism. Levinas asserted that rationality used with pious words invites a dangerous seduction that masks violence and foments "contempt for the other" (177). Rationality without a spiritual awakening is the dwelling place of Pascal's "hateful I" that speaks "for Oneself," missing the human vocation of saintliness that forgets the self (21–29).

Without the forgetting of self, one construes a "hateful I" that enacts violence toward the face in three ways: (1) attempting to possess the face of the Other, even when there is a "good" spirit that propels the action; (2) returning to one's own face without attending to what redirects us toward an ethical echo of responsibility; and (3) the eclipsing of the face of the Other, which obscures an ethical echo. In the enigma of the face, one finds redirection as one attends to a call to responsibility. Chouchani was an exemplar of the power of enigma; he disclosed little about himself and performed a communicative warning about self-disclosure. He embraced a mystery that presented a lesson—ethics begins with the enigma of the face.

The Saying and the Said in Communication Ethics: Chouchani and the Face

The face is an enigma that cannot be possessed or reified; the nudity of the face moves us to an ethical echo. Assumed undue familiarity with the face of the Other misses the call to responsibility. The task was to learn from Chouchani, not to violate the infinity of learning. To understand from the enigma of Chouchani, one had to watch and learn without the assurance of one's assessment of this man of difference. Part of his teaching was performative and could not be represented by a given code or script of the Said; his instruction lived with the Saying.

Attending to an archaic voice.—Malka states that Levinas learned from Chouchani a thorough and respectful way to understand the Talmud, which invited a phenomenological midrash of interpretive meetings of the text. From Chouchani, Levinas learned to refuse to meet the text as an "archaism."[16] The text brings new life each time one questions the manuscript—interpretation is an act of respectfully meeting alterity with resultant transcendence that transforms the interpreter. Chouchani displayed the importance of respect for the text and the transcendent reality that offers a "surplus of signification" that recognizes an abundance of meaning discovered with each interpretive visit (Malka, *Emmanuel Levinas*, 27). Chouchani brought fresh eyes to each interpretive engagement.

Possession of the Other as demonic.—Details about Chouchani were known by few. Chouchani's real name, place of birth, home, and his formal education were unknown to virtually all who knew him. Levinas offered little personal information about Chouchani. Levinas comprehended the importance of the human face—such information does not belong to the inquirer. Levinas witnessed Chouchani as a man reacting against possession and "totalization"; he chose to honor the ambiguity of his face. Levinas engaged Chouchani in a manner that was "otherwise than totality" (Malka, 51).

Chouchani went so far as to try to pass himself off as an Arab; he carried "fake papers" that indicated Moroccan nationality. Some contended that he was not even a "believer," and others said they had witnessed him praying. Chouchani could easily move one to the temptation of psychologism, which attributes motives to another and seeks to possess the attributes of another by description of those motives. Buber referred to this act of motive possession as "demonic."[17] The danger of such exploitation, for Levinas, is that infinity is "reduced" to what I control (*Alterity*, 75). One of the greatest personal enticements is the attempt to seize the meaning of another whose actions appear odd and different.

Limits of proximity.—Levinas and Chouchani were counterparts; Malka called them "antipodes" of one another (239). Yet, Malka attributed to Simone, Levinas's daughter, a different assessment. Malka indicates that she asserted, "No, it is not true that the two men were antipodes of each other. Something bound them, profoundly, in spite of their belonging to two different worlds" (239). What joined the two men was something contrary to closeness; it was a commitment to learning from the Talmud. Their connection was not one of proximity, but of "profound[ity]" (238–39). They belonged to distinct worlds; their relationship was a human testimony to a "dis-interested" engagement with a "you" (*Alterity*, 171). One cannot require that the Other conform to one's own expectations; ethical proximity lives within disinterested attentiveness.

Uniqueness of response.—Chouchani was rapid in his movements, which moved briskly from laughter to anger; he displayed a full range of human passions. However, his encounter with the Talmud was "beyond pathos" (Malka, 248). After a spiritual awakening to the alterity of person or text, one must discern how to respond. Thinking and rational discernment constitute a substantial part of Levinas's project, an orientation that he held in common with Chouchani. A "bad conscience" is resisted in two ways: one, by attending to the text and/or person at hand that initiates a call into responsibility; and, two, by using education, experience, and rational discernment in considering appropriateness of action.

What Levinas seized in his engagement with Chouchani was a love of the Talmud. Such a love was an essential caress of wisdom after the Holocaust devastated a people. The Talmud renewed the hearts of Jewish scholars. For Levinas, "the encounter with this man [Chouchani] gave me back a trust in the books" (Malka, 158). Violence emerges in rational universality that assumes one can determine all answers. In the Talmud, one witnesses a call for multiple interpretations, which permits another to discover the particular ever anew.

Chouchani assisted Levinas's return to the Talmud with a love and trust that permitted conversation to arise once again. There was trust, not tied to a single person, but tied responsively to existence, the narrative ground on which we walk. The soil under our feet, narratively constituted, shapes our identity. This narrative ground invokes "existential trust."[18] Chouchani assisted Levinas by contributing method and rational commitment to the engagement of sacred stories that paved a path to existential trust. The result was not merely an educating of Levinas but rather a welcome to a text that shapes life and identity. Chouchani was a performative example of the face remaining an enigma and refusing to offer answers, while at the same time beginning a call of responsibility. It is in the immemorial ethical call that one discovers ground under one's feet that demands adherence enacted in an upright posture that utters a message of responsibility: "here I am." Responsibility necessitates a response that only "I" can offer, calling forth uniqueness in a heartfelt reply and unending obligation. The face is a Saying that summons one with an ethical call manifested in an ethical action of the Said. Communication ethics begins with attentiveness to the face of the Other. Communication ethics responds to an ambiguous, originative command accompanied by no rules or regulations. The life of Chouchani is an enigma that displays the challenge of communication ethics—responding to an enigma with responsibility without assurance.

CHAPTER 4
Proper Names: Saying, Said, and the Trace

Reduced to its essence, language is perhaps the fact that one sole word is always proffered, which does not designate a being that is thought, but accomplishes a movement beyond being, and beyond the thought in which being looks at and reflects itself. More precisely, the proffering itself moves beyond thought.

—Emmanuel Levinas, *Proper Names*

. . . the silence of the face points to the unsaid and unsayable—it reminds us of the ineffable, inexhaustible infinity of the saying . . . That is to say, perhaps my encounter with the other manifests neither in the separation of vision nor in the invocation of voice, but in my attentive attunement to the speech of the other.

—Lisbeth Lipari, *Listening, Thinking, Being: Toward an Ethics of Attunement*

Emmanuel Levinas's ethics has two fundamental places of origin: one visual (the face of the Other) and the other audio (an immemorial ethical echo). Both of these originative homes of ethics announce the power of Saying as a revelatory reality. Saying refuses taming, coercion, and direction; it is speaking propelled without the willful approval of a communicative agent. The Said solidifies through public, social, and cultural agreement that dwells in education, institutions, and laws associated with justice. Within any congealed sense of the Said, there is a trace of the Saying. Levinas's *Proper Names* is a gathering of stories about persons of importance to Levinas; his interpretive descriptions offer a sense of the Said of their projects with a trace of Saying that yields revelatory insight capable of emerging when least expected.[1] This chapter continues the theme of Levinas's careful engagement with another. He attends to proper names, again protecting the Other and resisting the impulse to impose. This chapter is a case study in the recognition of and attentiveness to the proper name of another without my voice and expectations eclipsing the uniqueness of another.

Introduction

The power of proper names resides in the Said, a memory of another and his or her accomplishments. The trace of a revelatory Saying remains within each proper name. In a moment of desperation with a friend, you call out your friend's name once, twice, thrice in hopes that the very articulating of the name might elicit a revelatory Saying of personal responsibility. A name speaks beyond the Said of letters and simultaneously houses a Saying that calls out identity and responsibility.

This chapter centers on the power of proper names. In the first section, "A Prelude," I describe the importance of this Levinasian contribution with a recapping of a short essay by Thomas Trezise, which announces the importance of reading that is attentive to the Saying lodged within the Said. I then explore, in "*Proper Names*," Levinas's book chapter by chapter, ending each interpretive rendition with a discussion of the relationship of the Saying and the Said. The final section, "The Saying and the Said in Communication Ethics: The Performative Power of Name," outlines the Said of this chapter with an emphasis on traces that continue to suggest the revelatory power of the Saying of responsibility.

Levinas reveals the mediating importance of proper names. It is with our names that we learn to respond to the particularity of address. My mother and father have been gone too long, but I still hear my mom addressing my dad in a voice that called forth the man she knew and loved with just one word, his proper first name!

A Prelude

Trezise's review of Levinas's *Proper Names* in *Comparative Literature Studies* sets the tone for understanding the significance of a human name as a form of mediated communication.[2] Trezise asserted that the compelling theme of *Proper Names* resides within the Saying of a particular face; the essays call attention to the "irreducible singularity" of voices from Buber to Blanchot (355, 359). The work is an entrance into conversation with a number of Levinas's compatriots. The book is a collection of significant faces and voices that witness to ethical listening that attends to the Other, represented by persons significant to Levinas's intellectual journey. In the volume Levinas does not totalize the Other; he participates within a Saying that responds to the Other. Levinas minimizes the Said; he resists trying to capture precise words, ideas, and meanings set forth by the Other.

Trezise states that the essays offer a "trace" of the Other's voice, which compels resistance to treating the particularity of the human face as an object, the Said, without revelatory implications. A proper name differs from the Same and resists imposition. A surplus of infinity reaches beyond engagement with the Other. One must be willing to meet "questions beyond the pursuit of answers" (355). For instance, Trezise states that if one attempts to totalize a proper name, the action assures simple answers—such is one of the reasons Levinas rejected the notion of reciprocity in ethics (356). Trezise reminds the reader of Levinas's insistence on justice, which brings the third or the unseen Other into the conversation and decision making, which necessitates the vitality of the Said and reciprocity. Institutions of justice require reciprocity of protection for all persons. Institutions are carriers of the morality of the Said and are unsettled by Saying inherent in proper names. Saying signifies faces, and proper names suggest faces that speak in a manner that reconfigures the Said with a trace of Saying.

The last essay in *Proper Names* moves to "Nameless," introducing the reader to a Same where difference and distinctiveness are no more. "In 'Nameless,' Levinas affirms the resistance of Saying to the Said, the persistence of a plurality beyond what Kenneth Burke once called, in reference to Nazism, a 'sinister unifying' of voice. He [Levinas] affirms, in short, the survival of the ethical relation and hence of the possibility of 'proper names'" (360). By attending to a proper name, the particular speaks. One does not meet another in abstraction but through a real human face beyond possession. Saying calls me forth, recalibrating my responsibility.

Engagement with Levinas's book requires a textured reading. As we attend to faces, real proper names, we must avoid the impulse to align relationally with a particular subject. This impersonal appraisal invites an attending to Saying that emanates from the Other and minimizes imposition of meaning. Levinas understands that proper names require space for a Saying that calls forth listening and attending to the Other. The impetus for such focused recognition of the power of a proper name invites Saying, response, and responsibility, with each tied to listening that begins with a real person with a real name. Levinas's understanding of *Proper Names* is a case study about attentive listening that opens space for Saying within the power of the Said. Before turning to Levinas and *Proper Names*, I explicate a powerful literary example of the disruptive ethical power of proper names.

The summoning forth of persons by proper names reflects the genius of Harper Lee (1926–2016) in the writing of *To Kill a Mockingbird*. Lee wrote the novel in 1960. It received the Pulitzer Prize for Literature in 1961 and has never been out of print. Lee participated in only eight interviews until 2010,[3] when she agreed to take part in an interview for the novel's fiftieth anniversary. *To Kill a Mockingbird* remained the only book Lee published until the 2015 publication of an earlier draft of the manuscript titled *Go Set a Watchman*.[4] The book names persons and outlines the power of such gestures. Atticus Finch, father of the main character, Scout, is a lawyer defending Tom Robinson, an African American man accused of raping and beating a white woman. One night when Atticus leaves for the county jail to visit Robinson, Scout, along with her brother Jem and friend Dill, follow their father to find him sitting outside Robinson's cell. Shortly after, a mob arrives. Mistaking the crowd for strangers, Scout jumps among them. Scout then recognizes persons in the crowd and calls out one, Mr. Cunningham, by his proper name. At first Cunningham ignores Scout's call, but the young girl persistently continues to distinguish him; she then identifies his son stating, "I go to school with Walter. . . . He's your boy, ain't he?"[5] The presence of Scout using proper names dispersed the mob. The power of the Said resides in a proper name that houses a trace of a Saying of responsibility. Lee's novel is a literary exemplar of the interplay of Said, trace, and Saying, which frames the heart of Levinas's project.

Proper Names

The foreword to *Proper Names* connects the work to dramatic changes in the West during and after World War II—a world of "disappointment" that must confront the "bankruptcy of humanism" in an era of "anxiety" of "apocalyptic proportions" (3–4). Levinas contends that we live in an era of interruptions when "signifiers" no longer point to the "signified" and result in a lessening of confidence in "representation" and "genealogy." The world announces increasingly less attentiveness to "traces" of responsibility when signifying disruption is normative fare. Levinas reminds us, however, that Saying consistently resides within a human face and is, at times, accessible via proper names: "Perhaps the names of persons whose *saying* signifies a face—proper names, in the middle of all these common names and commonplaces—can resist the dissolution of meaning and help us to speak. Perhaps they will enable us to divine, behind the downfall of discourse, the end of a certain *intelligibility* but the dawning of a new one. What is coming to a close may be a rationality tied *exclusively* to the being that is sustained by words, the *Said* of the Saying . . ." (4–5). Levinas explicates proper names as traces of Saying. He contends that rationality of the Said no longer guides hope; traces of Saying illuminate disruptive transformations. For this reason, Levinas views Hegel as the last philosopher of the Same who celebrates a relentless march toward progress. A paradigmatically alternative perspective propels Levinas.

Levinas visits the "absolute" in a different key through the work of Wahl, who unites this term with "separation," in order to understand the shifting historical moment from Hegel to the time of Wahl. In this historical moment, Levinas embraces Marcel's rejection of "self-sufficiency," displaying how this era of disruption demands that we lean toward the Other and welcome the *thou*. Spirit is not the Said but functions as traces of Saying within a Said that continues to demand an "awakening," which ruptures undue confidence in the "self" or "universalization." Levinas ends the foreword to *Proper Names* with a stress on "rupture" and "awakening" in order to secure our attention (5–6). Levinas states that no longer can one expect the Said of the past to answer all questions. Saying opens the "passage from the Same to the Other, where there is as yet nothing in common" (6). Meeting between persons commences with indifference that is a nonindifference. There is the offering of a gift from the Other, which demands sacrifice on the part of the recipient. Saying interrupts, awakens, and ruptures; it alerts both self and Other, which requires reflection on the neighbor and all those who are stateless in the moment of awakening—"an awakening that is neither reflection upon oneself nor universalization. An awakening signifying a responsibility for the other, the other who must be fed and clothed" (6). In such a moment, one listens to the Saying, knowing that answers dwell in the revelatory emergence of human faces. I now turn to proper names that shaped the identity of Levinas, framing the Said through trace and Saying.

SHMUEL YOSEF AGNON (1888–1970)

Shmuel Yosef Agnon was born Shmu'el Yosef Czaczkes in the city of Buczacz, in the historical Galicia region in 1888. In 1908 he traveled to Jaffa and adopted the pen name Agnon after the publication of his story "Agunot."[6] From 1913 until 1924, Agnon lived in Germany and then moved to Jerusalem in 1924, which became his "adopted city, his new Buczacz," where he legally changed his name to Agnon and returned to Orthodox practices until his death in 1970 (Band, 25–26). Agnon was a major Hebrew novelist and writer of short stories. He, along with Nelly Sachs (1891–1970), shared the Nobel Prize for Literature in 1966.

Agnon was born into a family of Jewish and Polish rabbis and scholars. He had great admiration for the Hebrew language and the Jewish intellectual tradition. He wrote his works in Hebrew and Yiddish.[7] His literary style required multiple revisions; he attended carefully to the details of each manuscript. Agnon was a storyteller; he often alluded to a large corpus of Hebrew literature in his stories and brought to life the intellectual tradition of his people. Agnon's subjects were often persons of great faith and character. Literary connections between his writing and that of Miguel de Cervantes (1547–1616) and Franz Kafka (1883–1924) were evident as he brought a classical voice distinguishing between good and evil to his novels (127–29).[8] His characters responded to direction required for their lives in action.

Agnon spent his entire life as a writer with support from a "permanent annual stipend" that he received from his publisher, Schocken House.[9] He was one of the major masters of Hebrew literature but was little known outside of Israel due to the tedious nature of translating his novels into other languages.[10] Some authors are readable only in their own literary language. Agnon's characters struggled to be faithful, meeting the demands of spiritual homelessness and disorientation without losing the guidance of faith. He was an extraordinary author, capable of writing with existential texture that brought insight without missing the demands of the ambiguity of the moment. From 1913 until 1924, Agnon lived in Germany, working as a research collaborator with Buber on Hasidic tales, to whom he later paid tribute in 1928, 1958, and 1963 (Hochman, 25).[11] Buber called Agnon the "Hebrew Homer of modern literature" after reading Agnon's *And the Crooked Will Be Made Straight.* Later in the 1930s, the phrase "Hebrew Kafka" became a designation for Agnon (Alter, 105). His images of detailed action surpass existentially the passive narrative of the novel. His heroes manifest a sense of helplessness as they discern the direction necessary to address penultimate actions, not ultimate goods.

Agnon was an ardent reader of great writers such as James Joyce (1882–1941) and Rainer Maria Rilke (1875–1926) and also, of course, the Talmud—he functioned as an existential craftsman of the faith (Alter, 106). His style reflected a Medieval Hebraic midrash tradition that did not fall prey to unnecessary, ornate, and elaborate writing of the medieval West. Agnon's ability to deal with ambiguity in meeting the demands of life also revealed connections to insights of Gustave Flaubert (1821–1880) (Band, 22). Agnon provided images of the homeless and the dispossessed without giving readers false answers; his novels reveal characters responsive to demanding choices driven by the faith. His sense of hope eschewed denial and met existence in a shrewd, tough-minded enactment of the faith.

Levinas posed the question, does Agnon belong to the Jewish tradition, or is he primarily a witness to the end of the modern world? Agnon is untranslatable, as stated above; in *Proper Names* Levinas clarifies that the ambiguity and lack of translation rests with the importance of background information from the culture and language. Was Agnon undertaking "unshakable certainty," "refuge," or pointing to the "end of the world"? (*Proper Names*, 10). His work is a Saying, making the assurance of a Said a misrepresentation. He understood the power of "unrepresentability" (12). Agnon responded to the crisis in Western humanism with poetry that called for association with an immemorial past, a tradition alive with a trace that reaches "beyond those limits" (16). Agnon's poetry unleashed the power of Saying via tradition resistant to death and solidification. He suggested a tomorrow that begins with a particular tradition responsive to an immemorial past that provides traces of insight for next steps. Agnon offered direction in a path that is ever in need of clearing. Saying dwells in an abode that houses multidirectional actions—yes and no, now and not yet, all pulling simultaneously with a demand for revelatory Saying that testifies with a glimpse of insight.

MARTIN BUBER (1878–1965)

The story of Buber's life, documented in Maurice Friedman's three-volume work, indicates that Buber's mother left his father when Martin was three years old.[12] The responsibilities for raising him fell to his paternal grandparents. His grandfather, Solomon Buber, completed a critical edition of the midrashim[13]; he was interested in the rabbinic lore of the midrash, which functioned as a counter to the legal framework of the Talmud. His grandmother, intellectually situated in the nineteenth-century Enlightenment movement of Eastern European Jewry, permitted the unity of contraries to guide Buber's early life. Buber developed a great love of literature, leaning more toward stories of the faith than to intricacies of the law. In 1899 he married a Zionist writer, Paula Winkler, who had converted to Judaism before their marriage (*Proper Names*, 49). Buber embraced Zionism, even as he parted ways with Theodor Herzl (1860–1904),[14] who emphasized laws and rules. Buber desired a Zionism that invited a spiritual heart. Buber left Germany for Palestine in 1938, at the age of sixty, as Nazi nationalism grew in power and overt expression. Known for his intellectual leadership in Hasidism, philosophical anthropology, and dialogue, Buber complied with the state of Israel's request to work with the Institute for Adult Education, which he founded in 1949 and directed until 1953.[15]

Levinas dedicated two essays in *Proper Names* to Buber: the first centered on Buber's *Knowledge of Man*, edited by Friedman, and the second was a dialogic response to Buber. Only Blanchot had more essays devoted to him in this volume. Levinas contends that Buber's main point was that truth is not tied to "content" but to the "subjective" (19). The self for Buber is not a substance but a relation; his

94

position is in accordance with Husserl's emphasis on intentionality. Levinas explains that Buber understands the human being in and through "meeting" (19, 23–24). This form of communicative engagement takes one to alterity where truth resides as a "living truth" in the face of the Other. Levinas rejected Buber's center of a formalized I-Thou relation that assumes the necessity of reciprocity. Levinas questioned the placement of ethics in an I-Thou meeting, which diminishes the power of ethics (17–35). In Levinas's second essay on Buber, Levinas reprinted one of his negative responses about the privileged status of the I-Thou, reciprocity, and formalization.

Buber had earlier contended that Levinas mistakenly understood his work as living in abstraction, within "ether" that exists on a "purely spiritual" plane (*Proper Names*, 33, 36). Levinas, in retort, restated his case. Buber once again differentiated their perspectives and ended with a thank you of the French *remercier* and the Hebrew *hodot*, with the latter suggesting that concrete support emerges first and only then is followed by thanks (38–39). Levinas leaves the essay exchange with Buber having the last word. I suspect Levinas had a twofold motive. First, he had great respect for Buber, and second, Buber's comments verify Levinas's concern about reciprocity—for Levinas's ethics, concrete acts of ethical support require no thanks. In Levinas's reading of Buber's Said, there is a trace of the Saying of responsibility beyond reciprocity. Levinas's ethical framework is otherwise than Buber's. Saying morphs into the Said when one waits for response. Saying lives in response to an existential demand that answers the Other through acts of responsibility. Saying does not wait for thanks; it calls forth unending responsibility.

PAUL CELAN (1920–1970)

One of the significant Jewish literary voices after World War II was Paul Celan. He witnessed atrocities, both distant and familial. The Nazis sent him to a forced labor camp in Bukovina in 1941 as they murdered his parents in Transnistria. Celan's first two books of poetry, *The Sand from the Urns* (*Der Sand aus den Urnen*), published in 1948, and *Poppy and Memory* (*Mohn und Gedächtnis*), published in 1952, responded to the horrors of Nazi occupation. He was the recipient of two major awards: the Bremen Literature Prize in 1958 and the Georg Büchner Prize in 1960. In 2004 the *New German Critique* published a special issue on the poetry and work of Celan. Amir Eshel states that Celan attended to the Saying with the Other.[16] Eshel emphasizes a famous moment in Celan's career and life—on October 26, 1960, Celan gave his Büchner Prize speech, known as the "Meridian" speech, where he addressed the German Academy of Language and Literature. The speech articulated the Saying of poetry: "The poem intends another, needs this other," said Celan (Eshel, 57). Celan spoke of the Other in a dual and contradictory fashion—the "impersonal" Other and the "personal" Other (58). Within the unity of contraries, poetry develops a dialogue that moves between the personal and the impersonal Other. Eshel stressed the historical importance of the award in Germany, reminding readers that only nineteen years before Celan was in a forced labor camp (59).

The postwar environment continued to offer all too frequent reminders of Nazi power. One well-known German critic, Günter Blöcker, stated that any concerns about Celan's use of German "'may live in his ancestry.'" The reference was to Celan's Jewish heritage—Blöcker noted, "The poet is not a native speaker, is not from here, is other, is a Jew" (Eshel, 59). Celan responds to the critic in a poem about his murdered mother—published in a posthumous volume (60). Celan understood the intimate connection between aesthetics and ethics, with the poem speaking on behalf of foreigners. The poem itself took on a sense of Otherness that met the world. Poetry, as the Other, offers a dwelling for Saying from the depths of foreignness. His works announce a depth of Saying in a "turning back" in response to the rest of the world that is running toward a progress that eclipses the ethical (72).

Levinas uplifted Celan's admission that he saw no difference "between a handshake and a poem" (*Proper Names*, 40). From the impersonal, the dateless, comes the impact of the Said of action; in either handshake or poem, one detects a trace of a Saying that affects the personal. In the movement of a nonplace that is impersonal, poetry calls one out personally into the meeting of the transcendent reality of a poem. This impersonal landscape makes a domicile for the stranger and the neighbor while motioning to a history older than the first reading and first human encounter. Saying speaks when the poem welcomes the Other in an impersonal and strange embrace with a trace that charges personal response.

JEANNE DELHOMME (1911–1983)

Pierre-Antoine Marie stated that Delhomme presented a philosophy in response to the challenge of Friedrich Nietzsche (1844–1900).[17] The question raised by Delhomme is whether it is possible for thinkers to free themselves from a second system of beliefs. Philosophers do not simply reference reality but rather are engaged in an act of intelligibility through thinking as a creative and necessary art. Thinking assumes an aesthetic dimension. Without creative thought, the philosopher and the artist would simply reproduce a preexisting world. Without doubt, Delhomme's philosophy was the forgetting of a philosophy centered on Being. For Levinas, the attraction to this intellectual orientation is a mode of thinking beyond Being, a freedom of laughter that is unbounded from Being and tied to a "laughter of irresponsibility" (*Proper Names*, 54). Delhomme contended with Being and its conformity to constraints.

Levinas attended to Delhomme's understanding of philosophy as in contrast to Being and totalizing efforts that sought to systematize. Philosophy is a freedom that is the "polar opposite of life." Philosophy is performative thinking—"the hard work of intelligent thought" (48). The task is not one truth, but the opening of multiplicity of legitimacies. The search embodied within Husserl's *epoch* from one perspective misses the mark of multiplicity. Philosophy played out in something other than consciousness, and intentionality dwells in language. Delhomme contends that philosophy interrupted by history requires a philosopher engaged in the discerning of ideas and direction. Delhomme does not abide by the conventional phenomenological assertion of "consciousness of"; instead, she emphasized "concept of" (50). The "I" of a philosopher alone does not interrupt history; concepts uttered by a philosopher are the only way to escape a deterministic version of history.

This conception of philosophy invites spontaneity responsive via language and beyond Being. Intelligence is a "narcotic" that propels revolution outside of Being: "Thought, appearing not as a *thesis*, but as a *manner*, while not dominating history, interrupts it. The freedom of escape!" (51, 53). Levinas contends that this position requires rejection with its attunement to a negativity of Otherness. The work of philosophy becomes a "sarcastic laughter of irresponsibility" propelled by

97

an "unbounded" freedom (54). In such a case, the Saying is abusive of the Said; indeed, history interrupted is contrary to history ignored. Within history is a trace of revelatory Saying, which can emerge with full knowledge that it eventually fades into a performative Said with traces of Saying resting dormant and awaiting recognition.

JACQUES DERRIDA (1930–2004)

Derrida was born in Algeria to Jewish parents. He was educated at the École Normale Supérieure; he later taught at the Sorbonne (1960–1964), returned to the École Normale Supérieure (1964–1984) for a twenty-year commitment, and concluded his career at the École des Hautes Études en Sciences Sociales (1984–1999). Derrida, as one of the primary philosophers of deconstruction, sought to critique the binary and hierarchical oppositions that he considered inherent in Western philosophy, which he contended came from the ancient Greeks. He argued that such oppositions are not natural; however, they remain constructs present throughout the history of the West. For example, Derrida rejected an oppositional understanding of speech and writing. However, as one understands the oppositional construction of a text's *différence*, one engages the manner in which meaning manifests itself in analysis. Derrida's early work outlines the linguistic scholarship of Ferdinand de Saussure (1857–1913), whose works he questioned along with those associated with structuralism. Meaning emerges in contrast. Differences between words result in limitless possibilities; Derrida sought deconstruction of certainty and ideological assurance.

Derrida's scholarship was interdisciplinary and wide-ranging. He wrote on linguistics, literature, theatrical drama, Marxism, and psychologism. Additionally, he addressed political, legal, and Jewish questions—often in response to Levinas. Derrida's masterpiece *Of Grammatology* unmasked the construction of texts.[18] Richard Klein's interview with Derrida assumes that one should be suspicious of Derrida's willingness to accept an interview, considering the multiplicity of possibilities that might emerge from the conversation. Derrida's theoretical position made him unpredictable even in discussion of his own work. Derrida rejected the Hegelian presupposition of "formal [analysis]" and "thematic analysis."[19] Derrida, like Nietzsche, used "materialism" as a lever against the problematic power of the metaphysical; he sought to dismantle anything that resembled idealism. Klein stated that Western philosophy centered on the city-state or the countryside, in contrast with Derrida's "suburbs," which suggest unwillingness to commit to a particular tradition. The title of the interview, insisted on by Derrida, uses the word position(s) in relation to Derrida (Klein, 31–33). Deconstruction is unending, leading to one position after another, unwilling to land in one city or countryside.

The refusal to rest in one location illuminates the "otherwise" character of Derrida's project. Derrida reminds us that the history of philosophy is best understood as engagement in the difficulty of thinking. Levinas stated that Derrida takes us to a "no-man's land" void of certainty. Derrida aspired to overthrow "logocentric" logic. Levinas stated that he envisioned the "1940 exodus" whenever he read Derrida. The doing of philosophy with language seemed only to invite "defeat"; it demanded acts of "desertion." *Différence* deconstructs presence without the possibility of a designation. Levinas stated that the constant act of deconstruction misses the power and insight of the Saying and the Said, living somewhere between in an unknown abyss. Such activity opens to "pathless 'places.'" Derrida fought against a return to metaphysics with a philosophy that stressed perpetual motion, understanding Being as a "verb" (*Proper Names*, 55–62).

Levinas comprehended Derrida as freeing time from the present, which invited a Saying not controlled by a solidified conception of the immediacy of the moment, the Said. Saying correlates with the Said and with the reality of the trace, which remains in each Said. Freeing Saying from the present permits one to understand a voice from an immemorial past. Saying does not establish dimensional limits and relies upon the Said; Saying bursts forth in interruptive responses in and through the existence of the Said.

EDMOND JABÈS (1912–1991)

Jabès was born in Cairo; he was the son of wealthy Egyptian Jews. While living in a European community in Cairo, Jabès received a French education. His first literary connection was with the French poet Max Jacob (1876–1944). In the 1950s Jabès's life abruptly shifted with Egyptian president Gamal Abdel Nasser's (1918–1970) rise to power in 1956, during the Suez Canal struggle that commenced in the same year. Nasser nationalized the canal, which heightened tensions between Egypt and Israel. In 1956, because of the heightened tensions, Jabès's family "voluntarily" exiled themselves to France, never returning to their native Egypt.[20] Before that juncture, Jabès was a cultural Jew. With a new identity as a displaced person in France, Jabès turned to Jewish writing to discover his Jewish roots. Jabès struggled for literary and Jewish identity. He wrote poetry that lent his voice to Jewish and human questions as a poet survivor of exile who embraced an intense interest in Jewish identity. In his writing he referred to the Nazi legacy of horror and the Holocaust as metaphorical warnings. He bore witness to Jewish questions. His three-volume *The Book of Questions* includes a story about a Jewish woman deported to a concentration camp, a tale about a writer who commits suicide, and a focus on interaction between words and a writer. Throughout much of this major work, he relied on a Talmudic structure of commentary by fictional rabbis; the stories announced the power of the word and the necessity of conversation about implications and meaning. He wrote allegorically in his rendering of a picture of the twentieth century.

Jabès responded to Theodor Adorno (1903–1969), who stated that to write poetry following Auschwitz was barbaric. Jabès contended that writing must coincide with a return to the Jewish tradition, which employs strategies of "commentary and interpretation" to address "the collapse of human values" (Hawkins, 156). Such writing signifies an existential condition defined by a plethora of choices. Warren F. Motte Jr., in *Questioning Jabès*, describes the narrative style that guides Jabès's work as reliance on questioning that deliberately undercuts blind adherence to authority. One of Jabès's most insistent theoretical intents was to put the notion of authority into question *within* a book.[21] Jabès offers a literary version of the canonical Jewish texts. He submits a glimpse of how a rabbi contributes to the insight of a sacred work by keeping the Saying alive for those not present in the conversation. The Saying continues to register in a space without placement that is available to those not present—attending to voices from the past and those not yet.

Levinas contended that Jabès was a poet doing his work in an era with a lost sense of place. The task of a poet is to open space constructed of a "bottomlessness or height." Jabès gave life to poetry that transcended "breathlessness," giving life and meaning to the unspoken. Levinas quoted Jabès as stating that he was merely the "spoken word," the "word" that gave him a "face." Jabès presented the world in a literary version of a "Judaism of wandering." The "joy of a minor poet" is reliance on a tradition that houses a trace of Saying devoid of the unreflective solidification of the Said. The trace begins a Saying that functions as a "vertigo" of the Said; it disrupts insight and place (*Proper Names*, 63–65).

SØREN KIERKEGAARD (1813–1855)

Kierkegaard is a founder of existentialist study. He wrote as a Protestant critic who highlighted the deterioration of the faith narrative. Where Nietzsche rejected and deconstructed the Christian narrative, Kierkegaard worked within the faith story. Kierkegaard connected the faith narrative to existence, moving it out of a realm of mere abstraction. Kierkegaard came from a wealthy family known for its gloomy outlook and intense argumentative reactions to God. He was distant from his father for much of his adult life. In response to this environment, Kierkegaard found his intellectual strivings honed at the University of Copenhagen, where he began to study theology, only to find his greatest interest in literature and philosophy. In an 1835 journal entry, Kierkegaard stated that he wanted to discover ideas worthy of shaping a life.

Kierkegaard was interested in literary figures that detailed homelessness and struggles with obsessions, represented by Don Juan and Faust. His own existence represented this story line. For instance, Kierkegaard's love life is well known; he walked away from Regina Olson and broke off his engagement with her. This relationship and its brokenness never ceased to affect him. The presence of that memory stayed, and he continued to suffer. There are contending speculations about the exact reasons for his action, but there is agreement on the fact—his life, like his philosophy, found shape in disruption and interruption. He quarreled with many, from his father and newspaper writers to members of the Church of Denmark (Lutheran), and often wrote under a pseudonym. Kierkegaard considered his labor religious and within a prophetic tradition. He desired to correct the degenerating Christian narrative. Kierkegaard did not seek to dismiss the Christian narrative; he coveted that narrative's genuine return to existential life.

Peter F. Drucker offers insight into the exceptional contributions of Kierkegaard in an essay aptly titled "The Unfashionable Kierkegaard."[22] Drucker claims that Kierkegaard was not a psychologist or a poet but a man deeply concerned about religious experience; Kierkegaard passionately asked questions about existence in an era defined by Rousseau's and Hegel's focus on society. Kierkegaard refuted the version of society assumed by Rousseau, who understood human existence as determined by and only possible within "society's objective need of survival," whereas Kierkegaard insisted that human existence resides in the tension between life as a member of society and as an individual "in the sight of God" (Drucker, 587–90).

Kierkegaard had few companions in the struggle against the direction of the nineteenth-century West. His work has kinship with Nietzsche and Honoré de Balzac (1799–1850) in that they shared his trepidation about the direction of the nineteenth century. The difference, however, was that Kierkegaard offered a religious, prophetic answer. Kierkegaard examined the tension between the "individual in the spirit and as a citizen in society," which gives birth to human existence via contrast (589). The interplay of spirit and citizen connects, respectively, with the eternal and the everyday dealings with the world. Human existence emerges through the unity of contraries.

Kierkegaard contested the optimism of the nineteenth century, contending that such a moment found identity in gloomy sentiments of fear, trembling, anxiety, and despair. He viewed human existence as tragic and the nineteenth century as heading toward disaster with its focus on optimism and progress (593). The creed of progress gave support to unexpected developments such as Nazism and communism. Drucker states that the nineteenth century sought to lessen the power of death with the institutionalization of life insurance. Kierkegaard opposed that moment—naming it despair emanating from a refusal to be a genuine individual. Kierkegaard called the individual to a faith of existential courage. While living in "fear and trembling," one does not stop, quit, or live a life of lament—one presses forward in faithfulness. Abraham was a symbol of such faith—faithfulness in the face of the absurd (596, 599). Kierkegaard suggests no way out of loneliness and human pain; he does render, however, a picture of a faith fashioned by courage to continue when the reason is unduly unclear. For Kierkegaard, one is not what Rudyard Kipling (1865–1936) termed a son becoming a man but rather a human becoming a person of faith.

Levinas devotes two essays to Kierkegaard, with each underscoring Kierkegaard's connection of ethics and faith to existence and human living. Levinas stated that Kierkegaard kept subjective internal life alive in an era dominated by an imposed exteriority of objectivity. No objective truth can lessen the "thorn in the side" of a human being who must meet despair, anguish, and the need or necessity of carrying on (*Proper Names*, 67). Kierkegaard protests against systems that deny the Saying of a human life that emerges from a trace of insight within an anguish of Said. Belief is a truth that offers direction in the midst of suffering. For Kierkegaard, the ethical does not triumph; it is faith in action in the face of absurdity that ultimately defines a fuzzy and determined sense of direction. Kierkegaard's responsibility rests in the "I" before the Other, for whom I am solely answerable. No matter what the absurdity of life, God calls and I answer in the meeting of the Other in ethical responsibility demanded by the absurdity of faith.

Levinas asserted that Kierkegaard's effort is ultimately a "polemics against speculative philosophy" and against "ethics" in his assertion of faithfulness in the midst of the absurd (76). The images of the National Socialist movement generate pause as one considers the subjective Saying of faith in the depths of the absurd. The only way to keep the Saying vibrant is to attend to its misuse, which rests within the false assurance of the Said of ideology. One cannot permit the unpredictability of the Saying of the absurd to become a strange trace of an unquestioned promise. Saying speaks within the unexpected and in unwanted interruptions of the absurdities of existence. Saying reifies into the Said of ideology when its revelatory implications become demanded expectations.

JEAN LACROIX (1900–1986)

Lacroix's work ties to spirituality, Catholicism, and personalism. Lacroix emphasized "personalism" as the impact of the spirit upon the person as consciousness about existence.[23] He was part of a generation of French Catholics tied to this theoretical work, which followed Bergson's orientation, which influenced French Catholicism. He was a founding member and contributor to the review *Esprit* and was active in numerous center-left movements of Catholic intellectuals. With Emmanuel Mounier, Lacroix created *Esprit*, a significant Catholic review that gave voice to personalism and provided direction for many disenfranchised and "disoriented" individuals (Hellman). Additionally, Lacroix popularized a philosophy of personalism, writing a weekly philosophical column in *Le Monde* from 1945 to 1980.[24]

Lacroix called Christians to attend to a uniting link with atheists, a demand for human responsibility. He contended that it is the task of Christians to demonstrate that faith and responsibility are compatible (*Proper Names*, 9). The notion of responsibility is central in his interpretation of Kant. Lacroix contended that Kant fought against a "fatalism" and "scepticism," as he underlined the interplay of "human freedom, morality, and religion."[25] Personalism opens one to the spirit that animates an individual within a life, moving one to the sphere of the person, which is a subjective life attentive to existential demands.

Lacroix conceptualized a "vicious circle" composed of a unity of contraries[26]; to break it, he proffered belief in the agreement of ideas and objective reality. He rejected true ideas originating between subject and object. Likewise, the truth of ideas does not rest in human contact. Truth of ideas themselves generates faith and has an "intrinsic character." Truth lives within the "*acquisition* of the idea, not a *relation* between idea and object" (Wald, 200). One tests the truth of an idea in confrontation through practice. Truth is not a possession or property; it emerges in ongoing action. Lacroix "would argue that humanism's construction of man as an absolute amounts to idolatry."[27] The Said of ideas carries a trace of Saying that stirs within practices that guide and constitute human actions.

Levinas's short essay on Lacroix discusses "extreme consciousness" that is greater than consciousness itself. Extreme consciousness moves from the realm of subjectivity to *logos*, to a Saying that is before consciousness. Lacroix's philosophy of "insufficiency," which engaged personalism of the spirit, guides a faith that fills gaps in philosophy and brings life to a third dimension of participation (*Proper Names*, 80–81, 89). The religious evokes responsibility called forth by a consciousness that is beyond consciousness. The Saying of this consciousness makes personalism of the faith possible and permits us to perceive traces of textured depth of meaning that the Said of rationality can only begin to suggest.

ROGER LAPORTE (1925–2001)

Laporte was born in Lyon and taught philosophy at the University of Montpellier. Laporte, known for his critical insight, was the recipient of the literary prize Prix France-Culture in 1978. His works had a biographical focus without entailing dates or events. He explained his own thinking, giving insight into "repercussions in his mind."[28] He examined the interaction between words and subjectivity that gives rise to language. His writings are factually unbiographical and, at the same time, deeply biographical in that the reader witnesses his practices of thought. He "pa[id] homage" to self-consciousness; he examined connections between and among words and subjectivity (Sheringham, 71). He arguably submits the most intellectually engaging form of autobiography since Rousseau. Laporte focused on discourse. He examined words and subjectivity. Laporte moved from self-questioning to ongoing linguistic examination of deconstruction that illuminates differently than conventional autobiography does.

Levinas contends in *Proper Names* that, for Laporte, the word is "*par excellence*" (90). In search of the right word, he attended to a voice "that approaches in becoming more distant, like an echo or a rhyme, hovering at the edge of silence and forgetfulness" (91). Writing becomes an act of searching for precision that seeks not to dispel uncertainty but to witness to the power of Saying. Levinas points to a Saying that emerges from a persistent search for traces within the Said of a given word or image; Saying demands our ongoing effort of engagement to respond to the trace within the Said.

MAX PICARD (1888–1965)

Picard's parents were of Jewish origin. Picard converted to Catholicism in 1939; although he was born in Germany, he spent the majority of his life in isolation near Switzerland. Picard was a "sage," not a philosopher.[29] He was a surgeon who committed himself to contemplation, philosophic thought, and writing. He manifested a humble and simple form of "majesty." His dignity came from his knowledge of being bound to his divine creator. He did not overemphasize his place in the cosmos, which underscored his love of communication with a wide variety of persons. Picard understood the entire world as off-center and in flight from God (Marcel, ix–xi). Marcel said the following about Picard: "Picard is amongst the few who can resist the universal vertigo and who appear capable of redirecting the remnants of the thinking élite. Without such a redirection it is impossible not to despair of mankind" (xiii). Picard had a deep sensitivity to the moral crisis of the West.

Picard made no pretense about being scientific. His task was to address the despair of the human condition in the West. The confusing nature of the world requires "contemplative" action, not just raw impulses to rush in with unreflective solutions.[30] In an age of crisis, the impulse is flight, and Picard's counter was contemplative consideration. He questioned all that abolishes opportunities for silence, from machines to exaggerated ideas. Picard craved a human capable of reclaiming a sense of balance in a fragmented era. Picard functioned as a Neoplatonist; he insisted that truth and justice existed well before the first human.

Levinas stated that he corresponded for a number of years with Picard; he encountered his face as a poetic experience. The face is enigmatic, devoid of human clarity and pointing to something more than the reality of an empirical person. The face beckons us to an obligation to and for a specific person. Picard rejected the modern world as a point of constant noise and activity. He called for "silence" as the dwelling place of meaning. In silence and stories that enrich an inner life, there is a trace of a sanctuary, a "refuge from contemporaneity itself" (*Proper Names*, 97–98). Silence is the home of Saying. Nonstop action and motion is the Said displayed in the noise of place and people.

MARCEL PROUST (1871–1922)

Proust, considered one of the most important French novelists of the twentieth century, suffered from ongoing ill health. He responded to issues of domination and oppression generated from an aristocratic class. Proust was an outstanding student. He graduated from the Lycée Condorcet, and he studied law and graduated from the Sorbonne. His parents were bourgeois, but his allegiances connected him to those without power. Proust, whose mother was Jewish, was one of the main figures who fought for a retrial for Dreyfus, the Jewish captain wrongly accused of treason. Dreyfus, twice convicted, endured the fact that officials knew that another, not Dreyfus, passed documents to Germany. The French government eventually pardoned Dreyfus; Proust was at the center of much of the controversy. This event took a sizable toll on Proust, who suffered ill health from depression and asthma.

Proust's greatest novel was the multivolume *Remembrance of Things Past*. He was very interested in the work of John Ruskin (1819–1900), which reflected his great concern for artisans who construct the world around us. Both Ruskin and Proust shared sensitivity to and for "physical sensation[s]."[31] Proust explored reconstruction of memory, and

Ruskin described the reconstruction of architecture. Like Ruskin, Proust engaged unconventional views of "action"; he connected memory and story to life, which together shaped his literary heart (Murray, "Marcel Proust," 41). Throughout his life, Proust was fragile; then, in 1922, after coming down with a cold, he was given two adrenaline shots. The second one either killed him or coincided with his death. Proust resisted physical action even as he contended that it was remembered physical sensations that structure the events of human memory.

Levinas recounted the rise and the fall of interest in Proust, noting that the latter emerged from Sartre's critique of Proust's psychology. Proust's grand analysis faded into problematic theory. Levinas, however, had a different take on Proust; he contended that his work was not a psychology of human relationships but rather a rendering of and about "communication" between persons (*Proper Names*, 104). Solitude, in Proust's work, is a dwelling in which the trace of a possibility of communication dwells. For Levinas, solitude was not the failure of communication but the gathering of sensations that open opportunities for Saying between persons. Saying nurtured in the Said of solitude of human life permits discovery of communicative potentialities. Proust lent insight into solitude's functioning as a communicative dwelling for the awakening of Saying.

FATHER HERMAN LEO VAN BREDA (1911–1974)

Father Van Breda wrote his dissertation on Husserl; he completed his PhD in 1941 at the Catholic University of Leuven in Belgium.[32] When he initiated his dissertation research, Father Van Breda went to the University of Freiburg in 1938. Due to the date of his arrival, five years after the election of Hitler as the German chancellor, Father Van Breda took Husserl's papers back with him to Leuven. With the help of the University of Leuven and the Belgian government, he smuggled the documents out of Nazi Germany. His contribution was extraordinary; he saved a legacy, the life's work of the founder of phenomenology. Father Van Breda joined the university as a faculty member and provided a home for the international study of phenomenology.

Levinas noted that, in 1938, German National Socialism was a dominant force and viewed itself as representing the heart of civilization, yet it was a thoughtful Catholic priest who saved Husserl's manuscripts. Father Van Breda secured the manuscripts right out from under the Nazis' undisciplined watch with the help of Husserl's former research assistants, the Catholic University of Leuven, and the Belgian government. He transported the papers to Brussels and became a hero of phenomenology, known for telling the story of his securing the documents with humility and humor. Father Van Breda built the Husserl Archives at University of Leuven. He organized multiple international meetings on phenomenology; his work kept the conversation alive. Levinas emphasized the generosity of Father Van Breda's heart, a generosity that made conferences possible. Father Van Breda made friends everywhere. Levinas stated that Father Van Breda created a future for phenomenology; his work permitted the "non-said" to continue to influence the world (*Proper Names*, 109). He engaged a life in which he preserved the Said of manuscripts and conferences on phenomenology, which housed traces of Saying that kept conversation vibrant between and among friends as he nourished the legacy of Husserl's project.

JEAN WAHL (1888–1974)

Wahl spent much of his professional life at the University of Sorbonne from 1936 until 1967. The only interruption was a stay in the United States from 1942 until 1945, which provided a safe haven after he had escaped from the Drancy internment camp for Jews that was located outside of Paris. He was initially attracted to the work of Bergson and William James (1842–1910); Wahl introduced Hegel to France in the 1930s, and he wrote on Kierkegaard. His work, although not systematic, influenced numerous scholars, particularly Levinas. In the United States, during his exile, Wahl assisted in the establishment of a "university in exile."[33] Levinas's first word on Wahl is "sensibility": "To seek a homeland for oneself *outside*—in the realm of ideas and human works—all that is meaningful only in the final analysis as the life of feeling. 'Ideas are valid only if they cease being ideas'" (*Proper Names*, 110, 117). Wahl conscientiously avoided comprehensive systems; he was attracted to the embodiment of ideas in everyday human action.

In discussion of Wahl, Levinas tenders a story that cites Aristotle's discussion of the free man who desires a "minimum" of material goods in order to pursue happiness. Long before Karl Marx (1818–1883), Aristotle's critique of undue accumulation was part of an ongoing argument about the development of the West. He questioned accumulation committed to exteriority and materiality as tools for mastery of self and the universe. For Levinas, this accumulative sense of "I" dwells at the heart of totality. An alternative to exteriority dominated Wahl's perspective; he stressed feeling that demands attention and necessitates response. Wahl was interested, not in warmth of response, but intensity of engagement. He explored feelings that were "savage, dense, opaque, dark" (112, 114). Wahl embraced an "I" akin to that of the cynics, one that recognizes the difference between me and the world of things, in contrast to an "I" that seeks to dominate. Levinas asserted that Wahl turned toward ideas and the fragmentary (traces) to interrupt the Said of possession, a turn that unleashed Saying and revelatory insight.

Wahl was attracted to a realm of ideas that only becomes real and meaningful within the house of feelings. Ironically, one finds a home for such feeling in the exteriority of ideas that separate the "I" from ongoing events of the world. Wahl reminds us of the Saying of an "I" that embraces private conviction/feeling that refuses solidification into the Said of "implements" and "heritage" (118). Wahl moves us toward an "I" that lives within a Saying of unbounded intensity of feeling.

NAMELESS

This essay by Levinas addresses the multitude of nameless victims of Hitler's Germany. Levinas stated that between 1940 and 1945, institutions for justice did not exist. One felt "hapless" and in "despair," living in a historical moment of "abandonment." The political left was completely lacking in its protection of human rights; their presence was virtually nonexistent. The nameless had to fend for themselves, to open their own possibilities. Each day was lived within the realm of "insecurity" (*Proper Names*, 119–20).

For the nameless, the war announced three truths. First, people found that they need less of almost everything than "civilization" tells them is necessary. Second, at times, the only possible hope for human dignity is the courage to wait for its return. Third, one must teach the next generation to be "strong in isolation"; they must acknowledge the necessity of "resistance." Resistance begins with one's inner life, which undergirds strength of hope when all hope seems lost. The Jewish condition reflects humanity on the brink of "morality without institutions" (121–22). The election of the nameless is a hardship that gathers a voice for an immemorial cry for justice. The Saying of justice continues within a people who lived without human rights, bereft of champions of support, and void of institutions that could render protection. The Saying of justice stands steadfast; it is rooted in traces of an immemorial echo of "I am my brother's keeper." No institutional Said stood forth to protect the nameless; however, there was and is the Saying of an archaic ethical command that generates hope amid the despair of waiting for justice to enter existence once again. The nameless carried a trace of an ethical echo in their lives and faces; they awaited justice of a Said that would stand firm in their renewal.

MAURICE BLANCHOT (1907–2003)

Blanchot was a man of contradictions. Before World War II, he was a right-wing author, and after the war, he became an antigovernment protestor who contested the occupation of Algeria. He was significant in the thinking of postmodern writers from Derrida to Foucault; his influence was purposely quiet. Seldom seen in public, this man, who once supported conservative causes, became an important influence in Levinas's life and became a great representative of French existential atheist literature.

When Levinas delivered his thesis defense in 1961 at the Sorbonne, the jury consisted of Wahl, Vladimir Jankélévitch (1903–1985), Ricoeur, Marcel, and Georges Blin. They listened to Levinas defending *Totality and Infinity* in June of 1961. One person in the audience was Blanchot, who was "always the friend, the unique and brotherly interlocutor" for Levinas.[34] Blanchot visited Levinas at his home the next morning following his defense, which was their last meeting, but in the words of Levinas's son, their continuing "correspondence . . . was sublime and essential." Levinas repeatedly returned to Blanchot, offering a "philosophical reading" of his work (M. Levinas, 651). Levinas offers three essays that reveal the nature of the Levinasian response to Blanchot.

Levinas reacted to the particular manner in which Blanchot brought people into a poetic realm. He did so through the impersonal; his work was "outside the realm of the Day" (*Proper Names*, 129). Blanchot brought impersonality to his work and time; he pointed to a way of knowing beyond responsiveness to empirical existence. The work suggests an independence and authenticity in its own right. The artist knows that the "nontrue," the least responsive to the environment, is the actual realm of "authenticity." Levinas cites the following insight from Blanchot: "The artist and the poet seem to have received this mission: to call us obstinately back to error, to turn us toward that space where everything we propose, everything we have acquired, everything we are, all that is disclosed on earth ... returns to insignificance, and where what approaches is the nonserious and the nontrue, as if perhaps thence sprang the source of all authenticity" (135). There is authenticity in exile that avoids the wretchedness of control by others, who act out of an "idealism of the haughty." Blanchot's view of art and the "I" that stands in impersonal response to Being acts to "[uproot] the Heideggerian universe" (138–39).

Blanchot outlined the keys to engaging art in the form of "waiting" and "forgetting," as opposed to "remembering" (145). Forgetting oneself and relaxing while engaging art permits an "I" to become a question in existence without a sense of worry. Levinas stated that Blanchot's "I" lives somewhere between "seeing" and "saying" (148). Blanchot found access in interspaces in time that are unresponsive to past, future, and present. He placed his feet on soil, refusing to float above existence, while at the same time refusing to be a captive of the world.

Levinas responded to André Dalmas on the subject of François Collins's book on Blanchot.[35] Levinas discussed the manner in which Collins understood Blanchot's understanding of the presence of absence without being confused with "negation." Blanchot "reminds that world that its totality is not total" (*Proper Names*, 152, 154). As Collins suggested, Blanchot's writing does not destroy; it disputes. Blanchot wrote with an impersonal spirit that disrupted totality of existence, underscoring an "I" responsive in its own accumulated history. The "derivative I" emerges from spaces of disruption. Blanchot wrote *The Madness of the Day* after the end of World War II. The novel seemed to fit events of 1968, particularly demonstrations throughout the West in opposition to war. He wrote without concern for "temporal limitations." His works revolve within a space between "renewal" and the reality of "repetition" (159). Blanchot, drawn to darkness, understood that transparency often wounds. Blanchot chanted at the end of *The Madness of the Day*—"No stories, never again." In the "refusal" there is an "I" that begins to tell a story, not through imposition, but through a dance in the madness and darkness of existence that is a Said with a trace played out in the dance that permits the Saying to speak again (170).

The Saying and the Said in Communication Ethics: The Performative Power of Name

Proper Names outlines the Saying of particular human faces significant in Levinas's project of lifelong engagement. Levinas provides a Said in the form of a distinct chapter within *Proper Names* as he simultaneously responds to the trace of Saying within a given person's work. Levinas does not seek to totalize his subjects; he suggests and points. Saying dwells within particular moments—modest glimpses of gestures and poetic lines offered in response to the Other. Within the particularity of Saying, a momentary window to infinity emerges through the performative and revelatory power of Saying.

Saying illuminates beyond the event, the object, the person, and the moment. The revelatory authority of Saying performs in silence, in the quiet of a dwelling of poetry that moves beyond the page, working within darkness in a manner that makes light visible and within the nudity of a human face. The Said defines the structure of life, with Saying giving substance, character, and signification to a proper name. Saying continues to beckon after death, if only to announce "finite freedom" (Levinas, *Alterity*, 15). Through finiteness, Saying speaks. In death, Saying reverberates, awakening the Other to a unique responsibility to utter and live—"here I am" (31). In *Proper Names*, we discover the power of Said, trace, and Saying:

The revelatory.—Poetry invites the Other to attend to a present that is not apparent. The Said of the written page, guided by creative ambiguity, metaphorical implication, and an orality that speaks from the page itself, houses a trace of a revelatory Saying that can reenvision and reshape the reader's world.

Obligation.—The human face of the Other is a Said claimed by a proper name with a trace that redirects me to the Saying of an ethical echo present long before this meeting, calling me into personal responsibility for the Other. The face is the Said that houses a trace of revelatory hope of human responsibility.

Creative tradition.—The ground of tradition that guides human lives in constructive directions does not possess, but suggests. Such a conception of tradition is a Said, publicly known, with a trace of creative, new possibilities that open the Saying of the unexpected and the not yet connected to a tradition publicly acknowledged.

Discerning orientation.—Direction sought within darkness and confusion seeks a trace of insight that propels a Saying of guidance. One finds direction through the telling of stories that become a Said that houses within it the power of trace and Saying that later unleashes new direction and clarity that refuse starkness of appearance.

Guidance without undue assurance.—Ethics finds voice in the meeting and interplay of Said, trace, and Saying. This trinity of public direction and revelatory shifts permits communication ethics to guide a life without a false assurance of artificial clarity.

The uttering of a name enacts a performative Saying of a life that gives meaning to the trace within the Said of a name. As stated in the beginning of this chapter, it was not just the words, or the tone, but the performative Saying of my mom to my dad that I recall. She called his name in a manner that framed his identity in a performative Saying. The revelatory power of Saying acts as a spiritual awakening via the proper name of another!

Like Harper Lee's book, *Proper Names* is a reminder of the power of a name connected to a particular face. Levinas's book witnesses to an existential fact: it is possible to meet intellectuals who are working with complex ideas and differences and attend to a proper name with a texture that refuses to eclipse the Saying of the Other. *Proper Names* testifies to the power of the human face in scholarly form and simultaneously verifies for me why I still hear the echo of my mother calling my father's first name with all the responsibility it invoked. Communication ethics sometimes dwells in a human utterance that invokes the name of another, inviting the Saying of responsibility and the discovery of my responsibility and identity.

CHAPTER 5

The Impersonal and the Sacred: Igniting Personal Responsibility

The idea of a society putting religion between parentheses in the name of religion itself is concretized in the idea of the foreigner: the "*ger.*" We are reminded more than forty times in the Pentateuch that we must respect strangers. The law will be the same for foreigner and native; this is justified by both human fraternity and the community of human misery ("because you were strangers in the land of Egypt"). The rights of a person are founded outside his membership in the state religion.
—Emmanuel Levinas, *Unforeseen History*

Levinas' thought experiment leaves him with an indeterminacy like the impersonal "it" of the expression, "it snows." . . . It is not absolute negativity, for this would presume there were something that might be the object of negation's action . . . It is, rather, a kind of positivity or fullness that is anonymous, like the way the darkness of the night seems full though it obscures all objects in a room.
—Bettina G. Bergo, *Levinas between Ethics and Politics: For the Beauty That Adorns the Earth*

Emmanuel Levinas's "ethics as first philosophy" commences with burden and obligation to and for the Other, forgoing the temptation and social danger of ethics tied to the personal. Levinas's ethics relies on "impersonal attentiveness" as an ironic guide for an initial ethical optic that meets the Other. It is the particular Other who awakens an impersonal attentiveness charged by an ethical demand that dwells within an immemorial ethical echo. Levinas's ethics of impersonal attentiveness originates with an archaic call, "I am my brother's keeper," that results in a "derivative I" charged with the responsibility of "if not me, then whom?" In order to explicate the importance of the "impersonal" in Levinas's ethics, this chapter relies on two quite different figures: Kant, the premier ethicist of the Enlightenment, and Gregory Bateson (1904–1980), an anthropologist and semiotician known for originating the theory of double bind. Both of these scholars, from the eighteenth and the twentieth centuries, respectively, countered a tyranny of universal reason and the perils lurking within a singular focus on the personal.

Introduction

The sacred met with an impersonal attentiveness avoids the impulse of personal possession. The impersonal makes ethics possible as one is redirected to an audio ethic that is an immemorial demand upon me that calls forth a "responsive I"[1] of "here I am." The impersonal calls forth personal responsibility. This sequence of events includes four elements or steps: (1) the impersonal call of the face that (2) directs one to an ethical echo that (3) returns one to the particular face with a charge of personal responsibility that (4) is ultimately disrupted by justice, turning one's attention to the unseen and unknown third. Ethics totalized requires justice to function as a routine act of disruption. Levinas does not begin with the communicative agent telling or commanding. The face of the Other demands that one attend to an immemorial ethical echo, which charges an ethical call of personal responsibility that constitutes a "derivative I," in contrast with the "originative I" of a communicative agent.[2]

This chapter addresses the pragmatic limits of a personal consideration that seeks to possess certainty of answers for the Other, which misses the revelatory and the sacred, the heart of Bateson's last book, *Angels Fear: Towards an Epistemology of the Sacred.* This chapter explores the limits of possession and its relationship to the impersonal through four different perspectives. The first section, "Bateson's Pragmatic Turn to the Sacred," offers an interpretive summary of Bateson's last scholarly project. The second section, "Chalier on Kant and

Levinas," attends to Catherine Chalier's thoughtful examination of the interplay of Kantian and Levinasian thought. The third section, "Levinas on Kant and the Impersonal," examines Levinas's citing and referencing of the notion of the impersonal in reference to Kant. The chapter concludes with "The Saying and the Said in Communication Ethics: The Impersonal and the Sacred," a section that explicates ethics as first philosophy—a pragmatic communication ethics resistant to the act of possession.

There is distinct irony in Levinas's ethics—the impersonal makes personal responsibility possible. If one begins with the personal, one is likely to do what benefits one's own self-image. Ethics, for Levinas, forsakes representation, image, or self-assessment of my own goodness. Ethics commences in an impersonal attending to the Other that calls forth personal responsibility. Ethics as a sacred performative responsibility dwells in the impersonal, which demands personal responsibility from me alone.

Bateson's Pragmatic Turn to the Sacred

This section focuses on the final days of Bateson's life, during which he offered a concluding record of his ideas that his daughter completed after his death. Bateson and Mary Catherine Bateson wrote *Angels Fear* in collaboration. Mary Catherine finished the manuscript after Gregory's death; she also added sections of her own. This collaborative book opens a door to apprehension of Levinas's view of the impersonal, a communicative position that is unconventional in a communicative culture where personal possession of another's sense of meaning is normative.[3] Following the title of Bateson's book, this chapter examines a conceptual space where even angels fear to tread, a place constructed in acts of personal possession that seek to dominate the communicative landscape.

Bateson contended against acts of personal possession, claiming that such action is contrary to the sacred. He engaged the sacred as an atheist, offering witness to the wrongheadedness of imposed certitude. Bateson displayed "distrust" of those claiming assurance of knowledge beyond temporal interrogation. He recognized gaps in knowledge, which nurtured places that celebrate the unknown, while responsibly addressing "the hungry, overpopulated, sick, ambitious, and competitive world [that] will not wait, we are told, till more is known, but must rush in where angels fear to tread."[4] Bateson described a world that angels seek to protect and promote, a space void of false assurance.

Bateson affirmed genuine learning that originates with one assumption: whatever we discover conceals more than it discloses. The unseen, the "not yet" noticed, makes it impossible to gather all accumulated data. Bateson celebrated "difference" as a "signal" for the commencement of knowledge. Bateson emphasized the difference between "Pleroma" and "Creatura," with the latter based on clear and precise descriptions of disparities and the former situated with distinctions without meticulous precision (Bateson and Bateson, 17). Pleroma consists of "no maps, no names, no classes, and no members of classes" (21). Pleroma is difference within a poetic space that argues with general senses, rather than through narrow specifics. Creatura is a conceptual movement focused upon a "thing" or object (27). Pleroma attends to "relations" between and among things (28–29). The home of such relational connections resides in language and "metaphor," which acts as a temporal lodging of an implied story that suggests "models" and "structures" that organize human perception (30, 37). The key for Bateson is that different textures of events invite consideration of models and structures via stories that reject universal statements of undisputed truth. Bateson encountered the unknown as "gaps" and "limits" that preserve structures and models from undue certainty (39). To illustrate this understanding in action, he depicted dissimilarities between "feedback" and "calibration," with the former permitting precise changes and the latter requiring an ensemble of generalized practices that entail multiple skill sets that must be performed simultaneously (42). Feedback assists one in playing notes; however, if one is to play music with others, calibration is necessary. Calibration is attentive to multiplicity gathered in "pattern" and "gestalt"; this understanding of variability is contrary to uniformity, which is "toxic" to the discovery of novel insights (60, 116).

Pattern without undue homogeny permits one to arrive at unexpected places as one meets the unanticipated. Additionally, meaning tied to gestalt emerges in forms that announce themselves through the irony of "noncommunication" (81). The sacred cannot and should not center discussion. An inability to discontinue communicating makes inevitable the exploits of undue certainty. As one seeks to disclose all about a given thing or topic, there is inevitable loss of the sacred, which relies upon the "inarticulate."[5] For instance, consider what happens when one is experiencing a great time with friends and someone yells, "Is this not great or what?" At that moment, all gaze at one another in disbelief, thinking: "Why did you make this wonderful moment so explicit? It is now gone!" Designing an experience too explicitly destroys the sacred in everyday life. The attempt to possess the power of the moment leaves only an artifact of a living moment. Gaps, limitations, and sensations of pattern, when rendered unduly perspicuous, eclipse experience into a concentrated, self-confident gaze. Bateson warns that communicating to the point of reification emerges within a patterned sense of possessive meaning. Wisdom about the inarticulate, however, assumes that meaning vanishes when overly dissected; signification simply fades away. For Bateson, life is composed of both clarity and "secrets" that require protecting to shelter the "sacred" (86). The hallowed emerges through the interplay of "complex relations" that transpire between and among events, persons, and objects (98)—supported by gaps and limits that texture and particularize stories.

Gaps and limits permit creativity, giving rise to unforeseen consequences. For instance, Bateson argued that the Treaty of Versailles at the conclusion of World War I and subsequent treatment of Germany led to unforeseen responses: "It is said that in the 1920s when Germany was restricted by the Treaty of Versailles to a parade-ground army of ten thousand men, very strict tests were applied to the men who volunteered for this army. They were to be the cream of the rising generation not only in physique but also in physiology and dedication" (111–12). The precision of specimens selected for the "parade-ground army of ten thousand" led to an unexpected future. The Treaty of Versailles inaugurated a rationale for an "ideal" German prototype (111–12).

Too much specificity and "quantity" of thinking becomes "toxic," shifting attention from "pattern[s]" of excellence (116–17). Through the "interface" of specific and amorphous senses of pattern, one locates a communicative relation between Pleroma and Creatura (123). This interface is an *impersonal* "force" that furnishes power and significance through relational difference:

The Greek idea of necessary sequence was, of course, not unique. What is interesting is that the Greeks seem to have thought of *anangke* as a totally impersonal theme in the structure of the human world. It was as if, from the initial act onwards, dice were loaded against the participants. The theme, as it worked itself out, used human emotions and motives as its means, but the theme itself (we would vulgarly call it a "force") was thought to be impersonal, beyond and greater than gods and persons, a bias or warp in the structure of the universe. (137)

This impersonal force is a metaphorical pattern of creative ambiguity that permits one to engage something or someone with less than a direct gaze. "Metaphorical connections" rescue us from the demand of possession (144). Such insight into the world of metaphor focuses attention on gaps between and among persons and the world before us, forgoing a mandate of possession and the performative assurance of a direct gaze. We become what we practice—to rehearse possession fuels the fear of loss, making the reality of J. R. R. Tolkien's Gollum and "my precious" a principal shaper of identity.[6] On the other hand, to practice the recognition of limits, the necessity of gaps, and the importance of metaphors that maintain an appreciation of fuzzy clarity constitutes a contrasting realm of meaning. For Bateson, such is the reason that we become that which we "pretend," and we enact what another "imposes" on us when our responses are continually practiced (182). Practice shapes direction and identity.

Bateson's commitment to the sacred embraces ambiguity and practices that nourish and enlarge the world as we affirm four elements: (1) what we do not know, (2) the reality of unforeseen consequences, (3) the importance of acknowledging gaps and limits in knowing, and (4) metaphorical understanding that does not seek to possess. Bateson's insights frame the importance of an impersonal force that eschews undue certainty and tempers the temptation of illicit proprietorship and possession. The significance of the impersonal, pointed to by Bateson, undergirds the projects of Kant and Levinas. Such an exploration witnesses the interplay of the two worlds detailed by Bateson—one more analytic (Kant) and the other more poetically demanding (Levinas). Together these perspectives display the complexity of protecting the sacred.

Chalier on Kant and Levinas

The examination of the relationship between Kant and Levinas is described in *What Ought I to Do? Morality in Kant and Levinas* by Catherine Chalier, professor of philosophy at the University of Paris, Nanterre. Chalier tacitly lends insight into Bateson's reminder that fuzzy edges support the sacred as she illustrates the importance of the impersonal for both Kant and Levinas. Chalier's work provides another vocabulary, which attends to ideas similar to what Bateson called the Pleroma and Creatura, poetic and analytic conceptual space, respectively; Chalier's project has her functioning as the director of an ethics orchestra composed of Levinas and Kant. She illuminates Kantian and Levinasian commonalties and differences in an era termed "[t]he crisis of the subject," an era in which a Cartesian, Archimedean point from which one can discern truth has lost its philosophical and practical power; this historical moment is defined by the loss of undue certainty.[7] Chalier suggests that both Kant and Levinas discount the assumption that knowledge accumulation augments moral uprightness; she illustrates this point through contrasting cases of the French Revolution and the Third Reich. Chalier argues that Levinas and Kant embrace the viability of practical reason, with Levinas more attentive to "sensibility" and Kant responsive to a transcendental understanding of "timeless choice." Kant anticipates that virtue will lead to happiness, and Levinas offers a demanding existential encounter with "infinite obligation" on to death and beyond (Chalier, 7–8). One such example of Levinas's perspective emerged in Nazi Germany through the actions of the White Rose, a group largely composed of students from the University of Munich who opposed the Nazis. Each member of the group lost his life on February 22, 1943.[8] For Levinas, these students lived out ethics that demanded great sacrifice; they embraced ethical clarity, not in theoretical abstraction, but in the face of suffering and ultimate death.

The critique of abstract intellectualism and knowledge accumulation unites Kant and Levinas, particularly after Kant stressed the importance of the individual being treated as an end in himself, rather than as a mere means. This position, according to Chalier, creates a divide between Kant and Levinas, with Kant propelled by ethical "principle" and Levinas by an ethical anarchy (31). Kant engaged the finite hope of "good will" with enlightened self-interest, and Levinas underscored an infinite set of obligations toward the Other played out in the particular, not within an abstract conception of ethics in existence. Their positions suggest disparate routes of access to a universal morality that trumps the particularity of a given person. Levinas refused to tether his understanding of ethical action solely to a universal of an immemorial call. The archaic ethical echo only generates a spiritual awakening that demands responsibility. For Levinas, the universal calls one to responsibility without dictating a specific course of ethical action. Ethics performed in the midst of precarious circumstances finds no assurance in a clarity of code and procedure; the responsibility for ethical decision making and action is mine alone (33–34).

Kant launches his ethics project with access to the universal. Levinas, on the other hand, inaugurates ethics with the concrete face of the Other that eventuates a return to the particular Other charged with ethical responsibility. Each encounter with another is an "ethical awakening" for Levinas. The face is the carrier of an image of those without, the dispossessed, and those demanding responsibility from me. The key for Levinas is not the immediate relationship alone but attentiveness to an ethical responsibility. This grander call of responsibility comes from "the epiphany of the face" understood within a loftier context of an ethical echo that commands concerned action for a particular Other (37).

Both Kant and Levinas understand the good as a priori to what is termed evil and ultimately as more powerful than the action of evil. Kant emphasized a "radical" evil in human nature, following an Enlightenment protocol of abjuring the term *original sin* (49–50). For Kant and Levinas, the human ego is the locus of attacks on the good: "The ego is held liable on three charges: 'the *temptation* of the ease of breaking off, *erotic attraction* . . . [or] the* seduction of irresponsibility, and the *probability* of egoism'" (54). Kant uses "self-interest" and the maxim of "good will" to temper the impulse of the ego. Levinas states that the one cannot control the self-centered focus of the ego with an enlightened reasoning, which I have termed an "originative I." Contrarily, the "derivative I" is called out by the face of the Other.[9] Levinas situates evil within the view of the Enlightenment ego, an "originative I" that functions as a prince or sovereign unjustifiably "preoccupied with the self" (Chalier, 55).

Kant's counter to evil assumes a subject using finite reason that attends to a good beyond the immediacy of the moment. For Kant, ethics does not originate in Being but emerges through thinking attentive to the categorical imperative. Levinas also works otherwise than Being. "'It is not by chance,' Levinas maintains, 'that this manner of conceiving of a sense beyond being is the corollary of an ethics'" (59). Both Levinas and Kant announce conceptions of ethics that are not dependent on Being alone—Kant is guided by the principle of the categorical imperative and Levinas by infinite obligation to the Other.

Obligation shapes both perspectives with ethical debt played out in contrasting fashion. The chemistry between autonomy and heteronomy (rule by another) contours both ethical perspectives. Kant emphasizes "self-interest" that lends itself to good will toward others as well as "respect" for the self. His project adheres to the moral perspective/demand that permits the human to turn to a categorical imperative of action that must stand the test of a universal law. The categorical imperative permits autonomy and freedom in discernment of judgments in everyday practical reasoning: "That is why one of the formulations of the categorical imperative requires that every person treat the humanity in his own person and in others '*always at the same time as an end, never simply as a means*'" (65). Unlike Rousseau and his emphasis on the social contract and freedom, Kant associates autonomy and freedom with acts that eventuate in respect for the self and that adhere to the demands of a universal moral imperative. In short, Chalier contends that Kant rejects the tyranny of "heteronomy" without forgoing restraint compelled by a categorical imperative (60–62); ethical action emerges in freedom and is propelled through self-evaluative respect for the self, as one functions as an autonomous moral being engaged in self-legislation.

Levinas does not adhere to Kant's ethics of self-legislation. Additionally, Levinas rejects tyranny that assumes a master-slave relationship; Kant understands the weak and the downtrodden as forming a healthy heteronomy that holds us hostage and demands our responsibility. In Levinas's project, this relationship includes concern for the "third," or the neighbor—disquiet generated by a unique face, disrupted by a larger existential attentiveness to justice inclusive of the unknown or unseen neighbor. Levinas does not labor within self-interest; instead, he stresses the pragmatic importance of "disinterestedness" inherent in answering an ethical call/demand (66). Chalier states that there is a Kantian movement in Levinas. The moral subject does not merely attend to the Other. To do so is to eclipse responsibility to and for those not proximate: "Responsibility does not rest on a heart-felt and partial impulse or on intimidation in the face of distress; it remains inseparable from justice toward a third party" (82). The notion of justice, attentiveness to those not present, offers common ground for Kant and Levinas, with their projects gathered together by disinterestedness.

Disinterestedness attends to the Other within a context of distant Others, ever responsive to an archaic ethical echo. For Levinas, ethical action is a vocation, not a matter of self-interest or regulation within a categorical imperative. Kant defends autonomy, and Levinas offers an unusual form of heteronomy that attends to another from a position of infinite obligation. Neither Kant nor Levinas permits a relationship of proximate familiarity to govern final ethical decisions. The impersonal attends to a standard outside the immediacy of encounter; for Kant, it is the categorical imperative; for Levinas, the impersonal meeting of a human face shifts attentiveness to an immemorial ethical echo that charges one with personal responsibility.

Kant does not rely on an audio ethic; instead, he places confidence in individual access to the universality of reason: "The subject's capacity to disregard sensible, cultural, and social data and to think and judge for itself, places it face to face with autonomy as the criterion par excellence of a human being's humanity" (85). Kant seeks to emancipate the person from the particulars of a given culture. Levinas rails against the tyranny of reason that goes unregulated by "the obligation toward the stranger" (87). Kant works from self-love and self-response that assumes an expectation of "reciprocity." His position is contrary to that of Levinas, who discusses the a priori demand of "vulnerability" situated within asymmetrical obligations. Perhaps fundamental differences between Kant and Levinas rest with their respective weight placed on the "sublime" and on "disinterestedness." The sublime, for Kant, requires magnanimity in reflection on moral laws tied to a universal understanding of the categorical imperative. Levinas, on the other hand, concentrates on demands of the Other that are not personally ascertained. Levinas contends that an individual is "elected," called forth by a genuine Saying that commences in the face of the Other, who directs one to an immemorial ethical past, and then, once charged with responsibility, returns to the person (91–93, 97, 107).

Kant seeks the sublime in shaping an "intelligible character" with a "transcendental freedom" that also emanates from an "immemorial" a priori outside practical temporality. Transcendental freedom is grounded in "natural necessity," "[t]he law of natural causality" (112–13, 115–17). It is this sense of intelligible character that precedes temporality and guides practical reasoning, keeping it connected to moral reasoning that attends to the categorical imperative as a beckoning standard that requires discernment—"[e]thics is always lived in the plural" (129). Thus, there is agreement between Kant and Levinas on the importance of the immemorial, with a profound difference in how Kant and Levinas understand its constitution: "The name of the immemorial thus differs in Kant and in Levinas. Their philosophies are profoundly *affected* by that difference. Transcendental freedom announces the promise of autonomy: in all circumstances, the Kantian subject will be marked by the concern 'not to go outside itself'" (130). Levinas turns directly to exteriority and Kant to self-legislation; both are attentive to an archaic past.

Levinas's understanding of the immemorial begins with an ethical call that alerts one to an ethical awakening about an anarchical election initiated by the Other, who calls forth a "responsive I" in "me" that demands my accountability for the Other: "The significance of anteriority exempt from memory differs in the two philosophies. Kant understands it in terms of a free establishment of character; Levinas understands it in terms of an anarchical election . . . when one is confronted with the present vulnerability of one's neighbor" (124). Levinas's ethical awakening is prompted by the face of the Other and a world larger than those in close familial proximity.

Kant broke tradition with Aristotle, who defined happiness as connected to contemplation and metaphysical life in action. Kant frames happiness with the virtue of self-legislative ethical decision making driven by the moral standard of the categorical imperative. A desire for happiness aligned with self-love and self-interest can propel one to impose a given attitude and demeanor on others (124). Kant's attentiveness to the categorical imperative rejects both moral fanaticism and metaphysics of self-interest, providing a practical reason of self-legislation that invites "dignity," "worthiness," and respect that, as a by-product, yields happiness. Kant stressed the worthiness to be happy, which is quite different from "the expectation of happiness." For Levinas, the emphasis is not on happiness; instead, he accentuates "enjoyment," which entails learning from difference in all of existence (138–42). For Levinas, the heteronomy of the face demands concentration on the Other, not on the desire for happiness. The Other initiates a demand to attend to an "opening of dis-inter-estedness, of sacrifice without reward . . . An opening of the self to the infinite, which no corroboration can match, which proves itself only by its own excessiveness" (149). Neither Kant nor Levinas abides by a consumptive conception of happiness. Kant viewed the human as liberated from the manic desire for happiness when happiness is constituted as an aftermath of self-legislative dignity; Levinas bypasses happiness, connecting joy to the meeting of existence that is caressed as one attends to an ethical echo that dwells within the anarchy of an immemorial past and within the immediacy of the right now.

Both Kant and Levinas forgo ethical systems that seek to console—neither treats the human being as a consumer. Both Kant and Levinas refuse a godhead that determines the validity of individual action. Kant emphasizes autonomy and a disinterested response to duty: "Practical knowledge [for Kant] is equivalent to the imperative and disinterested petition of an inner duty that does not depend on the empirical state of the world and of the person" (158). Levinas responds to an election from the Other, an immemorial ethical echo, and an awareness of obligation to the neighbor in one performative statement: "here I am" (161). Kant and Levinas do not embrace God, reason, or the Other directly. Both stress a disinterestedness that focuses attention on something outside the immediacy of the moment, a categorical imperative or the interaction of an ethical echo and a third party (the neighbor). The impersonal counters a direct gaze, eschewing a Narcissus-like fascination with one's own image.[10] The next section continues exploration of linkages between Levinas and Kant through the lens of Levinas's own scholarship.

Levinas on Kant and the Impersonal

Levinas references or cites Kant one hundred seventy-one times throughout his work. Additionally, *God, Death, and Time* includes three essays dedicated to Kant: "The Radical Question: Kant against

Heidegger," "A Reading of Kant (Continued)," and "Kant and the Transcendental Ideal." Only three of Levinas's books (*New Talmudic Readings, Nine Talmudic Readings,* and *On Escape: De l'évasion*) omit references to Kant. Due to the large volume of citations of Kant in his work, I turn to sections of four of Levinas's books that concentrate most keenly on Kant.

In *Totality and Infinity*, Levinas connects Kant to a metaphysics tied to interhuman relations that function, on the one hand, as a "forever primitive form of religion."[11] On the other hand, in Kant, the "I" meets the need for "happiness" by earning such a right. Levinas argues with Kant's positions, stating that Kant's view of infinity embraces finitudes (*Totality,* 119, 196). Levinas stated that, since Kant, only the notion of "finitude" has trumped in philosophical discourse.[12] Levinas contended that, unlike Heidegger, Kant did not assume finitude as the only possibility. Of the four questions central to Kant's project (What may I know? What must I do? What am I entitled to hope? and What is man?), the second and third questions align with a practical philosophy not directly snarled within the notion of finitude. Additionally, Levinas resisted Kant's concentration on the interhuman, happiness, and relational reciprocity; only Kant's idea of infinity permits the finite to gather praise in its affiliation with sensibility that is "detached from concrete conditions" (*Totality,* 126). For Levinas, existential engagement is the realm of enjoyment, not happiness. Kant's practical philosophy reveals that Heidegger's reduction is not obligatory, pointing toward a signification otherwise than finitude. Levinas uncovers in Kant meaning that refuses to be dictated by Being and the notion of finitude (61, 65).

In *The Theory of Intuition in Husserl's Phenomenology*, Levinas claims that Kant and Husserl differ on the phrase "to the things themselves," with Kant having "an internal determination of this existence" with a commitment to "synthesis" in the "contents of consciousness" and Husserl stressing exteriority.[13] Levinas contends that Kant's project does not maintain exteriority as a central issue[14]; instead, it frames a categorical imperative intimately linked to personal autonomy and self-respect. Levinas understands an "idealism," which drives both the work of Kant and Husserl as well as differences that arise with transcendental Kantian "reason" and Husserl's transcendental conception of "intentionality" (Levinas, *Discovering,* 92–94). Both Kant and Husserl, according to Levinas, suggest that transcendental glimpses permit the human to experience genuine "wakefulness" (166). Kant rejected Gottfried Wilhelm Leibniz's (1646–1716) view of analytic logic and stressed, instead, a synthetic logic, rebuffing the linking of concepts. Husserl was closer to Kant than to Leibniz even as Husserl scorned Kant's focus on the a priori. Husserl sought direct access to a given phenomenon, asserting the importance of the inexact over precision in association with Kant's conception of idea: "Husserl's essential idea is to assert the primacy of inexact morphological essences over exact mathematical essences. This primacy can easily be explained by the fact that exact essences are only idealizations of inexact ones" (Levinas, *Theory of Intuition*, 118). The key for Levinas is exteriority, which he reviewed in both Kant's and Husserl's projects.

Levinas recognized that Kant reveals the importance of finding "meaning to the human" outside of "ontology."[15] Additionally, the notion of essence emerges through self-recognition, given birth as an "afterward" (*Otherwise*, 179). Kant conceives reason outside typical Western conventions of knowledge accumulation, enclosing a limit on rationality with a "vigilance" that is a re-return to one's own identity, leaving no "consciousness outside itself" or within a "diachrony of time."[16] Kant's description of temporality distinguished "thinking" (including idea and reason) from "knowing" (including concept and understanding), with the latter tied to accumulation and the former to abstract judgment (Levinas, *Of God*, 122). Even though "Kant's criticist philosophy seriously shakes the foundations of the idea of totality" and aims beyond totality toward infinity, embracing a "spatio-temporal nature,"[17] the project, nonetheless, falls short for Levinas. Kant's repositionings are insufficient in that they return us to Being with practical reasoning celebrating "the Ideal of pure reason," in a failed attempt to replace Being with "freedom" (123).

In *Otherwise than Being*, Levinas responded to Heidegger, stating that Kant's emphasis of the "temporalization of time" includes a moment when sensations reveal themselves in "temporal" impressions (34). One then responds from a Kantian and Levinasian position of disinterest. Levinas defines this perspective as "disinterestedness [that] is beyond essence" (58). The "I" is no longer conceptualized as an essence; it goes beyond essence and apprehends the "neighbor" as a genuine phenomenological reality, no longer enveloped by an Idea in the Kantian sense of the term (87). Disinterest, as understood by Levinas, is otherwise than reification of ideas or knowledge.

In *Of God Who Comes to Mind*, Levinas continues this theme, stating that ideology fills a gap between subject and reality consistent with Kant's understanding of reason in what he termed a "transcendental dialectic"; the alternative, for Levinas, is a passivity propelled by "disinterestedness" (4–5). This fundamental difference between Levinas and Kant rests in the original dwelling that each contends gives rise to ethics. For Kant, a universal standard functions as a guide for ethics in the enactment of practical reason. For Levinas, ethics lives in the face of the Other, which moves us from an individual gaze to an audio attentiveness about responsibility for the Other. Levinas's response to and for the Other precedes a mind/body split, a position unfriendly to Descartes's perspective and more in line with David Hume's (1711–1776) emphasis on sensations, which naturally shape sympathy. When the Other suffers, I have sympathy, the origin of love (146). Kant's contribution to transcendental philosophy was a stress on sensory content that emanated from experience (209). Kant and Levinas embrace the notion of the impersonal from divergent perspectives. For Kant, the impersonal links to the categorical imperative, and for Levinas, the impersonal is awakened by the demand emanating from the face of the Other, which moves one to attend to an ethical echo of "I am my brother's keeper."[18] Levinas's impersonal ethic cannot attend to the color of another's eyes.[19] Ethics resides within a realm before and beyond the familial. The sacred dwells within an impersonal space that calls forth personal response.

The Saying and the Said in Communication Ethics: The Impersonal and the Sacred

Bateson's insights initiated this chapter, differentiating the sacred from undue assurance. For Levinas, the sacred embraces ethics devoid of reification and imposition. Ethics has an impersonal cast of disinterest that nourishes the sacred dimension of the human condition. Levinas's understanding of impersonal disinterest has multiple, textured, and diverse dimensions.[20] He removes from the table of assurance "impersonal reason" that functions as a warrant for universal truth. Levinas disunites the impersonal from reason. The impersonal intertwined with reason has begotten colonization, imposition, and hegemony; it eclipses uniqueness of human responsibility. Levinas turned away from impersonal reason and endorsed an impersonal ethic that demanded concern for the disadvantaged and dispossessed.

For Levinas, the impersonal escorts my attention from the face of the Other to an ethical echo. Attending to the face of the Other begins with the impersonal and moves to acts of personal responsibility. Levinas understands the notion of the impersonal as essential in the act of tempering an "egoism" that vies for the chance to substitute for a profound obligation to the Other. Levinas does not offer us an "I" heroically attempting to care for another; Levinas's ethics begins with an "I" directed by the face of the Other that then attends to an archaic directive—"I am my brother's keeper." If the engagement with the face is dismissive or possessive, then one fails to attend to an ethical audio command; instead, one acts on a series of abstract principles tied to a standard of conduct connected to a universal ethical warrant. Levinas's assertion is that the face of another awakens an "ethical ear" that hears a morally upright echo that began long before a given encounter and will endure long after. Impersonal disinterest makes the transition from an ethics of optics to an ethics of ancient audio command possible. The ethical echo of "I am my brother's keeper" resides within a world that is timeless, a place that we could call the universal. The crucial point of Levinas's project is that he does not begin with the universal but with the particular. Levinas's ethics engages the universal after commencing with the particular. The impersonal is the fulcrum upon which the Saying of ethics commences. The following material outlines the different ways in which Levinas underscored the Saying and Said of the notion of the impersonal.

Il y a.—This French grammatical construction of "there is" proclaims the existential component of the impersonal. The utterance "there is" is an acknowledgment of an impersonal within the beyond of existence. Levinas refers to this conception as "absolutely impersonal" (*Alterity*, 98). *Il y a* announces the fact of being without objects that claim attention; *il y a* makes "apprehension" possible, a seeing without objects (*Totality*, 45). *Il y a* is "a nothing that is not a nothing" (*Alterity*, 99). The "there is" grounds the existential background of subject and object. "There is" reflects an impersonal nature toward Being that announces "dis-inter-*estedness.*"[21] *Il y a* is like *il pleut* (it is raining) or a fundamental opacity (*Totality*, 42). The "there is" is not a form of representation; faceless background makes recognition possible. Levinas states that "vision" is only possible when *il y a* becomes a forgotten background (*Totality*, 191); *il y a* functions as a hidden milieu that renders objects visible. The impersonal shapes the present in that the present fades before it can ever mature. The present is an "anonymous instant" given life by *il y a* (Levinas, *Collected Papers*, 9). This perspective suggests an ambiguous background that makes all other events visible. The notion of a forgotten background houses Bateson's understanding of the sacred.

Counter to impersonal reason.—Levinas, in *Totality and Infinity*, counters Kant's stress on impersonal reason with an impersonal ethics attentive to the Other (87). For Levinas, universal reason is the dark side of reason and invites an impersonal coldness that ignores the reality of real people, faces, and third parties that claim responsibility without empirical presence. The universal presented impersonally is another form of "inhumanity," disengaged from "particularism" (46, 52). Impersonal reason totalizes an individual within a given history and fails to attend to the particular face before him or her. Levinas does not attach reason to the universal but to the sociality of "society" (208). Reason emerges from a given perspective; it is not pure or impersonal in actuality. The links between ideas and discernment of action are integral to the social nature of being human. No undisputable form of assurance can emerge from impersonal reason falsely/ideologically linked to the universal. Reason emerges from locality and addresses the particular. If impersonal reason were to access the universal, we would discover institutions without flaws and capable of building perfect states that unify all "multiplicity" (217). Institutions are the product of will that desires to counter the natural reality of death (237). Efforts that seek purity totalize institutions into images of perfection, which result in a "tyranny of the universal" (242). Such schemes for perfection lead to dismissal of difference and eclipse authentic human responsibility. Levinas envisions a "[f]ecundity [that] evinces a unity that is not opposed to multiplicity, but, in the precise sense of the term, engenders it" (273). Beginning with the universal leads to imposition on the particular and opposition to multiplicity. Levinas's ethics originates and gathers momentum from the particular. Bateson's understanding of the sacred performed and enacted in the particular responds to the uniqueness of the demands of a given historical moment.

Dis-inter-estedness.—The impersonal guides ethics and frames justice as one attends to the unseen and unknown. This conception of impersonal ethics is contrary to what Levinas calls the Heideggerian "philosophy of the Neuter" in *Totality and Infinity* (298). Levinas understands impersonal ethics as alertness to a face that does not permit a gaze to linger on the face. The "nudity" of the face unmasks me, simultaneously removing me from above and below existence, transporting me to an audio ethical call that is more ancient than the notion of the past (299). This notion of the impersonal requires an active disinterest that functions as a fulcrum for sociality that situates an ethics otherwise than logical and synchronic presuppositions in an engagement of responsibility for the Other. An "impersonal language" of disinterest moves ethics within the sociality of persons in *Proper Names* (41). The impersonal of disinterest is not "arbitrary"; it is, however, beyond "imagination" and situated within a "coherent" command (72, 118). There is "impersonal speech" of disinterest without a "you" that dwells in an a priori anarchy—not via eternity but through something more ancient and ever present, the "incessant" (131–32). Such speech is an old, yet new, story that has no beginning or end; it simply reminds and informs while demanding from me a unique sense of responsibility. In *Totality and Infinity* Levinas writes, "The face fades, and in its impersonal and inexpressive neutrality is prolonged, in ambiguity, into animality" (263). For Levinas, it is only this impersonal sense of disinterest that can lead, ironically, to a "personal God" and to genuine obligation for another initiated by a primordial and prefigured call for responsibility (78). The impersonal is the realm of the sacred that invites wonder without claiming certainty about what a given person, animal, or object "actually means." The sacred claims us; we do not claim it. Bateson and his daughter used the metaphor of an angel well; out of the disinterested care of an angel, the sacred lives in the doing of ethics and of tasks impersonally, for the good of all, resisting the impulse to limit one's care to a given group. The task is to do good for all, not just those affirmed and accepted by a given group.

In *Difficult Freedom* Levinas offers one of the most well-known stories from his prison camp experience—the story about a dog named

Bobby.[22] The essay "The Name of a Dog, or Natural Rights" illuminates the power of disinterested ethics that yields personal responsibility. The description of the story is brief, with Levinas accentuating how his French uniform assisted him and others in the prisoner of war camp in Hanover, Germany, where an imposed "subhuman" category defined the prisoners (153). Levinas was in a camp labeled with the number 1492, the year Spain, under Ferdinand V, expelled the Jews from their territory, which is either a coincidence or horrific intentionality. Levinas stated that racism and anti-Semitism are "archetype[s] of all internment" (153); they deny habitation, leaving one nowhere. The famous quote of this three-page essay comes in the final paragraph: "Perhaps the dog that recognized Ulysses beneath his disguise on his return from the Odyssey was a forebear of our own. But no, no! There, they were in Ithaca and the Fatherland. Here, we were nowhere. This dog was the last Kantian in Nazi Germany, without the brain needed to universalize maxims and drives. He was a descendant of the dogs of Egypt. And his friendly growling, his animal faith, was born from the silence of his forefathers on the banks of the Nile" (153). Ethics and the impersonal permitted Bobby to address others, regardless of their ethnic pedigree. Levinas stressed desire for the impersonal displayed by dogs in camps, and on the banks of the Nile during Jewish captivity, who displayed a "friendly growling" and "animal faith." The dogs were part of an enemy habitat and simultaneously recognized "captives" as human beings, engaging in an impersonal disinterest that was unresponsive to power or a privileged place. The dogs looked, but they did not see a "rabble of slaves" (152–53); the dog Bobby, as an exemplar, witnessed and responded to ethics in the face of real men of difference, reminding us of the power of the impersonal that calls us forth in responsibility.

The power of Levinas's "ethics as first philosophy" reposes in his conception of impersonal disinterest that makes recognition of the sacred possible. His work offers theoretical ethical insight into Bateson's *Angels Fear* in which Bateson emphasized four major terms: angels, sacred, gaps, and noncommunication, with each pointing to linkage between the impersonal and the sacred. Angels come unexpectedly, sometimes in the guise of a friend, occasionally in the semblance of a teacher, and sometimes in the form of a stray dog that reaches out to the forgotten. Bateson did not use the term *angel* literally; it is an image of a person meeting existence impersonally—with a result that is ever so personal. The sacred cannot be totally explainable or understandable; it is associated with places, things, and persons that remind us of an impersonal obligation that propels us to a greater sense of moral height. Gaps and limits retain a reality—we cannot control existence, no matter how hard we attempt to gather certainty. Gaps are impersonal reminders of limits that contain within them the joy and responsibility of unexpected dimensions of being human. Finally, noncommunication is often an ambiguous call from an impersonal place that cannot be defined, labeled, or totally understood; it is a space where human beings continue to follow, even where angels fear to tread. People move forward accompanied by one repetitive, sacred ethical echo—"I am my brother's keeper" and "if not me, then whom?" With only an ethical echo in one's soul, humans tread where angels fear to wander, and, somehow and someway, people answer a call of responsibility. The places where angels fear to tread is the terrain where humans must somehow find the courage to follow an ethical call—like poor lost dogs that respond to and witness for the reality of an impersonal ethic that recharges the world. Levinas's impersonal permits the acknowledgment of a space that is sacred; it calls us into personal responsibility. Communication ethics, for Levinas, lives within an ironic space—my personal responsibility demands impersonal care. It is not the color of another's eyes or my familiarity with him or her that demands my responsibility. Ethics as first philosophy resides in an immemorial echo shaping the human condition.

CHAPTER 6

Imperfection: Ethics Disrupted by Justice—The Name of the Rose

---

. . . the order of justice of individuals responsible for one another does not arise in order to restore that reciprocity between the I and its other; it arises from the fact of the third who, next to the one who is an other to me, is "another other" to me.

> —Emmanuel Levinas, *Is It Righteous to Be?*
> *Interviews with Emmanuel Levinas*

The asymmetrical structure of love as a gift is a testament to the transcendent status of the gift of love, transcending the economy of person to person relations that is stimulated by a distributive justice that defines human relationships as symmetrical, equal, and reciprocal . . . While love may be freely given as a gift, love cannot be commanded.

> —Pat Arneson, *Communicative Engagement and*
> *Social Liberation: Justice Will Be Made*

Emmanuel Levinas employs a distinctive understanding of justice that requires attentiveness to those not empowered or present in a given moment of decision making. Levinas is concerned with both the proximate Other and those unknown and unnoticed. For Levinas, the task of a community and of education is to alert persons to those not present and to offer knowledge about the how and why of assisting the disadvantaged. The theme of justice examined in this chapter follows a Levinasian engagement with Eco's 1980 novel, *The Name of the Rose.*[1] The novel wrestles with the question of justice through consideration and action on behalf of those without power and influence. As Levinas stated, justice is a "struggle with evil," a fight on behalf of those not present at the moment of decision and action who are, nevertheless, directly or indirectly affected by a given set of choices.[2] Justice interrupts ethics, and ethics disrupts justice; in the tension of imperfection between ethics and justice, one must act responsibly without assurance. "Here I am" dwells in imperfection—the jarring intersection of ethics and justice. Again, one cannot turn Levinas's ethical project into an odd form of martyrdom. Ethics requires attentiveness to the Other, and justice can never, ever forget all involved in the conversation, proximate and ever so far away in distance and in time, including oneself. Ethics matters, people matter, and we must remember that justice not only demands attention to those not at the table of conversation but also to oneself—sometimes the defense of our own space is an act of justice.

Introduction

Levinas's understanding of ethics as first principle works in creative tension with his conception of justice; human responsibility attends to ethics within the realm of proximity, and justice is responsive to the forgotten and marginalized. Levinas's formulation of justice clarifies his disavowal of Buber's emphasis on reciprocity tied to dialogic ethics. Justice, for Levinas, recognizes the importance of institutions, which depend on reciprocity. Justice includes concern for the disadvantaged by building institutions that assure reciprocity and expectation of mutual support. Levinas's understanding of justice begins with a consideration of those not present or able to affect decision making. Justice dwells outside the propinquity of the moment and proximate participants. Such a formation of justice underscores the story line of Eco's novel *The Name of the Rose.*

Eco's novel is an exemplar of Levinas's conception of justice in action. Examination of justice, in this chapter, begins with a section titled "Eco and *The Name of the Rose.*" The second segment, "The Novel," recounts the characters and events of the story. The third section, "Levinas on Justice," offers an exploration of Levinas's own insights on justice throughout his scholarly corpus. The chapter concludes with "The

Saying and the Said in Communication Ethics: Temporal Legislation of Justice," in which justice is tied to the third and to communication ethics. Within Eco's novel we witness flawed characters making decisions that attempt to include those without power and outside the realm of conventional influence.

Levinas's explication of justice is performed within Eco's medieval setting, which repeatedly announces the necessity of acting on behalf of those not present, those unable to shape a conversation or directive in order to assure their interests. *The Name of the Rose* places justice within the role and responsibility of a medieval monk who functions as a sleuth, a medieval Sherlock Holmes. He engages the particulars of crime and murder with rationality illuminated "within the framework of a story."[3] The reader discovers in the act of uncovering clues the detection of injustices that demand concern for the forgotten and lost.

Eco and The Name of the Rose

Eco unites the study of history, semiotics, literature, and philosophy.[4] Eco's semiotic work joins the synchronic and diachronic, making the old new and the new uncertain and unresolved with repeated reliance on irony that contours semantic engagement. *The Name of the Rose* is a medieval story with postmodern underpinnings. Eco is a humanities scholar observant of context and meaning. He submits an understanding of semiotics that brings the reader into a literary narrative as an interpretive participant. Eco's exertion demands both interpretive enhancement and correction from the reader. Eco offers insight into the semiotics of everyday life; he does "narrative semiotics" composed of constant interruptions that transport the reader through intertextual conversations between and among contrasting historical moments.[5] Eco renders a model of intellectual engagement that explores "the 'new' without refusing the importance of the 'old.'"[6] Eco's hermeneutic orientation is consistent with his education at the University of Turin, Italy, where he studied medieval philosophy and literature.

Eco completed his thesis in 1954 on Thomas Aquinas. He moved contra to a faith commitment during his graduate education without losing interest in the interplay of medieval and church life, which is aptly represented in *The Name of the Rose*. His scholarship "resolved into . . . [a] sort of humanist secularism that has characterized his writing ever since (but nobody who has had such an education, he says, ever entirely loses a sense of the religious)" (Caesar, 1). Eco, as a philosopher trained in medieval history and literature, engages the setting of an unknown abbey that dictates examination of the demands of justice. Eco provides the reader with semiotic insight into perennial issues of the human condition; he illustrates the background for such illumination via his story set in the fourteenth century.

Gioacchino Balducci, in "Umberto Eco in New York: An Interview," stated that Eco was cognizant of the hefty gap between the avant-garde and mass communication, with the former defined by openness and ambiguity and the latter by fixed formulas and schemas. Eco's scholarship assesses both avant-garde and conventional communication through semiotic positioning for the reader. Eco's view of semiotics explores signs as "anything which stands for something else to somebody in some respect."[7] As Charles S. Peirce stated, signs have three partitions: (1) "symbols," conventional relationships to objects; (2) an "index," a physical connection to the presence of some object; and (3) an "icon," which has resemblance to a given object.[8] Eco admired the insights of Peirce; Eco contended that they were played out with eloquence in the works of Joyce. Eco is a professional and personal admirer of the semiotic complexity in Joyce's writing.[9]

The Name of the Rose relies upon semantic density; throughout the novel, the reader encounters multiple ideological positions, which promote communicative pause about the danger of doing something with undue "good intentions"[10]; the reader witnesses the reality of unintended consequences associated with good actions. In the novel we observe an initial conventional relationship with the abbey (symbol) that relies on a physical connection to such a religious place (index) that gives way to the recognition of the abbey as a resemblance of a religious dwelling (icon). Two major semiotic focal points guide the reader: the abbey and the library, with each following the pattern of symbol to index to icon. Both the abbey and the library, within the novel, are void of openness and learning. Instead, they portray "a labyrinth with secret passages, booby traps, skull switches, and rat-infested, skeleton-covered dungeons."[11] The novel takes the reader into the darker side of two major medieval dwellings, reminding us of the creative and potentially destructive power of institutions.

Eco's *The Name of the Rose* generated the following assessment from Agnes Heller—the novel is "the first well known contemporary, postmodern historical novel."[12] Eco connects postmodern insights to irony within a medieval setting as he engages intertextual conversations; he recognizes that no one instant is without copresent moments situated within differing historical eras. Historical eras, for Eco, are vibrant and not steeped within a single linear conception of history. This absence/presence motif of differing historical eras is central to "irony as a special postmodern sign."[13] Eco invites the reader into differing historical epochs dwelling within his description of the events of this fourteenth-century crime investigation.

The Franciscan friar, William of Baskerville, leads the inquiry. His name is suggestive of two differing eras and persons. First, William of Ockham (c. 1288–c. 1348) was famous for his logic, lack of formal education, and continual run-ins with Pope John XXII.[14] William of Ockham was a Franciscan who contended that the Church should be composed of leaders willing to live a life of poverty, like the original apostles. Second, Sherlock Holmes in *The Hound of the Baskervilles* conveys logic and personal flaws throughout his investigative work. Eco suggests that literary significance emerges through semiotic engagement of "archetypes."[15] The ultimate theme of struggle between the Franciscans and the Church is played out in the novel with the inquisitor Bernard Gui and a Sherlock Holmes–like figure within a medieval detective mystery.

The Name of the Rose is widely read; it sold over fifty million copies worldwide. Additionally, the novel became a 1986 movie with Sean Connery in the lead role as William of Baskerville. With the first James Bond portrayer starring as William, the gross box-office income was just under $5.6 million in the United States. The movie was far more successful in Europe, grossing over $70 million. The name of the novel is interesting and by no means specified within the story; we never discover the why behind the name of the rose. The reader is left to wonder if there is a medieval connection to the Freemasons. Stonemasons and builders of cathedrals in medieval England were associated with the rose. To become a member, one had to be an adult male, believe in a supreme being, and understand the soul as immortal; this group became the world's largest secret society. The Freemasons continue to attract us to a lore that endures in contemporary popular culture;

we can turn to a variety of recent books and novels enamored with their mythology. The Freemasons use three roses to articulate their commitments, representing love, life, and light.[16] The roses promise a direction that identifies Freemasons in their less than transparent associations. Like the secrecy of the Freemasons, the reader imagines larger implications for the name of the rose. I now examine *The Name of the Rose* as an exemplar of Levinasian justice—demanding that we assist those outside the scope of conventional power and influence.

The Novel

The Name of the Rose is replete with symbolic meaning, beginning with the fact that the novel divides into seven days—day one, day two, day three, etc. The narrator is a monk, Adso of Melk, who divulges information about an event that took place in 1327. The monk is, of course, the "fictional" author and character in the manuscript. Eco invites the reader into a reading of fiction that requires multiple suspensions of disbelief in order to engage an authentic medieval murder mystery set in the context of struggles of the fourteenth-century Catholic Church. Eco commences with an illusory story about the work that recounts the supposed discovery of the manuscript. A "translator" comes upon the manuscript in 1968 after it has experienced a number of mysterious turns and events. A monk, Adso of Melk, is the fictional author of the original document, with Abbé Vallet "faithfully" translating Adso's original text into French (Eco, *The Name of the Rose*, 1). After transcribing the translation, the "narrator" loses the manuscript, only to rediscover it in 1970 when he comes across a version of Milo Temesvar's *On the Use of Mirrors in the Game of Chess*. Portions of the manuscript were within Temesvar's book; in his version the narrator discovers quotes from Father Athanasius Kircher, a seventeenth-century German Jesuit priest, with no reference to Adso or Vallet (3). However, the narrator discovers that in the translation of Adso's text, Vallet "took some liberties" in omitting some important segments (4).

The point of this fictional background to the discovery of the novel is to offer a performative introduction to problems in translation and accuracy, which plunge the reader into even greater ambiguity and questions. The "translator" of 1968 details how previous persons took possession of the manuscript, enacting interpretative freedoms to the point that reliability about the main characters and events could no longer be trusted. The translator involves the reader in real-world events in Prague on August 16, 1968. Occupation of Prague occurred within five days. On August 21, Soviet tanks rolled into the city, which captures the imagination of an informed reader intent on understanding the larger context and implications of the work. The reader then returns to the fictional time of the actual drama, which simultaneously continues to interact with real events. Eco begins his tale in a world of clouded ambiguity. We do not know what is true or false—such moments call for justice situated within the imperfect. One must navigate historical and contextual ambiguity.

The prologue to the novel continues to beckon the reader further into this medieval plot about the imperfections and necessity of engaging justice. The old man who pens an imaginary prologue is Adso of Melk; his task is to prepare the reader for a story arranged around a Franciscan monk and his companion. On the initial day of the novel, Adso, then a "young Benedictine" from the monastery of Melk, placed under William's direction by his parents (13), enters, alongside William, an abbey "whose name it is only right and pious now to omit" (11). The abbey houses one of the finest libraries of the Catholic Church. Eco inaugurates the drama with the chemistry of strange characters and unstated power allied with a medieval archive. The library garnered enormous influence in an era defined by the scarcity of books and the anguishing number of hours required to handwrite manuscripts. The library houses books of the Church and, additionally, those from Greek culture and authors, which remain hidden. The library functions as a dwelling place for mysterious and dangerous ideas that require painstaking control. Additionally, this drama is set within another ongoing subtheme. William, charged by the emperor to participate in a debate between the papacy and the Franciscan order, requires conversation about the Church reconsidering its commitment to the accumulation of wealth.

On the first day, Adso and William learn that a young monk, Adelmo, linked with the great library, either had jumped or had been thrown out a window from the east tower. The abbot Abo asks William to assist in discerning what had transpired. The hope is for a quick judgment; guests are soon to arrive with the objective of working out the Franciscan relationship with the Church. The next day we find Adso and William at morning prayer, where they ascertain that another member of the library has turned up dead—discovered in a barrel of pig's blood. The monk Venantius is a translator and a friend of the first dead monk. With two dead monks, both connected to the library, Adso and William walk to the library in search of clues about their deaths. Adso and William quickly discover a book they believe both monks had read. However, while they are investigating the library, someone steals the book and pilfers William's glasses. The only thing that goes well for William is that he uncovers a secret entrance from the main library that exposes a large area that is off limits to all but the librarian and the assistant librarian.

The next day includes more deception, and Adso experiences his first sexual experience with a girl no older than twenty. The girl is a representative of those not at the table of power and influence; she goes unnamed. The girl, described as young and speaking a language different from that of Adso, confesses the event to William the following day. At the same time, the two learn that yet another monk, Berengar, the assistant librarian, is dead in one of the baths. Adso, William, and another monk, Alinardo, locate Berengar after he had gone missing for a day and after he had talked openly about the deaths occurring in the abbey. This incident augments intrigue and lack of trust. We find a mixture of innocence and secrecy undermining "existential trust"[17] that resides within the abbey, a place increasingly defined by lack of confidence in the environment. Under the guise of an official investigation, Bernard Gui, who is a well-known inquisitor, approaches the abbey with Cardinal del Poggetto; they arrive charged with the task of discovering acts of heresy. Gui knows that William was once an inquisitor. Gui promptly produces three people that he charges with acts of heresy: the girl who was with Adso (she is called a witch); Salvatore (a hunchback who was a member of the Dolcinians); and Remigio, who, like Salvatore, was part of this same heretical group, the Dolcinians.[18] The Dolcinians, a sect considered sacrilegious, used violence against the Church. The sect's namesake leader, Fra Dolcino of Novara (1250–1307), was burned at the stake by decree of Pope Clement V (1260–1314, the first of Avignon popes). Both men (Salvatore and Remigio) were former members of this deviant group that used violence to challenge the privileges of the Church. Into this environment of distrust, the abbey welcomes the Franciscan delegation charged with blasphemy and the challenge of arguing against the pope's perspective on poverty.

The following day finds debate centered on the Franciscan viewpoint, which is contrary to the position of the papacy. With this background, the novel turns to Remigio Severinus, the herbalist who has the "lost" book from the library in his possession; he finds the book with Berengar, the assistant librarian who had died in the baths. Severinus, the herbalist, dies at the hand of Malachi, who gives the book to Jorge before he dies in prayer. Jorge, the monk, who is the keeper of the library, hates laughter and views such frivolous expression as wicked blasphemy. Jorge wants no one to read the book because it encourages merriment. For Jorge, laughter is heresy. The book that Jorge dislikes is supposedly the only work remaining that contains Aristotle's views on comedy—considered to be his lost second book of the *Poetics.*

The novel then finds William and Adso navigating their way into hidden chambers of the library, where they discover Jorge hunched over this book of comedy that has been at the center of so much tragedy. Jorge had placed poison on each page of the manuscript: the poisoned pages were the weapons that killed his fellow monks. With William and Adso watching, Jorge begins to kill himself by eating the folios of the book, while he puts to fire other "questionable" books. As flames consume the library, William and Adso escape. William and Adso walk out of the library, only to find the inquisitor Gui burning his three "heresy" captives at the stake: Remigio, Salvatore, and the girl who had been involved with Adso. The girl is the only one who escapes the flames during the chaos of the library fire. William and Adso then part from the abbey the next day, never to see each other again.

The novel welcomes the reader into a murder mystery genre with intrigue, characters that possess dubious pasts, and a plot laden with numerous clues. The background of the novel includes the Catholic Church and four major issues influencing the Church in the fourteenth century. First, Emperor Louis IV (1282–1347) appointed William to this detective task; William's past behavior had placed him at odds with the pope. Second, there is allusion to Pope Clement V, who burned Fra Dolcino at the stake; Clement also suppressed the Knights Templar by killing many of them as he shifted the Curia from Rome to the Avignon (France) papacy.[19] Third, there was a dispute between the Franciscans and Pope Clement V, who sought to persecute the Franciscans. More than a century later, in 1432, when the novel is set, the reality of distance between the Franciscans and the papacy remains; the argument continues to focus on the question of poverty and the Church's role in alleviating anguish in a material as well as a spiritual fashion. Pope Martin V (1368–1431) unified the Franciscans within the larger Church, which had returned to Rome in 1378 with Pope Gregory XI and the Council of Pisa in 1409, which resolved the location dispute, moving authority from Avignon (1309–1377) to Rome once again.[20] Clement was tied to the death of the Templars and to the century-long dispute about Catholic authority and the location of the papacy. Fourth, the library functions as the center of action within the novel. It is a place where ideas of an earlier culture persevere, along with great works of the Church. The library is a place of light and darkness steered by undue privacy and secrecy. The library is not open to all; it is accessible to but a select number of persons. Hidden away in surreptitious rooms are thousands of books sequestered from everyday view by the monks. The library does not represent literacy for all; it signals privilege, power, and the withholding of ideas from all but a few. The semiotic importance of each of these themes emerges in the interaction of persons within "the field of social practices in their materiality and historicity."[21] We discover a murder mystery located in a library and social practices that limit access to ideas, led by Jorge, considered a composite of "heretical" views on laughter.[22] The book attributed to Aristotle poisons through social practices within the abbey that carry "venomous power" (MacKey, 38).

Leonard G. Schulze suggests that the novel has an ethos that is only understandable within the context of law and culture of a particular place. The novel functions as a literary exemplar of "ethical energy" that responsively unites locality of context and reader, who must step up to this interpretive responsibility.[23] This enthymematic style wrests control from the narrator and voids any attempt for accuracy that is akin to a "machine . . . generating interpretations."[24] The reader enters an interpretive space where ethical meaning emerges between text and reader.

The enthymematic semiotic task for the reader involves sorting through a multiplicity of social poisons that lurk within everyday practices of this medieval drama that continue to taint contemporary life.[25] Carl Rubino states that William Blake's 1794 poem "The Sick Rose" refers to an "invisible worm" that connects the ancients and the moderns, stating that truth "is not innocent, it is not pure."[26] The pursuit of truth is temporal—"Eco knows, as does Prigogine [theory of thermodynamics], that all structures have a history. Modern science, like the religion it displaced, presents the face of the absolute and timeless in its canonical coordinates and universal mechanism."[27] Eco refuses to embrace either an old world religion or a new world science; he walks between them, creating a baseline for the hope of justice that dwells "outside" ideologies that blindly encircle the old and/or the new.[28]

Justice, within the novel, does not reside within a given agent or monk, even though at first consideration the major villain of the drama is Jorge, who is actually a "stalwart of his religious order."[29] The younger monks look to Jorge for spiritual guidance. Evil reposes in responses to given events, such as Jorge's understanding of Aristotle's work as a "source of all evil."[30] Evil resides in responsive practices, exemplified by Jorge.[31] Ultimately, justice, or its absence, must abide within the context of actions and responses within the abbey.

Eco contends with any stance of "passive complicity"; instead, he offers a responsive style that is "interventionist."[32] Deborah Parker contends that Jorge of Borges is actually the Argentinean writer Jorge Luis Borges (1899–1986), an author to whom Eco is both indebted and critically reactive. Leo Corry states that Eco relies on Borges throughout the novel, offering consistent meta-allusions to Borges' literary corpus, which provide an intertextual dialogue. Eco's meta-allusions to Borges's work give clarity to the title of Corry and Giovanolli's essay "Jorge Borges, Author of the Name of the Rose."[33]

For Eco, Jorge of Borges is not just a protector of knowledge and books; he is a hoarder of information. We find, in *The Name of the Rose*, "[a] world in which a blind librarian" denies opportunities for learning, burns books, and destroys through purification.[34] Jorge's presence is a performative insistence that an ideology is a destructive form aimed at survival against all other perspectives.[35]

Eco's literary insights shift the conversation beyond the immediate moment. The novel operates as "an echo" that suggests previous documents.[36] The emphasis on papers written, other pamphlets, multiple authors, and competing historical events furnishes insight into Husserl's notion of "genetic phenomenology," which details a layered development of a given phenomenon through shifting historical moments.[37] Eco offers a literary layering, stated in the postscript, confessing to his following a path set by Thomas Mann (1875–1955). Eco used a raconteur similar to Serenus Zeitblom, the narrator in Mann's *Faustus*.[38] Both "Mann and Eco resort to intertextual quotations to condense several centuries of culture, thereby suggesting that the past and the present are the same, while at the same time different."[39] Semiotic theory shifts from sign to text to reader as Eco offers a novel that compels interpretation via enthymematic significance of events.

Interpretation requires the full involvement and participation of the reader. Eco contends that semiotics is no longer an elaborate disclosure of patterns that facilitate appreciation of signs and texts; his position criticizes numerous semiotic theories. Eco requires the reader to discern signs within text.[40] Eco never abandons the text but stresses the necessity of chemistry between text and reader. Eco argues that each text relies on a secret code that gives rise to a "model reader" capable of engaging multiple interpretations and simultaneously surrendering assumptions when the text illuminates a given perspective.[41] Eco employs this dialogic and rhetorically disruptive meeting between text and reader as an ironical device aimed at unsettling the viability of "semantic reductionism."[42]

Eco moves beyond a semantic prison, offering instead a commitment to both the interaction of the limited and the unlimited. Eco's style is akin to William of Ockham and Thomas Reid (1710–1796), who engaged realism in rejection of semiotic idealism.[43] Eco embraces the dialogic nature of limits, acknowledging their presence without reifying them. Eco recognizes the reality of restraints without boundaries and the unlimited with restrictions. To read Eco's work in a manner otherwise than his self-intended contradictions is to miss the interpretive significance of his project, which counters the universal/particular debate and a modern/postmodern opposition. Eco understands that the concept of postmodernity is not a category that stands alone; the term is an explication of intertextuality that announces the reality of multiple eras that are present together and mutually informing.

Eco offers a dialogue of many texts, which takes the readership to multiple intertextual connections. This dialogue of texts results in the writer being embedded within a layered set of histories that critique raw communicative agency and invite the reader into a dialogue with textual "traces."[44] The trace within *The Name of the Rose* is an "'intrusion' of laughter"[45] that disrupts understanding of a world maintained by silence, authority, and learning within controlled parameters. Eco disrupts this standpoint as he points to the messy enactment of justice. *The Name of the Rose* is a novel about signs that remind the reader of something that was and is not yet. Eco reminds us that we cannot adapt a metaphysics that reifies the meaning and reality of signs because they shift, change, and "govern the making of meaning from the perception of phenomena in external reality as conveyed through the sign system of language."[46] Signs suggest traces of justice that are not immediately understandable within the shadowy presence of the present; signs are important to the meaning of lives in a given historical moment constituted by change and disruption, which requires our participatory engagement.

A trace consists of the not present and the ever present, which moves the conversation to Levinas and his examination of justice tied to those no longer or not yet at the table of decision making. Levinas is attentive to justice located within a community that considers the unknown third as the heart of judgment and discernment. Attending to those not present is at the core of justice. Together, Levinas and Eco detail communal responsibility charged with maintaining a trace of justice that attends to a presence that is absent and requires elucidation.

Levinas on Justice

A communal view of justice shoulders the importance of having concern for the neighbor; justice assumes a burden for those not present. Justice "relates back to the infinite original right of the neighbor, and to responsibility for the other . . . the third party."[47] Levinas refers to the notion of justice in twenty-three out of his twenty-four books, using the term at least three hundred forty times. His perspective acknowledges the communal nature of justice. Levinas's contention is that justice dwells within a community constituted by a commitment beyond law. This sense of community has phenomenological proportions and includes those not immediately proximate. The third party, the unknown neighbor, provides a rationale for the use of violence in defense of "the third party."[48] Justice increasingly arises as "multiplicity" calls us to attend to those not proximate to us (Levinas, *Is It Righteous*, 223). Multiplicity commences with attentiveness to "singularity" as one acknowledges those not present at the immediate table of decision making (262); justice concentrates on the uniqueness of needs, hopes, and demands of unseen neighbors. In ethics, the uprightness of the face of the Other moves one to responsibility. In justice, participation in a covenant that extends beyond our reach demands responsibility for an unseen Other. Justice demands action out of moral height that embraces responsibility for an unknown Other. In contrast to this expanded conception of a community situated within justice, one finds evil living wherever there is hapless despair on the part of the ignored, forgotten, and abandoned—the unseen and unheard neighbor.[49]

With justice, contrary to the common tendency to disremember and ignore, one discovers no statute of limitations that relieves one of the particularity of concern and care for the neighbor. Levinas describes "the endless requirement of justice hidden behind justice, the requirement of an even juster justice, more faithful to its original imperative in the face of the other" (Levinas, *In the Time*, 121). The act of justice, however, is not charity. Charity, when rightly engaged, cries for justice that attends to care for an unknown Other. Justice is distinct from charity in that it introduces a form of equality and measure (131). At the same time, justice without charity morphs into a legalistic action of abstraction that trumps genuine concern for the neighbor. Justice tied to a community assumes concern for an unknown Other, education, and the admission that the perilous nature of justice emerges beyond law and/or charity.

Justice is the center of Levinas's conception of truth, for truth emerges only when freedom becomes a question. The realm of justice works as a restraint on absolute freedom. One is subordinated to the Other, which nourishes the reality of conscience. Justice is possible when conscience inhibits self-concerned exploitations of one's freedom. The critique of my own freedom commences with my welcome of the Other, which puts "in question my freedom."[50] The lie of an "evil genius" frequents the "interspace" between the illusory and the serious; it is the realm of mockery that eclipses the face of the Other (Levinas, *Totality*, 91). This space houses an "originative I" that misses the Other by failing to take notice of the yes that emerges from the Other, which calls forth an uncommon sense of a "derivative I." Speech is the origin of signification that begins with the Other. The Other teaches me that my freedom is not the final word, for *I am not alone.*[51] The reality of sociality commences the march toward justice with a limiting of my own freedom and a demand to attend to the Other who calls me forth into a world larger than me and mine.

The reminder to attend to the neighbor does not abide in slogans and adages but within ongoing practices that constitute community. Ethics assumes an unlimited responsibility for the Other and limited attentiveness to one's own ego, the "originative I." Ethics is naturally responsive to proximity and finds disruption by justice—concern for the "neighbor, [who] is also a 'third party' in relation to another neighbor, [who] invites me to justice, to weighing matters, and to thought. And the unlimited responsibility, which justifies this concern for justice and for self and for philosophy[,] can be forgotten."[52] The third is the neighbor who, for one reason or another, cannot join us at the table of conversation. Justice is both an accompaniment to and a disruptor of ethics. The reality of justice unmasks self-righteousness as a mistake—curtailing confidence in my own goodness, which enhances my own ego while eclipsing the face of the Other.

The neighbor does not don a reified form or mutate into an object of abstract justice. The neighbor, the third, requires the imagination and implementation of justice in order to protect the unseen Other in everyday action. Kant differentiates between fantasy and imagination, with the latter responding to the real and the former invoking optimistic demands. Levinas's understanding of justice requires imagination that sees farther than the near, attending to a larger sense of community—protecting those beyond proximate obligations. Pat Gehrke reminds us consistently in his writings on Levinas that ethics and justice complement and simultaneously disrupt each other.[53] This interplay of demands of responsibility rejects any polarity between ethics and justice. For it is the tension between them and the obligations of both that call forth the life worth living. The key to justice is an imagination fueled by a community that refuses to ignore those not physically present at the table of conversation. Community and the face of the Other keep one from falling into the trap of "abstract justice" unresponsive to real persons (Gehrke, "Being," 105). Community requires stories that remind one of a world beyond the immediate, taking one farther than the face of the Other into the realm of justice.

Levinas considers the face of the Other the beginning of truth and the commencement of philosophy. In "Philosophy, Justice, and Love," collected in *Entre Nous*, he renders insight into the development of justice via pursuit of truth through philosophy initiated by the face of the Other, which leads to social recognition that there are others who require concerned action beyond the immediate, proximate Other (*Entre Nous*, 103–22). This moment of acknowledgment opens the door to justice. Levinas argues that the moment of reflection about what is just or not just is the beginning of theory. Philosophy assists in the weighing and discerning of ideas that opens the door to theory and justice.

In justice, one combats evil; resistance to evil makes violence inevitable. Levinas situates self-righteousness within the roots of evil: "Evil is the order of being pure and simple" (114). There is no manner of protecting justice that avoids the necessity of violence in the protection of the unseen Other. The third party interrupts undue concern for the person before me. Justice, for Levinas, comes from love that expands beyond the immediate moment and the proximate Other. Levinas rejects the unity of the "One," assuming instead the reality of multiplicity, which requires philosophical thought in pursuit of truth and works to restrain evil with recognition that violence is, at times, needed to protect those who cannot safeguard themselves. For this reason Levinas cannot reject any violence associated with Marxism that takes the Other seriously; however, he does contend against a utopianism that assumes one can invite a world void of political power. Such nonsense made Stalinism possible and a finitude of abstract truth.

Justice is both different and intertwined with charity; "charity is impossible without justice, and . . . justice is warped without charity" (121). Justice interrupts ethics and charity interrupts justice by dislodging a habitude of evil where self-righteousness makes questioning and reflection impossible. In his play *No Exit*, Sartre offers the famous line "Hell is other people."[54] For Levinas, hell finds constitution in the forgetting of the unknown, the unseen, and the unnoticed. The dwelling of justice does not reside in institutions alone but also in actions of responsibility for the unknown Other. Justice through institutions tempered by interpersonal relations (ethics and the face) limits undue reflection upon self-preservation and self-absorption (Levinas, *Of God*, 177). Justice does not dwell within a utopian sense of the good.

Levinas frames the danger of justice as an ideology of self-righteousness in *Entre Nous* (224). Levinas returns to Bergson's emphasis on *durée* that offers an understanding of proximity that is not special but that opens the door to concern for those who are not empirically close. Levinas respected events that shape the moment beyond hope of possession. He concurred with Adorno that Heidegger's notion of "authenticity" smacks of elitism and aristocratic blood (226). For Levinas, there is nothing more authentic than attentiveness to the Other; a summoned "derivative I" seeks to assist the Other, in contrast to an "originative I" that embraces an ambiance of self-righteousness. Uniqueness, discovered in my being called, generates my responsibility by and for the Other.

Justice disrupts the realm of ethics, which can remain forever dominated by the proximate Other; justice moves beyond the personal and the unique into the judgment of a genus. The demand for justice is the curtailing factor contra self-righteousness:

> The *I*, precisely as responsible for the other and the third, cannot remain indifferent to their interactions, and in the charity for the one, cannot withdraw its love from the other. The self, the *I*, cannot limit itself to the incomparable uniqueness of each one, which is expressed in the face of the each one. Behind the unique singularities, one must perceive the individuals of a *genus*, one must compare them, judge them, and condemn them. There is a subtle ambiguity of the individual and the unique, the personal and the absolute, the mask, the face. That is the hour of inevitable justice—required, however, by charity itself. (229)

The protectors of justice do not function as the bearers of "righteousness." They are not persons of self-righteousness—a criterion that makes justice possible.[55] The hour of justice rests within the universal, unlike that of ethics within the personal and particular. Justice is a gathering of human memory that informs how we should treat one another. Justice is unfinished legislation; as we learn more about the human condition, our responsibility to one another changes and necessitates legislative change. Levinas's conception of justice is akin to Seyla Benhabib's call for incremental justice and change.[56] The neighbor, the unknown third, is a rational commitment that institutionally extends my responsibility. Justice finds life and energy within the Saying of the needs of justice and a public presence of a Said that institutionalizes justice.[57] Levinas suggests that justice relies on learning from ethics, which forms a temporal legislation of the Said. Our obligation to and for the Other is immemorial and simultaneously unique with every contract; it is the unknown third who makes laws and institutions necessary. We temporally gather the Saying of ethics within the Said of legislation (*Entre Nous*, 233).

Justice, for Levinas, requires walking "into a covenant with the transcendent will" that focuses on an enlarged sense of concern (*In the Time*, 47). The notion of covenant burdens, keeping alertness alive for the neighbor—the transcendent sustains the image of the covenant as ever expansive and increasingly inclusive. Resistance to injustice unearths and unleashes legitimate force when another attacks the neighbor: "The absolute that upholds justice is the absolute of the interlocutor. Its mode of being and of making its presence known consists in turning its face toward me, in being a face" (*Entre Nous*, 22). Defense of the neighbor activates expansive obligations. This view of justice does not find solace in "reward and punishment" but in infinite obligation to the Other (*Of God*, 129). The neighbor, the third, arouses the thought of "consciousness" of justice (Levinas, *Basic Philosophical*, 95). The realm of justice begins with an oral ethic of "I am my brother's keeper." Levinas writes, "The other and the third party, my neighbors, contemporaries of one another, put distance between me and the other and the third party. 'Peace, peace to the neighbor and the one far-off' (Isaiah 57:19)."[58] Justice concentrates on those "far-off" from everyday conversation, vision, and consideration.

Justice reaches out to the Other with an obligation of countering fascination with ourselves alone. Justice accounts for a third party who is not present or cognizant of an ongoing conversation (*Entre Nous*, 21). Levinas rejects justice associated with "for oneself" and a sacred interpersonal space, such as the dwelling of "I-Thou."[59] Levinas discards the notion of a special place of justice (the I-Thou) where reciprocity limits obligation to turn taking. Justice for the stranger does not rest within the confines of a mystical interpersonal space; justice lives in the world of the Said, of rationality, of consciousness that furnishes our sense of obligation to unknown others incapable of reciprocity.[60] Justice tied to learning attends to the Saying of obligation gathered in institutional memory.

Levinas states that unlimited responsibility for the Other can be forgotten as consciousness becomes unduly significant, eclipsed by a "pure possession of self by self."[61] Justice does not rest with the self, but with plurality. Levinas places justice well above the "aspiration of individual piety."[62] Due to difference and multiplicity, one continually learns about and from persons and ideas that are different from one's own; such a reality makes a commitment to learning and to "knowledge" an important part of discovering and enacting justice.[63] Levinas ties knowledge and learning directly to justice, which shapes and informs "institutions" that must attend to the face of the unknown Other. Justice requires education.

Levinas rejects the privileged social place of justice by looking to the third, the neighbor, the unseen and unknown Other, which requires looking beyond proximity. The task of education is to take us beyond where we are—learning about the unknown. "Prophetism is in fact the fundamental mode of revelation"[64]; education assumes a prophetic role of taking one beyond the self. Justice and the self require judging oneself otherwise than current convention (Levinas, *Nine Talmudic*, 100). Justice requires constant learning and education. Justice pursued without an ethical impulse for particularity is "rotten with perfection."[65] Conscience understands the difference between reasonable politics and absolute justice, with the former tied more closely to violence than to those outside our reach (*Nine Talmudic*, 107). Levinas's project yields linkage with the study of narrative when aligned with justice. Petite narratives embrace practices, a story, and some form of agreement from a larger community. For Levinas, justice dwells within the narratives of institutions. The righteousness of justice, however, is disrupted by ethics and the face of the Other. Our obligation to the Other does not rest within a narrative but within the proximate demands of ethics to an Other. Ethics disrupts justice, and justice calls ethical attentiveness to the proximate into question. Human life, for Levinas, embraces the unity and the difference of justice and ethics.

Justice lives in the story-shaped action of a community that restrains the "righteous" individual. Levinas rejects persons who are so happy with their own actions that the needs of the unseen neighbor go unknowingly ignored (*Nine Talmudic*, 186). Levinas assumes that the moment one considers oneself to be the "just" one, an unexpected fact emerges—one "is no longer just" (*Basic Philosophical*, 17). Levinas refuses to confuse learning about obligation for Others with the doing of justice; he is not tempted by the "idealism of the haughty" (*Proper Names*, 138).

The Saying and the Said in Communication Ethics: Temporal Legislation of Justice

The following material connects Levinas's conception of justice with Eco's illumination of his characters functioning within an intertextual dialogue of ethics and justice as recorded in *The Name of the Rose*. The work offers a glimpse of Levinas's conception of the Said of justice in acts of protecting those not at the immediate table of deliberation.

COMMUNITY AS THE ORIGINATIVE DWELLING PLACE OF JUSTICE

This form of community frames a lodging that welcomes the stranger and keeps before us the needs of those not present. *The Name of the Rose* illumes Levinas's understanding of justice, situating actions within the midst of decisions with consequences of import. Communities, like persons, are imperfect. Lack of perfection makes justice a necessary interruption to ethics. In *The Name of the Rose*, William, charged by the emperor, participated in a debate between the papacy and the Franciscan order centered on the role of poverty and the Church's right to accumulate sizable wealth. Throughout the novel, we witness imperfections and dangers of self-righteousness. The struggle against righteousness of self-assurance announces the necessity for justice. The novel debunks justice as resting within a person alone; justice is an action learned within a community from stories and actions that attend to the stranger. *The Name of the Rose* continually reveals a trace of community that calls forth a cry of justice, which permits constructive actions by William and Adso to assist the abbey. These two main characters in the novel are products of stories about justice that remind them of the necessity to protect those beyond their own immediate interests.

THE STRANGER

Justice defined attends to the stranger, the unknown neighbor. The ordering of justice begins with attentiveness to the stranger, which arises from the Saying, a "spirituality of awakening" that gives insight into a primordial sense of equality that calls for justice, which demands that we nourish the Said of justice.[66] Justice fueled by the Saying becomes temporally fixed within the Said of concern for the unseen Other, which spawns additional Sayings of justice discerned within the particular of the face of ethics. In *The Name of the Rose*, William walks into a dispute between the Franciscans and the papacy; he is a voice of the Said of justice. William's task is the public presence of justice. In Levinasian terms William personifies "if not me, then whom," where the "I" is called forth by the story of justice in a particular place. William, as a former inquisitor, personifies the Saying of a spiritual awakening that gives rise to the Said of justice. He acts on behalf of the disenfranchised.

EDUCATION, BOOKS, AND THE LIBRARY

Levinas discusses the importance of dwelling in a manner that invites discussion about justice. Education is vital to Levinas's non-mystical project. *The Name of the Rose* yields insights into the vivacity and limits of education via the library, which moves one from self-absorption into a world of books about an unknown world of exteriority and learning. Levinas reminds us that there is an "inextinguishable concern for justice"[67]; indeed, the library is the secular symbol of such a search. William found himself at risk as he fought evil within the library. His battle with evil in the library reminds the reader of the rightful function of a library, which gives insight into unknown worlds and persons. In the burning of the library, Eco suggests that signification rests, not with the dwelling of the library as a place, but within the reality of ideas and people that are not physically present. The library is a sign of the sojourner of learning; it is the beginning of justice. Eco discloses the library as impure, while acknowledging its dynamic role in the long movement toward justice. As Levinas stated, "Justice is impossible to the ignorant man" (*Difficult Freedom*, 6). In the novel the library is the principal dwelling place of the story of justice, which requires consciousness about ideas and actions that link one to a world beyond the self. A world without learning from difference eclipses the stranger and invites a resultant absence of justice.

IMPERFECTION OF JUSTICE

Justice is never pure; it is the first step of violence, in that it involves the comparison of one principle pitted against another (*Is It Righteous*, 136): "The call to justice is a high task, even if—and especially because—the road is long and the outcome unsure."[68] Justice cannot stop violence; however, justice works to invite dwellings where concern for the unknown neighbor trumps narrow allegiance (*Proper Names*, 167). Justice requires places that are open to the Other. Such institutional places are not pure, but without them justice is increasingly less likely. Violence is always with us as we occupy space that another might inhabit. One cannot pursue justice for the third without the possibility of violence resisting evil. Violence is inevitable as we seek to defend another, the neighbor, against another: "Now, there is the appearance of the third who is a limitation on this measureless *hesed*. Because the other for whom I am responsible can be the executioner of the third who is also my other" (*Is It Righteous*, 100). Justice is not simply an add-on to ethics; it is a disruptive protector of ethics. Eco's novel announces repeatedly that justice does not live in perfection but rather in real places. We live in a world of imperfection void of self-righteous assurance.

Human obligation, for Levinas, is ethics, responsibility for the Other, disrupted by the demands for justice and the concerns for those not present—making our self-righteous assurance of good deeds and actions impossible. Justice, for Levinas, resists universal process, procedure, and doctrine. The moment we assume that we are unquestionably right for all, the disruption of ethics from the face of the Other calls our colonial plans into question. Again, ethics and justice are central to Levinas; when either reifies into unquestioned certainty, self-righteous assurance emerges with the inevitable consequence of failed responsibility and action.

JUSTICE AND THE IMPERSONAL

Levinas unites the impersonal with justice, which eschews connection to liking; justice has social lineage in its commitment to fairness for all. Justice lives when one is willing to assist an unknown other. Justice is a performative act of impersonal care for those who are unable to offer defense for themselves or others.

The image of justice in the West is a woman with eyes blindfolded, a sword in one hand, and the "scales of justice" in the other hand. The Greek mythological goddess Themis suggests this originative image of justice. She was an oracle at Delphi and became the goddess of divine justice, who offered advice to Zeus. The image of the blindfolded and impersonal justice is akin to Levinas's concern for obligation beyond familiar friendship patterns; justice is disruptive of an optical ethics of proximity.[69] Levinas's understanding of justice shifts justice from our kind, clan, type, or nation to those outside our vision.[70] The doing of justice requires an impersonal alertness that works to assist those not connected to or seated at the points of power. Such is the reason Levinas repeatedly stated our obligations to the disadvantaged.

Levinas's conception of justice personified in *The Name of the Rose* offers a conclusion that highlights William and Adso living out a commitment to impersonal justice. It ends simply: when their task is completed, the two separate without seeing each other ever again. Impersonal justice does not build personal relationships; it constructs dwellings that serve the unseen. Justice is a house that permits others to build homes. Justice provides a dwelling for others, offering existential trust between and among persons.[71] Justice takes us beyond the familial, the relational, and the proximate, tying us to an impersonal commitment that constructs a house of justice from which many can build meaningful homes together. In ethics we find the trace of justice, and in justice the trace of ethics—otherwise, the self-righteous person becomes an oppressive guide. Communication ethics becomes a vital force for good when rejected as the only moral action demanded of each one of us. There is more than me, more than the Other, and more than institutional commitments—to embrace only one dimension of our responsibility makes us less and diminishes the human condition. The power of communication ethics resides in its temporality of application, constantly interrupted by demands for justice that move one's gaze to obligation.

CHAPTER 7
Possession and Burden: Otherwise Than Murdoch's Information Acquisition

Thematization and conceptualization, which moreover are inseparable, are not peace with the other but suppression or possession of the other. For possession affirms the other, but within a negation of its independence.
> —Emmanuel Levinas, *Totality and Infinity: An Essay on Exteriority*

The rhetoric of telling and the desire to control, to colonize a creative moment, moves a people from learning from the Other into a milieu that atrophies into acts of possession and posturing—moving from the praxis of genius to a rhetoric of self-congratulatory pretentiousness.   —Ronald C. Arnett, "A Rhetoric of Sentiment: The House the Scots Built"

Possession, as outlined within an examination of Rupert Murdoch's *News of the World* scandal, explicates the problematic nature of an "originative I." This avaricious action is in contrast to communicative action propelled by a "derivative I," which is fundamental to Emmanuel Levinas's understanding of "ethics as first philosophy." The news artifact that guides this inquiry emerged from acts of illicit information acquisition involving the *News of the World* (1843–2011; Murdoch-owned 1969–2011), a tabloid in Great Britain that found itself in the center of information hacking via the cell phone messages of celebrities, politicians, and other citizens. The motivation for acquiring knowledge from targeted cell phone users was news and entertainment that permitted the *News of the World* to preempt competitors. Murdoch's *News of the World* generated a story that unites the hope of commercial success with information possession that falls outside an ethical arena detailed by Levinas. After clarifying the activities of the *News of the World*, I deconstruct their actions, interrogating the metaphor of possession via conceptual insights of Levinas.

Introduction

Possession of another's private information is an increasingly common reality in an era when technological possibility too easily morphs into self-granted permission. Jacques Ellul (1912–1994) challenged an emerging technological/communication actuality when he asserted that high-tech capability is an insufficient warrant for invasive human conduct; the question of capability or "can" does not automatically equate with an ethical "should."[1] Attentiveness to an ethical "should" separates capability from unreflective communicative routine.

Information acquisition as possession propels a communicative agent, witnessed in caricature form by the shadowy figure of Gollum in the *Lord of the Rings*[2]—this sinister character announces the dangers of possession that were played out in real life through the action of investigative journalism engaged by a now defunct British tabloid, *News of the World*. The varied performative implications of the notion of possession constitute the following three major sections. The first section, "The *Guardian*'s Tale," provides a detailed overview of the *News of the World* controversy, as reported by the *Guardian*—the newspaper that broke the phone-hacking story. The second section, "Levinas and Possession," offers an examination of Levinas's use and understanding of possession related to totality. The final section, "The Saying and the Said in Communication Ethics: Possession Otherwise," considers the contrary ethical implications of aligning possession with a call from the Other rather than imposing on the Other. Levinas's insights deconstruct the seemingly natural alignment of possession with the increasing ease of technological surveillance.

Examination of possession related to communicative privacy invasion explores an increasingly problematic reality in this historical moment. Framing the issue of privacy invasion with a retelling of

the events that led to the collapse of the *News of the World* emphasizes the reality of this privacy invasion moment. The main point is
twofold—the problematic nature of possession and the "otherwise
than convention" usage offered by Levinas. His orientation counters
a conventional understanding of possession tied to personal gain;
Levinas offers a conception that is otherwise than convention by linking possession and responsibility with a communicative agent finding
identity through a "derivative I" charged by the Other.

The Guardian's *Tale*

The *Guardian*'s story begins in the final days of Murdoch's *News of the
World* with the discovery, investigation, and unmasking of tactics that
united technological capability and invasion of privacy. I examine the
News of the World controversy by following a story about information
exploitation and possession that eventuated in the ruin of the *News of
the World* on July 11, 2011, and the jailing of several *News of the World*
editors, executives, and other employees. The actions of the *News of
the World* displayed information possession overreach that violated
privacy. Communicative acts of possession eclipse what Arendt called
public points of separation or "interspaces" that maintain and nourish differences of opinion within the public domain.[3] The actions of
the *News of the World* provide but one example of communicative
gestures that violate interspaces of separation between persons in
the public domain. The story of the *News of the World* functions as
an exemplar of Levinas's critique of the West as seduced by the demand for totality. This story displays possession at work with little
resistive creative thought that invites space for ethical reflection on
the "should"; instead, decisions emerge from a technological "can"
alone, as Ellul has described.

THE GUARDIAN (JULY 8, 2009)

The *Guardian*'s initial article by Nick Davies appeared July 8, 2009[4]; it
disclosed Murdoch's *News of the World*'s initial actions of a seeming
cover-up—with at least one million pounds in legal settlements dispersed to phone-hacking victims. The headline that day in the *Guardian*, "Murdoch papers paid £1m to gag phone-hacking victims," indicated that money suppressed phone-hacking victims from publicly

stating their concerns about personal information violation. The term "gag" frames the title of this initial *Guardian* exclusive stressing financial compensation used to keep people quiet. This "hush money" found identity in a corporate effort to secure "secrecy over out-of-court settlements" (Davies, para. 2). The *News of the World* sought to silence those who ". . . threatened to expose evidence of Murdoch journalists using private investigators who illegally hacked into the mobile phone messages of numerous public figures as well as gaining unlawful access to confidential personal data, including tax records, social security files, bank statements and itemised phone bills. Cabinet ministers, MPs, actors and sports stars were all targets of the private investigators" (para. 2). The *Guardian* alerted the public to "suppressed evidence" (para. 3). For many, the payments to victims of the hacking equated to a public admission of ethical culpability.

This early stage of the *Guardian* investigation unmasked "difficult questions" for various individuals such as Andy Coulson,[5] who, at the time of the 2009 article in the *Guardian*, was the director of communications for the Conservative Party under the leadership of David Cameron, who became prime minister the following year (Davies, para. 4). Coulson was editor of the *News of the World* during the phone-hacking allegations. The exposé indicated that the suppressed legal cases led to the arrest and four-month sentence of a *News of the World* reporter, Clive Goodman, in January 2007. Authorities convicted Goodman of hacking into the mobile phones of three royal staff members, "an offence under the Regulation of Investigatory Powers Act" (para. 8). At that time the *News of the World* indicated that Goodman acted alone; however, officers later uncovered evidence of the news group using multiple private investors to hack into "'thousands' of mobile phones" (para. 9).

This July 8, 2009, article stated that Cameron should rid himself of Coulson as director of communications. At that time Cameron, the Tory leader, did not seem particularly concerned about the revelations.[6] Additionally, Murdoch claimed he did not know anything about the incident. As the controversy unfolded, the facts mounted against the newspaper. First, there was the *News of the World* private investigator Glenn Mulcaire, imprisoned for phone hacking in 2007.[7] Second, there was evidence that at least thirty-one journalists connected with Murdoch's News International subsidiaries, the *News of the World* and the *Sun,* had conned public agencies into providing confidential information for news stories. Third, former *Sunday Times* editor Andrew Neil stated that the case involved more than one problematic journalist and/or private investigator. He suggested that deception was "systematic throughout the *News of the World,* and to a lesser extent the *Sun.* . . . [It was] a newsroom out of control" (Davies, para. 27). Public interest followed a story of unraveling public trust.

On the same day (July 8, 2009), the *Guardian* published a chronology of events that resulted in an initial public disclosure of the phone-hacking scandal. The review begins with the events of August 2006 when antiterror police arrested *News of the World* reporter Goodman and private investigator Mulcaire on suspicion of illegal interception of phone messages. Shortly thereafter the *News of the World* suspended Goodman. Then, in November 2006, Goodman admitted to conspiracy, pleading guilty to allegations of phone hacking. At that same time the *News of the World* editor, Coulson, publicly apologized; he stated that measures were in place to curtail such action forever. However, the *News of the World* rapidly lost public trust. In January 2007 Goodman received a sentence of four months' imprisonment, and Mulcaire received a sentence of up to six months. In January 2007 Coulson resigned as editor of *News of the World,* claiming "ultimate responsibility" for the events.[8] In March 2007 Les Hinton, chairman of News International, *News of the World*'s parent company, stated that Goodman had acted alone, and at the same time, Hinton "defend[ed] phone-tapping, arguing it can be in the public interest" (Robinson, "*News,*" para. 5).[9] In May 2007 the Press Complaint Commission gave the *News of the World* a clean bill of health, with Goodman and Mulcaire portrayed as aberrations and with Coulson no longer providing evidence in support of the *News of the World.* In 2007 Cameron appointed Coulson director of communications for the Conservative Party (2007–2010). The chronology from the July 8, 2009, article concluded in December 2007, when Hinton moved to New York to become chief executive of the *Wall Street Journal,* another newspaper owned by Murdoch (para. 5). Following this chronology of events, in July 2009 the phone-tapping case appeared potentially controlled/suppressed by the *News of the World*; the paper had seemingly used sufficient money for settlements. The paper generated necessary secrecy, while the public seemed satisfied with limited imprisonments for Goodman and Mulcaire. Additionally, the public witnessed the continuing success of certain individuals associated with the *News of the World*, particularly Coulson. The cover-up appeared successful until the exposé—as the phone-hacking story of Milly Dowler became known. This revelation renewed the investigation and left the readership of *News of the World* in ethical disbelief.

IRRESPONSIBILITY AND DEATH

Hélène Mulholland and James Robinson, on July 4, 2011, reported that the *News of the World* had hacked the cell phone of Milly Dowler, a missing thirteen-year-old girl. When Dowler disappeared, the *News of the World* team initiated, as it had in the past, an investigative journalism effort that accessed the voice mail of Dowler. She had disappeared on her way home on March 21, 2002. In September 2002, authorities reported discovery of her body. In June 2011, Levi Bellfield, convicted of her murder, received a sentence of life in prison. When the public became aware of the *News of the World*'s involvement in the hacking of Dowler's voice mails, the controversy surrounding the *News of the World* became a focal point of public attention.[10]

An article by Dan Sabbagh stated that during the week of July 7, 2011, the news world was attentive to the astonishing number of revelations related to phone hacking by Murdoch's battered newspaper. At that point Murdoch's News Corporation, the United Kingdom's largest newspaper publisher, had few friends left. The resignation of Rebekah Brooks, News International's chief executive, might have helped, but James Murdoch, Rupert Murdoch's son and chairman and chief executive of News Corporation, made another choice; he closed the *News of the World*.[11] Rupert Murdoch supported his son's judgment. The closing of the *News of the World* had another human consequence, generating the loss of more than two hundred jobs because of "the sins of a previous regime."[12]

The news about the violation of Dowler's cell messages was the catalyst for revisiting "privacy" and the *News of the World*. It was not the philosophical principle of privacy that charged the conversation with a sense of public shame. It was the news about the young girl Milly Dowler. As people learned that the paper hacked into voice mails of a murdered schoolgirl, there was an energizing public reaction. Competing newspapers within the industry stated that phone-hacking actions were a genuine threat to public trust.[13] Additionally, the Labour Party challenged any suggestions of future connections between British leaders and owners of the *News of the World*. Without question the case of Milly Dowler ultimately shifted this phone-hacking case of investigative journalism into increasing cries of public outrage. Journalists deleted voice mail messages in the first few days after Milly's disappearance in order to free up space for more messages. Because of this discovery of eliminated messages, friends and relatives of Milly concluded wrongly that she might be alive. It was only later that the family and public discovered that the hacking may not actually have been responsible for deleted voice mails; however, the image of such disrespectful action was already firmly set in the public mind (Sabbagh, "*News*").

Even James Murdoch's decision to close the *News of the World* on July 7, 2011, could not stop the continuing revelations and aftershocks emerging from this story. Brooks continued as a News International executive, but there were increasing public cries for her resignation. Cameron, the United Kingdom prime minister, then met with Ed Miliband, the Labour Party leader, which resulted in an official inquiry into the "phone hacking scandal" on July 8, 2011.

At the time of the closure of the *News of the World*, the Murdoch Corporation was attempting to finalize a BSkyB deal. The BSkyB, or formally British Sky Broadcasting, is a satellite broadcasting company that airs programming in the United Kingdom and Ireland. Murdoch's News Corporation owned a 39.1 percent stake in the company[14]; he presented a bid to take over the BSkyB in June 2010. Questions about James Murdoch and Brook's association with the wrongdoing of News Corporation evoked increasing resistance to Rupert Murdoch's effort to purchase this satellite broadcasting service. Then, on July 7, 2011, Amelia Hill reported that Coulson, the former director of communications for the Conservative Party (2007–2010) and the former head of communications for Prime Minister Cameron (2010–2011), who was under suspicion of possibly approving payments to police officers during the scandal, found himself under police custody.[15]

On July 10, 2011, the *Guardian* reported that payments had been offered to the Metropolitan Police for assistance with the stories, according to information detailed in recently surfaced News International memos from 2007. These memos, written shortly following the arrests of Goodman and Mulcaire, revealed the pair as not the only two involved in phone hacking.[16] Following the news of potential payments to police officers, British citizens put enormous pressure on the government to terminate the BSkyB deal because of Murdoch's sizable role in the BSkyB project. On July 11, after one hundred sixty-eight years, the *News of the World*, which Murdoch owned for forty-two years, beginning in 1969, put out its final paper, selling more than four million copies of its last issue.[17] James Murdoch shut down the paper, and it was unlikely that another might purchase the *News of the World* brand. On July 13, the News Corporation withdrew its BSkyB bid, although News Corporation still held 39.1 percent stake in the company. Then, on July 15, the *Guardian* reported that after twenty-two years with News International, Brooks resigned as chief executive. On that same day, July 15, the *Guardian* reported the resignation of Hinton from his position as chief executive officer of Dow Jones & Company and publisher of the *Wall Street Journal*; his service with the News Corporation had spanned fifty-two years.

In that same news cycle, Rupert Murdoch wrote an apology advertisement carried by Britain's national newspapers. The *Guardian* published the advertisement, stating that they donated proceeds to charity.[18] Two days later, on July 17, Sir Paul Stevenson resigned as commissioner of the Metropolitan Police Service due to accusatory links related to Metropolitan's connections with News International at its most senior levels. On that same day, authorities arrested Brooks. On July 19, Rupert Murdoch once again denied any knowledge of the details of the scandal. On September 6, 2011, the *Guardian* stated that no one could suggest that the problems were "confined to 'one rogue reporter.'"[19] Lisa O'Carroll reported that James Murdoch knew about the phone-hacking issues, with September 27 resulting in the resignation of James Murdoch's press secretary. Then, on November 23, James Murdoch resigned from the board of the *Sun* and the *Times* but remained executive chairman of News International. The *Guardian*'s coverage of the *News of the World* story ceased on January 2012, as followed in this chapter, although the controversy continues to unfold.[20] The communicative actions of the *News of the World* offer an exemplar of information acquisition falling into the dark side of possession. Rupert Murdoch continues to deny any knowledge of phone tapping and bribing actions of the *News of the World*.[21]

Even if one accepted Murdoch's assertions at face value, one must still ask questions about the character of the public dwelling Murdoch supported. For Levinas, dwelling "exceeds the knowing, the thought, and the idea in which, after the event, the subject will want to contain what is incommensurable with a knowing."[22] The events of the *News of the World* illuminate the shadow side of possession and its problematic influence on a social dwelling charged with assisting the public good.

Levinas and Possession

A signature phrase associated with Levinas is the title of his major work, *Totality and Infinity*; the term *possession* is textured by each of these key metaphors (153). The commonplace assumption is that Levinas's project only affirms infinity and carries a hostile rejection of totality. Such a reading misses the finesse of Levinas's thought. Levinas's scholarship qualifies his argument with an assertion that infinitude without acknowledgment of totality embraces limitlessness, which becomes a totalizing assumption. Consistent with Levinas's larger project, the alignment of possession and totality requires understanding the contrasting communicative implications of possession that associate more closely with infinity. The infinite seems, at first blush, the home of Levinas's view of ethical truth; however, the moment one attempts to possess the purity of the infinite, its power ceases. Consistent with this philosophical perspective, Levinas flees from the impulse to eradicate all totality; to do so misses the reality of the human condition.[23]

Levinas works out the interplay of totality and infinity in a discussion of serenity pursued with undue intensity. Such a determined quest for quietude embraces a totality of possession propelled by the "need" to grasp and own contentment. Need is a form of accumulation that does not ultimately satisfy. Desire, on the other hand, remains distant from the possessive effort to accumulate. Levinas's conception of desire is "a distance more precious than contact, a non-possession more precious than possession, a hunger that nourishes itself not with bread but with hunger itself" (*Totality*, 179). Desire, in stark contrast to the demands of need, refuses to eclipse the reality of separation and uniqueness between and among persons, events, and objects that we meet (102). Levinas discards need as the shadow side of possession.

A PEJORATIVE VIEW OF POSSESSION

Levinas's negative assessment of possession is multilayered; however, the consistent principal concern throughout his work is that possession obliterates alterity. Levinas equated determined effort to control the Other with an act of possession. He stated that the emergent or spontaneous act of possession cannot be "justified by virtue of its own spontaneity."[24] Whether premeditated or immediate, the need to possess is contrary to the call for responsibility that originates in an ethical mandate that emanates from the Other.

Levinas responded contrary to Hegel's *Phenomenology of Spirit* (published in 1807), in which history gives rise to consciousness that permits absolute thought and a "full possession of self."[25] Levinas witnessed the global results of linking possession to history and to the self; he contended with the impulse for personal and historical need. Levinas asserted that Hegel's position discounted the Other, which permits possession and consumption to drive encounters with the Other.[26] Such a perspective seeks to possess the Other through an authority that ignores an immemorial obligation to the Other (*Basic Philosophical*, 9). Possession happens in the act of fusion, a synthesis that leads to the seductive myth of progress that eclipses difference (159). The fable of progress grants permission, encouragement, and freedom to possess someone or something in the world in the process of embracing the new and the better (164).

The communicative act of possession is a passage into the realm of erasure, which actively dismisses the uniqueness of another.[27] Possession is an unresponsive disregard for the revelatory. The mythology of progress seeks a possessive synthesis propelled by an instinct for "integration" and "security."[28] The demand for progress and the pursuit of accumulation attempts to possess time, which loses the temporal reality of interruption as a defining feature of the human condition.[29] The communicative act of possession ultimately leads to fatigue emanating from a need to grasp and contain the distinctiveness of the Other.[30] Levinas cited Wahl's contention that life is an engagement of possession when confined to the immediate and temporal (*Proper Names*, 113). Additionally, possession united with accumulation and the universal is akin to what Blanchot called obsession energized by the "pagan" and rude (138). Need-driven possession dominates and discounts whatever is other than one's own expectations and outside the domain of one's own control.

Levinas contends that obsession with domination and control permits racism to pivot on the fulcrum of ownership, which turns qualitative differences and attributes into possessable values that discount the fact that one can do nothing to secure or accumulate such attributes. Possession is a communicative act that "denies" the reality of a distinctive experience with existence; it is an act of existential violence.[31] Interpersonal "flattery" serves as a possessive form of violence (*Totality*, 70). Possession denies uniqueness of another human being, whether propelled by artificial gestures of care or overt acts of domination.[32] The temptation to enact flattery and social domination emerges from a human fact—the solitary subject can possess nothing; sociality makes possession a temptation of need. We cannot acquire the present, which limits possession to acts of recollection and accumulation.[33] Possession energizes enthusiasm that drives the need to usurp the memory and recollection of another. This manner of possession colonizes another by limiting responsive imagination to the "not yet" and the unexpected.[34] Possession dwells within a house enthusiastically decorated with remnants of a dominated, collected, and organized past.

ENTHUSIASM

Levinas warns about the needful wish to be a god, a wish constituted by misdirected energy of sheer enthusiasm. This conception of a god garners a needy wish that goes unchallenged and unquestioned. Uncontrolled enthusiasm makes possession a goal that eschews demands for responsibility that emerge from alterity outside of our domination (*Difficult Freedom*, 54). Levinas rejected an "originative I" as the possessive persona of a "hateful self."[35] He even rejected Descartes's understanding of servitude as an attempt to possess care within the realm of the infinite; in this case, the "hateful self" of possession cloaks its true nature through an appearance of caring (*Totality*, 93). Levinas deprivileged possession in the pursuit of the sacred (*Difficult Freedom*, 216). Levinas cautioned against any sense of the universal good possessed by the communicator. Possession legitimates denial of necessary time and distance between persons and events; such action ignores thoughtful and necessary choices about what is temporally good in a particular historical moment (*Collected*, 134). A universal good that does not commence with the uniqueness of the particular is an act of possessive imposition.

For instance, one cannot demand that a friendship suddenly take hold. One does not possess a friendship—consciousness of possession destroys the friendship.[36] Things can be possessed; authentic relationships cannot (*Totality*, 131). To possess the Other eclipses alterity of uniqueness, difference, and separation of the Other from oneself. One "de-face[s]" another through the act of possession (*Basic Philosophical*, 168). Levinas, in response to Husserl, understood intentionality as a "signifying intention," which suggests that a phenomenological construct or thing cannot be possessed by an onlooker.[37] Possession preys upon the personal and proximate. Levinas suggests, "The act of possession is kept at bay by the acknowledgment of distance" (*Existence*, 39). Possession is a form of possessive greed that flourishes whenever there is an unleashing of uncontrollable personal enthusiasm.

Greed, when related to objects of whatever sort, manifests a "possession of possession" (*Collected*, 45). Possessive greed announces itself when accumulation of something becomes more important than responsibility for the Otherness that one encounters. Greed lurks within the shadows of information acquisition, arising when the need to accumulate a knowledge base eclipses responsibility for the Other.[38] Levinas warned that possession propelled by enthusiasm confuses accumulation of knowledge with responsibility. When one follows the demand for more alone, responsibility for meeting and engaging alterity morphs into possession, and creativity diminishes via imitation.

CREATIVITY

The result of the dark side of possession shapes the literature of Tolkien, Proust, and Charles Dickens (1812–1870), who depict dangers of possession when acts of creativity fall prey to possession. One must reach beyond the moment and respond to a genuine call of responsibility from the Other; otherwise, creativity is obliterated and yields to possessive need. Levinas contended that creativity responds to the rhythm of duration: "Duration in which the instance is not self-possessed, does not stop, is not present, is what makes music like a game" (*Existence*, 22). The inventive movement begins with possession, but in order for creativity to arise, one must reach beyond possession (20).

Levinas understood genuine creativity as dwelling within possession that pulls one out of the routine of life; interruptions demand that we take notice. Possession can extract one out of an immediate understanding of history, distance, and disengagement; possession is then an initial call for creativity that awakens responsibility. It is impossible to enjoy the world without an awakening by possession. One who genuinely meets ideas and questions often finds oneself possessed by the inquiry. However, when momentarily possessed by a given project, one recognizes the independence and force of that which one creatively meets (*Entre Nous*, 19, 41, 69).

Levinas differentiates between possession associated with need and possession that temporally gathers one's attentive energies and demands that one take notice. Levinas argued for the importance of this latter creative and temporal form of possession, which invites enjoyment of and satisfaction with existence. This form of possession is in contrast to the need to control, which loses all distance and forfeits independence of both self and Other (*Entre Nous*, 126). Levinas repudiated equation of possession with truth. He did not correlate the "modes of enjoyment, sensibility, and possession" with truth but rather with a sense of awakening (*Totality*, 172). A possessive awakening is a temporal moment that gathers attention and begins an unending journey of engagement.

Levinas's conception of creativity begins with possession that comprises distance in response to Otherness in the act of responsibility for a person, idea, and/or act. This understanding of creation sustains a focus of attention through possession that simultaneously maintains complete independence of self and Other (*Collected*, 50). Independence requires freedom and distance from and for the Other; insistence on the need of possession denies freedom of both self and Other. A self caught in obsessive reflection "ends up" on the other side of freedom (*Discovering Existence*, 74).

Creativity in the doing of labor invokes the interplay of possession and distance/separation. Labor, for Levinas, as articulated in *Totality and Infinity*, is action propelled by desire, not need for possession; the linkage of labor and possession acknowledges alterity as a nutriment calling forth responsibility (129, 159). "Possession tied to need" eclipses the Other while "possession tied to desire" awakens responsibility and embodies a generosity of responsiveness to alterity. Awakening human responsibility is the core of Levinas's ethics: "It is in generosity that the world [is] possessed by me—the world open to enjoyment" (75). Dispossession of the self through responsibility for the Other is a communicative act of responsibility that divests the self of possession in the meeting of Otherness (213). The Other is a "dimension of height" that demands our obligation. Ethical height is the "epiphany of the face as a face" (75). The epiphany of the face calls forth a "derivative I" possessed by a desire to be responsible for the Other.

EPIPHANY OF THE FACE: POSSESSION
OTHERWISE THAN CONVENTION

The epiphany of the face shifts the focus of attention from possession that dominates the Other to an awakening of responsibility inclusive of a possession of me by the Other; this possession generates responsibility and is otherwise than convention. The face of the Other generates a desire to be responsible that calls forth a "derivative I" that is held "hostage" by one's responsibility for the Other (*Basic Philosophical*, 79). The "I" called out by the Other is a "derivative I" responsive to the ethics of alterity in existence (*Existence*, 39). This "I" of responsibility is an "original possession of being" that constitutes an infinite radical attentiveness to and responsibility for the Other (79).

Levinas describes a recovering of self-possession via the "derivative I" as the ultimate response of responsibility to and for the Other (*Totality*, 54). Levinas's responsive ethical "I" is in contrast to a conventional conception of communicative agency.[39] Levinas's ethical perspective is akin to postmodern rejection of the "originative I" that seeks to possess and dominate. Levinas engaged otherwise, pointing to a "derivative I" possessed and held hostage in the act of responsibility for the Other, which indirectly frames one's identity, purpose, and direction. Unlike the possession of an "originative I," where relation with the Other never nullifies separation, the "derivative I" is responsible and attentive to distance between and among persons (*Totality*, 256).

In answering a summons from the Other, one becomes "self-possessed" with attentiveness to and responsibility for the Other as an ethical first principle (*Otherwise*, 56). This ethical self-possession propels a "derivative I" that assumes responsibility within an ethical charge—"if not me, then whom." The ethical practice of self-possession permits the human to counter the impulse to dominate with responsibility to and for alterity (*Totality*, 199). This uncharacteristic view of possession is contrary to a provisional demand that weighs one down with thoughts and actions responsive to me, not the Other (271).

The "derivative I" finds identity through a possession of me by the Other, which demands my responsibility; such a perspective begins with attentiveness to the face, which is the origin of sociality—a community that counters domination of the Other.[40] For Levinas, a phenomenological act of prayer attends to the face of the Other and is contrary to possession (*Totality*, 51); it commences with an unwillingness to "decipher" information about the life of another (*Nine Talmudic*, 32).

Responsibility calls forth self-possession within "universal trembling" and "in the midst of corruption." We do not know the "right" action of responsibility to and for another (*Difficult Freedom*, 254). The borders of ethical assurance make justice and its limits result in decision making devoid of a guarantee of righteousness (*Otherwise*, 161). Lack of assurance shapes both ethics and justice. In working with Psalm 80:14, Levinas disrupts both ethics and justice with difference; he quotes, "*Rage against and repel the wild beast and keep for your own possession the community* [of Israel]."[41] The wild beast, for Levinas, consists of acts, thoughts, and ideas "that are written with only one pen" (*In the Time*, 89); he appeals to multiplicity of voices. Levinas's view of community authorizes responsibility without possession of the Other, making multiple voices possible. Levinas understood promises that offer "possession and enjoyment" as analogous to attempting to hold sand in one's hands.[42] Infinity reminds one that existence is "alien to the grasp, to possession" (*Outside*, 41). Levinas rejected uniting "presence," "possession," and "self-consciousness"; he articulated the impossibility of such a project (*Proper Names*, 57). His ethics emerges from exteriority that reshapes interiority; ethics originating from the exteriority of the face of the Other restructures the interiority of the communicative agent. This unconventional conception of possession called forth by the Other shapes my identity and responsibility to and for the Other.

The desire of responsibility for the Other propels a creative and conscientious caretaker of existence and dwellings. Levinas stated that we must till real parcels of land in order to build sites of "hospitality" (*Collected*, 149). Contrary to the act of possession of the Other, this separation invites the Other into a dwelling that offers hospitality where one functions as a host attentive to the Other (*Totality*, 299). Such a dwelling is a place where enjoyment resists possession ignited by need (162). Dwellings are composed of possessions of recollections of events, ideas, and persons that invite genuine "enjoyment" (123, 170). As we acknowledge that the earth cannot be possessed, the desire to welcome the Other lends reason for construction of a dwelling defined by joy.

Dwelling situated within a communicative milieu of nonpossession shapes Levinas's discussion of fecundity; he reminds us that a father cannot possess his own child. For the child to remain connected to the father, the notion of the stranger must simultaneously exist in the relationship. Levinas discussed the failure of Eros in that it seeks to possess, missing the power of the Other who holds the ego hostage by possessing me. Levinas's example of fecundity emphasizes that a child defines the identity of a parent as the parent demarcates the child; identity derives one from another (266–67). Fecundity negates ownership or understanding of another as relational property.[43] For Levinas, it is this unconventional view of possession that makes family possible.

A dwelling of a family, a place of friendship, the church, or a gathering of persons requires self-possessed persons charged by another with the task of constructive building of places of welcome; the builder is held hostage by responsibility for the Other. From such a dwelling, one heeds an immemorial echo of responsibility that bears testimony within a given place. One cannot possess truth. On the contrary, it is truth that holds us upright in the act of responsibility to and for the Other (*Collected*, 129). To be "for-the-other" is dissimilar to the act of possession of the Other; it is a possession by the Other of me in the demand for responsibility that builds dwellings of welcome. Such dwellings come from actions called forth by burden and responsibility for the Other, ever so much in contrast to the *News of the World*'s fascination with information possession that seeks to dominate.

The Saying and the Said in Communication Ethics: Possession Otherwise

Levinas would understand the danger of possession reflected in the investigative journalism of the *News of the World*. One can envision Levinas's disgust with the actions that define this story—information possession aligned with the hope of securing data that might have given the paper an edge over competitors. For Aristotle, the fulcrum point of error rests in the extremes of deficiency or excess[44]—in this case, too much concern for personal success. Levinas offers another form of excess: an ethics that dwells in a home composed of unending responsibility for the Other. The demise of justice commences with intrusion into "the private sphere, which is 'no one's business'" (*Nine Talmudic*, 76). Justice demands possession accompanied by responsibility that moves beyond the use of another's lifeworld for the possessive purposes of voyeurism and/or career advancement. Levinas outlines a conception of possession that cannot escape the demands of an unending excess of responsibility.

Self-possession for soi-même.—Levinas suggests an alternative locus of the call for responsibility; it does not begin with me but with the Other. For Levinas, alterity calls forward a "derivative I," which requires possession in order to secure our attention. The face of the Other awakens an ethical responsibility. Additionally, one must awaken to the third, the unknown neighbor—a stirring of ethical responsibility for those not seen and not present at the table of conversation and decision making.

Contrasting need and desire.—Levinas's understanding of need unites possession and accumulation. Desire emerges from a possession of me that unites with unending desire. There is no end to responsibility. Dangerous possessive energy that emanates from need must give way to a possession via desire if constructive ethical responsibility is to frame one's actions toward the Other. Desire propels ethics in action for the Other in the form of a "derivative I."

Moral uprightness.—The ongoing performance of ethics does not begin with me but with attentiveness and responsiveness to the Other. The Other calls me into moral uprightness; I am propelled to respond. Moral uprightness is not my choice, but rather it is my obligation to another.

No end . . .—There is no conclusion to ethics, burden, and responsibility. There is no moment of accomplishment or victory. Just as air is necessary for life, burden is essential for ethical conduct; we assume responsibility for the Other—it is the heart of the human condition. Responsibility does not cease; only the particular characteristics of how and whom to assist alter over time.

Levinas offers an ethical vision that is broader, deeper, and considerably more demanding than the tunnel vision of career recognition. The "derivative I" testifies and witnesses for the unseen, the unknown, and the voiceless. The tragic story of Dowler, from the vantage point of Levinas's project, announced public outrage that demanded concern for the voiceless; knowledge about the tragedy of this young girl sent the *News of the World* to its demise. At that moment we witnessed "moral uprightness" that demanded concern for the unseen neighbor and forgotten voices. An ethical outcry of indignity and anger collapses a dwelling carved out of needful possession. There is no final totality of goodness. In the *News of the World* story, we witness the phenomenological reality of Levinas's conviction that only when we meet the face of the Other can ethical responsibility be called out. From the grave, Dowler's voice testified, demanding that people bear witness to a justice that refuses to forget those not present at the table of discussion and decision making. As communicative agents build dwellings that welcome the stranger into places of public trust, one finds oneself possessed by responsibility directed by the Other. Enacting such responsibility builds dwellings of public trust, guided by an unspoken desire to carry forth obligation for the Other and directed by an immemorial echo of "I am my brother's keeper." Communication ethics from a Levinasian orientation embraces possession tied to responsive obligation that originates in the face of the Other. A Levinasian conception of communication ethics presupposes that each one of us is held hostage by an immemorial demand to enact responsibility to and for the Other.

CHAPTER 8

The Ethical Parvenu: Unremitting Accountability

Heidegger invited me to go to Davos. I did such a great job [at ridiculing the opponent;] Cassirer was too easy to mimic, in fact; he had hair like an ice-cream cone. I'm afraid I did much better than I would have liked to. . . . I always said that if I came to the United States I would ask pardon of Mme. Cassirer. I had no idea, we could not have known, what would take place in 1933.
     —Emmanuel Levinas, as cited in Peter E. Gordon's
      Continental Divide: Heidegger, Cassirer, Davos

Just as events of discourse and action require for their intelligibility an insertion into the history of discursive and institutional practices, so also the face-to-face encounters of the self with the other take on meaning only against the background of a tradition already delivered and the foreground of one yet to be enacted. It is this historical perspective that provides the proper space and parameters for the self in community. Self-understanding entails an understanding of oneself as a citizen of a polis, a player in an ongoing tradition of beliefs and commitments, a participant in an expanding range of institutions and traditions.
     —Calvin O. Schrag, *The Self after Postmodernity*

The famous conversation/debate between Cassirer and Heidegger took place during the International Davos Conference (Internationale Davoser Hochschulkurse) with the theme "What Is Man?" The conference in Davos, Switzerland, was extensive, lasting from March 16 through April 6, 1929. The conference occurred four years before Hitler's rise to power and Heidegger's assumption of the rectorship of Freiburg University as well as his admission to the Nazi Party in 1933. The discussion at Davos was simply titled "A Discussion between Ernst Cassirer and Martin Heidegger." The event gave rise to a lifelong communication ethics memory that significantly influenced Levinas's project of obligation to the Other that begins with acknowledgment of a human face. As this chapter will relate, Emmanuel Levinas was a student at the conference, and his actions after the debate remained with him throughout the remainder of his life.

Introduction

The debate between Cassirer and Heidegger was the centerpiece of the second annual International Davos Conference. The International Davos Conference convened multiple times between 1928 and 1931. The conference was a colloquial gathering of European intellectuals, which served as a cultural bridge between France and Germany. The meeting consisted of lectures and public dialogues, culminating in a "discussion evening" between select numbers of internationally recognized intellects who presented their ideas in a highly formal and structured format. The Cassirer and Heidegger symposium was distinctive; it was a newly introduced "working seminar" (*Arbeitsgemeinschaft*), which was less structured and more conversational. Cassirer and Heidegger were the key presenters for the second annual conference, which the organizers hoped would exceed the "intellectual excitement" generated by the conference's inaugural speaker, Albert Einstein.[1] Cassirer and Heidegger were to focus on Kant, with each scholar offering his perspective on Kant's project. At the time of the debate, Cassirer was fifty-five years old and had recently finished his work *The Individual and the Cosmos in Renaissance Philosophy* (published in 1927). Cassirer contended that the importance of neo-Kantianism rested in posing questions and not within the development of a "substantive doctrine." Heidegger was thirty-nine years old and had recently published *Being and Time*. Heidegger's conviction was that neo-Kantianism was a "mere epistemology or theory of knowledge" (Gordon, 137, 139). Cassirer and Heidegger had considerable expertise on Kant's project, although Cassirer was the more well-known Kantian expert. During the debate Levinas was an ethical participant in a manner that he would understand only much later in his life.

This chapter commences with two scholars with contrary perspectives on Kant; the debate was unknowingly on the future of the West. The communication ethics implications center on Levinas missing the face of the Other. The first section, "The Debate," reviews the events of this significant scholarly exchange, highlighting pragmatic implications about incommensurable directions within the West. The second part, "Cohen on the Debate," centers on Levinas's lament about his actions at the conference. The third section, "Humanism: Otherwise than Convention," continues with the Levinas work that contains Cohen's foreword on the debate. Finally, in "The Saying and the Said in Communication Ethics: An Ethical Parvenu," Geoffrey Waite's response to the debate underscores the revelatory importance of a lamented moment.

The differences between Cassirer and Heidegger are historically important in that they offer a glimpse of upcoming consequences of dismissing the face of the Other. Additionally, the ethical learning of Levinas shifts the signification of the parvenu within the realm of ethics as unending obligation. My contention is that the debate between Cassirer and Heidegger centered on humanism, with the former tying it to culture and the latter rejecting this assumption. A third alternative on the question of humanism emerges in the writing of Levinas that was the unexpected consequence of this event. Waite contends that Levinas embraced a lifelong lament about his reaction to the Cassirer and Heidegger debate. Waite maintains that Heidegger acted as a provocateur, demonstrating a vibrant personality. In retrospect, however, this personal attribute was not sufficient for claiming victory over the more careful reader of Kant, Cassirer. In *Humanism of the Other*, Levinas critiques an "originative I" that imposes on and eclipses the Other, of which Heidegger functioned as an exemplar. Heidegger knowingly violated the Kantian project, while Cassirer worked diligently to explicate the implications of Kant's work.

The Debate

As the conversation between the two scholars commenced, Cassirer challenged Heidegger's understanding of neo-Kantianism. Cassirer argued that neo-Kantianism is "a direction taken in question posing" rather than a philosophical dogma; Cassirer, "rather surprisingly," discovered neo-Kantianism in Heidegger's work (Gordon, 137). Heidegger, however, rejected the scope of neo-Kantianism as mere epistemology. Heidegger argued that neo-Kantians such as Hermann Cohen (1842–1918) read Kant's first critique as mere "epistemological inquiry into the formal-methodological foundations of the natural sciences" (142). Heidegger argued that Kant was less concerned with epistemology than with the problem of metaphysics and thus the problem of ontology, which was central to Heidegger's project (129).

Kant offers a seemingly negative assessment of metaphysics and ontology, which Heidegger countered with the assertion that Being (*Sein*) is a "positive problem"; he intended to move the principal ideas of Kant's assertions in *Critique of Pure Reason* into a focus upon "ontology."[2] Heidegger sought to go beyond Kant's negative expression of the relationship between appearances and the "nature of human being" and to stress a "more positive . . . 'ontological' doctrine" that united human being and appearances (Gordon, 143). This movement distinguishes Heidegger from neo-Kantians, who turned to Kant for "the mathematico-physical theory of knowledge"; however, it was never Kant's intention to provide such a theory of natural science (Cassirer and Heidegger, 193). Heidegger's critique focused on the work of Cohen in *Kant's Theory of Experience*, which validated an interpretation of Kant's work as "natural scientific experience" (Gordon, 143). Cassirer responded to Heidegger's critique, arguing that Cohen writes historically, not as an epistemologist (Cassirer and Heidegger, 193). Cassirer asserted that Cohen's work on Kant via the mathematical sciences of nature represents only a paradigm, not "the whole of the problem" addressed by Kant and neo-Kantians. Cassirer, in this respect, expressed agreement with Heidegger, citing Kant's productive imagination.

Both Cassirer and Heidegger stressed the importance of imagination. Cassirer accentuated the importance of the "symbol-concept," and Heidegger emphasized truth as relative to Being. They both recognized the importance of schematism within Kant's work. Their differences rested in the relation of schematism to Kant's ethics. Cassirer stated that one finds a modest sense of typology in Kant's "schematism" that illuminates "practical reason." In the ethical realm, one reaches a point where reason is no longer the primary driver for decision making. Thus, Cassirer asserted that within Kant's ethical work, practical reason becomes a typology and not a schematism (193–94). Cassirer explains, "For Kant the schematism is a *terminus a quo* [starting point], not a *terminus ad quem* [ending point]" (194). Cassirer questioned Heidegger's conception of finite beings as "relative and confined" and therefore unable to obtain knowledge and truth. Cassirer posed, "Does Heidegger wish to renounce this complete objectivity, this form of absoluteness, which Kant placed within the realms of the ethical and theoretical in the *Critique of Pure Judgment?*" (194). Heidegger countered by calling the notion of objectivity into question with a stress on finitude. Cassirer then refuted Heidegger with an assertion that outside a finite being there is the "beyond," which is present in the categorical imperative (194–95).

Heidegger stated that the "imagination of the schematism" is an originative, but finite, power whereas Being is aligned with the infinite.[3] The "understanding of Being" as infinite includes finite assistance from *Dasein*. For Heidegger, keeping oneself open to "things-which-are" is the basis of "Being-in-the-truth." The finitude of *Dasein* generates both a "Being-in-truth" and a "Being-in-the-untruth." Truth becomes relative to a given position of *Dasein* via time. Heidegger stated that the task of exposing the temporality of *Dasein* rests with "understanding of Being." Truth in relation to temporality intends toward Being's "radical futurity." Heidegger's emphasis on death and *Dasein* exposes both a "radical futurity" and "dread [*Angst*]" that finds meaning in the inevitability of nothingness that is recognized in "Nothing or Dread," which illuminates an understanding of Being. The comprehension of "Being and Nothing" gives rise to an original question, "why," which is a fundamental interrogation within the human condition. For Heidegger, the question "how is freedom possible?" is not relevant to philosophy; such inquiry misses the problem of origin and results in a "philosophizing over-all view of life [*Weltanschauung*]" that mistakenly hopes to "[transcend] *Dasein* itself" and ignores the radical reality of finitude. The origin question provides an "over-all view of life," which Heidegger contended was not the task of the philosopher (Cassirer and Heidegger, 195–97).

Cassirer, on the other hand, stated that the human must participate in infinity; finitude does not define a human being. Cassirer agreed, however, that it is not the task of philosophy to assist the human being with "liberation from dread." For Cassirer, one must understand the power of finitude in relation to the human's desire to experience a glimpse of the infinite. The fulfillment of finitude necessitates infinity—such a proposition is at the heart of a "profession of faith" (198–99). Cassirer asserted that philosophy permits the human being to acknowledge and experience freedom from the limits of finitude—philosophy, thus understood, is a door to a transcendence that curtails the power of the finite.

The two men continued their disagreement, centered on a topic fundamental to Cassirer's project—the notion of culture. Heidegger rejected Cassirer's emphasis on the "philosophy of culture" as a dwelling for the human being. Heidegger vetoed all of Cassirer's efforts to appease, rejecting Cassirer's emphasis on culture as dwelling. Heidegger contended that philosophy tied to culture is an act of inauthenticity, propelled by a desire to escape finitude. Instead, Heidegger emphasized meeting finitude with rationality that is historically relative to the task of *Dasein*; it locates disclosure of *logos* within finitude. For Heidegger, finitude offers the possibility of freedom; it is the primal act of "thrownness" into the reality of limits; freedom is only possible as one avoids metaphysical flight (200).

For Heidegger, the temporality of *Dasein* situated within an authentic meeting of finitude assumes both dread and recognition of nothingness, which engenders a philosophy that explicates an existential fact: the human is thrown "back into the hardness of his fate" (201). Philosophy cannot appease; it only describes the demands of the human condition. Freedom found not in metaphysical union, but within acceptance of the hardness of fate, is a celebratory revolution of freedom that functions as a return to finitude. Heidegger wrote, "I have not given freedom to myself although I can be the self that I am only through being free . . . *Dasein* is the really fundamental event in which the act of existing of man, and with that, every problematic of existence as such essentially comes about" (200). Being, in Heidegger's understanding, "cannot be translated" with the semantic sense of Cassirer and his announcement of the fundamental nature of culture in the *terminus a quo*. Heidegger's understanding of Being works apart from philosophical divisions; he rejected traditional divisions as "the greatest snare in the way of getting back to the inner problematic of philosophy" (200). The question of metaphysics, for

Heidegger, transcends empiricism, finding its place in the underlining of philosophical disciplines.

Language, in relation to Kant's notion of the transcendental, offers a profound divide between Heidegger and Cassirer. For Cassirer, the transcendental makes language meaningfully understandable. Cassirer understood *unity* tied to the transcendental. Heidegger, on the other hand, traced the concept of the transcendental back to the Greeks and *difference*; the etymology of transcendence revealed the importance of difference—"differentiating of standpoints . . . is the root of philosophical work." Distinguishing of standpoints is key to Heidegger's work; difference pushes a being "beyond himself" into the whole and "nothingness of his *Dasein*" with Being the point of temporal transcendence (201–3).

Numerous essays and books trace the differences between Cassirer and Heidegger[4]; their exchange is significant in the history of philosophy and most assuredly affected Levinas's later life. Fundamental differences between Cassirer's and Heidegger's contrasting commitments revolve around the following concepts: unity and multiplicity, the role of finitude and the infinite, and the dissimilarity between the symbols of culture and the *alethic* of Being. In reflecting upon the debate at Davos, Levinas contended that the contrasts between Heidegger and Cassirer prompted three ongoing and repetitive personal reflections. First, Levinas thought Heidegger articulated the correct side of the argument. Second, following the debate, Levinas played the role of Cassirer in a student play staged by participants at the Davos debate; his performance mocked Cassirer. Third, later in life Levinas regretted taking the side of Heidegger against Cassirer, both conceptually and within the student drama. When questioned about the Davos encounter during an interview with François Poirié in 1968, Levinas stated, "During the Hitler years I reproached myself for having preferred Heidegger at Davos."[5] Levinas repeatedly reflected upon this event—the failure to attend to the human face of Cassirer plagued him long after the encounter.

The power of the human face demands my obligation; this reality shapes Levinas's frequent return to the Cassirer and Heidegger debate. These later reflections by Levinas announce the authority of the face of the Other as more enduring than philosophical dominance. The Cassirer incident prompted Levinas's moral conscience throughout the remainder of his life. According to Richard Cohen, during a 1973 trip to the United States, Levinas "inquired of the whereabouts of Mrs. Cassirer, so that he might be able, in his own words, 'to ask pardon of her.'"[6] Levinas, however, was unable to fulfill the apology; unfortunately, Mrs. Cassirer had died in 1961 (Gordon, 327). Following this recognition of the ethical lament, Levinas announces repeatedly the power of the Other in calling forth our ethical responsibility—explicated in *Humanism of the Other.* However, before leaving the debate between Heidegger and Cassirer, I wish to recount the points of emphasis articulated by Cohen, director of the Institute for Jewish Thought and Heritage. Cohen wrote the introduction to *Humanism of the Other.* Heidegger is the core to which Levinas responds in *Otherwise than Being,* which frames a reason for "ethics as first philosophy."[7] Cohen states that the encounter between Cassirer and Heidegger explicated profound differences between ethics tied to the human face and Heidegger's fascination with Being.

Cohen on the Debate

Richard Cohen, in his introduction to *Humanism of the Other,* frames the 1929 encounter in the following fashion. Two distinguished scholars known for their interpretive expertise on Kant met in debate. Cassirer's credentials were beyond dispute on the subject, yet, in the eyes of the audience, Heidegger was the victor. At Freiburg, Heidegger trained with Heinrich Rickert, who, at the time of the debate, was a leading representative of neo-Kantians (Gordon, 137–38). From 1912 until 1918, Cassirer was the general editor of an eleven-volume collection that brought together the complete works of Kant; additionally, Cassirer wrote a biography of Kant.[8] There is little question that Cassirer's scholarly version was closer to the horizon of Kant's project than that of Heidegger, whose focus was not on what Kant said but on how he might use Kant's insights to further explicate his understanding of Being. The argument within the debate centered on incommensurable interpretations of Kant's views on "interpretation" and "reason." Cassirer asserted a place for pure logic, with Heidegger declaring against pure logic. Cohen stated that "Cassirer defended the possibility, across discourse, of discovering 'infinity,' 'ideality,' or 'objectivity' of cultural formations. Heidegger, in contrast, defended the necessity of a steadfast return to the 'finitude,' or historical situation, of all that is meaningful," which knowingly violated the spirit of Kant's inquiry. Heidegger professed that such intellectual violence against the spirit of Kant's inquiry was an essential act in creative thought. Cassirer disagreed, calling Heidegger a "usurper." (Cohen, introduction, xi).

Cohen holds that Heidegger's reading of Kant placed imagination at the center of "sensible existence" and "the syntheses of understanding and the unifying idealism of reason" (xii). From this interpretation Heidegger challenged Cassirer's reading of Kant. Cassirer's effort to use reason to unify Kant's project beyond the realms of ethics and aesthetics was the fundamental dividing line between Heidegger and Cassirer, with the former understanding reason as derivative of a given historical situation and the latter connecting reason to the innate capacity of the human being (xii).

Cohen stated that *Dasein* discovers freedom in the meeting of the historical situation and encounter with finitude. Heidegger sought to reverse the Copernican Revolution present in Kant's thought. Cassirer and fellow neo-Kantians understood the Copernican Revolution, within Kant's work, as primarily in the production of a cultural realm and in the use of language (xiii). Heidegger conceptualized human meaning as emerging from Being, not from humans themselves. For Heidegger, freedom rested in *Dasein*'s "freedom to appropriate the finitude of its fate and its place within its historical destiny" (xiii), while Cassirer worked within the framework of Kant's Copernican Revolution that connects human freedom to a symbol-making capacity. In addition to highlighting the fundamental differences between Cassirer and Heidegger, the debate served as a warning about events that were beginning to unfold.

Levinas does not embrace Cassirer's scholarship on humanism; nevertheless, Levinas acknowledged his failure to recognize Cassirer's story about the "noble ethics of humanism" in a moment that was giving way to Hitler's Nazism. Levinas later asserted that Cassirer acted at the "height of nobility" (xxxvi), but his own mocking of Cassirer functioned as an eclipse of the face of the Other. Cohen underscored Levinas's role in the skit performed after the 1929 debate. With a powdered white wig, Levinas played the role of Cassirer. Cohen turned to Levinas's own words to reveal the profanity of this moment: "As you know, it was following this historic confrontation that the thoughts inspired by Kant and the heritage of the Enlightenment, primarily represented by Cassirer, disappeared from Germany. . . . For my part, I played (*j'incarnais*) Cassirer, whose positions Heidegger constantly attacked. And to convey Cassirer's noncombative and somewhat woebegone attitude, I continually repeated: 'I am a pacifist'" (xv). In Levinas's defense, at the time of the debate, he was a student and graduate assistant. He attended the conference at the invitation of Heidegger while he studied with Husserl at Freiburg (1928–1929). Levinas was translating works for Husserl, taking classes with him, and, like his fellow students, read *Being and Time*.

Levinas did not recognize what Cohen explicates in retrospect: the debate was far more than a discussion about Kant and the state of philosophy as a discipline (vii). What was at stake was the struggle between two contentious worldviews. Cassirer offered a cosmopolitan perspective, a "philosophy of culture." Heidegger, on the other hand, immediately proposed "a critique of 'the metaphysics of presence'" with an emphasis on Being; the argument centered on humanism and antihumanism, not principally on Kant. The quarrel was "over the meaning of the West," which functioned as a dividing line between Heidegger's project and Cassirer's work (vii).

The clash between Heidegger and Cassirer was significant, displaying a fundamental conflict of ideas of import to the future of the West. Cassirer was the first Jewish rector of the University of Marburg in 1930, and in May 1933, four years after the Davos conversation, Cassirer fled Germany with his wife and child (xiv). At the same time, on May 5, 1933, Heidegger delivered his famous rector speech, "The Self-Assertion of the German University," at the University of Freiburg; the address publicly announced Heidegger's alignment with the Nazi regime.[9]

Cassirer influenced Levinas's work, even though Cassirer is formally absent in citations. Cohen speculates that Levinas did not mention Cassirer in an attempt to separate his project from neo-Kantianism. Cassirer's insights are present within Levinas's understanding of "signification," which becomes apparent in "Signification and Sense," an essay in *Humanism of the Other* (xv). As stated, Levinas deeply regretted his role in the student farce. After Hitler came to power, Levinas understood what was at stake—Cassirer's emphasis on persons and culture lost in debate against Heidegger's contention that the human is secondary to Being.

Cohen recounts that Cassirer's humanism is present in Sartre's early work that outlined a "conscious philosophy" that sought freedom in a "self-reflective consciousness." Sartre's understanding of humanism consisted of responsibility for all persons (xvii–xviii); humanism was understood as a claim that invokes human solidarity. Sartre's position ultimately lingers between those of Cassirer and Heidegger with an emphasis on the tension between solidarity and individuality. After the Cassirer disagreement, it is not surprising that Heidegger later offered an antihumanism refutation of Sartre in a "Letter on Humanism" in 1946. Heidegger stated that he had nothing in common with Sartre and, implicitly, with Cassirer (xvi).

Cohen argued that Heidegger's disavowal of humanism was a natural extension of his project: the very existence of *Dasein* commences with thrownness (*geworfen*) into the world situated in "mood and temporality," which frames the "mortal embodiment" of *Dasein*. The temporal and thrown nature of *Dasein* accounts for the historicity (*Geschichtlichkeit*) of being human, which contrasts with "Sartre's monadic for-itself . . . [and] the vast cultural productions of Cassirer's *animal symbolicum*." Heidegger contended that "the task of the philosopher, the authentic human being, is neither to project meaning existentially nor to re-present meaning intellectually, which tasks are 'mere willing,' 'domination,' and 'decadence,' but rather to hearken attentively to the meaning that is given by being." Being is the dwelling place of possibilities illuminated by *Dasein* in acts of care and responsibility. Signification of life emerges from and within Being alone, which constitutes the fundamental undertaking of *Dasein*. For Heidegger, the human being plays a secondary role to Being, functioning as a servant, a "mouthpiece" or the "guardian" of Being (xix–xxi). Cassirer rejected the assumption that the human being rests in the shadow of Being. For Cassirer, essential dignity associated with humanism was not present in Heidegger's project. Cohen, in summarizing Cassirer's perspective, writes, "Humanity's freedom is sacrificed on the altar of historical being" (xxiii). Cohen cogently illuminates Cassirer's conception of humanity as the primary reason for his opposition to Heidegger.

Cohen clarified by differentiating Cassirer's position as contrary to both Sartre's "for-itself" and Heidegger's Being. Cassirer, in contrast, embraced neither a mystical *Volksgeist* nor an inexplicable truth about civilization in its pluralism and universality. Cassirer interprets civilization more broadly than does Kant, not only in terms of reason, but more fundamentally in terms of "symbolic forms," including myth, art, language, religion, and science—viewing each as the free achievement of individuals in society. Unlike Sartre's narrow rationalist construction of a for-itself trapped in a monadic world of meaning or Heidegger's "ponderous naturalist ventriloquism," Cassirer understood that the human being could not escape human achievements and that they should liberate, not confine. Cohen stated that Cassirer's project embraced a philosophy of culture responsive to diversity within the human community, while Heidegger's conception of Being was propelled by an "arrogant and irresponsible . . . romantic naturalism" (xxiii–xv). Cohen contended that Levinas's project is responsive to and distinctive from the work of both Cassirer and Heidegger.

Cohen asserted that Levinas's insights do not rest within culture or naturalism but within what Edith Wyschogrod (1930–2009) termed "ethical metaphysics" (xxvi). Levinas's project does not privilege Being over the human being's responsibility called forth by the face of another. Attentiveness to one's unique responsibility to and for the Other is a response to the call from the Other. Levinas's first philosophy is an ethical imperative; it is a "humanism of the Other" that takes one to an ethical echo that has primordial roots (xxvii)—"I am my brother's keeper." Levinas agrees with Cassirer that ethics has an anthropological base; however, Levinas's ethical echo does not permit one to equate ethics with Cassirer's notion of "symbol." Levinas unites ethics with a priori "signification." He registered disagreements with Cassirer, but time revealed that he was fundamentally more at odds with Heidegger. Levinas does not abide by Heidegger's underscoring of the "voice of being"; for Levinas, ethical responsibility emerges in the face-to-face meeting of persons, not via an encounter with Being.

Levinas, according to Cohen, witnesses to an ethical imperative signified by the face of the Other, which moves one into an immemorial burden of obligation and responsibility for a particular Other. This call is in opposition to Heidegger's "'ownmost' (*eigentlich*) character or individuating 'mineness' (*Jemeinigkeit*) of being-toward-death" (xxxiii). Instead, Levinas's project rests in vulnerability and suffering for the Other (xxiii). Cohen emphasized that suffering and burden for the Other are integral to Levinas's metaphysics of ethics. He stated,

"Levinas is fond of quoting Rabbi Israel Salanter, the nineteenth-century Eastern European rabbi known for his zealous commitment to ethical self-examination and self-improvement: 'The other's material needs are my spiritual needs.' The first body is the body of the other, from whom my own embodiment . . . takes on its significance as moral compassion" (xxxiv). For Levinas, the origin of human meaning rests in concrete responsibility for the Other—the commission of responsibility is never complete, not even at the point of death. For Levinas, it is not culture or Being but our obligation to the Other that shapes his unconventional understanding of humanism. Levinas's *Humanism of the Other* explicates the vitality of the human face that directs us to ethical obligations. When we miss and/or eclipse the face of the Other, we fail to attend to an audio ethic—the repeated call to enact ethical responsibility as our brother's keeper.

Humanism: Otherwise Than Convention

Cohen and this author contend that *Humanism of the Other* is a continuing response to the 1929 Conference at Davos centered on Levinas's dismissive responses to Cassirer. In *Humanism of the Other*, we witness the power of the Other in the initiation of an ethical turn that commands the "I" to shift from an ethics of optics to an audio ethic that offers an unending echo that demands personal responsibility.

Levinas's unconventional conception of humanism does not commence with the communicative agent or "originative I."[10] *Humanism of the Other* begins with Levinas's admission that the term *humanism* has been legitimately called into question. Levinas's inquiry incorporates an alternative perspective: a humanism that inaugurates with the Other and moves the "I" into ethical responsibility that attends and responds to an immemorial ethical echo. The movement from the face of the Other to an ethical echo assumes the importance of "proximity" framed by an "impersonal" engagement with the Other. The "derivative I" finds identity in obligation to the Other in an urgency to live with a sense of uprightness that announces "here I am" for the Other.[11]

In *Humanism of the Other*, Levinas explains that in response to burden and obligation through acts of responsibility, one finds signification that dwells within an "embodied" and situated sense of meaning (16). Signification surrounds us; Levinas's conception of signification returns to the importance of culture, suggesting a partial kinship with Cassirer: "*Signification can not be inventoried in the interiority of thought.* The thought itself intervenes in the Culture through the verbal gesture of the body that precedes and surpasses it" (16). Although Levinas sides with Cassirer against Heidegger, he does not view signification as separate from the accesses that make an embedded life possible (20). For Levinas, the Other is "neither a cultural signification nor a simple given" (30); the fundamental phenomenon of ethical signification can only be introduced through the face of the Other.

Levinas recounts Plato's view of signification as preceding language. The anti-Platonic assumption of modern philosophy links signification with intellect and thought, which subordinates expression to knowledge and a world of optics. Anti-Platonists situate intellect as superior to a priori expression. Contemporary philosophy views the "face to face" as a "limit-abstraction," observing that the "intellect sighting the intelligible would itself stand on the being that the sighted only claims to illuminate" (*Humanism*, 19). Bergson emphasized that access to signification begins with a story lived long before one engages or perceives a given object; illumination transpires within history brought forth into perceptual attentiveness. Perception grounded in "multiplicity" permits us to learn from those who perceive differently and engage contrasting stories, which, as Levinas stated, permits a Frenchman to learn Chinese without dismissing perceptual differences as a mere mistake on the part of one or the Other. "Non-sense" is a series of significations without a "consciousness" gathered into an ensemble of meaning. One encounters what appears to be non-sense when one hears a language alien to one's own mother tongue. However, it is a sense of individual forms of signification that make learning another language possible. Sense does not originate in the ego; it provides signification for existence within which the ego dwells. For Levinas, sense can, however, become a "universal allergy" if tied to a unity that misses the power and importance of particularities that give rise to a multiplicity of meanings (26). Levinas understood that the only path to the universal is through the particularities of uniqueness. Levinas emphasized plurality of senses, not the universal alone.

Levinas's *Humanism of the Other* refers to the notion that thought moves toward the Other without returning to the selfsame as "work thought" (26). The generosity of thought toward the Other simultaneously requires ingratitude from the Other, which maintains separation and difference as one learns from the Other. Such learning does not impose the Same upon the Other. Levinas refers to this obligation to the Other as a departure without return. The communicative act of generosity toward the Other without return dwells within the heart of Levinasian ethics. Levinas states that gratitude is laden with responsibility. This gratuitous gesture toward the Other shapes signification for Levinas; it is a "liturgical orientation of the work" (28). This liturgy guides the long haul of a life and is resistant to immediate engagement nestled within undue proximity that becomes dependent upon reciprocity. Levinas articulates a liturgy of desire for the Other that eschews the demand for reciprocity and attends to a burden of unique and unending responsibility.

Levinas separates from Cassirer as he emphasizes the epiphany of the face of the Other as a signification no longer dependent on culture alone. One meets the nudity of the face as signification not dependent on culture. One meets the nudity of the face void of all cultural ornaments. The ego does not consciously decide to respond; the face demands rejoinder, calling forth desire for responsibility for the Other, an interminable requirement that cannot be quenched. The more responsible the ego, the more responsibility is called forth. For Levinas, "will" rests in the call of the Other originated in exteriority and in the anteriority of an ethical echo.

Levinas offers a dramatically different account from Cassirer's will in action. Levinas's conceptions of will lives within a servant's humility, not within the power of a communicative agent or an originative ego. Levinas discusses a consciousness, without a return to self and without a martyr's obligation of responsibility. This burden demands ethical work without compensation, trumping culture and aesthetics with signification of the face being an a priori morality that does not emerge from culture; however, this immemorial ethic permits one to judge a culture. Morality of ethical responsibility acts as "elevation" of the human; it propels one to a vaster moral height. This moral sense permits one to challenge cultural expansion that seeks to impose, such as colonialism or imperialism, which inevitably leads to exploitation and violence (36). If one does not start with culture but with a priori signification, then attentiveness to and for the Other commences with an immemorial call for ethical responsibility.

Levinas refers to the immemorial demand for ethical responsibility in *Humanism of the Other* as a call "before history." One listens to a "trace" of this call as one responds to the "epiphany" of the face of the Other (38). Levinas reminds us that the face is abstract; its "wonder" lies not in physicality but within an audio message that references/signals "I am my brother's keeper." The face is the "absolutely absent" that moves one to this audio ethical command (39). "The beyond whence comes the face signifies as the trace. . . . No memory could follow in the trace of this past. It is an immemorial past" (40). An ethical trace disturbs the world of everyday convention; it prompts signification of an immemorial past that charges us with an unquenchable desire for responsibility. Recognition of responsibility beyond the face of the Other awakens obligation for the Other with the "illeity" of "irreversibility" (41).

The face is a sign that directs one to a trace that reminds one of signification of an ever-so-ancient ethical call. The trace takes us to an immemorial past call of responsibility. Beyond the sign of the face of the Other is a trace that unites past, present, and future, resulting in transcendent change. It is not the Other, however, that changes me; it is the performative engagement of responsibility. There is illeity of presence, an irreversibility of responsibility; even death cannot silence the ethical call that originates with another. Responsibility lives in an illeity beyond all economies, cultures, calculations, and reciprocities. One hears the demands of an irreversible immemorial past as an ever-new voice that whispers an inextinguishable *ancienne* responsibility; this ethical performance dwells in a desire that has no kinship with "need" or totalization manifested in accumulation, self-possession, and the demand for reciprocity.

Levinas contends that without attention to an ethical trace we are vulnerable to ideology. The immemorial trace within the human face commands without precluding flexibility of response. Levinas uses this manner of thought to describe metaphysics as a death proclaimed only to embrace ideology in another form. An ethical trace of responsibility calls the human toward a human realm nourished by appreciation and gratitude. Just as a tourist can attempt to see too much and miss genuine wonder, a person inattentive to an ethical trace can miss the profound and burdensome sense of responsibility. Levinas contends that the notion of trace permits one to apprehend Kant's writing. Kant never traveled far from Königsberg, his native town; he did not have the impulse of a tourist. In Levinas's language, Kant attended to traces of profundity and responsibility united with wonder in the meeting of alterity; such attentiveness permits one to differentiate uniqueness from acquisitive engagement.

Levinas's humanism assumes that a trace of an immemorial ethical echo is in the face of the Other; this conception of humanism dwells within responsibility, not efficacy. His humanism embraces "passivity" that yields to the command of an originative echo that gives birth to a "derivative I." At such a point, a responsible "derivative I" is then held "hostage" by the Other, who demands enactment of this primordial sense of responsibility. A hostage held in responsibility discovers a re-framed sense of "interiority" that pushes a "derivative I" into ethical action: "The unutterable or incommunicable of interiority that cannot hold in a Said is a responsibility prior to freedom. The unspeakability of the unutterable is described by the preoriginality of responsibility for others, by a responsibility prior to all free engagement, before describing itself by its inability to appear in the *said*" (52). Levinas understands radical passivity of a call as the transforming guide of identity; such a transformation is not located within standards and social dictates but is rooted in responsiveness to an "anarchic situation of responsibility." This responsibility is an "axiologic bipolarity" that unites "freedom" and "non-freedom" and demands action propelled by ethical responsibility for the Other (53–55).

Humanism, for Levinas, is a responsibility ignited outside the scope of laws and cultural mores. This call and demand is without beginning, "more antique than the principle," and bears a noninterchangeable sense of obligation (54). Levinas does not begin with an egoistic position of modern humanism, and, at the same time, he simultaneously disagrees with modern antihumanism's failure to seek what is lost in history and in human order—"the trace of this pre-historic an-archic saying" (57). Levinas points to humanism carried forth by a "derivative I" beckoned by an ethical trace housed within a human face.

Levinas concurred with arguments against humanism that place the person at the originative forefront of action. He agreed that the "originative I" of the ego too often imposes a good upon another; such is the home of colonialism and totalitarianism. Levinas's conception of humanism places an ancient voice of ethical responsibility at the vanguard, with the human "I" constituted as a derivative consequence. Levinas offers human identity with "no place" to stand (59); the only guide is an ethical echo. No method or prescript can shape such an understanding of humanism. For Levinas, humanism attentive to the Other emerges from response and obligation that cannot be scripted. The humanism of a "derivative I" rejects ideology and listens to those who came before and those who will follow, each informed by an immemorial ethical echo.

Heidegger, according to Levinas, framed an antihumanism model. Heidegger leaves the inner world of the subject and "radicalizes Husserl's anti-psychologism," making the human a worker for the enhancement of Being. Both Heidegger and the social sciences turn toward "exteriority" as they seek answers. Humanism, in contrast, embraces the role and value of "interiority" in enacting learning from exteriority. Levinas's understanding of "interiority" is called forth by the face of the Other. The vulnerability of the face and one's ultimate submission to the ethical echo situate Levinas's view of "sincerity" in *Humanism of the Other* (64). Levinas's project commences with exteriority of the face that moves one to an ethical echo that reframes the interiority of the person into obligation and responsibility. Levinas offers a humanism of a "derivative I."

The interiority of this calling is without foundation and remains within a permanent sense of the Said; it is a trace of an ethical home demanding constant attentiveness. This ongoing and permanent echo outlines traces of an ethical home that contours the interiority of the person, which finds nourishment via posterior and anterior, and past and future, in responsible action. Levinas points to responsibility without escape. The "I" is called by an ethical echo that fosters an interiority that makes one a "hostage" of unending responsibility (68). This responsibility dwells within an ancient past and, when activated, "disturbs" interiority with "non-interchangeability" of responsibility.

Levinas's humanism is a response to an immemorial call that finds clarity of response in the interiority of the self, which fashions a "derivative I" that is called forth into performative action. Humanism otherwise than convention demands an "authenticity" grounded in "vulnerability" and manifested in "sincerity." Levinas's humanism that is otherwise than convention is without thickness of veneer; it calls forth ethical vulnerability as the core of "humanity" (68–69).

I now return to the Cassirer and Heidegger debate with assistance from Waite's thoughtful analysis of the Davos debate in "On Esotericism: Heidegger and/or Cassirer at Davos." Waite frames this event as a latter moment of ethical call in the life of Levinas. Waite announces the power of a human face and dangerous consequences that arise when it is eclipsed. In the debate there was a general point of agreement centered on ethics: Cassirer's undertaking moved ethics to a point of silence, and Heidegger's project "declared [that] ethics is impossible."[12] Waite considered the debate to be about a "postethical human subject" (604). Waite reminds the reader of the kinship among nihilism, fascism, and extreme relativism; Mussolini embraced Nietzsche, and Hans Vaihinger was "the leading neo-Kantian Nietzschean." In regard to Vaihinger's philosophy of the as-if, Waite wrote, "We *know* that relativism and fascism are ungrounded systems but we decide to act *as if* they were grounded, so that this very ungroundedness *in effect* becomes our ground" (606). Waite contends that the debate pushed ethics to a point of exotericism and esotericism (607–08).[13]

The Saying and the Said in Communication Ethics: An Ethical Parvenu

Waite claimed that Heidegger explicated an extreme relativism reminiscent of an *Alice in Wonderland* quality of not knowing what is up and what is down until experts articulate the standards. Levinas rejects esotericism and pronouncements discernible by experts. Heidegger won the debate as the world order was in Nazi turmoil—propelled by arrogance of "ethical imposition" on others. Waite's focus on ethics frames the final section of this chapter. Both Heidegger and Levinas ignored the face of Cassirer, eclipsing the Other. This action obliterated the possibility of attending to the practical origin of ethics. Disregarding the face of the Other misses the initial source of ethics. In the Heidegger and Cassirer exchange and the mocking performance of Levinas, we witness the eclipse of the face of the Other, which makes ethics impossible. The danger of the parvenu game rests with devastation of persons who hope for inclusion. The Said of domination obliterates the Saying of ethics as suggested by the following insights.

Ignoring/eclipsing the face of the Other.—Ignoring the face of the Other curtails the hope of ethics awakened by a human face. Leo Strauss, Cassirer's student, who completed his dissertation on Spinoza, stated that style, not content, won the day for Heidegger. With ethical grounding as unachievable, the only foundation was that of style (Waite, 617–18). Heidegger did not reject the ideas alone—he rejected the man, Cassirer. Ethics was vacant in Heidegger's philosophy and void of interpersonal engagement as he dismissively met Cassirer. Rejecting the face of the Other results in the impossibility of an ethics of responsibility. Levinas understood humanism as an inner world called out by the face of the Other. Such a perspective was in contrast to Heidegger's ignoring of the Other; the eclipse of the human face places ethics within the realm of nonsense. Levinas's humanism requires the presence of the face of the Other, which then moves one to an ethical echo. If one omits the presence of the Other, then the ethical passage toward responsibility remains dormant.

Forgoing access to an immemorial ethical echo.—The immemorial ethical echo is the fundamental counter to inattentiveness to the face of the Other—without an ethics of optics, an audio ethic goes unheard. Heidegger understood an era in which rationality and ethics were both under siege; persuasion rested with "eloquence and silence" transmitted via style. One witnessed performative action in operation: Cassirer acknowledged Heidegger, but Heidegger refused to utter Cassirer's name (624). In the debate between the two men, Cassirer actually attended to Kant and ethics, while Heidegger remained silent on the subject. Heidegger contended that Kant's first treatise, *Critique of Pure Reason*, undermined rationality and, consequently, any hope for a foundational ground of ethics. For Heidegger, Kant's general failure was not confronting his own "premises and conclusions." Specifically, through the *Critique of Pure Reason*, Kant threatened "Logic." Throughout the lecture, Heidegger undercut Cassirer with "*ad hominem*" criticisms, pointing to Cassirer's life as shallow and inauthentic in a thinly "veiled personal attack." Heidegger stressed the nothingness of *Dasein*, which throws the human back onto a "hardness of fate" (627–28). For Heidegger, this thrownness unmasks those unwilling to live authentic lives.

Unrealized responsibility.—Obligation fails to commence when the face of the Other goes unacknowledged, when one misses the call and burden. On the point of Heidegger's thrownness and "hardness of fate," Cassirer responded, "Little is to be accomplished through arguments that are purely logical" (627). Heidegger understood the limits of the rational demonstrated in personal attacks on Cassirer; Heidegger tricked Cassirer into unknowingly applauding his argument. Waite contends that Cassirer never understood the nature of Heidegger's attack on him. Cassirer even continued the debate in further essays and in his 1931 review of Heidegger's *Kant and the Problem of Metaphysics* and, additionally, in Cassirer's third and fourth volumes of his *Philosophy of Symbolic Forms.* Sadly, Cassirer incorporated some of Heidegger's phrases into his own work without knowledge of the depth of Heidegger's dismissive critique. Waite writes, "Cassirer's exoteric 'die *Sprache*' (*the* language) should never be confused with the later Heidegger's exo/esoteric '*die Sprache spricht*' (language speaks), or with the Lacanian *ça parle*. The last word, the checkmate, of the Davos transcript is Heidegger's. He turns away from Cassirer to look into the eyes of an audience already won over to him, whether it knew it or not" (630). Heidegger's final dismissive gesture of turning away from Cassirer defines the relationship between Heidegger and Cassirer in a way contrary to a humanistic awakening of a "derivative I" pointed to by Levinas.

Fixation on an "originative I."—Self-centered fascination trumps responsibility for the Other when no human face redirects one's phenomenological and ethical attention. Waite argues that Heidegger enjoyed "forensic success," using a silent eloquence that laid a path of ad hominem attacks (632). Heidegger refused to debate Cassirer again; however, he did invite him to speak at Freiburg in April 1932 before the Academic-Literary Society on "The Problem of Jean-Jacques Rousseau." Cassirer once again failed to understand the game he had entered with Heidegger. Heidegger invited Cassirer into an evil social game carried forth by social oppressors who preyed on those who wanted to be accepted and then found continual exclusion at the last moment—such is the life of a parvenu. This deceitful social game of potential inclusion requires those in power continually to invite back the person they seek to reject. Heidegger tempted Cassirer with a visit to his campus while continuing an unending contempt for his work. Thus Waite ends discussion of Heidegger and Cassirer: "In 1929 Davos, Ernst Cassirer had met his enemy face to face—absolutely clueless about how to combat him effectively" (635). Levinas witnessed evil in action: a social game of invitation and rejection that keeps the parvenu on the outside wanting desperately to be included. However, the debate announced the phenomenological power of a human face, which long after the events at Davos concluded continued to call Levinas to responsibility.

Levinas's humanism and the Other require an otherwise than conventional return to the notion of the parvenu. Conventionally, the parvenu is propelled by an eternal hope of affirmation and acceptance from a powerful social group that insincerely invites one to join, only to remind the other that he/she forever falls short of the needed standard for inclusion.[14]

The persistence of the face.—The call of the face does not cease—the power of its appeal continues long after a given meeting. Levinas, years later, continued to hear an ethical echo that originated from a face ignored; Levinas's performative caricature of Cassirer continued to remind him of his lack of ethical action. Levinas's eventual recognition of Cassirer's face moved him from being a spectator in a social game that ignored the face of the Other to having an unending ethical obligation—to assume that one's responsibility has concluded invites collapse into an abyss of complacent self-righteousness. Levinas avers that the face holds one ethically hostage, creating what I term an *ethical parvenu* who is unable to relieve the self of ethical obligation and never achieves ethical perfection or conclusion.

The heart of Levinas's project of ethics finds one point of origin in the donning of a flowing white wig as he made fun of a man who was unable to comprehend that he was a parvenu participant in a wicked social game of invitation and exclusion. Heidegger knew the rules of this parvenu game well. Levinas, unfortunately, participated in that game at Davos, yet we witness the enduring presence of the face of Cassirer and his calling forth of responsibility. The face of Cassirer at Davos remained with Levinas for a lifetime. Levinas's ethics project reminds us to attend to an ongoing and persistent whisper that originates with acknowledgment of the face of the Other. Levinas's *Humanism of the Other* is an invitation into an unending obligation to and for the Other, not in a self-righteous manner, but as an ethical parvenu. Just as the parvenu cannot fulfill the wish of genuine inclusion, a person called to responsibility has no final juncture of conclusion. It is the Said of the performances at Davos that pointed to a trace of an ethical Saying that arises in an eventual return to the face of the Other. Levinas did attend to Cassirer's face. In an ethical Saying housed within the Said, a trace of responsibility began to shape a communication ethic of obligation to and for the Other without end; such is the communicative life of an ethical parvenu. The ethical parvenu implements communication ethics from the vantage point of Levinas, shaping a life of unending obligation.

CHAPTER 9

Heidegger's Rectorate Address: Being as Mistaken Direction

Heidegger does not only sum up a whole evolution of Western philosophy. He exalts it by showing in the most pathetic way its antireligious essence become a religion in reverse. The lucid sobriety of those who call themselves friends of truth and enemies of opinion would then have a mysterious prolongation! In Heidegger atheism is a paganism, the presocratic texts anti-Scriptures. Heidegger shows in what intoxication the lucid sobriety of philosophers is steeped.   —Emmanuel Levinas, *Collected Philosophical Papers*

Contemplation that enables one to return to the things themselves which come before our self-knowledge or self behavior is a natural position. It becomes through this position that people transcend their physical body. —Annette M. Holba, *Transformative Leisure: A Philosophy of Communication*

Emmanuel Levinas's insights are otherwise than Being in that he situates "ethics as first philosophy." From the perspective of Levinas's project, Heidegger's rector address witnesses to the necessity of Levinas's ethical undertaking. Levinas counters Heidegger's philosophical worldview, which is otherwise than an immemorial call to ethics and responsibility to and for the Other. Heidegger's address offers an example of the limits of a worldview situated within supreme confidence; Heidegger's rector's address commences and concludes with an "originative I."

Introduction

Heidegger's famous speech, delivered on May 27, 1933, at the University of Freiburg, continues to generate controversy. The speech displays Heidegger's hope of influencing the Third Reich with his ideas. For many, the address is an announcement of Heidegger's commitment to an inexcusable political expression.[1] Additionally, Heidegger never offered an apology for the speech or for his membership in the Nazi Party.

I examine Heidegger's rector speech of 1933 through Heidegger's voice and that of Levinas. I situate the 1933 address between two Heideggerian responsive bookends: his 1966/1976 interview in *Der Spiegel* and his 1945 reflection upon the address. In the first section, "*Der Spiegel* Interview," I turn to Heidegger's own response to his address. This material provides interpretive insight into the second section, "The Rector Speech and Heidegger's 1945 Response," which examines the talk along with Heidegger's own responses to the speech. I then explore Levinas's understanding of Heidegger's discourse and his commitments in "Continuing Responses and Levinas's Alternative"; this section includes the insights of other Levinasian scholars as well. The essay concludes with reflections on communication ethics and mistaken paths in "The Saying and the Said in Communication Ethics: Direction without Clarity or Assurance."

On the one hand, Heidegger's rector address was, at best, his amateurish effort to influence the direction of the Third Reich. On the other hand, it was an affirmation of a mistaken direction that inflicted an ethical blight on the West. Where Heidegger seeks to participate with the demands of Being, Levinas counters with two fundamental admissions. The face of the Other matters, and an immemorial command to care for the Other defines the human task.

Der Spiegel *Interview*

Before examining the rector address, I turn to Heidegger's interview in *Der Spiegel*, a weekly magazine published in Hamburg, Germany. This preeminent newsmagazine is among the most circulated publications in Europe with a distribution of over one million copies per issue. *Der Spiegel* has a long history of intellectual significance; since its first publication in Hanover, on January 4, 1947, the newsmagazine has interviewed a number of major political figures, authors, and scholars. Throughout the interview Heidegger talks without a hint of apology. The 1966/1976 interview transpired thirty-three years after the actual delivery of his 1933 University of Freiburg address and ten years before his death in 1976.

In 1966 Heidegger granted an interview to *Der Spiegel* conducted by Rudolf Augstein and Georg Wolff. Heidegger's request was that the press let the interview go unpublished during his lifetime; five days after Heidegger's death the magazine published the interview on May 26, 1976, under the title "Only a God Can Save Us." Much of the interview centers on Heidegger's short and infamous stint as rector of the University of Freiburg (1933–1934) during the early reign of the Nazis.[2] This document serves as a last statement concerning the most controversial interval in Heidegger's intellectual and personal life. The interview begins with the assertion that Heidegger's rector period of only ten months is so historically formidable that it "overshadowed" his philosophical work in the judgment of many.[3]

In *Der Spiegel*'s interview, Heidegger asserted his lack of political activity. Friends and colleagues convinced him to take the rectorship; they wanted to retain integrity in German academic life. This desire influenced his decision to accept the position, following his friend Wilhelm von Möllendorf (1887–1944), professor of anatomy, who was rector on April 15, 1932, and removed from office within two weeks. The reason for Möllendorf's release involved refusal to display a poster that stated, "Jews unwelcome here." The minister of culture of Baden fired Möllendorf; this decision left the university without an authority committed to scholarship.[4] After his dismissal Möllendorf encouraged Heidegger to become the next rector. Heidegger's defense for accepting the post was the objective of assisting the university with *thinking* that moved beyond the "technical organization of universities and faculties" ("Only a God," 47). Heidegger's rector speech objective was announcement of public intellectual ambition made evident in his first lecture at the University of Freiburg on July 24, 1929—"What Is Metaphysics?" Heidegger contended that the rector speech was a continuing effort to link academic freedom and "negative freedom" with a promise to preserve "reflection and meditation" as fundamental to scientific inquiry. Heidegger desired even greater reflection and meditation in the "rooting of the sciences in their essential ground."

However, when Heidegger commented on his statement in the lecture that centered on the "greatness and glory of this new era," his response was parsimonious: "Yes, I was also convinced of it." Heidegger argued that twenty-two political parties could not contend with the national problem of unemployment within Germany in the 1930s; he asserted that that historical moment demanded a pragmatic response—a "national" and "social attitude" capable of uniting the entire country. Concern about technical divisions and the limits of negative freedom undergirded Heidegger's rector speech, "The Self-Assertion of the German University." Heidegger sought to counter the "politicizing of science." The university had to renew itself with Heidegger's proposed three pillars of rebirth: "service by labor," "service by arms," and "service by knowledge" (47–49). The National Socialists affirmed all but the third of his suggested pillars.[5]

In 1933 a Heideggerian quote in a local student newspaper read, "Let not doctrines and ideas be the rules of your Being. The Führer, himself and he alone, is today and for the future German actuality and its law" ("Only a God," 49). Heidegger acknowledged in the interview that he knew he would have to make compromises as he assumed the position of rector. Then he stated, "The sentences you quote I would no longer write today. Such things, as that, I ceased saying by 1934" (49). In 1933, however, he conceived of the Third Reich as offering a constructive reassertion of the country. As the interview continued, Heidegger refuted accusations of participation and sanctioning of Hitler's Youth Movement, who organized burnings of books by Jewish authors removed from the library (50). Heidegger asserted that in his role of rector he never encouraged such action. Additionally, he refuted the claim that he lost friendships with Jaspers (who had a Jewish wife) and with Husserl (the Jewish predecessor of the philosophy chair). In *Being and Time* Heidegger recorded a dedication to Husserl in the front matter, but in the fifth edition, published in 1941, Heidegger relegated his thanks to Husserl to page thirty-eight of the text.[6] Heidegger also denied that he had refused Husserl access to the university during his rectorship. When confronted with the 1938 fact that he did not attend Husserl's funeral, Heidegger attributed his action to "human failure" (52).[7]

Heidegger resigned as rector in 1934. In the interview Heidegger offered the following description of his resignation:

One day I was called to Karlsruhe where the Minister, through one of his Councillors, demanded, in the presence of the Student District Leader, that I replace the deans of the legal and medical faculties with other colleagues who were acceptable to the Party. I refused this request and offered my resignation from the rectorate if the Minister insisted on his demand. That's just what happened. . . . While the national and international press commented on my assumption of the rectorate in the most diversified fashion, not a word was said about my resignation. (52)

After the resignation, Heidegger limited his work to philosophy, focusing on Friedrich Hölderlin (1770–1843) and Nietzsche with what he affirmed was an ongoing "confrontation with National Socialism" (53).[8] The Schutzstaffel Security Service, the SS, scrutinized his actions and his Hölderlin lecture, which was "maliciously attacked in the review of the Hitler Youth Movement, *Wille und Macht.*" Then, in the summer of 1944, there was a mandate for academics to join the front, dividing scholars into three groups: (1) "completely expendable," (2) "half-expendable," and (3) "not expendable." German authorities placed Heidegger in the first group and sent him to do "manual labor on the Rhine" in 1944 ("Only a God," 54).

Heidegger also commented on his philosophizing about technology; he contended that as early as 1935 he was concerned about technicity; he left out such comments in his rector speech due to his audience's inability to engage "proper understanding." Heidegger states that technicity is not a tool; however, it seeks power over the human. Technicity lives wherever tasks or relationships are "merely technical ones" (55–56). Heidegger countered technicity with poetry and thinking. He then offered a disturbing statement: "Only a god can save us [via] . . . thinking and poetizing [that] prepare[s] a readiness for the appearance of a god . . . in view of the absent god we are in a state of decline" (57). The alternative to technicity is waiting with a sense of readiness. Creative waiting counters the advance of technicity. Planetary technicity is "unthought" that dominates action (59–60). Heidegger had not worked out all the coordinates related to technicity, but he called attention to two separate essays: "What Is Called Thinking" (1954) and "The Principle of Identity" (1957).[9] In the latter essay Heidegger contended that the task of meeting the challenges of technicity is largely a German responsibility, given the German language's special kinship with the Greek language—the origin of technicity. The key to thinking, for Heidegger, is connection with the original sense of thought—Greek culture and language. Heidegger found no answers in modern "poetry" and contemporary "art," which he considered more of a "cultural business" than an opening of thinking ("Only a God," 65). Heidegger lamented that there was no longer a great thinker able to restrain the power of technicity. Heidegger longed for a thinker capable of moving the world with big thoughts. The contention of this chapter is that Heidegger viewed himself as such a thinker, which made him vulnerable to the concept of a führer and to the Nazis, whom he thought he could influence.[10]

Der Spiegel's interview of 1966/1976 offers a context for understanding Heidegger's 1933 inaugural rector address. The interview continues to fuel fury about the address. Contention has centered on Heidegger's stressing the fundamental importance of German thought and language, underscoring the necessity of a great thinker, and outlining the essential task of uniting German culture and thinking to rectify the malaise of the prewar historical epoch. Such change, he asserted, made compromise inevitable. Interpretive evidence from the interview underscores Heidegger's provinciality (which he denied) and his waiting posture that yearned for the right person with the correct thoughts. His comments give credence to a hermeneutic suspicion tied to his infamous rector speech.

The Rector Speech and Heidegger's 1945 Response

Heidegger's rector speech, "The Self-Assertion of the German University," delivered on May 5, 1933, at the University of Freiburg, continues to generate controversy after his short stay in leadership, from 1933 until 1934.[11] As the translator of the address, Karsten Harries states that "Heidegger's thinking is a thinking 'on the way.'"[12] He deliberates in stages that illustrate an opening for more profound thinking. Hermann Heidegger, Heidegger's son, in his preface to the English translation, calls the reader's attention to several facts about the speech subsequent to its delivery in 1933. First, the Nationalsozialistische Deutsche Arbeiterpartei (National Socialist German Workers' Party, or Nazi Party) withdrew the rector address from the public after Heidegger's resignation;

second, after 1945, many words such as "National Socialism," "National Socialist," "Führer," "Chancellor of the Reich," and "Hitler" were falsely attributed to the speech; third, Heidegger admitted to being caught up in the mood of the moment, even as he prohibited book burnings and stopped the "posting of the 'Jew Notice'"; and, fourth and finally, it is important to examine Heidegger's retrospective essay written after the collapse of the National Socialist regime in 1945, which he titled "The Rectorate 1933/1934—Facts and Thoughts." Having contextualized Heidegger's 1933 address with later reflections, I now turn to the famous speech itself.

Heidegger begins his rector speech by stating that leaders in Germany must attend to an "unyielding spiritual mission that forces the fate of the German people to bear the stamp of its history." Heidegger brought together the words "self-governance" and "self-examination" in an effort to lead a university to "self-assertion" that prepares a marriage of science and "German fate" (Heidegger, Harries, and Heidegger, 470–71). Heidegger asserted that all science has a philosophical foundation. He then connected the Greek conception of science to the privilege of "pure contemplation"; he underscored the viability of theory, disregarding concern for practice and its implications. This perspective contrasts with the modern concern with utility and "progress" (472–73). The loss of pure contemplation required, according to Heidegger, a return to the insights of early Greek life: "Only if we resolutely submit to this distant command to recapture the greatness of the beginning, will science become the innermost necessity of our being (*Dasein*)" (473). Attending to the importance of pure contemplation could awaken spiritual vision in the people. Such action permits "our ownmost being (*Dasein*) itself [to stand] before a great transformation," allowing questions to emerge that prevent the rigid specialization of the sciences. Such an awakening authorizes an answer to the modern problem outlined by Nietzsche's statement "God is dead," which suggests that the dismissal of the "spiritual" results from an "inescapable" accumulation of facts. Returning to Greek origins acknowledges "questioning" about "uncertainty" within a spiritual world (474). Heidegger stated, "Only a spiritual world gives the people the assurance of greatness." It is within this Greek infusion of the spirit of Being that Heidegger sought to situate the German university; today, the following Heideggerian quote from his speech generates immediate alarm:

For what is decisive if one is to lead is not just that one walk ahead of others, but that one have the strength to be able to walk alone, not out of obstinacy and a craving for power, but empowered by the deepest vocation and broadest obligation. Such strength binds to what is essential, selects the best, and awakens the genuine following (*Gefolgschaft*) of those who are of a new mind. But there is no need to first awaken this following. Germany's student body is on the march. And *whom* it seeks are those leaders through whom it wills to so elevate its own vocation that it becomes a grounded, knowing truth, and to place it into the clarity of interpretive and effective word and work. (475)

The spirit of Heidegger's assertions garnered significance from their location and his statement that the ideas were already "on the march."

Heidegger referred to the importance of students organizing themselves—"to give the law to oneself is the highest freedom." Additionally, Heidegger made his famous gesture toward banishing "academic freedom," which ignored the heritage of the German university as the home to academic freedom. This academic freedom included two primary freedoms: *Lehrfreiheit*, freedom for teachers while teaching; and *Lernfreiheit*, freedom for students while learning. His contention claimed that academic freedom was not genuine and found identity only in the "negative." Heidegger argued that we must listen to the German student who teaches us about a freedom by choosing to impose law on himself/herself. This bounding of oneself to the law and labor of the community is the first act of a "Labor Service" (475–76).

The second bond that Heidegger pronounced was "the honor and destiny of the nation," which requires a readiness to defend and, if necessary "to give all," with "the entire being (*Dasein*) of the student shaped by '*Armed Service*.'" For Heidegger, this second bond required students to "rise to the highest clarity" in their disciplines while integrating an understanding of the state. This meeting of will and clarity of understanding must consistently be "preserved as battle" (476, 479).

The third bond of the student body was unique to Heidegger's project, connecting students to an understanding of the beginning of the Greek spirit, which has the ability to make life before us anew. Heidegger analyzed a dull understanding of "Knowledge Service"; he demanded that people resist the ultimatum of knowledge to serve professions. Application of knowledge is not central; rather, the key is a questioning, courageous spirit that learns when surrounded by uncertainty without subordinating thinking to a given outcome. Heidegger called for questioning as "we submit to the distant command of the beginning or our spiritual-historical being (*Dasein*)." Students and faculty "must be *seized* and *remain* seized by the concept of science." The "faculty" must be committed to shaping the insights and power of *Dasein* into the "spiritual world of the people." Additionally, the "specialty" of each faculty member must tear down artificial boundaries of disciplines and professions and give rise to a commitment to a "primordial essence of science" that centers on a questioning that gives birth to a conception of knowledge understood by the Greeks. Heidegger asserted that one could not envisage such an insight in one semester of study, or even one century; he considered this spirit-filled contemplative obligation to be the central and ongoing task of a German university (477–78).

Heidegger concluded his call to thinking within Greek origins with a pledge to shelter the heart of learning and knowledge, which demands courage to restrain oneself in a community of freedom. Restraint through questioning embraces self-limits and a self-examination that yield a new Greek beginning within the German university. To fail to enact Greek questioning assures a spiritual collapse of the West and a demise of culture that bequeaths only "confusion and lets it suffocate in madness." Heidegger left his audience with an exhortation—"Whether this will happen or not depends alone on whether or not we, as a historical-spiritual people, still and once again will ourselves. Every individual *participates* in this decision, even he, and indeed especially he, who evades it" (480). Heidegger summoned students, faculty, and the university community to an exclusive mission in a unique moment in German history marked by Hitler's claim to power. Heidegger announced that the students must will themselves into a type and character of their own German future. His final word returned to the importance of "thoughtfulness" and the necessity of reenacting "ancient Greek wisdom" via thinking and questioning within the halls of the German university (480).

Heidegger's response, written in 1945, "The Rectorate 1933/34: Facts and Thoughts," was a retort to his own rectorate address. His 1945 rejoinder was twice as long as the original 1933 speech. Soon after the Nazi Socialist regime lost power in 1945, Heidegger composed comments on his rector address. Heidegger emphasized four major tropes in his 1945 response: his own administrative academic naiveté, the hope of political compromise, his rejection of party demands, and the party's rejection of him and his work.

Heidegger entered the rectorship empowered by Greek philosophy, not practical experience in political administration. In reflection Heidegger emphasized that his 1933 rector address sought to charge the university with the responsibility of embracing the power of Greek thinking and knowledge, to connect his project to German soil, and to warn about the deterioration of the West propelled by a lack of genuine thinking.

Heidegger's 1945 remarks, first published in France in 1982, underscored the needed task of the German university—to engage Greek thinking and questioning. Only such a conceptual move could activate a genuine science that would jettison the "technical organization of universities and faculties." Heidegger asserted that he had little contact with political parties; he was convinced to run for the office of rectorate by the two previous rectors—Möllendorf and canon Joseph Sauer; each served only one year in that capacity. Others persuaded Heidegger that his thought might breathe new life into the German university through his understanding of early Greek contemplative life. Heidegger announced such a perspective in 1929 as he explored "What Is Metaphysics." The 1933 address had scholarly connections to the corpus of his work; he contended that the "the roots of the sciences in their essential ground have withered." Addressing this slippage was the "most pressing concern" of the German university, according to Heidegger (Heidegger, Harries, and Heidegger, 482).

By 1933, translations of Heidegger's "What Is Metaphysics" appeared in French, Spanish, Italian, and Japanese. He declared that knowledge rooted in thinking must found anew the university in a "primordial manner." Heidegger acknowledged, in 1933, that although the public was aware of his thoughts on problems facing the German university, it was the inaugural address that called for thinking objectives that many considered "impossible." The reaction to Heidegger's rector address united both the old and new guard in opposition to him; they sought to "get rid of me [Heidegger]." Heidegger's project to recover the "primordial" Greek thinking as a science evoked a "no" from both timeworn and new constituencies within the German university (482–83).

Heidegger accepted his rector mission as a conceptually safer course than remaining on the sidelines. He believed that the West had become a mirror of Nietzsche's God-is-dead assertion, which was an admission of the loss of an "effective force in history." Heidegger sensed within the Nazi movement a chance to reclaim a spirit of thinking and creative engagement if the movement was tempered. Heidegger asked, "What would have happened and what would have been prevented, had, around 1933, all capable forces aroused themselves and joined in secret in order to gradually purify and moderate the 'movement' that had come to power?" In Heidegger's words he assumed the rectorship with the hope of steering a creative path within the university and the West, which urged him to serve in spite of his wariness of "party functionaries" of the Third Reich (485–86).

Heidegger reiterated the emphases in his address: (1) the prominence of grounding creative thought within science; (2) linking science to a Greek view of thinking that has no end or final goal; (3) the preservation of the Greek heritage of thinking; and (4) an alignment of beginning Greek culture with Germany. He stated that each of these objectives rejected the "'political science' proclaimed by National Socialism," which he termed a "cruder version" of Nietzsche. For Heidegger, the main cause of misunderstanding of his address surrounded the title, "The Self-Assertion of the German University," and the German political sciences. Heidegger explained that confusion arose from use of the word "battle," which he tied to Heraclitus (487–89).[13] Battle, understood philosophically, announces "reciprocal recognition" of "setting-apart" of opposing parties during a confrontation in the pursuit of clarity, which "preserves" the essence of Being via the demand for reflection. Contending deliberation would permit the German university to carry "itself, by its own strength, unto its essential ground, a ground accessible only to the knowing that it cultivates." Grounding battle in reflection, not in politics, nourishes the essence of the university. Heidegger contended that those unable to trace his ideas to Greek thought and Heraclitus misunderstood his position (Heidegger, Harries, and Heidegger, 489–90).

The reaction to the rector speech, according to Heidegger, from the vantage point of National Socialist Party officials, was that the address was unacceptable. Heidegger learned this information from minister Otto Wacker, Baden's minister for education, culture, and justice, at a party banquet in the "Kopf." The reaction was negative for three reasons: one, the speech "circumvented" the programmatic direction of the party; two, the speech failed to ground ideas in race; and, three, the speech rejected the party view of "political science." In addition, there was irritation that Heidegger had positively singled out the previous rector, Sauer, and verbally credited his foundational scholarly commitments in education. This negative party reaction accompanied Heidegger's first official act as rector; he prohibited the posting of the "Jew Notice." The reaction of the ministry announced incompatibility between Heidegger's ideas and the German university. Additionally, his refusal to post the "Jew Notice" mobilized the Reich Student Leadership. Eight days after his refusal to post the notice, Heidegger experienced pressure from SA (Sturmabteilung) leadership, which later became the SS; they insisted that he post the notices. The SA's demand announced adherence to a narrow party line that Heidegger wanted to eliminate from the university. Heidegger stated that he had joined the party to protect the university; his error was political innocence (491–93). Heidegger stated that he did not engage in any decision making for or with the Nazi Party, which led to suspicion about him.

Heidegger was a novice player in a high-level academic office. His address was more like a lecture; not one of his colleagues commented on the rector address upon its conclusion; it was as if Heidegger had "spoken into the wind" (493). While lecturing at the University of Heidelberg during the summer of 1933, Heidegger discovered that an increasing number of "empty" faculty chairs gave opportunity for National Socialist Party members to rise to the rank of dean. Heidegger attempted to ward off National Socialist appointments by proposing a change in the university constitution that would make "decanal appointments in such a way that the essence of the faculties and the unity of the university could be saved." The proposed change in the university's constitution minimized appointments based on personal preference and lessened the Nazi transformation of the university (494).

Heidegger began to understand the gravity of the situation at the German university even more intensively when he attended a retreat with faculty at the "Todtnauberg Camp" in the winter semester of

1933/1934. At that gathering Heidegger provided another speech that he hoped would clarify his earlier rector address. However, as the students and faculty assembled to listen, uninvited guests overran them—the Nazis came to hear Heidegger. Heidegger had to accept the interruptions; Heidegger argued that they were there to destroy the camp. From that moment onward, the pressure from the party, faculty, and students to hire deans from the party catapulted. During the 1933 winter semester, Heidegger received an order from the ministerial counselor to relieve Möllendorf and Erik Wolf of their posts. Heidegger refused and resigned on April 12, 1934. Additionally, those opposed to National Socialism were willing to conspire with the ministry's effort to push Heidegger out of office. The minister contended that Heidegger did not have a philosophy compatible with the National Socialist Party and wanted his resignation to occur without fanfare. Heidegger discovered limits to his ability to shape conversation within the Nazi movement. His rectorate objective was to stop movement toward technicity in education. The only hope, according to Heidegger, was to assist in recognition of the "nihilism" of the moment and the necessity of "self-affirmation" as the only prudent form of response (496, 498).

Suspicions voiced against Heidegger degenerated into public insults, displayed in Ernst Krieck's journal *Volk im Werden* and the Hitler Youth's journal *Wille und Macht*. Heidegger stated that his rector address became a popular target of polemics in the Camps for Teachers. Heidegger contended that his treatment was "disgusting"; he and his work were held in disdain. Eventually party scrutiny entered his classroom in the summer 1937 semester with Dr. Hancke, a former student in Heidegger's winter 1936–1937 course, enlisted as an informer; Hancke eventually confessed that he was working for Dr. Scheel of the Security Service. There was also a comment that Heidegger was in league with members of the Jesuits and the Franciscans, who continued to attend his lectures. The Gestapo was concerned about the Catholic members of Heidegger's seminar and his openness to non-Aryans. Heidegger wrote, "Since 1938 it was forbidden to mention my name in newspapers and journals; similarly it was forbidden to review my writings." The German government subsequently barred Heidegger from major international conferences. Heidegger understood German history as a "catastrophe" that "has engulfed us" (499–502).

He discovered that his response was deemed inadequate by numerous, if not all, constituencies within the university.

Heidegger's failed address announced both administrative inexperience and the determined nature of Nazi domination of the academy. Heidegger courted disaster in his effort to compromise, and his resignation was an act considered to be both too little and too late. According to Heidegger, he endured continuing rejection; he found that government party agencies and a university community were unwilling to join him in reframing the academy in a "primordial manner" (481). Heidegger compromised himself with the hope of influence; instead, he gathered rejection from university and party officials.

Continuing Responses and Levinas's Alternative

Critical scholarship on Heidegger continues, with one of his principal critics suggesting that "the radically discriminatory and racist principles upon which Heidegger's work rests demand a complete re-evaluation of the status of that work. It is not, in its foundations, a philosophy, but rather an attempt to destroy philosophy."[14] The following essays evoke the sentiment of unmasking Heidegger's Nazi connections.

For instance, Fred Dallmayr, in "Postmetaphysics and Democracy," establishes a critical tone about Heidegger's participation with the Nazi regime, reminding readers of a "militant populism" employed by Heidegger in his rector rhetoric that emphasized "People-as-One" as he stressed one party and one leader. The weight given to "national resurgence" through "labor," "military training," and "learning" framed a populism that "shipwrecked" Heidegger's rectorship.[15] Dallmayr suggests that events of 1933 and 1934 eventually led Heidegger to his famous *Kehre*, or turn, which countered "technical business" or what Heidegger called "machination" (120–21). Dallmayr continues, "According to Heidegger, ideologies are an outgrowth of modern metaphysics and as such partake in, and even solidify, the relentless sway of machination . . . [thinking] is from the very beginning replaced by machination or managerial business (*Betrieb*)" (121). However, Heidegger's attraction to the Greeks and a world tied to the local was closely associated with the Nazi story that rejected modernity and uplifted the local machinelike characteristics of the Nazis.

Dallmayr's questioning of Heidegger continues in Tom Rockmore's essay, "Philosophical Literature and Intellectual Responsibility."[16] Rockmore states that philosophers often lack the ability to discern between "truth and falsity," which he argued is manifested in the case of Heidegger (119). Rockmore contends that the stature of Heidegger's philosophical work makes his participation with Nazism very troubling. Additionally, Heidegger seems to have adopted a Nazism that never existed, except in his own mind. In his essay "Heidegger after Farías," Rockmore refers to Victor Farías's *Heidegger and Nazism* as a deconstruction of Heidegger that explicates Heidegger's Nazism as an extension of *Being and Time* and emphasizes that Heidegger never refuted National Socialism after the war. Heidegger's thought dwells within "chauvinistic, and anti-democratic tendencies widely present in Germany."[17] Rockmore refers to *Der Spiegel*'s interview and the 1945 Heidegger response to the rector address as mere "gloss" (84). Rockmore's allegation is that Heidegger was positioning himself, not in the margins, but potentially at the center of a new version of German education. "Heidegger is not rejecting National Socialism; rather, he is offering the university as a place of science and himself to lead the Nazi movement," argues Rockmore (90). Heidegger did not follow the "official" Nazi line; instead, he framed his own "eccentric" view of Nazism (92). Rockmore notes, "Heidegger has lost, if indeed he ever possessed, . . . [a] philosophy to discriminate between good and evil" (98). The tone of Rockmore's argument is akin to Joseph Grange's "Heidegger as Nazi: A Postmodern Scandal," which casts Heidegger as "[a] convinced Nazi, a philosopher whose genuine interest in Nazism *survived* his apparent disillusionment with Hitler's particular form of National Socialism."[18] Grange accentuated that Heidegger's project could not differentiate truth from falsity due to its marginalization of any metaphysic of ethics.

For Levinas, Being without a questioning temper of the primacy of ethics is simply dangerous. Dallmayr states that in a time of historic "paradigm shifts," Heidegger was one of the few capable of offering theoretical insight into those changes.[19] This perspective moved Heidegger toward Nazism as a challenge to nihilism, which accompanied his refusal to permit Husserl to use the library in the philosophy department.[20] Richard Wolin, in "The French Heidegger Debate," further challenged Heidegger's contribution: "Heidegger's later [antihumanist] philosophy . . . serves once more to deny the specifically German responsibility for these crimes by attributing them to the dominance of an abstract, supervening, world-historical process" (158). In assessing Heidegger, one must choose between a critical tone related to the man and his politics and Rorty's argument that philosophy trumps Heidegger the man; Rorty rejects those that question the philosopher because of the man.[21] Derrida states that one can contend against Heidegger's effort to "spiritualize" National Socialism; Heidegger sought to break the "ideological" forces of his time,[22] which permitted him to counter the professionalization of the university and its "disciplinary compartmentalization."[23]

Samuel Moyn asserts that Heidegger's allegiance with Nazism may seem novel to some, but for many it has been part of the public record since 1933.[24] When the "new" Heidegger controversy erupted in the 1980s,[25] Levinas "kept a relatively low profile," as he did in the earlier eruptions of concern about Heidegger in the 1940s and the 1960s. Moyn writes, "Levinas's critique has its root . . . in the conviction that Heidegger collaborated to some extent with the Nazis, not just as the Rector of the University of Freiburg, but also as a philosopher who shared in their mentality and who aided and abetted in their endeavors" (27). In his 1989 essay, "As If Consenting to Horror," published in the *Le Nouvel Observateur*, Levinas outlined three major points: (1) he learned of Heidegger's involvement with the Nazis after 1933; (2) he was greatly disappointed with Heidegger; and (3) subsequent events removed the distance between *Mein Kampf* and *Sein und Zeit* (*Being and Time*).[26] Unlike Wahl, who publicly repudiated *Being and Time*, Levinas engaged the work with reflective ambiguity whenever asked if there was the "diabolical" in the work of Heidegger ("As If," 488). Levinas remembered the debate between Heidegger and Cassirer at the 1929 philosophy conference in Davos, Switzerland, a memory defined by Heidegger's and his own mocking of Cassirer.[27] Levinas stated that he felt great pain each time he heard Hitler's voice on the radio—it reminded him of Heidegger and that face-eclipsing event. Yet, such memories contributed to Levinas's "ethics as first philosophy" in response to a "personal crisis" of dismissal of the Other, which was awakened upon reflection (Moyn, 29).

Levinas entered Freiberg University in 1928 to study with Husserl, who retired in 1934, only to discover that scholarly attention centered on the emerging work of Heidegger. Levinas considered *Being and Time* one of the finest works of philosophy in the twentieth century; the work requires all who philosophize to attend to its implications. Levinas considered himself a phenomenologist, not an existential phenomenologist, who critically engaged the Heideggerian project; Levinas engaged Heidegger's work without a totalizing embrace. Moyn states that some wanted to call Levinas a Heideggerian during the 1930s (34); Levinas rejected the label and asserted that he did not follow Heidegger. Derrida recounted that as Levinas sat beside Heidegger, he found himself growing ever so "uncomfortable." Moyn cites Levinas's essay "Some Reflections on the Philosophy of Hitlerism," in which the limits of Heidegger's rejection of the transcendental is exposed in race-driven theory that finds corporality within the life of Nazi Germany (40). In 1935 Levinas wrote "L'Evasion," which Moyn describes as the question of "how to evade Heidegger, without at the same time avoiding him" (40). In response to Heidegger, Levinas's corpus is a "*re*-transcendentalizing response" (49). Levinas unites responsibility for the Other and learning from the Other as the heart of everyday transcendence in direct response—he offers ethics as the counter to Being as primary.

Levinas credited Heidegger with calling into question the modernist project[28]; Levinas enters a conversation that recognizes connections between Being and the corporality of Hitlerism. In response Levinas calls for an ethical reawakening; evil is unleashed by a failure to recognize that "meaning" is intimately connected to suffering for and responsibility to and for the Other.[29] In 1934, shortly after Hitler assumed power, Levinas wrote "Some Reflections on the Philosophy of Hitlerism," which was published in *Esprit*. In 1990, five years before his death, Levinas wrote a "prefatory note" before republishing the 1934 article in *Critical Inquiry*. In that essay Levinas stated that the barbarism of National Socialism did not reside within some "anomaly within human reasoning" or "ideological misunderstanding" but rather dwelt within a form of "*elemental Evil*" that emerges from a logic against which the West has no defense. The focus on Being eclipses the "face" of the Other, which is the "original 'site' of the Revelation" and the primordial counter to elemental evil.[30]

Levinas refers to the philosophy of Hitlerism as "simplistic"; it touches "elementary feelings" that awaken the German soul. Levinas's project rouses primeval ethical responsibility for the Other. Hitler's philosophy evokes elementary feelings that "predetermine" the adventure of the soul and its reaction to the world out of a commitment to "racist particularism"; this philosophy speaks of "human destiny" that has "no history." Hitler's philosophy embraces the "liberal" belief in reason, which unites "destiny" with "choice" without burden and limitations of "history" ("Some Reflections," 64–65). For Levinas, emancipation from history echoes in the theory of Marxism's intuition that the soul has an "inevitable relation to a determined situation." Levinas asserts that Marxism rejects the view of the soul as "pure reason" and "pure freedom" that seeks to float "above any attachment" (66–67). What is missing in the Western project, whether from the political right or left, is a connection to the body; there is a desire to float above the human condition and ignore the fact that the body appropriately weighs one down, keeping one's feet entwined within existence, resisting an idealism that is capable of housing crude elementary feelings.

Modern liberalism embraces an "eternal strangeness" toward the body. One cannot confuse materialism with the body without putting the spirit at risk. Body diminishes with an emphasis on materialism, idealism, and Hitler's dangerous equation of body with "blood." The spirit embodies a rebellious action against pain; identity requires body and a rebellious spirit in resistance against material conditions. The appeal to body tied to blood and heredity puts at risk human freedom, which resides within spirit. Levinas contended that a society that seeks to eradicate spirit loses contact with freedom and turns to degenerated "forms of the ideal" (67–70). In Hitler's world the collapsed form consisted of "the Germanic ideal of man . . . [the] promise [of] sincerity and authenticity" (70). The human is no longer "confronted by a world of ideas" that requires responsible choice. Instead, direction comes from a "concrete being, anchored in his flesh and blood" with a German spirit chained to him, unable to escape and unable to engage in transcendence. Thought and ideas fuel the spirit that nourishes freedom and permits the person to avoid an a priori conception of the body via racial heredity. Levinas scorned efforts to ignore the body through idealism, materialism, and racial heredity. Levinas argued that the body in existence continually shapes ideas, history, and community. Hitlerism brought forth an ideological and imposed conception of the body used for "war and conquest" (70–71). The imposed racial emphasis of Hitlerism is not a democratic aberration for Levinas but a manifestation of a Western error that privileges Being over the human face that houses freedom that nourishes a spirit of rebellion. Hitlerism advocated a body eclipsed by hereditary and racial demands and fueled by ideological assurance.

Levinas's message about the danger of ignoring the interplay of the body and spirit is a critique of an "originative I" of the West that focuses on Being. Levinas's work is otherwise than Heidegger's and the "originative I" of the West. Levinas contended that both are vulnerable to becoming a part of a "we" that avoids the uniqueness of personal responsibility. Levinas understood the importance of spirit within poetic expression; the key for Levinas was the danger of putting the "we" before the "I." Levinas understood the debate related to poetry after the Holocaust played out by a number of scholars and poets.[31] Levinas turned to Celan to counter the poetic interests of Heidegger. Celan, a Jewish poet who had contact with the intellectuals at the École Normale Israélite Orientale, responded to Heidegger with the poem "Todtnauberg," which Celan wrote after first meeting Heidegger. Celan, unlike Heidegger, did not privilege "a single national culture or historical moment over another"; Celan credited Shoah with being a revelatory ethical awakening in the West. Levinas asserted that Heidegger presupposed a "we" prior to an "I"; for Levinas, the "I" is called forth by a separate and distinct Other.[32] It is the "derivative I" called forth by the face of the Other that carries ethical responsibility.

Levinas's argument with Heidegger is ironical in that Heidegger critiques the "herd."[33] Levinas asserts that Heidegger's "we" situated within Being misses the identity of an ethical "I." Peperzak stated that Levinas's ethics, unlike a focus on ontology, privileges the face of the Other.[34] Levinas understood Heidegger's Being as a totalizing factor that swallows the Other.[35] Levinas rejected a view of the world as a "system of tools"; his focus was not on using. He stressed enjoyment of existence.[36] Enjoyment comes from desire that cannot be satiated, which is in contrast to Heidegger's *Dasein* that is "never hungry" (*Totality*, 134). Cohen stated that Levinas spurned the Heideggerian project because of a "foundation" of Being that refused to engage "alterity."[37] Alterity, for Levinas, lives before us in a presence that is "not yet" and simultaneously immemorial—continually calling us into ethical responsibility. Attending to an immemorial ethical echo deprivileges the rational hope of standing above existence.[38]

The emphasis on neighbor moves Levinasian ethics to questions about justice, requiring attentiveness to those not present at the table of decision making and influence. The stress on the Other and the neighbor is at the heart of Cem Zeytinoglu's explication of the difference between Heidegger's call to conscience and a Levinasian attentiveness to the Other that involves both active and passive communication. Heidegger's call to conscience is an "Ek-static existence" concerned with the Other through disquiet with oneself.[39] A Levinasian attentiveness to others presupposes that one is "held hostage" by the face of the Other. In being held hostage, Zeytinoglu explains, "the most 'assertive' I can be is when, as a hostage, I am fulfilling responsibility to the Other" (282). Levinas does not begin with an "originative I" but with the Other who calls a "derivative I" into responsibility. Levinasian attentiveness to the Other is an ethics of being a "keeper-of-my-brother" as a "hostage" in service of the Other; it is the human as a hostage of ethical responsibility that is called forth into action by the Other (282).

The ethical hostage recognizes that efforts to evade transcendence must expel all exertions to locate an "Archimedean point" that permits discovery of wisdom united with the "unchangeable," a time "without a history" and a "community" of constant "commentary" (Moyn, 51). Heidegger emphasized the importance of thinking, which assisted in the disclosure of Being; Levinas countered with a "precognitive source of meaning" that furnishes an initial ethical awakening.[40] Levinas contended that "Being dictates," which misses the call of responsibility for the concrete Other (*Proper Names*, 3, 41). Levinas's understanding of the concrete presupposes responsibility to a unique and particular Other. Levinas reminds us of the face of the Other as a beginning ethical optic without clarity or precision about or for a given person that moves "me" to an audio ethic, "I am my brother's keeper." It is this call that moves one back to ethical responsibility within a spirit of anarchy, contentious toward any metaphysical suggestions for the doing of good. The call is a spiritual awakening that requires responsiveness to a real person situated in unique circumstances; it is to and with this specific person in a particular historical moment as a concrete Other that demands my figuring out the how of responsibility. The stress on the concrete suggests an aversion to abstract metaphysical claims, for it is the real, particular Other that calls forth ethical responsibility that cannot be discerned in advance of the moment. Being offers "seductiveness" to the reader related to the ontological tightness of the argument (*Proper Names*, 71).

Attentiveness to the concrete, for Levinas, includes both the Other and an immemorial ethical demand. Levinas understood ethics as dwelling within the concrete in contrast to Heidegger's notion of dwelling, which is "spare" and seeks to "preserve"; Heidegger's understanding of dwelling is a utopia.[41] It is the "centric" understanding of dwelling that houses the "we" that connects Heidegger's project to Nazi aspirations. Levinas asserted that such a dwelling results in estrangement from an ethical call: "Place, then, before being a geometric space, and before being the concrete setting of the Heideggerian world, is a base."[42] Levinas rejected all exertions that structure life within utility and use.

Levinas contended that Heidegger's view of home assumes a "system of implements" (*Totality*, 171). Levinas's "appeal to ethics" is contrary to Heidegger's conception of Being (*Proper Names*, 137). Levinas scorned the privileging of Being over the face of human beings; he refused Heidegger's emphasis on "solitude." Levinas's stress on sociality links to "solidarity" and the "authentic" (*Time*, 40, 93). This connection shifts the conversation from Heidegger's "thought of Being" to the origin of ethics (*Totality*, 111). Heidegger's theory, for Levinas, only knows objects, with even care centered in "cognition" (*Existence*, 81). And Heidegger critiques technology and "technicity" as dangerous in opening an unreflective glorification of the "privileges of enrootedness." In leaning toward the Other in responsibility, one finds a sense of dwelling before and beyond a specific location. Levinas refuses to subordinate the concrete Other to locality or to Being.

The Saying and the Said in Communication Ethics: Direction without Clarity or Assurance

Levinas's response to Heidegger's project is a case study in the dual actions of the Saying and the Said. Levinas's argument with Heidegger's address centers on the Said in interaction with the ongoing power of Saying, the implications of the speech. For Levinas, the address eclipses ethics and misses an immemorial audio ethical command by following a fascination with locality, Being, and authenticity that eclipses responsibility to and for the Other. Levinas's project of ethics dwells in decision and sociality, not in locality of person or place.

Attentiveness to a specific place.—Locality resonates throughout Heidegger's address, with Levinas choosing the ambiguous space of technology over the intimacy of a given dwelling. Levinas's response to Heidegger's speech concludes in stunning irony—Levinas chose technology over the enrootedness of Heidegger's sense of place. Levinas, as the philosopher of the face, embraced technology over Heidegger's locality; technology lives in no space. It is akin to an audio ethical echo. The concrete immemorial ethical echo moves one to offer a place of dwelling for another. Levinas does not begin with dwelling but with an ethical echo. The origin of ethics is not in a person or place but in the performative engagement of responsibility for the Other. The revelatory in the Saying of ethics counters the temptation of locality of the Said.

The importance of "we."—Heidegger's project countered a Levinasian stress on the particularity of responsibility from the "derivative I." The "originative I" lives within dwellings that enhance the ego through idealism, materialism, heredity, and locality. The concrete, for Levinas, is not the Said but the immemorial voice of ethics. This archaic voice is a Saying that calls me into responsibility. The spirit of imposition within Nazi life eclipses ethics with a demand to follow, ironically, the practical manifestation of Being as the herd of the Third Reich.

Compromise.—Heidegger's gestures toward the Reich found opposition in Levinas's reminder that we are held hostage by the Other and that ethics demands fullness of response from me alone. Compromise is not the word of ethics. For Levinas, burden, obligation, and unending responsibility define a life of ethics. Compromise is a totalistic abstraction of Saying that refuses to put one's feet on the ground and take a public position. Care for the Other is not compromise but an obligation with one's whole person.

The focus on Being.—Heidegger's speech finds Levinas returning to the human face. Heidegger aspired for human beings to be responsible for Being, and Levinas contended that human beings must be responsible for the concrete Other person, the "I-for-the-other."[43] Levinas's focus was not abstract Being or heredity but the Other before us. Levinas's uniting of existence, enjoyment, responsibility, and the unique face of the Other opens the reality of "infinity," a place before, beyond, and above[44]—the dwelling of ethics.

Heidegger appealed to German faculty and students about a fundamental responsibility for thinking, science, and education. Levinas, on the other hand, speaks of a human face that calls "me" into responsibility. The focus on "my" unique responsibility rejects the Said of ideology that composes a "should" imposed on another. Instead, Levinas turns to an immemorial ethics that calls each of us singularly into a responsibility that bids ethical action without any sense of imposed clarity of action. Levinas's ethical "saying" offers direction so profound that there are no clear directions. Levinas does not stress direction; to the contrary, he offers unending responsibility. Levinas's response to the rector speech is a rejection of clear direction; instead Levinas propels each one of us individually to a more fundamental path—one that dwells forever in ambiguity and in unending obligation refusing predefinition. For Levinas, communication ethics does not pivot on political compromise. The task of communication ethics is an awakening to an immemorial call of responsibility. The test of our ethical action dwells in the public square. For Levinas, Heidegger's choices failed, announcing the necessity of ethics as first philosophy.

CHAPTER 10
Adieu to Levinas: The Unending Rhetoric of the Face

We encounter death in the face of the other.
> —Emmanuel Levinas, *God, Death, and Time*

Deeds can be done in eloquent silence, and ideas conveyed through a wide range of symbolic means beyond the spoken or written word.
> —Lester C. Olson, "On the Margins of Rhetoric: Audre Lorde Transforming Silence into Language and Action"

Decades after the death of my mother, I still can sense the moment of a depth of pain penetrating the core of my soul as I stood outside my parent's house. I was confused and wondered why the world had not stopped to mourn the loss of my mother. Cars still moved. Branches still tossed in the wind. Small children still played. How could all this commotion continue after the death of my mother? Emmanuel Levinas might suggest that life continued with the face of my mother persistently demanding responsible action from me. A Levinasian understanding of death reminds us of the particularity of a face that demands unique responsibility from me alone. In such moments one discovers temporal access to the universal through a particular face that calls for ethical action long after an empirical presence is no more; the call continues to interrupt our lives, demanding responsibility through an ethical awakening.

Introduction

I conclude this project with an unending sense of communication ethics as a signification stronger than death. The Other interrupts and awakens the living—calling the "I" into responsibility. When one experiences the death of another, one is jarred by the face of the Other who demands ongoing responsibility of me. As long as one responds to the face of another, death cannot eclipse the Other's power upon me. Evoking a call beyond death does not lessen weeping and raw lament for the loss of another who no longer physically walks among us, but death cannot curtail the power of the face speaking from the grave with a personal call of responsibility.

I conclude with a review and reminder of Levinas's account of death. The first section, "Adieu as the Unity of Contraries," turns to Derrida's *Adieu to Emmanuel Levinas.* Derrida reminded those present at Levinas's physical end of the paradoxical implications of *adieu;* Derrida emphasized that the term is inclusive of both hello and goodbye.[1] Adieu is "a farewell to temporal despair and a welcome to tenacious hope."[2] With this dual conception of adieu guiding understanding of Derrida's reflections, in the section "A Word of Welcome," I examine Derrida's responses after Levinas's death. First, Derrida gave the *Adieu* address at the burial of Levinas in Pantin, a suburb of Paris, on December 27, 1995. Then, a year later, he offered "A Word of Welcome" at the beginning of "Homage to Emmanuel Levinas," a memorial that took place on December 7, 1996, in the Richelieu Amphitheater of the Sorbonne. In the third section, "*God, Death, and Time,*" I recount Levinasian insights on death in his collected work *God, Death, and Time.* The final section, "The Saying and the Said in Communication Ethics: The Trace within Totality," comments on the communication ethics implications tied to Saying, Said, and trace.

Ethics communicates with a power stronger than death. Levinas's project details a rhetoric of ethics that surpasses the physical end of a person. Communication ethics begins with the face of another, propelled by an immemorial echo, and endures beyond death. Ethics speaks, and the face of another carries a rhetorical demand of responsibility.

Adieu as the Unity of Contraries

As Derrida delivered a tribute to Levinas in his *Adieu to Emmanuel Levinas*, he expressed his fear about such a day; he had envisioned it with trembling of voice and heart. What bequeathed Derrida some solace was Levinas's use of the term *adieu*. Derrida stated, "I would like . . . [to reflect on Levinas's understanding of *adieu*] with unadorned, naked words, words as childlike and disarmed as my sorrow" (1). The responsibility of saying adieu is the necessary "work of mourning." Levinas emphasized *droiture*, a "straightforwardness," an "uprightness" that is "stronger than death," while unable to console those remaining. The acknowledgment of death calls forth a movement toward the Other that never returns to its point of origin; one must understand and accept that the person is no longer. For Levinas, such moments remind us of "'unlimited' responsibility," moments that provoke a yes that is older and bolder than any form of naïve spontaneity. Death via the face of the Other demands responsibility, which remains the first and last word of action. Derrida reminds witnesses about the oeuvre of Levinas, which affirms the "holy" and the "promised" within a context of "nakedness" and "desert." Levinas, twenty years prior to his own death in "Death and Time" ("La mort et le temps"), stated that death is a nonresponse and a "patience of time" situated within the face of the Other and demanding a unique ethical response from the living (2–5).

Levinas contended that Shakespeare's Hamlet was wrong as he posed the question of "to be or not to be."[3] The key to life is not existence alone but enactment of "entrusted responsibility," which requires one to live life through a "duty beyond all debt." Derrida sketched the duty of "hospitality" as manifested in friendship and in Levinas's love of France. Derrida argued that Levinas altered the intellectual landscape within France with his personal and intellectual dignity. Levinas detailed the power of responsibility invoked by the Other by underlining the "traumatism of [me that is awakened by] the other." The Other shocks us out of routine and into ethical obligation responsive to ethical action and responsibility. Levinas described the necessary ethical response to the Other as commencing with "here I am." In such a moment one assumes an "immense responsibility" for the Other (Derrida, *Adieu*, 6–8, 11–12).

Derrida referred to Levinas's admiration for Heidegger's project, even as he rigorously refuted the fundamental base of the work. The difference between the two men and their work is that, unlike Heidegger, Levinas calls forth respect and thanks without regret. Derrida's disagreements with Levinas never eclipsed genuineness of respect for the person. One can sense the depth of the veneration for Levinas in Derrida's closing words:

> The question-prayer that turned me [Derrida] toward him [Levinas] perhaps already shared in the experience of the *à-Dieu* with which I began. The greeting of the *à-Dieu* does not signal the end. "The *à-Dieu* is not a finality," he says, thus challenging the "alternative between being and nothingness," which "is not ultimate." The *à-Dieu* greets the other beyond being, in what is "signified, beyond being, by the word 'glory.'" "The *à-Dieu* is not a process of being: in the call, I am referred back to the other human being through whom this call signifies, to the neighbor for whom I am to fear."
>
> But I said that I did not want simply to recall what he entrusted to us of the *à-Dieu*, but first of all to say *adieu* to him, to call him by his name, to call his name, his first name, what he is called at the moment when, if he no longer responds, it is because he is responding in us, from the bottom of our hearts, in us but before us, in us right before us—in calling us, in recalling to us: *à-Dieu*.
>
> *Adieu*, Emmanuel. (13)

Adieu invokes the reality of a genuine end that simultaneously has no conclusion; the term reminds us of the unity of contraries of a life well lived—a uniting of sorrow with a nagging demand for responsibility engendered by an awakened life. *Adieu* in the midst of death acknowledges goodbye, while reminding us of the face of the Other that never stops startling and awakening us. Even in death, the face of the Other beckons us toward unending responsibility and obligation.

A Word of Welcome

Derrida begins his second statement of *Adieu to Emmanuel Levinas* centered on Levinas with *bienvenue*. He highlights the power of welcome with his own understanding of "hospitality" (15–16). Welcome requires one to be in a position to address the Other, which gives credence to enabling the capacity of *moi-même* (myself). Hospitality functions as a politics of capacity for Derrida; it is the *pouvoir*, the power of a host who becomes a guest in the act of welcoming the Other—power resides in welcoming initiated by the host-guest. The uniting of the constructs of host and guest moves the communicative gesture of welcome from an act of possession and paternalism into an obligation to attend to the Other. This form of welcome gives and receives, turning teaching into a simultaneous interplay of offering and reception.

Derrida stated that the reversal of the host, who then becomes the guest, moves welcome from ownership to temporal participation within a dwelling of responsibility. Such a move keeps hospitality within an act of "opening" (19). Derrida asserted that for Levinas, hospitality connects to Sinai and to the face (63–70)[4]—to law and to particularity of obligation. There are both law and particularity of obligation tied to hospitality. For Derrida, there are, in the writings of Levinas, both an ethics and a law of hospitality: "[There is a relationship] between an *ethics* of hospitality (an ethics *as* hospitality) and a *law* or a *politics* of hospitality, for example, in the tradition of what Kant calls the conditions of universal hospitality in *cosmopolitical law*: 'with a view to perpetual peace'" (19–20). Ethics emerges in the face of the Other, and law houses concern for those not present in a given moment. Like many of Levinas's insights, the interplay of the particular and the universal offers guidance, providing a textured conception of hospitality responsive to ethics and law.

Derrida stated that in Levinas's *Totality and Infinity*, he seldom uses the word *hospitality*, stating it approximately six times in this important volume. Nonetheless, the theme of hospitality is central throughout Levinas's major work. Hospitality is a communicative act witnessed in the opening of oneself to the visage, the face, of the Other. The face welcomes and bids responsibility for the Other. This welcome originates in the human face, which generates a burden of accountability for the Other that cannot be understood within the realm of "thematization." The welcome of the face opens one to "infinity," to a "yes" that transforms a life. The cry of this affirmation necessitates acceptance of welcome that lives in "anarchy" within a world without limits defined by a responsibility that is "pre-orig-inarily welcomed." The "yes" and the "welcome" emanate from the Other, shaping a unique view of agency that derivatively responds to an immemorial communicative environment that is already and always under way. Even when there is no response and one remains in a "solitary cry of distress," there is still the "promise of a response." The response abides within an acknowledged welcome that origi-nates with a particular human face (22–24).

Interestingly, welcome is not a primal first gesture; welcome, like the face, rests in a "passive movement," which makes "ethics as first philosophy" possible (25). Ethical relation depends on the reception of the welcome that guides awareness of ethical responsibility, which is unresponsive to reciprocity. This welcome is a door to the home of ethics within exteriority and infinity, demanding that we cross the threshold of this door of ethical obligation, which leads to re-sponsibility for the Other (55). Welcome acknowledges the human being while demanding attentiveness to an immemorial ethical echo that invites ethics and responsibility without assurance of correct responses. Human responsibility requires existential discernment in the doing of ethics, which nurtures a dwelling of acumen and ongo-ing responsibility.

Welcome involves a "thinking of recollection," which makes possi-ble the notion of "dwelling"; it is recollection and collection that makes the act of recollection possible. The *bienvenue* of ethics commences with the face of the Other. Ethics awakened finds disruption through justice, which temporally deprivileges the face-to-face nature of eth-ics. Justice demands attentive regard for those not empirically present at the table of conversation and decision making. Justice moves one outside proximity of the face to face, *dehors* a sense of "immediacy" of contact (28, 31–32).

Levinas frequently spoke of a "primordial word of honor," which is sensed as one engages in an "attestation of oneself" that announces the "uprightness of the face to face." The proximity of ethics embraces a companion form of hospitality—the intrusion of justice is an al-most "intolerable scandal." "Justice commits perjury as easily as it breathes; it betrays the 'primordial word of honor' and swears [*jurer*] only to perjure, to swear falsely [*parjurer*], swear off [*abjurer*] or swear at [*injurier*] . . . [T]his ineluctability . . . imagines the sigh of the just," writes Derrida (34). Concern for the just emerges with recognition that enactment of justice demands without directions for clear action. Just as Levinas offers no easy framework for ethics, he also refuses such a move in justice. Only in the nourishing of structures and laws can one hope to approximate justice.

There is an ongoing oscillation between ethics and justice, with each interrupting the Other. The face is an ethical reminder for *moi-même* of responsibility that originates in both proximate (ethics) and distant (justice) obligations. Derrida emphasized that hospitality emanates from the "trace of the face, of the visage," and is a *"visitation"* that "disjoins and *disturbs."* The visitation of the face is unprogrammed and undemanded; it is "unexpected" and "awaited beyond all awaiting." Perhaps one can liken the visitation of the face to a "messianic visit" that is not tied to a past or the present but rather to responsibility for ethics within proximity, with justice disrupting obligations to a particular human face (62).

Derrida's view of hospitality operates within a background guidance of justice that shapes and interrupts ethics. This form of hospitality enacts radical separation, essential for space between persons that disrupts the comfort of the proximity of ethics (47). Derrida alludes to the justice connection as a major reason for Levinas's rejection of the I-Thou sphere of Buber; Levinas contends that there is no exclusive sphere of justice in the dialogic and dyadic construct. Justice dwells in attentiveness to exteriority, an Otherness that is outside a special ethical location between persons (60).

Separation, or what Levinas called "disinterestedness," makes hospitality, ethics, justice, and welcome possible, displacing any sense of hospitality that seeks to mask acts of interpersonal domination.[5] Hospitality entwines with the infinite, not with the totality of ideological assertions about a particular set of unwavering assumptions. Separation within hospitality interrupts the self, making it a "paradox" capable of attending to an ethical import of a particular face that turns one to an immemorial call without an impulse to unmask the Other, who remains an enigma. Levinas suggests a hospitality of disclosure and continued veiling. Without separation, proximity that abides in the face-to-face trace of ethics seeks to eclipse the equally important obligation of justice. The "face as a trace" propels ethics and justice within an ethical dwelling that maintains separation (Derrida, *Adieu*, 52–53).

In *Adieu to Emmanuel Levinas*, Derrida understands that the unity of contraries undergirds the welcome of hospitality via (1) ethics and justice, (2) particular and universal, (3) proximate and distant, (4) meeting and separation, and (5) visual attentiveness to the Other and audio recognition of an immemorial responsibility. There is an ongoing interruption, as the host becomes the "hostage" of the Other, where the host becomes a guest within a dwelling that ceases to be one's own. The hostage endures "substitution," assuming responsibility for the Other (56). The act of substitution is a profound interruption of the self (61). Derrida connects the Sinai Peninsula to a dwelling of interruption, a place where conflict defines the day with contrasting and competing histories and disputed boundaries (65). Derrida contends that three major terms undergird Levinas's project, with each pointing beyond the self within a responsibility of "*fraternity, humanity, hospitality.*" These concepts are at the heart of the Torah. Even for those unwilling or unable to offer a message of the Torah, all are reminded of life "*before* or outside of the Sinai*" by attentiveness to a human face (67).

The defining assertion of Levinas centers on fraternity; this ethical command thrives throughout his work and life. Fraternity and justice move one from concern for the proximate neighbor to the distant third. This form of hospitality is more radical than Kant's rendition of hospitality displayed in a *Perpetual Peace*.[6] Hospitality, for Kant, was attentive to interspaces within the public and civic domain. Levinas, on the other hand, understands hospitality as a "dwelling" that offers an "asylum," an "inn" for the Other. Hospitality is an abode of welcome attentive to the proximate (ethics) and the distant (justice). Such a dwelling, for Levinas, is a "place offered to the stranger." This *espace* gathers and collects persons near and far around the vitality of fraternity, humanity, and hospitality. Levinas discloses an immemorial welcome for the Other. An unending burden of ethics and justice welcomes the proximate and the distant, the neighbor and the stranger. Levinas's ethics, when misunderstood, is a *cosmopolitical* hospitality in the Kantian way; the term *hospitality* is better tied, however, to justice, which interrupts ethics of the face to face (Derrida, *Adieu*, 68, 71).

According to Derrida's *Adieu to Emmanuel Levinas*, Levinas's project evokes a memory that is prior to a conception of God. This immemorial ethical echo is a voice before and beyond the Torah that meets Sinai by calling forth welcome, responsibility, and interruption of justice. Levinas illuminates hospitality, beyond the nation-state, that welcomes from a ground of ethics that is more ancient than time itself. Additionally, Levinas crafts "politics beyond the political" (79). For Levinas, peace exceeds the political. Peace arises in the welcome and the receiving of the Other from a "magisterial height" assumed by a host who becomes a hostage attentive to responsibility for the Other; the command of ethics demands construction of a temporal dwelling prepared for the guest (85).

The hostage becomes a derivatively formed self that leads to transcendence of the self through the act of substitution for the Other, which then revisits the Other charged with responsibility. This derivative self is hostage to the Other, shaped via "substitution," and acts with absolute passivity, not in a Heideggerian sense of the possibility of the impossibility, but out of "infinite responsibility" that obligates me toward the neighbor; a "passivity is not only the possibility of death in being, the possibility of impossibility. It is an impossibility prior to that possibility, the impossibility of slipping away" (Levinas, *Otherwise*, 128). Our responsibility, awakened by the death of another, reminds us of an ongoing obligation (Derrida, *Adieu*, 83).

The hostage of whom Levinas spoke understands the danger of rhetoric that invokes "careless idealism" (84). Additionally, Levinas rejected Kant's contention that all begins with war. For Levinas, genuine human hope resides not in idealism or in the dark reality of war but in the human face functioning as the visual origin of ethics and, ultimately, justice. The human face demands tending to places of "non-violence, peace, and hospitality" (92). This visual and audio understanding of ethics and responsibility finds prominence within a peace that embraces radical separation and distance between and among persons in the act of responding to the call of the face of a particular Other.

Derrida continues with an outline of Kant's perspective on peace, which assumes that the pivotal point of the human condition is war. Kant's assertion demonstrates that peace is something other than a utopia; peace is a state that requires constant vigilance, work, and action. If, during a moment of peace, one reflects on the possibility of war, then war, not peace, is the point of origin. Peace is simply not natural (86–87). In addressing the nonnatural reality of peace, Kant discussed the importance of universal hospitality that offers a dwelling larger and more expansive than a given state or residence; he wanted to provide a scope of institutional sustenance capable of supporting physical sustenance and safety. Levinas understood this cautionary perspective on the state; he frequently referred to dangers that lurk within the "tyranny of the State." Such dominations deform the "I" by missing directives within the face of the Other. Eclipsing the face of the Other allows political hospitality to morph into "tyrannical violence" (97).

The political does otherwise with hospitality, moving it from the authentic to the temporally artificial. An act of political hospitality engenders brilliant illumination. One discovers later that such light blinds one to all persons, events, and ideas; it covers and obscures with an ironical form of darkness. Political light obfuscates for Levinas, ignoring the reality of genuine holy sparks. Levinas, like Kant, rejected a civil view of peace that was dependent on a government alone. Kant's cosmopolitan position supports a dwelling for the sojourner. Levinas, on the other hand, did not suggest the term *cosmopolitan*, due to its ideological connotations used to render credence to "modern anti-Semitism" (87–88). Hospitality, for Levinas, is both proximate and distant, with each interrupting the certainty of the Other. This ongoing interruption includes an excessive love for the stranger accompanied by an unwillingness to announce oneself; there is a "holy separation" between the human and God, which permits one to love the stranger. Derrida suggests, "The Saying *à-Dieu* would signify hospitality. This is not some abstraction that one would call, as I have just hastily done, 'love of the stranger,' but (God) '*who* loves the stranger.'" Derrida asserted that the call of *adieu* is a desire to rest and dwell in God. A city of refuge was contrary to Levinas's view of dwelling; responsibility originates beyond and before the immediate proximate moment. The dwelling within death has an active demand for responsibility from the face of the Other; with the interruption of death, the face continues. Levinas pointed to an ethical dwelling that houses an echo that carries the burden of responsibility and a "promise" of holiness by responsibility for the Other (104–5, 113). Adieu is a goodbye and, like in seventeenth-century France, a hello to the Other within a realm of ethics and responsibility that has no end. For Derrida, adieu is a continuing form of signification—the face of the one for whom we grieve still calls forth responsibility for the living: death is another form of ethical awakening. Adieu, as understood by Derrida, included an immemorial call, which Levinas defined as one's relationship to God, death, and time. I now examine this threefold engagement of immemorial responsibility in a series of Levinas's lectures, *God, Death, and Time*, compiled by Jacques Rolland.

God, Death, and Time

There are forty-seven essays in *God, Death, and Time*; they are the product of two lecture courses taught by Levinas in the 1975–1976 academic year. My task in this section requires adhering to the wisdom of Benjamin—functioning as a "pearl-diver" searching for performative characteristics of adieu, the goodbye and the hello that acknowledges the face of the dead while calling forth responsibility. This series of lectures centers on the "word beyond measure" that gives structure to what Levinas understood as an immemorial echo of ethics as first philosophy.[7] Levinas understood this primordial word as an ethical trace stronger than death itself. In his lectures we witness a trace of Levinas's face; he is lecturing, talking to students, and now conversing with us, the readers. For each essay I offer a brief statement about an idea imperative to Levinas and then follow with a response in italics. Note that not all essays address death, but each points to the fact that totality is not ultimate; death as the greatest exertion of totality fails in response to the face of another who continues to call us into responsibility.

PART I: DEATH AND TIME

INITIAL QUESTIONS—FRIDAY, NOVEMBER 7, 1975. Time is "duration," with death assuming the patience of all time (7). Death is a departure to the unknown; it appears as a passage from being to no longer being. Duration in death is a "fission" that reunites one with an a priori that is before the a priori (10). The death of another is not the same experience as my own death; spiritual awakening calls forth my responsibility. *The death of another awakens my ethical responsibility, and my own death calls forth responsibility in another.*

WHAT DO WE KNOW OF DEATH?—FRIDAY, NOVEMBER 14, 1975. Death is the "stopping of expressive movements." However, one is awakened by the Other with recognition that I am the "survivor." The meaning of life flows beyond the moment of death, offering "surprise" that heals by announcing the ethical impotence of the inevitability of death (11–14). Mortality is the recognition of duration defined by the transience of a single one. *The Other's death informs us; our own death, at the least, reminds us of duration in its infinite calling and in its finite sense of stoppage.*

THE DEATH OF THE OTHER [*D'AUTRUI*] AND MY OWN—FRIDAY, NOVEMBER 21, 1975. Levinas counters both Husserl and Heidegger, suggesting that emotion cannot be limited to intentionality or "rooted in anxiety." Death, better understood as "disquietude," is a finite moment that defines infinity as life continues. Death is a "nonsense" that must be met (17–18, 21). *A life of finitude confirms the infinite, connecting us to those before and those not yet.*

AN OBLIGATORY PASSAGE: HEIDEGGER—FRIDAY, NOVEMBER 28, 1975. Levinas offers his voice in discussion of death's disquieting restlessness and the awakening we receive from the death of another that is "beyond measure" (22). For Heidegger, the point of Being in relation to *Dasein* is a "mineness" associated with a potential loss of being (25). Heidegger later reflected on the question of time, noting that "it is a being." Existentially, Levinas ends with the question "*Who* is time?" (27). Time dwells within the acknowledgment of a human face and responsiveness to an ethical echo, not within the abstraction of Being. *Levinas reminds us of a call that the Other renders from the grave. On the other hand, Heidegger reminds us of a sober note—it is "me" who dies. For Levinas, death disquiets and calls out responsibility.*

THE ANALYTIC OF *DASEIN*—FRIDAY, DECEMBER 5, 1975. In addition to nature and natural science, the human offers a "rupture" in the advent of Being, reason, and the claim to objectivity outside existence (28). The human, awakened by the face of the Other, directs one to an archaic sense of ethics. Heidegger, on the other hand, explicates care that is routinely expected. The structure of Heidegger's care is threefold: "*being-out-ahead-of-oneself* (the project), *being-always-already-in-the-world* (facticity), being in the world as *being-alongside-of* (alongside the things, alongside of what is encountered within the world)" (30). Levinas stresses that time defines care as a project connected to the future, united with the facticity of the past, and engaged alongside the being of the present. The structure of things and time associates with care. Even the notion of despair fits within structure in that there is anticipation of more agony. *Dasein*, in the act of care, finds a lack, being death, and is intimately connected to time as one cares for structures on the way to death (32). *Heidegger's view of care is time-centered. Levinas's understanding of care allied with ethics is a response to an immemorial echo enacted in a responsibility before and beyond time that shapes human joy without primary anticipation centered on death.*

DASEIN AND DEATH—FRIDAY, DECEMBER 12, 1975.—Levinas contended that Heidegger's contribution centered on describing *Dasein* as moving toward death, which reframes our understanding of time and Being. Heidegger embraces an ontological preoccupation with "being-there" in the "proper" or "authentic" sense (33–34). Death becomes the end of "being-in-the-world" with Levinas being unwilling to forget the possibility of the "beyond," the "infinite" (37), *which leads Levinas to a natural claim—the face of the Other continues to speak after death.*

THE DEATH AND TOTALITY OF *DASEIN*—FRIDAY, DECEMBER 19, 1975. Heidegger asserts that death emerges as a totality of "being there" in the experience of the death of another. *Dasein* works with a debt, a "distance relative to itself," in response to death. The "being-out-ahead-of-oneself" is the movement of *Dasein* to death. Death is that which actually completes *Dasein* (38–41). *Levinas admires the recognition of the power of death and its import for us via experience of and response to the death of another. Unlike Heidegger's conception of death, Levinas contends that the visage of another continues to speak.*

BEING-TOWARD-DEATH AS THE ORIGIN OF TIME—FRIDAY, JANUARY 9, 1976. For Levinas, death, tied to signification of responsibility, announces the mortality of *Dasein*. However, death is not an abrupt end but rather an ongoing recognition of the "not-yet." *Dasein* lives as if close to the end in every moment of life; death is a defining characteristic of one's own being. Death shapes the "manner of being." Death is not an "unfulfilled future" but is the very root of being: "Just as *Dasein*, as long as it is, is always a 'not yet,' it is also always its end" (43). The movement toward death carries with it an ever-present recognition of the question of nonbeing. *For Levinas, on the other hand, the focus is on responsibility for the Other, not preoccupation with one's own death.*

DEATH, ANXIETY, AND FEAR—FRIDAY, JANUARY 16, 1976. One lives with the "to-be-in-question." *Dasein* responds to anxiety "for" and "of," which renders insight into being-toward-death. One flees death into the "They" of "idle talk" (46–48). The certainty of death makes all possibilities of life feasible, according to Heidegger. *Levinas agrees that flight from meeting existence is an escape and an eclipse of one's unique responsibility for the Other.*

TIME CONSIDERED ON THE BASIS OF DEATH—FRIDAY, JANUARY 23, 1976. Death is a "reversal of appearing"; it makes *Dasein* and time possible. In every moment in life, *Dasein* is in relationship with death (50, 53). *For Levinas, the human is in relationship with responsibility for the Other in each moment of life.*

INSIDE HEIDEGGER: BERGSON—FRIDAY, JANUARY 30, 1976. Levinas stresses Bergson's contribution to time via *duration*, which veers from the Western equation of time with measurement. Duration assumes a heaviness that descends into and with the self. Duration makes intersubjectivity between persons conceivable, as one attends to the "interiority" of another (55–56). *Levinas recounts that such a view of duration accounts for signification that transpires long after the empirical death of another.*

THE RADICAL QUESTION: KANT AGAINST HEIDEGGER—FRIDAY, FEBRUARY 6, 1976. Levinas explicates what he considers a fundamental difference between Kant and Heidegger with the latter focused on Being and the former on transcendence, which permits Kant to understand signification as contrary to Being. Kant's transcendental ideal apprehends meaning otherwise than finitude (60). *Levinas highlights an alternative to finitude with signification of the face that continues after death.*

A READING OF KANT (CONTINUED)—FRIDAY, FEBRUARY 13, 1976. This section continues differentiation between Heidegger and Kant with the latter's emphasis on a nonlinear sense of hope manifested in the doing of a universal maxim. This conception of hope offers signification that is more than and beyond Being. For Kant, hope is a product of happiness; the "rational character of a virtue" works with a universal imperative. Happiness intertwined with virtuous work is not morality of a "Sovereign Good"; it is the doing of ethical reasoning and action: "Therefore, neither happiness alone nor virtue alone— both of these injure Reason" (63–65). *Levinas concurs with the dangers of the reification of morality, happiness, and virtue; he recognizes the power of finitude and the reality of making ethical decisions without pure assurance of correctness; through such living, one finds meaning and hope beyond an impending sense of conclusion.*

HOW TO THINK NOTHINGNESS?—FRIDAY, FEBRUARY 20, 1976. Levinas asserted that the notion of nothingness has "defied" much of recent Western philosophy. Contrary to this perspective is Kant's understanding of "rational hope," understood as a counter to nothingness (67, 70). Rational hope is outside the temporal sequence of events. Rational hope is outside time; it assumes the power of self-legislation and is attentively aligned with the categorical imperative. *For Levinas, the joy of existence trumps nothingness; in existence, the face of the Other matters.*

HEGEL'S RESPONSE: THE SCIENCE OF LOGIC—FRIDAY, FEBRUARY 27, 1976. Levinas emphasizes that "pure being" as understood by Hegel is indeterminate, including its genesis, corruption, and decomposition, subsumed within the "absolute" (72–73). Nothing is new, and at the same time, annihilation never ceases. Nothingness is part of Being, with beginning ignited within nothingness that contributes shape to the absolute. *For Levinas, an inauguration before all beginnings is part of an ancient past; it is an origin before origins.*

READING HEGEL'S SCIENCE OF LOGIC (CONTINUED)—FRIDAY, MARCH 5, 1976. For Hegel, "'pure being and pure nothingness are the same'" (76). There is an identity of nothingness with being (77). One cannot name the difference between being and nothingness. *For Levinas, however, there is an origin of ethics that is fundamentally prior to an origin of being.*

FROM THE SCIENCE OF LOGIC TO THE PHENOMENOLOGY[8]—FRIDAY, MARCH 12, 1976. Belief is better understood theoretically as *doxa*. The thinking of being connects nothingness with thought, uniting one to a world beyond measure. "*I think*" permits consciousness to engage in reciprocal recognition. This consciousness becomes an ethical state that clarifies human and divine law. The double form of consciousness permits the spirit to function as an individual within a community (79–82). The universal is lost when an individual dies; only the individual glimpses the universal. *For Levinas, sociality is a defining shaper of our humanness—only through the particularity of personal responsibility is the possibility of the universal disclosed.*

READING HEGEL'S PHENOMENOLOGY (CONTINUED)—FRIDAY, MARCH 19, 1976. Hegel, like Kant, does not equate the individual with spirit or ethic. Universality, for Hegel, rests in the individual. Death of an individual is the continuing progress of thought. For Hegel, death is not a person or thing but a "shadow" that obscures the world of thought and appearances akin to Plato's allegory of the cave. Death is a nothingness that returns to the "ground of being" (84–87). *Levinas, on the other hand, unearths an immemorial universal ethical message through the particular, which permits a glimpse of an anarchical origin.*

THE SCANDAL OF DEATH: FROM HEGEL TO FINK—FRIDAY, APRIL 9, 1976. The nothingness of Hegel and Aristotle assumes that there is "already a beginning." Death is a "destiny" for the real that is always "destined for destruction." Death connects one to the beginning once again with self-grasping thought. Eugen Fink (1905–1975), contrarily, connects death to intelligibility. Death is a "rupture" that must be met in silence; death functions as a "scandal" in that it is estrangement from intelligibility (88–90). *For Levinas, death is far from a scandal; it links to an immemorial echo of responsibility that continues to call forth ethical action from another.*

ANOTHER THINKING OF DEATH: STARTING FROM BLOCH—FRIDAY, APRIL 23, 1976. Levinas contends that Ernst Bloch (1885–1977) engages a humanism that yearns for a "habitable site." What led many to socialism was the "spectacle of misery" that screamed for attentive concern about and for the neighbor. Bloch understands Marx as offering a philosophy about a progress toward the enactment of human dignity with alienation of labor representing an incompleteness of progress. "Social evil" manifests as a "fault" or obstacle toward progress. For Bloch, time is a dwelling of hope that lives within culture that "vibrates in sympathy" toward a progressive ideal of human dignity (94–96). *Levinas responds with affirmation to the role of the neighbor's suffering and enactment of eternal responsibility while addressing another's pain; such action is the keystone to attentiveness to and for justice.*

A READING OF BLOCH (CONTINUED)—FRIDAY, APRIL 30, 1976. Bloch assumes the importance of hope tied to a utopian future. Anxiety about death originates in the incompletion of one's work, a stoppage of progress. Bloch contends that when light emanates from utopia, it bursts upon the "obscurity of subjectivity" with a witness that calls forth "*astonishment*" (98–100). Through such amazement, one senses the penetrating reign of progress at work. *Levinas responds to hope, not via progress, but through an unending obligation to attend to a voice before all voices.*

A READING OF BLOCH: TOWARD A CONCLUSION—FRIDAY, MAY 7, 1976. The subject in a dark biosphere works for "a better world" with the fear of dying before necessary work is accomplished. Culture shaped by such work becomes a cultural revolution. "Astonishment" emerges in moments that glimpse a perfected utopia in which a uniqueness of person emerges. During such moments one understands work as "leisure." Bloch bonds astonishment with leisure as he refuses to equate leisure with "the unfinished or capitalist world" of empty and "sad Sundays" of false rejuvenation. Leisure connected with the temporal world of astonishment is stronger than "any possession or any property"; such amazement counters the world of melancholia (101–2). Bloch has the audacity to celebrate astonishment, culture, and leisure as coordinates of work that invites a glimpse of a dwelling for utopian hope. *Levinas recognizes the significance of the oeuvre of a life. Additionally, he understands the power of astonishment through the expressive voice of Saying announced in and through the work.*

THINKING ABOUT DEATH ON THE BASIS OF TIME—FRIDAY, MAY 14, 1976. Death opens the door to attentiveness to others; it functions as an interruption in time. The "*flux*" of time lives within interruptions that make understanding of the infinite possible (106–8). *Levinas understands the infinite as necessarily disturbed by the finite; the infinite must embrace totality. Without interruption, Saying morphs into a finite, continuous abstraction.*

TO CONCLUDE: QUESTIONING AGAIN—FRIDAY, MAY 21, 1976. Death is not of our current world; it is forever a "scandal" (113). Death unites us to an origin before origins while bringing us face to face with the finite. In response to the authority of death, however, there is yet a greater power—the face of the Other that calls us into responsibility. *When all analysis is complete, there is one fundamental remaining fact—the death of the Other calls me into responsibility.*

PART II: GOD AND ONTO-THEO-LOGY

BEGINNING WITH HEIDEGGER—FRIDAY, NOVEMBER 7, 1975. Levinas's perspective on death assumes that the face of another speaks with power greater than death; such a project requires final reflections on an unnamed God. Levinas examines Heidegger's question of Being after God. Heidegger's project became "Onto-theo-logy" within an epoch announcing a particular way of being. Being, differentiated from human being, aligns language with the "house of being" (122). Unlike Hegel, where philosophy aligns with progress, Heidegger moves backward in his interrogation of questioning and thinking about Being in order to burst the constraints of his time. *Levinas understands the move backward to Being as otherwise than toward a primordial ethics. Contrarily, Levinas stresses passive thought that attends to an archaic ethical echo in a disinterested and determined fashion.*

BEING AND MEANING—FRIDAY, NOVEMBER 14, 1975. Heidegger posits Being as the origin of meaning. Levinas states that to separate God from Onto-theo-logy means that the Same and the Other cannot be equated; the key is difference. For Levinas, this suggests that questioning and thinking about Being is no longer central; his emphasis is on difference and ethics, not Being. The Greeks tied meaning to discourse, but Levinas understands ethical meaning as a priori. Communication about Being comes long after an ancient commanding communication about ethics. *Levinas reminds us of an immemorial responsibility that existed long before Being and thinking about the importance of Being.*

BEING AND WORLD—FRIDAY, NOVEMBER 21, 1975. In the Western tradition, rhetoric functions as the carrier of meaning. Levinas asserts that Heidegger works within a rhetorical position in a questioning fashion, undoing metaphysics as he gestures toward another metaphysics in which the "Same is still the rational, the meaningful" (135). *Levinas's conception of ethics is prior to and beyond synthesis, metaphysics, and the rational; it is an archaistic and immemorial audio ethical command of obligation.*

TO THINK GOD ON THE BASIS OF ETHICS—FRIDAY, DECEMBER 5, 1975. Heidegger offered a rationality of disquietude as he questioned Being. Only through the questioning of Being does one engage and understand Being. Levinas privileges ethics within an origin prior to any disquietude of Being. Levinas understands the power and vitality of disquietude. *Unlike Heidegger, however, he understands disquietude as arising from the interruption of the face of the Other, which imposes on me and activates an inexhaustible patience of ethics that reshapes my own identity.*

THE SAME AND THE OTHER—FRIDAY, DECEMBER 12, 1975. Pure passivity of response to an ethical call emerges from the Other as one answers within the diachrony of time (141). Levinas repeatedly announces the importance of ethical meaning before knowledge within a duration before time. It is the Other that sobers the Same into an awareness of an ancient ethical call that is before, during, and after time. *The face of the Other acts as a spiritual awakening to a sacred command of responsibility.*

THE SUBJECT-OBJECT CORRELATION—FRIDAY, DECEMBER 19, 1975. Transcendence happens in response to the Other as a human face awakens and transforms the Same. Difference, not synthesis and correlation of subject and object, counters the Western impulse to absorb and assimilate. *Levinas's conception of ethics does not begin with an originative subject but with an awakened subject, a "derivative I."*

THE QUESTION OF SUBJECTIVITY—FRIDAY, JANUARY 9, 1976. The gathering of structures frames signification and constitutes the Said. Saying grows silent within the Said, while a trace of Saying remains lodged in the Said. Heidegger stated that the poet enlivens the Said of a poem, permitting it to speak; a poet awakens the voice of a Saying that dwells in the silence of the Said. The facticity, the Saidness of the Other, houses a trace of Saying that redirects responsibility as an "I" with obligations that are unique and carried forth in a particular manner. *Levinas understands the Said as the dwelling of the trace of Saying; the interaction between Saying and Said makes signification of responsibility possible.*

KANT AND THE TRANSCENDENTAL IDEAL—FRIDAY, JANUARY 16, 1976. The dialectic of transcendence suggested by Kant assumes thinking that is both empirical and general, which permits one to sense what is and what might be. In Western philosophy, communication announces the signification of representation of Being. Signification thematized lives within the Said; Saying is independent of such content and bursts forth into meaning that refuses reification. *The Other points us to a call of responsibility that dwells within Saying—an inarticulate, yet definitive, voice.*

SIGNIFICATION AS SAYING—FRIDAY, JANUARY 23, 1976. The signification of Saying fuels responsibility for the Other. There is no Said or clear programmatic answer that calls forth responsibility; the "I" of ethics lives within a dwelling of Saying that is forever moved to the particular. The call of responsibility charges an ethical "I" with obligation as a hostage indebted to the Other, who renders possible my identity. The manner in which this ethical debt emerges in practice has no formula; the ethical action demands a one-of-a-kind response each and every time. *Saying carries signification that cannot be packaged, framed, or duplicated in the hands of an "ethics technician."*

ETHICAL SUBJECTIVITY—FRIDAY, JANUARY 30, 1976. This form of subjectivity habituates within Saying and manifests itself in the uniqueness of response to the Other. Saying dwells prior to language in the before, above, and beyond. Signification emerges in inimitability of reply that emerges in answer to Saying. *Ethical subjectivity is performative, commanded by an archaic ethical echo.*

TRANSCENDENCE, IDOLATRY, AND SECULARIZATION—FRIDAY, FEBRUARY 6, 1976. When one relates transcendence to ethics, one discovers a "secularization of the sacred" (163). Ontology is the idolatry of our time, which Levinas understands as manifested in secularization. Levinas discusses secularization of transcendence as snarled within the pursuit of Being. When Being becomes an ideology, it cannot attend to the concrete needs of a world in hunger and in poverty. Even technology as a secularization "is destructive of pagan gods" (166). *Levinas understands the danger of false height as materialized through ideology, reification, secularization, and the local embraced without reserve.*

DON QUIXOTE: BEWITCHMENT AND HUNGER—FRIDAY, FEBRUARY 13, 1976. Levinas states that the world is always proportionate to knowledge, with God functioning as an ultimate metaphor of "dis-proportion" (167). One seeks to avoid dis-proportion through "bewitchment," which Levinas contends is at the core of the story of *Don Quixote*. One can be bewitched by any ideology or reification that misses the face of the Other; such action too easily accompanies those who live in a "well-fed slumber." Levinas underscores Don Quixote's enchantment with a transferable responsibility (171). For Levinas, responsibility is not transferable. *However, even in the midst of bewitchment, a trace of the Saying of ethics calls forth responsibility.*

SUBJECTIVITY AS AN-ARCHY—FRIDAY, FEBRUARY 20, 1976. Levinas's conception of ethics originates prior to a beginning in *"an-archy."* Ethical signification dwells in acts of responsibility. Unlike that of Heidegger, Levinas's version of freedom emerges from response to a demand for responsibility. Ethical subjectivity, detached from Being, connects to an ethical echo—"I am my brother's keeper." The ethical command for investiture in the Other is impersonal; such responsibility shapes personal identity. *Levinas does not equate ethics with a program or a set of skills; ethics is an originative anarchy that fuels uniqueness of responsibility for a particular Other.*

FREEDOM AND RESPONSIBILITY—FRIDAY, FEBRUARY 27, 1976. Freedom emerges in the act of responsibility for the Other; freedom is the enactment of *"uniqueness"* of responsibility that generates "super-individuation," which can be carried forth by no one other than me (176). This responsibility is a vocation and in contrast to a utopian posture; the vocation of ethics demands an inequality of me toward and for the Other. A call for responsibility heard via a demanding whisper continues to speak immemorially. *For Levinas, ethics is performed in an inequality of self in relation to the Other.*

THE ETHICAL RELATIONSHIP AS A DEPARTURE FROM ONTOLOGY—FRIDAY, MARCH 5, 1976. Ethics begins with a dis-inter-estedness, a dissymmetry of relationship with the Other that demands substitution of me for the suffering of another, which abandons the "free ego." Nevertheless, even the responsibility of ethics has limits. Justice attends to "the third party's intervening in the relationship of nearness" (182–83). Meaning dwells within the revelatory, which emerges in responsibility that originates beyond and before the assurance of technique, clarity of ethics, or confidence in a singular conception of justice. *Levinas reminds us that totality cannot subsume ethics, which must give way to justice. Our responsibility for the proximate Other is never sufficient alone. Justice interrupts ethics, just as ethics tempers the assurance of justice.*

THE EXTRA-ORDINARY SUBJECTIVITY OF RESPONSIBILITY—FRIDAY, MARCH 12, 1976. Levinas states that subjectivity is the "extra-ordinary" dimension of my responsibility for another. This responsibility is not a disclosure of an ethical act but a bearing witness by me in the performative utterance of "here I am" (188–89). *This call of responsibility is both extra-ordinary and simultaneously otherwise than the convention of Being.*

THE SINCERITY OF THE SAYING—FRIDAY, MARCH 19, 1976. Meaning begins with giving bread to another and requires practical material acts. Such gestures offer sincerity when they dwell within Saying; sincerity lives until it is absorbed into a programmatic Said. Sincerity is a witnessing that does not return focus of attention to oneself. Sincerity of Saying offers a "model without a world" (194). *Sincerity cannot name itself in the witnessing of Saying; sincerity lives beyond reflection and in practical acts for the Other.*

GLORY OF THE INFINITE AND WITNESSING—FRIDAY, APRIL 9, 1976. Inspiration witnesses to ethics and responsibility in response to the Other. It is not a form of representation or thematization; inspiration is a Saying that temporally manifests itself in a witnessing, a bursting forth of responsibility—"here I am" (197). *Witnessing begins with Saying that becomes the Said and then fades within a trace of Saying that can be called forth at a later time.*

WITNESSING AND ETHICS—FRIDAY, APRIL 23, 1976. Witnessing is the fulfilling of responsibility. One bears witness in the "here I am." It is a fulfilling of responsibility propelled by an "anachronism of inspiration." It is in witnessing for God without ever using the word *God.* God in action is "God . . . not uttered" (200–201). Witnessing is not in representation but performed in doing. *Ethics emerges from an immemorial sacred call but falters in representation and solidification of the Said.*

FROM CONSCIOUSNESS TO PROPHETISM—FRIDAY, APRIL 30, 1976. Bearing witness is not an act of making manifest but rather is being responsible in response to an immemorial command. The notion of God reminds us of a height of responsibility beyond being that does not pause in idolatry; it "speaks beyond being" (206). *To witness is to bear responsibility; the focus remains on our unique responsibility. Responsibility, not the prophet, must speak.*

IN PRAISE OF INSOMNIA—FRIDAY, MAY 7, 1976. Insomnia is tied to consciousness; it is an awakening tied to a diachrony of time. Insomnia is the Other awakening spiritual activity of the soul. Consciousness "descends from insomnia" (210). *Levinas points to a primordial consciousness that witnesses a presence in a spiritual insomnia that awakens us to responsibility.*

OUTSIDE OF EXPERIENCE: THE CARTESIAN IDEA OF THE INFINITE—FRIDAY, MAY 14, 1976. Within the West there is a privileging of Being and immanence. Even much discussion of God rests upon representation and immanence, which is a form of ontology. Such a focus misses signification prior to Being and immanence (217–18). *It is the ethical command before Being to which Levinas calls us to attend and witness.*

A GOD "TRANSCENDENT TO THE POINT OF ABSENCE"—FRIDAY, MAY 21, 1976. The final contribution in this series of essays announces with exceptional clarity the danger of turning the good and the infinite into a totality of assurance. One eclipses the power of the infinite when attempting to eclipse the finite. The infinite is ungraspable as a weapon of self-assurance. The infinite dwells within incomprehensibil-ity, housing personal calls for responsibility. The infinite is awakened in responsibility for the Other. The infinite arises in a "trauma of awak-ening" (220). The awakening is a love without eros, an unquenchable desire, a disinterested responsibility, and a signification that is both beyond and before Being. Such a view of ethics calls forth witnesses to God as transcendent to a point of absence. *Infinite responsibility is played out in a derivative me who stands and acts in "here I am" for the Other without assurance of righteousness.*

The Saying and the Said in Communication Ethics: The Trace within Totality

We witness in the words of Derrida the reality of Saying that lives in a trace that rests within the ultimate form of totality, the Said of death. Levinas's project articulates the inability of death to extinguish ethics, which is not tied to a person alone but to an immemorial time that houses ethics. Transcendence points to the absence of God, forgoing reliance on Being and immanence; acknowledgment of God is per-formed in responsibility for the Other. Levinas enunciates meaning beyond meaning, time before time, responsibility before necessity, and an obligation of ethics that speaks in spite of death with recognition of transcendence so powerful that self-assurance is forsaken. Levinas offers insight into an immemorial world of responsibility that connects us to a universal ethic, "I am my brother's keeper." This audio ethical echo elects one to responsibility for the Other—demanding that one witness through the performative act of "here I am." At such a mo-ment, personal decision making begins—one must discern how to be uniquely responsible for a particular Other. There is no blueprint for acts of responsibility, just an immemorial command to be responsible. Ethics is simply more powerful than death and totality, which inevitably holds a trace of Saying that calls forth responsibility.

The Said of death.—The totality of death houses within it a trace of Saying. Saying is a call to an ethical responsibility enacted uniquely by "me" alone. The Said of death is not the final word. Death houses a trace of Saying that evokes an ethical sense of responsibility.

The face of the Other.—The face of the Other speaks beyond the shadow of death. The Saying of responsibilities continues to disrupt all forms of self-assurance. The totalities of ideologies, procedures, and culturally imposed assumptions find themselves disrupted by an ethical Saying that implodes the power of totality. The face of the Other continues to demand responsibility from me.

Transcendence.—The face of the Other houses an ethical optic that moves me to an immemorial echo, "I am my brother's keeper." At that moment, the "I" of "me" transforms in my unique and personal enactment of responsibility to and for the Other. Transcendence transpires in ethical action called forth by the Other. This voice of ethics resists the power of death.

Death and God.—Both terms announce ultimate totalities for Levinas. However, they invoke a spiritual awakening within a trace of an ethical Saying that defies both the solidification of anguish and the power of self-righteous assurance. Death and God, for Levinas, do not immobilize; they unleash the Saying of ethics. Levinas rejects the reification of both death and God.

Ethics and justice.—Ethics and justice commence with attentiveness to the face of the Other, the unknown and unseen. They dwell within the adieu of goodbye and hello, a goodbye to self-assurance and a hello to an immemorial ethical echo. Adieu demands that each person stand and respond in uniqueness and particularity in performative ethical action. The unity of contraries within an adieu suggests that applause for ethical action and efforts to totalize justice dissipate in the face of the Other. For Levinas, the greatest fear in enacting "ethics as first philosophy" is self-righteousness. Such undue confidence morphs ethics and justice into dwellings of imposition.

Even the call of ethics has limits, as one considers those not at the table of decision making. The interruption of ethics makes justice possible. Finitude and infinity, Said and Saying, justice and ethics, universal and particular interrupt *l'un et l'Autre*, defining human identity with responsibility and ambiguity. No code, process, procedure, or rule ensures universal enactment of ethics and justice. There is, however, an unending demand to perform acts of responsibility for the Other, the neighbor, the unknown third—ever reminded of a "me" that originates in exteriority of responsibility unresponsive to self-righteousness and the demand for self-assurance. The "me" alone discovers and enacts communication ethics, awakened by a trace within the Said of totality, propelled by the Saying of responsibility, and tempered by unending obligation without assurance. Communication ethics, for Levinas, resists an a priori metaphysic, the imposition of a code or procedure, and, fundamentally, the self-righteous smirk of a knowing do-gooder. Communication ethics dwells in an immemorial space before, beyond, and ever more powerful than death itself.

NOTES

BIBLIOGRAPHY

INDEX

Notes

INTRODUCTION: EMMANUEL LEVINAS AND
COMMUNICATION ETHICS—ORIGINS AND TRACES

1. Emmanuel Levinas, *Totality and Infinity: An Essay on Exteriority*, trans. Alphonso Lingis (1961; repr., Pittsburgh: Duquesne University Press, 1969).

2. For more information on the originative I, see Ronald C. Arnett, *Communication Ethics in Dark Times: Hannah Arendt's Rhetoric of Warning and Hope* (Carbondale: Southern Illinois University Press, 2013), chap. 1. For more information on the hateful self, see Blaise Pascal, *Thoughts, Letters, and Minor Works* (New York: P. F. Collier & Son Company, 1910).

3. Arnett, *Communication Ethics in Dark Times*; see chap. 1.

4. Martin Buber, *The Way of Response* (New York: Schocken Books, 1966), 111.

5. Calvin O. Schrag, *Communicative Praxis and the Space of Subjectivity* (West Lafayette, IN: Purdue University Press, 2003).

6. Alasdair C. MacIntyre, *After Virtue: A Study in Moral Theory* (1981; repr., Notre Dame, IN: University of Notre Dame Press, 1984).

7. Emmanuel Levinas, *Entre Nous: Thinking-of-the-Other*, trans. Michael B. Smith and Barbara Harshav (New York: Columbia University Press, 1998), chap. 7.

8. Bettina Bergo, "What Is Levinas Doing? Phenomenology and the Rhetoric of an Ethical Un-Conscious," *Philosophy & Rhetoric*, 38, no. 2 (2005): 122–44.

9. Immanuel Kant, *Prolegomena to Any Future Metaphysics with Selections from the* Critique of Pure Reason, ed. Gary Hatfield (1997; repr., New York: Cambridge University Press, 2004), 10, 94–97.

10. Gary Hatfield, introduction to *Prolegomena to Any Future Metaphysics with Selections from the* Critique of Pure Reason by Immanuel Kant (1997; repr., New York: Cambridge University Press, 2004), xiv. For more information about the relationship between the projects of Kant and Levinas, see Catherine Chalier, *What Ought I to Do? Morality in Kant and Levinas*, trans. Jane Marie Todd (Ithaca, NY: Cornell University Press, 2002).

11. Aristotle, *Rhetoric*, trans. W. Rhys Roberts (Mineola, NY: Dover Publications, 2004), book 2.

12. The phrase, which I term *spiritual awakening*, derives directly from Levinas's language when describing the recognition of the face of the Other that charges one with responsibility by responding "here I am" to the immemorial ethical echo. Ronald C. Arnett, "Emmanuel Levinas: Priority of the Other," in *Ethical Communication: Moral Stances in Human Dialogue*, ed. Clifford G. Christians and John C. Merrill (Columbia: University of Missouri Press, 2009), 200.

13. Midrash is a form of biblical interpretation. Scholars contest definitions of midrash, with midrash readings of Jewish texts differing from European interpretations of the same texts. Daniel Boyarin, *Intertextuality and the Reading of Midrash* (Bloomington: Indiana University Press, 1994).

14. Claire Elise Katz, "Levinas—Between Philosophy and Rhetoric: The 'Teaching' of Levinas's Scriptural References," *Philosophy & Rhetoric* 38, no. 2 (2005): 159–72.

15. Boyarin, *Intertexuality and the Reading of Midrash*, viii.

16. Ronald C. Arnett, Janie Harden Fritz, and Leeanne M. Bell, *Communication Ethics Literacy: Dialogue and Difference* (Thousand Oaks, CA: Sage, 2009).

17. Robert John Scheffler Manning, *Interpreting Otherwise than Martin Heidegger* (Pittsburgh: Duquesne University Press, 1993).

18. Ronald C. Arnett, Janie Harden Fritz, and Annette M. Holba, "The Rhetorical Turn to Otherness: Otherwise than Humanism," *Cosmos and History: The Journal of Natural and Social Philosophy* 3, no. 1 (2007): 115–33.

19. See Emmanuel Levinas, "The Trace of the Other," trans. Alphonso Lingis, in *Deconstruction in Context*, ed. Mark C. Taylor (Chicago: University of Chicago Press, 1986), 348–59.

20. Thomas Merton, *Seven Storey Mountain* (New York: Mariner Books, 1999), 260–61.

21. See Martin Buber, "Guilt and Guilt Feelings," *Psychiatry* 20, no. 2 (1957): 114–29.

22. Dietrich Bonhoeffer, *Life Together: The Classic Exploration of Christian Community* (New York: Harper & Row, 1954).

23. Martin Heidegger, *Being and Time*, trans. Joan Stambaugh (Albany: State University of New York Press, 2010).

1. PRIMORDIAL GESTURE: THE DIFFICULT FREEDOM OF COMMUNICATION ETHICS

1. Emmanuel Levinas, "Ethics as First Philosophy," in *The Levinas Reader*, ed. Seán Hand (Malden, MA: Blackwell Publishers, 1989), 75–85; Emmanuel Levinas, *Difficult Freedom: Essays on Judaism*, trans. Seán Hand (1990; repr., Baltimore: Johns Hopkins University Press, 1997), xiv.

2. Emmanuel Levinas, *Time and the Other*, trans. Richard. A. Cohen (1979; repr., Pittsburgh: Duquesne University Press, 1987), 83.

3. See Edward. T. Hall, *The Silent Language* (New York: Anchor, 1973); Ray L. Birdwhistell, *Introduction to Kinesics: An Annotation System for Analysis of Body Motion and Gesture* (Louisville, KY: University of Louisville, 1952); Adam Kendon, *Gesture: Visible Action as Utterance* (Cambridge: Cambridge University Press, 2004).

4. George Herbert Mead, *Mind, Self, and Society: From the Standpoint of a Social Behaviorist*, ed. Charles W. Morris (1934; repr., Chicago: University of Chicago Press, 1962), 68.

5. Annette M. Holba, *Philosophical Leisure: Recuperative Praxis for Human Communication* (Milwaukee, WI: Marquette University Press, 2007), 127–70.

6. Mead's insights have propelled communication scholars, prominently Julia T. Wood. See Julia T. Wood, *Interpersonal Communication: Everyday Encounters*, 4th ed. (Belmont, CA: Wadsworth/Thompson, 2004); and Julia T. Wood, *Spinning the Symbolic Web: Human Communication as Symbolic Interaction* (Norwood, NJ: Ablex, 1992).

7. Mitchell Aboulafia, ed., *Philosophy, Social Theory, and the Thought of George Herbert Mead* (Albany: State University of New York Press, 1991).

8. Edmund Husserl, *The Crisis of European Sciences and Transcendental Phenomenology: An Introduction to Phenomenological Philosophy*, trans. David Carr (Evanston, IL: Northwestern University Press, 1970).

9. Amit Pinchevski, "Emmanuel Levinas: Contact and Interruption," in *Philosophical Profiles in the Theory of Communication*, ed. Jason Hannan (New York: Peter Lang Publishing, 2012), 348.

10. Ronald C. Arnett, *Communication Ethics in Dark Times*, chap. 1.

11. Michael J. Hyde, *The Call of Conscience: Heidegger and Levinas, Rhetoric and the Euthanasia Debate* (Columbia: University of South Carolina Press, 2001); Amit Pinchevski, *By Way of Interruption: Levinas and the Ethics of Communication* (Pittsburgh: Duquesne University Press, 2005).

12. Claire Elise Katz, "Emmanuel Levinas: The Rhetoric of Ethics," *Philosophy & Rhetoric* 38, no. 2 (2005): 100.

13. Laurie Johnson, "Face-Interface or the Prospect of a Virtual Ethics," *Ethical Space: The International Journal of Communication Ethics* 4, no. 1/2 (2007): 49–56.

14. Edmund Husserl, *Experience and Judgment*, ed. Ludwig Landgrebe, trans. James S. Churchill and Karl Ameriks (1948; repr., Evanston, IL: Northwestern University Press, 1973).

15. Amit Pinchevski, "Levinas as a Media Theorist: Toward an Ethics of Mediation," *Philosophy & Rhetoric* 47, no. 1 (2014): 48–72.

16. Spoma Jovanovic and Roy V. Wood, "Speaking from the Bedrock of Ethics," *Philosophy & Rhetoric* 37, no. 4 (2004): 332.

17. Spoma Jovanovic, "Difficult Conversations as Moral Imperatives: Negotiating Ethnic Identities during War," *Communication Quarterly* 51, no. 1 (2003): 57.

18. Kenneth Cmiel, "On Cynicism, Evil, and the Discovery of Communication in the 1940s," *Journal of Communication* 46, no. 3 (1996): 101.

19. David A. Frank, "The Jewish Countermodel: Talmudic Argumentation, the New Rhetoric Project, and the Classical Tradition of Rhetoric," *Journal of Communication and Religion* 26, no. 2 (2003): 163–94.

20. Angela Cooke-Jackson and Elizabeth K. Hansen, "Appalachian Culture and Reality TV: The Ethical Dilemma of Stereotyping Others," *Journal of Mass Media Ethics* 23, no. 3 (2008): 191.

21. Gerrie Snyman, "Rhetoric and Ethics: Looking at the Marks of our Reading/Speaking in Society," *Communicatio* 28, no. 1 (2002): 45.

22. Rochelle M. Green, Bonnie Mann, and Amy E. Story, "Care, Domination, and Representation," *Journal of Mass Media Ethics* 21, no. 2/3 (2006): 177–95.

23. Michael J. Hyde and Kenneth Rufo, "The Call of Conscience, Rhetorical Interruptions, and the Euthanasia Controversy," *Journal of Applied Communication Research* 28, no. 1 (2000): 4.

24. Stephen Coleman, "New Mediation and Direct Representation: Reconceptualizing Representation in the Digital Age," *New Media & Society* 7, no. 2 (2005): 177–98.

25. Sean Cubitt, "Immersed in Time," *Visual Communication* 6, no. 2 (2007): 220–29.

26. Stephanie Houston Grey, "Exhibitions in Life and Death: The Photography of Lucinda Devlin, Gunther von Hagens' *Body Worlds*, and the Disassembly of Scientific Progress," *American Communication Journal* 10, special edition (2008), http://ac-journal.org/journal/pubs/2008/Special%20Edition%2008%20-%20Aesthetics/Article_7.pdf.

27. Gary McCarron, "Undecided Stories: Alfred Hitchcock's *Blackmail* and the Problem of Moral Agency," *Canadian Journal of Communication* 33, no. 1 (2008): 65–80.

28. Boris Gubman, "Jacques Derrida on Philosophy, Language, and Power in the Age of Globalization," *American Journal of Semiotics* 18, no. 1–4 (2002): 288.

29. Susan Petrilli, "Semiotic Phenomenology of Predicative Judgment," *American Journal of Semiotics* 24, no. 4 (2008): 159.

30. Susan Petrilli, "On Communication: Contributions to the Human Sciences and to Humanism from Semiotics Understood as Semioethics," *American Journal of Semiotics* 24, no. 4 (2008): 193–236.

31. Susan Petrilli, "Working with Interpreters of the 'Meaning of Meaning': International Trends among 20th-Century Sign Theorists," *American Journal of Semiotics* 24, no. 4 (2008): 49–88.

32. Susan Petrilli, "Iconicity in Translation: On Similarity, Alterity, and Dialogism in the Relation among Signs," *American Journal of Semiotics* 24, no. 4 (2008): 237–302.

33. Jonathan Corpus Ong, "The Cosmopolitan Continuum: Locating Cosmopolitanism in Media and Cultural Studies," *Media, Culture & Society* 31, no. 3 (2009): 462.

34. Arnett, *Communication Ethics in Dark Times*, 117; see also chap. 9.

35. Christopher N. Poulos, "Accidental Dialogue," *Communication Theory* 18, no. 1 (2008): 117–38.

36. Michael J. Hyde, *The Life-Giving Gift of Acknowledgment* (West Lafayette, IN: Purdue University Press, 2005).

37. Hyde, *Call of Conscience*, 79–115.

38. Jeffrey W. Murray, "Toward a Post-Habermasian Discourse Ethics: The Acknowledgment of the Other," *New Jersey Journal of Communication* 9, no. 1 (2001): 1–19.

39. Emmanuel Levinas, *Ethics and Infinity: Conversations with Philippe Nemo*, trans. Richard A. Cohen (Pittsburgh: Duquesne University Press, 1985), 86–87.

40. Levinas, *Totality and Infinity*; for instance, see 14, 85, 89, 156–58.

41. D. Diane Davis, "Finitude's Clamor; Or, Notes toward a Communitarian Literacy," *College Composition and Communication* 53, no. 1 (2001): 131.

42. Lisbeth Lipari, "Listening for the Other: Ethical Implications of the Buber-Levinas Encounter," *Communication Theory* 14, no. 2 (2004): 122–41.

43. Jeffrey W. Murray, "An Other Ethics for Kenneth Burke," *Communication Studies* 49, no. 1 (1998): 44.

44. Jeffrey W. Murray, "Kenneth Burke: A Dialogue of Motives," *Philosophy & Rhetoric* 35, no. 1 (2002): 34.

44. Amit Pinchevski, "Ethics on the Line," *Southern Communication Journal* 68, no. 2 (2003): 153.

46. Jeffrey W. Murray, "The Paradox of Emmanuel Levinas: Knowledge of the Absolute Other," *Qualitative Research Reports in Communication* 3, no. 2 (2002): 39–46. Also see Robert John Sheffler Manning, *Interpreting*

Otherwise than Heidegger: Emmanuel Levinas's Ethics as First Philosophy (Pittsburgh: Duquesne University Press, 1993); Jacques Derrida, "Violence and Metaphysics: An Essay on the Thought of Emmanuel Levinas," in *Writing and Difference*, trans. Alan Bass (Chicago: University of Chicago Press, 1978), 79–153; Richard J. Bernstein, *The New Constellation: The Ethical-Political Horizons of Modernity/Postmodernity* (Cambridge, MA: MIT Press, 1991).

47. Murray, "Paradox of Emmanuel Levinas."
48. Michael J. Salvo, "Ethics of Engagement: User-Centered Design and Rhetorical Methodology," *Technical Communication Quarterly* 10, no. 3 (2001): 275.
49. Katz, "Levinas—Between Philosophy and Rhetoric"; Diane Perpich, "Figurative Language and the 'Face' in Levinas's Philosophy," *Philosophy & Rhetoric* 38, no. 2 (2005): 119.
50. Jeffrey W. Murray, "The Dialogical Prioritization of Calls: Toward a Communicative Model of Justice," *New Jersey Journal of Communication* 11, no. 1 (2003): 20.
51. Pat J. Gehrke, "Being for the Other-to-the-Other: Justice and Communication in Levinasian Ethics," *Review of Communication* 10, no. 1 (2010): 5–19.
52. Pat J. Gehrke, "Before the One and the Other: Ethico-Political Communication and Community," in *Philosophy of Communication Ethics: Alterity and the Other*, ed. Ronald C. Arnett and Pat Arneson (Lanham, MD, NJ: Fairleigh Dickinson University Press, 2014), 58.
53. Oona Eisenstadt, "Levinas versus Levinas: Hebrew, Greek, and Linguistic Justice," *Philosophy & Rhetoric* 38, no. 2 (2005): 145.
54. Arnett, *Communication Ethics in Dark Times*, chap. 1.
55. Hyde, *Call of Consciousness*; Gehrke, "Being for the Other-to-the-Other," 7; Lisbeth Lipari, "Rhetoric's Other: Levinas, Listening and the Ethical Response," *Philosophy & Rhetoric* 45, no. 3 (2012): 227–45; Pinchevski, *By Way of Interruption*, 213. Pinchevski also draws from the work of Bakhtin.
56. Stanley Deetz, "Reclaiming the Subject Matter as a Guide to Mutual Understanding: Effectiveness and Ethics in Interpersonal Interaction," *Communication Quarterly* 38, no. 3 (1990): 226–43.
57. Emmanuel Levinas, *Basic Philosophical Writings*, ed. Adriaan T. Peperzak, Simon Critchley, and Robert Bernasconi (Bloomington: Indiana University Press, 1996), 168.
58. Emmanuel Levinas, *Otherwise than Being or Beyond Essence*, trans. Alphonso Lingis (1981; repr., Pittsburgh: Duquesne University Press, 1998).
59. MacIntyre, *After Virtue*, 23–35.

60. Arnett, "Emmanuel Levinas: Priority of the Other," 200.

61. The Hebrew prophet Elijah advocated monotheism, claiming that the God of Israel was the only true god. His story is told in 1 Kings 17–19 of the Old Testament. See Levinas, *Difficult Freedom*, 38.

62. For a discussion of the religious roots of Levinas's project, see James Hatley, "Generations: Levinas in the Jewish Context," *Philosophy & Rhetoric* 38, no. 2 (2005): 173–89; and Katz, "Levinas—Between Philosophy and Rhetoric." For a brief discussion of an interpretation of Levinas's project as agnostic, see Bettina G. Bergo, *Levinas between Ethics and Politics: For the Beauty That Adorns the Earth* (Dordrecht, Netherlands: Springer, 1999), 16.

2. FOOTPRINTS AND ECHOES: EMMANUEL LEVINAS

1. Hannah Arendt, *Responsibility and Judgment*, ed. Jerome John (New York: Schocken Books, 2003), 8; Immanuel Kant, *Critique of Judgment*, trans. J. H. Bernard (New York: Hafner Press, 1951), 80, 91.

2. Levinas, "Ethics as First Philosophy"; Levinas, *Totality and Infinity*, 304.

3. Annette Aronowicz, "Introducing 'The Temptation of Temptation': Levinas and Europe," *Journal of Scriptural Reasoning* 11, no. 2 (2012), http://jsr.shanti.virginia.edu/back-issues/volume-11-no-2-december-2012-levinas-and-philosophy/introducing-the-temptation-of-temptation-levinas-and-europe/. Aronowicz notes that Levinas remained involved with the school until his retirement in 1979.

4. Philippe Nemo, foreword to *Emmanuel Levinas: His Life and Legacy*, by Salomon Malka, trans. Michael Kigel and Sonja E. Embree (Pittsburgh: Duquesne University Press, 2006), xi.

5. Raul Hilberg, *The Destruction of the European Jews*, vol. 3, 3rd ed. (New Haven, CT: Yale University Press, 2003), 1301–3. Published estimates varied between five and six million killed.

6. See Ronald C. Arnett, "Communicative Meaning: From Pangloss to Tenacious Hope," in *A Century of Communication Studies: The Unfinished Conversation*, ed. Pat J. Gehrke and William M. Keith (New York: Routledge, 2015), 262.

7. Arnett, *Communication Ethics in Dark Times*, chap. 1.

8. Michael Kigel, translator's notes to *Emmanuel Levinas: His Life and Legacy*, by Salomon Malka (Pittsburgh: Duquesne University Press, 2006), xxiv.

9. Salomon Malka, *Emmanuel Levinas: His Life and Legacy*, trans. Michael Kigel and Sonja M. Embree (Pittsburgh: Duquesne University Press, 2006), 57.

10. Hasidism is a Jewish religious movement that began in eighteenth-century Europe and persists today in Europe, the United States, and Israel. This form of Judaism stresses mystic traditions of Kabbalah and centers on holy men believed to hold a special relationship with God. Wendy Doniger, ed., *Merriam-Webster's Encyclopedia of World Religions* (Springfield, MA: Merriam-Webster, 1999), 415. The Musar movement originated amongst Orthodox Jews in Lithuania during the nineteenth century. The movement stresses personal piety as a "necessary complement to intellectual studies of the Torah and Talmud." Ibid., 759.

11. Maurice Blanchot was a French writer and critic in the early twentieth century. During the German occupation of France in World War II, Blanchot worked as a journalist traveling among groups of antidemocrats, anti-Marxists, and anti-Populars. Blanchot served as a literary association director under the Vichy regime. His writings were "dissident." Gerald L. Bruns, *Maurice Blanchot: The Refusal of Philosophy* (Baltimore: Johns Hopkins University Press, 1997), xi.

12. Meins G. S. Coetsier, *The Existential Philosophy of Etty Hillesum: An Analysis of Her Diaries and Letters* (Leiden, Netherlands: Brill Publishing, 2014), 294.

13. In May 1933 Heidegger delivered his inaugural rector address, "The Self-Assertion of the German University," at the University of Freiburg. The address reflected Heidegger's participation in the Nazi Party, particularly in claiming the "destiny" of the German people through leadership within the university. Tom Rockmore, *On Heidegger's Nazism and Philosophy* (Berkeley: University of California Press, 1992), 59.

14. The Alliance Israélite Universelle, a French political organization founded in 1860, worked for the "emancipation, welfare and improvement of Jews worldwide, especially in French territories in the Middle East." The alliance founded an extensive system of schools in North Africa, Palestine, and the Ottoman Empire to teach secular and religious subjects. Raymond P. Scheindlin, *A Short History of the Jewish People: From Legendary Times to Modern Statehood* (New York: Oxford University Press, 1998), 138–40, 150.

15. Between the wars France experienced an economic boom, which led to the reformation of naturalization laws and accommodated the needs of Eastern European workers. In 1940 the Vichy regime enabled the Commission of Revisions of Naturalizations to review all applicants following 1927 and to denaturalize anyone deemed unable to integrate into French society. Thomas J. Laub, *After the Fall: German Policy in Occupied France, 1940–1944* (Oxford: Oxford University Press, 2010).

16. Samuel Moyn, *Origins of the Other: Emmanuel Levinas between Revelation and Ethics* (Ithaca, NY: Cornell University Press, 2005), 90.
17. Ira F. Stone, *Reading Levinas/Reading Talmud: An Introduction* (Philadelphia: Jewish Publication Society, 1998), 5.
18. The dedication states, "To Marcelle *and* Jean Wahl."
19. The dedication states, "To Doctor Henri Nerson: A Friend. In memory of a teaching which exalts that friendship."
20. William J. Richardson, *Heidegger: Through Phenomenology to Thought* (Dordrecht, Netherlands: Martinus Nijhoff, 1963).
21. Jacques Derrida, *Adieu to Emmanuel Levinas*, trans. Pascale Anne Brault and Michael Naas (Stanford, CA: Stanford University Press, 1999).
22. Jacques Derrida, "Violence and Metaphysics: An Essay on the Thought of Emmanuel Levinas," in *Writing and Difference*, trans. Alan Bass (Chicago: University of Chicago Press, 1978).
23. Jean Beaufret was a French philosopher who studied at École Normale Supérieure. After the war Beaufret turned to phenomenology. Heidegger addressed his "Letter on 'Humanism'" to Beaufret. Ethan Kleinberg, *Generation Existential: Heidegger's Philosophy in France, 1927–1961* (Ithaca, NY: Cornell University Press, 2005), 158–62.
24. Martin Heidegger, "Letter on 'Humanism,'" in *Pathways*, ed. William McNeill (Cambridge: Cambridge University Press, 1998).
25. René Char, ed., *L'Endurance de la pensée, pour saluer Jean Beaufret* (Paris: Plon, 1968).
26. In a memorial piece written for Levinas shortly after his death, Ricoeur called him his "venerated friend." See Paul Ricoeur, "In Memoriam: Emmanuel Levinas," *Philosophy Today* 40, no. 3 (1996): 331–33. Both Levinas and Ricoeur held scholarly common ground, including a concern for the Other. They responded to each other's writings. For information about Ricoeur's interactions with Levinas, see Peter Kemp, "Ricoeur between Heidegger and Levinas: Original Affirmation between Ontological Attestation and Ethical Injunction," in *Paul Ricoeur: The Hermeneutics of Action*, ed. Paul Kearney (Thousand Oaks, CA: SAGE, 1996), 41–62.
27. Pope John Paul II (1920–2005) invited Ricoeur and Levinas for conversation; one sat at the pontiff's right hand and the other at his left. The pope had great interest in phenomenology and was a student of Roman Ingarden (1893–1970), a Polish scholar indebted to Husserl.
28. Jöelle Hansel, *Levinas in Jerusalem: Phenomenology, Ethics, Politics, Aesthetics* (Dordrecht, Netherlands: Springer, 2009).

29. Malka notes that French media outlets did not begin recognizing Levinas as a top French philosopher until the 1980 publication of *Textes pour Emmanuel Levinas.*
30. Maurice Blanchot, ed., *Textes pour Emmanuel Levinas* (Paris: Jean-Michel Place, 1980).
31. Philippe Nemo, preface to *Ethics and Infinity: Conversations with Philippe Nemo,* by Emmanuel Levinas (Pittsburgh: Duquesne University Press, 1985), vi–vii.
32. Richard A. Cohen, introduction to *Ethics and Infinity: Conversations with Philippe Nemo,* by Emmanuel Levinas (Pittsburgh: Duquesne University Press, 1985), 1–15.
33. See William Shakespeare, *Hamlet,* act 3, scene 1, line 56.
34. Richard A. Cohen, foreword to *Otherwise than Being or Beyond Essence,* by Emmanuel Levinas, trans. Alphonso Lingis (Pittsburgh: Duquesne University Press, 1998), xii.
35. In 1894 Alfred Dreyfus, a Jewish officer in the French General Staff, was convicted of espionage, suspected of delivering confidential military information to a German officer. Dreyfus was sent to Devil's Island for a lifetime. In 1895 Dreyfus's defense began when Colonel Picquart, head of the information division of the General Staff, declared Dreyfus innocent, stating that the real traitor was Major Walsin-Esterhazy, another officer in the French General Staff. At which point Picquart assumed a commission post in Tunisia. Georges Clemenceau, a journalist, publicly called for a reexamination of the case. In 1898 Emile Zola wrote "J'Accuse," published by Clemenceau's paper. When Clemenceau became the prime minister, he pardoned Dreyfus without a second trial. Hannah Arendt, *The Origins of Totalitarianism* (New York: Harcourt, 1968), 89–95.
36. Rosenzweig's *The Star of Redemption* influenced Levinas's rejection of totality in *Totality and Infinity* through its understanding of "revelation and redemption in their opposition to the 'Pantheistic Conception of All.'" See Emil L. Fackenheim and Raphael Jospe, ed., *Jewish Philosophy and the Academy* (Cranbury, NJ: Associated University Presses, 1996), 136.
37. Husserl, *The Crisis of European Sciences.*
38. Husserl, *Experience and Judgment,* 75.
39. See Paul Ricoeur, *Time and Narrative,* trans. Kathleen McLaughlin and David Pellauer (1983; repr., Chicago: University of Chicago Press, 1985); and Hans-Georg Gadamer, *Truth and Method* (1975; repr., London: Continuum, New York: Bloomsbury, 2013).

3. THE COMMENCEMENT OF RESPONSIBILITY: THE ENIGMA OF THE FACE

1. Levinas, *Ethics and Infinity*, 85.
2. References to this enigmatic teacher, in scholarly literature, appear as Shushani and Chouchani. For consistency I maintain the spelling Chouchani.
3. Alan M. Dershowitz cites Wiesel's work helping survivors of "a world-wide conspiracy of genocide" to "re-enter and adjust in peace to an alien world that deserved little forgiveness." See Alan M. Dershowitz, "Elie Wiesel: A Biblical Life," in *Celebrating Elie Wiesel: Stories, Essays, Reflections*, ed. Alan Rosen (Notre Dame, IN: University of Notre Dame Press, 1998), xi.
4. Elie Wiesel, *All Rivers Run to the Sea: Memoirs of Elie Wiesel* (New York: Alfred A. Knopf, 1995); Elie Wiesel, *Legends of Our Time* (New York: Schocken Books, 1968).
5. Salomon Malka, *Monsieur Chouchani: L'énigme d'un Maître du XXe Siècle* (Paris: J. C. Lattes, 1994).
6. Emmanuel Levinas, *Alterity and Transcendence*, trans. Michael B. Smith (New York: Columbia University Press, 1999).
7. Pierre Hayat, preface to *Alterity and Transcendence*, ix.
8. Levinas, *Ethics and Infinity*, 85.
9. Plotinus (205–270) was an ancient philosopher influential in third-century Rome whom many consider the founder of Neoplatonic philosophy. Plotinus likely studied philosophy at a very young age, leading him to Alexandria and the school of Ammonius.
10. Kant discusses schematism in *Critique of Pure Reason*, which examines the "sense and significance" of categories. See Immanuel Kant, *Critique of Pure Reason*, trans. Werner S. Pluhar (1781; repr., Indianapolis, IN: Hackett Publishing Company, 1996).
11. See Martin Buber, *I and Thou*, trans. Ronald Gregor Smith (Edinburgh: T. & T. Clark, 1937).
12. For an in-depth examination of the differences between Buber and Levinas on the question of reciprocity, see Ronald C. Arnett, "A Dialogic Ethic 'Between' Buber and Levinas: A Responsive Ethical 'I,'" in *Dialogue: Theorizing Differences in Communication Studies*, ed. Rob Anderson, Leslie A. Baxter, and Kenneth N. Cissna (Thousand Oaks, CA: Sage, 2004).
13. See Matthew 22: 36–39. The second commandment ordering to love your neighbor as yourself follows the first commandment to love God with one's whole heart, mind, and soul.

14. Levinas suggests that Buber's I-Thou is missing a third, the "Other," or illeity. Levinas challenges Buber's notion of reciprocity rooted in an understanding of alterity. While Buber considers justice possible in the I-Thou, Levinas looks to a third to render justice, which he considers a public, rather than private, dialogue. See Ronald C. Arnett, "Beyond Dialogue: Beyond Levinas and Otherwise than the I-Thou," *Language and Dialogue* 2, no. 1 (2012): 140–55.

15. See Lynn Hunt, ed. and trans., *The French Revolution and Human Rights: A Brief Documentary History* (Boston: Bedford, 1996), 77–79.

16. Malka, *Emmanuel Levinas*, 126.

17. Buber, *I and Thou*, 54.

18. See Maurice Friedman, *Martin Buber's Life and Work* (1981; repr., Detroit, MI: Wayne State University Press, 1988), 376.

4. PROPER NAMES: SAYING, SAID, AND THE TRACE

1. Emmanuel Levinas, *Proper Names*, trans. Michael B. Smith (1975; repr., Stanford, CA: Stanford University Press, 1996).

2. Thomas Trezise, review of *Proper Names*, by Emmanuel Levinas, *Comparative Literature Studies* 37, no. 3 (2000): 352–60.

3. Mary McDonagh Murphy, *Scout, Atticus, and Boo: A Celebration of Fifty Years of* To Kill a Mockingbird (New York: HarperCollins Publishers, 2010).

4. In July 2015 Harper Lee released *Go Set a Watchman*, an earlier version of *To Kill a Mockingbird*, written from the perspective of Scout as an adult. Lee wrote *To Kill a Mockingbird* because the editor requested a story from the perspective of a child.

5. Harper Lee, *To Kill a Mockingbird* (1960; repr., New York: HarperCollins Publishers, 2010), 253.

6. In the context of the story, *agunot* refers to "souls in limbo" and *agnon* refers to "some relationship to the state of limbo." Arnold J. Band, *Nostalgia and Nightmare: A Study in the Fiction of S. Y. Agnon* (Berkeley: University of California Press, 1968), 17.

7. For complete lists of works written by Agnon in Hebrew and Yiddish, see appendixes 1–3 in Band, *Nostalgia and Nightmare*, 525–39.

8. Band argues that the association to Kafka is "erroneous," arguing that "Agnon is Kafkaesque only because Kafka is the best-known exponent of a style of writing both he and Agnon inherited, which has its roots in German Romanticism or, more directly, in the late-nineteenth-century rebirth of the Romantic spirit ordinarily called Neoromanticism." See Band, *Nostalgia and Nightmare*, 27, 448.

9. Robert Alter, "The Genius of S. Y. Agnon," *Commentary* 32 (1961): 108.

10. Baruch Hochman, *The Fiction of S. Y. Agnon* (Ithaca, NY: Cornell University Press, 1970), x. Even Levinas describes Agnon's work as having an "untranslatable dimension." See Levinas, *Proper Names*, 10.

11. For references to Agnon's Hebrew tributes to Buber, see appendix 1 in Band, *Nostalgia and Nightmare*, 456, 473, 490.

12. Friedman, *Martin Buber's Life and Work*.

13. At the age of fourteen, Buber occasionally assisted his grandfather with his editions of midrashim—biblical exegesis or commentary on ancient Hebrew texts. Midrash essentially fills gaps in biblical narratives through their continued interpretation.

14. Herzl, known as one of the fathers of modern Zionism, assisted in the formation of the World Zionist Organization in 1897 and was an avid promoter of Jewish migration to Palestine in the effort to establish Israel as a Jewish state. See Mark Gelber, "Theodore Herzl," in *Routledge Encyclopedia of Jewish Writers of the Twentieth Century*, ed. Sorrel Kerbel (New York: Taylor and Francis, 2003), 443–44.

15. While in Palestine in 1938, Buber continued his commitment to adult education. For example, he advocated for adult education at Hebrew University and was part of the Committee on Adult Education. See Friedman, *Martin Buber's Life and Work*, 73.

16. Amir Eshel, "Paul Celan's Other: History, Poetics, and Ethics," *New German Critique*, no. 91 (2004): 57–77.

17. Pierre-Antoine Marie, "Sens et opinion selon Jeanne Delhomme," *Revue de Métaphysique et de Morale*, 73, no. 4 (1968): 492–506.

18. Jacques Derrida, *Of Grammatology* (1967; repr., Baltimore: Johns Hopkins University Press, 1997).

19. Richard Klein, "Prolegomenon to Derrida," *Diacritics* 2, no. 4 (1972): 30.

20. Beth Hawkins, *Reluctant Theologians: Franz Kafka, Paul Celan, Edmond Jabès* (Bronx, NY: Fordham University Press, 2003), 158.

21. Warren F. Motte Jr., "Questioning Jabès" *French Forum* 11, no. 1 (1986): 83–94.

22. Peter F. Drucker, "The Unfashionable Kierkegaard," *Sewanee Review* 57, no. 4 (1949): 587–602.

23. John Hellman, "Jacques Chavalier, Bergsonism, and Modern French Catholic Intellectuals," *Biography* 4, no. 2 (1982): 138–53.

24. Michael Kelly, "Jean Lacroix," in *The New Oxford Companion to Literature in French*, ed. Peter France (Oxford: Clarendon Press, 1995).

25. A. R. Louch, review of *Lectures on Philosophy*, by G. E. Moore, *Journal of the History of Philosophy* 6, no. 2 (1986): 182–83.

26. Henri Wald, *Introduction to Dialectical Logic* (Romania: Academieie Republicii Socialiste Romania, 1975), 200.

27. See Stefanos Geroulanos, *An Atheism That Is Not Humanism Emerges in French Thought* (Stanford: Stanford University Press, 2010), 253.

28. Michael Sheringham, "French Autobiography: Texts, Contexts, Poetics," *Journal of European Studies* 16, no. 1 (1986): 71.

29. Gabriel Marcel, "Max Picard," in *In the Flight from God*, ed. J. M. Cameron, trans. Marianne Kuschnitzky (1934; repr., Chicago: Henry Regnery Company, 1951), viii.

30. Siegfried B. Puknat, "Max Picard," *Books Abroad* 25, no. 4 (1951): 341.

31. J. Murray, "Marcel Proust," *Modern Language Review* 21, no. 1 (1926): 37.

32. The establishment of the Husserl Archives occurred before the Université Catholique de Louvain split from the Katholieke Universiteit Leuven in 1968. The archives remain at the Katholieke Universiteit Leuven.

33. The university in exile, founded with the help of the Rockefeller Foundation, was a place for Jewish intellectual refugees, stripped of their academic credentials, to study and work in New York. See Peter M. Rutkoff and William B. Scott, "The French in New York: Resistance and Structure," *Social Research* 50, no. 1 (1983): 185–214.

34. Michael Levinas, "The Final Meeting between Emmanuel Levinas and Maurice Blanchot," *Critical Inquiry* 36, no. 4 (2010): 650.

35. Françoise Collin, *Maurice Blanchot et la question de l'écriture* (Paris: Gallimard, 1971).

5. THE IMPERSONAL AND THE SACRED:
IGNITING PERSONAL RESPONSIBILITY

1. Arnett, *Communication Ethics in Dark Times*, chap. 1; Arnett, "A Dialogic Ethic 'Between' Buber and Levinas," 75–90.

2. Arnett, *Communication Ethics in Dark Times*, chap. 1.

3. Dana L. Cloud, *Control and Consolation in American Culture and Politics: Rhetorics of Therapy* (Thousand Oaks, CA: Sage, 1998).

4. Gregory Bateson and Mary Catherine Bateson, *Angels Fear: Towards an Epistemology of the Sacred* (1987; repr., Creskill, NJ: Hampton Press, 2005), 15.

5. Charles Taylor, *Sources of the Self: The Making of Modern Identity* (1989; repr., Cambridge, MA: Harvard University Press, 2006), 53.

6. J. R. R. Tolkien, *The Two Towers: Being the Second Part of* The Lord of the Rings (New York: Ballantine Books, 1954), 260–67.

7. Catherine Chalier, *What Ought I to Do? Morality in Kant and Levinas*, trans. Jane Marie Todd (Ithaca, NY: Cornell University Press, 2002), 1.

8. Inge Scholl, *The White Rose: Munich, 1942–1943*, trans. Arthur R. Schultz (Hanover, NH: Wesleyan University Press, 1983).

9. Arnett, *Communication Ethics in Dark Times*, chap. 1.

10. The Narcissus story from Greek mythology tells of a handsome youth named Narcissus who stares at his reflection in a body of water.

11. Levinas, *Totality and Infinity*, 79.

12. Emmanuel Levinas, *God, Death, and Time*, trans. Bettina Bergo (1993; repr., Stanford: Stanford University Press, 2000), 36.

13. Emmanuel Levinas, *The Theory of Intuition in Husserl's Phenomenology*, 2nd ed., trans. André Orianne (1973; repr., Evanston, IL: Northwestern University Press, 1995), 23, 35, 74.

14. Emmanuel Levinas, *Discovering Existence with Husserl*, trans. Richard A. Cohen and Michael B. Smith (Evanston, IL: Northwestern University Press, 1998), 122.

15. Levinas, *Otherwise than Being*, 129.

16. Emmanuel Levinas, *Of God Who Comes to Mind*, trans. Bettina Bergo (1986; repr., Stanford, CA: Stanford University Press, 1998), 16–17, 119.

17. Levinas, *Alterity and Transcendence*, 46, 66.

18. Cohen, foreword to *Otherwise than Being*, xii.

19. Levinas, *Ethics and Infinity*, 85.

20. Levinas references the "impersonal" on one hundred nine pages within twenty-one of his books.

21. Emmanuel Levinas, *Collected Philosophical Papers*, trans. Alphonso Lingis (Dordrecht: Martinus Nijhoff Publishers, 1987), 183.

22. Bobby belonged to a German guard in Stalag XIB, where Levinas was prisoner during World War II. According to Malka, "Bobby and his cheerful barks welcoming the exhausted inmates returning from work—something that lasted for a few weeks until the sentinels decided to chase him out of the camp—left the inmates with a fond memory." Malka, *Emmanuel Levinas*, 71. For more information on the relationship between Levinas and animals in regard to posthuman rhetoric, see D. Diane Davis, *Inessential Solidarity: Rhetoric and Foreigner Relations* (Pittsburgh: University of Pittsburgh Press, 2010); Pat Gehrke, "The Ethical Importance of Being Human: God and Humanism in Levinas's Philosophy," *Philosophy Today* 50, no. 4 (2006): 428–36.

6. IMPERFECTION: ETHICS DISRUPTED BY
JUSTICE—*THE NAME OF THE ROSE*

1. Umberto Eco, *The Name of the Rose*, trans. William Weaver (Orlando, FL: Harcourt, 1983). Eco's novel first appeared in Italian in 1980 and was translated into English in 1983.

2. Emmanuel Levinas, *Is It Righteous to Be? Interviews with Emmanuel Levinas*, ed. Jill Robbins (Stanford, CA: Stanford University Press, 2001), 167.

3. John Lyne, review of *The Name of the Rose*, by Umberto Eco, *Quarterly Journal of Speech*, 71, no. 4 (1985): 489.

4. The breadth of Eco's scholarship is detailed by Michael Caesar, *Umberto Eco: Philosophy, Semiotics, and the Work of Fiction* (Malden, MA: Blackwell Publishers, 1999); and Gary Radford, *On Eco* (Belmont, CA: Wadsworth Publishing, 2002).

5. Elissavet Evdoridou, "Multiscale Textual Semiotic Analysis," *Semiotica* 171, no. 1/4 (2008): 252.

6. Carlos Scolari, "Digital Eco_logy: Umberto Eco and a Semiotic Approach to Digital Communication," *Information, Communication & Society* 12, no. 1 (2009): 143.

7. Gioacchino Balducci, "Umberto Eco in New York: An Interview," *Communication Quarterly* 24, no. 2 (1976): 36.

8. Charles Sanders Peirce, "The Icon, Index, and Symbol," *Collected Philosophical Papers* 2 (1932), 274–307.

9. Umberto Eco, *The Role of the Reader: Explorations in the Semiotics of Texts* (Bloomington: Indiana University Press, 1979).

10. Robert A. Rushing, "From Monk to Monks: The End of Enjoyment in Umberto Eco's *The Name of the Rose*," *Symposium* 59, no. 2 (2005): 125.

11. Kornelia Tancheva, "Recasting the Debate: The Sign of the Library in Popular Culture," *Libraries & Culture* 40, no. 4 (2005): 534.

12. Agnes Heller, "The Contemporary Historical Novel," *Thesis Eleven* 106, no. 1 (2011): 93.

13. Marc-Oliver Schuster, "Bi-Paradigmatic Irony as a Postmodern Sign," *Semiotica* 183, no. 1/4 (2011): 359.

14. Pope John XXII served from 1316 until 1334. William of Ockham wrote at least one text, *Opus Nonaginta*, specifically "to overturn John XXII's attacks on Franciscan poverty." See Marilyn McCord Adams, *William Ockham, Vols. 1 and 2* (Notre Dame, IN: University of Notre Dame Press, 1987), 1200–1201.

15. Umberto Eco, "'Casablanca': Cult Movies and Intertextual Collage," *Substance* 14, no. 2 (1985): 10.

16. Jack Tresidder, *The Complete Dictionary of Symbols* (San Francisco: Chronicle Books, 2005), 418.

17. Martin Buber, *The Knowledge of Man: A Philosophy of the Interhuman*, ed. Maurice Friedman, trans. Maurice Friedman and Ronald Gregor Smith (1965; repr., Atlantic Highlands, NJ: Humanities Press International, 1988), 56.

18. Dolcinians are associated with Fra Dolcino, an egalitarian and violent leader in the Joachimite movement: "Dolcino headed a band of the Illuminated who plundered and destroyed and announced the reign of the Spirit. In 1507 they were vanquished by the 'forces of order'—that is, an army commanded by the Bishop of Vercueil." See Jacques Ellul, *Violence: Reflections from a Christian Perspective* (1969; repr., Eugene, OR: Wipf and Stock Publisher, 2007), 18.

19. Due to the political conditions of the time, Pope Clement V moved the papal capital from Rome to Avignon, France, in 1309. During the Avignon papacy, all seven appointed popes were French as well as the majority of cardinals. The pope's residence remained in Avignon until 1377 when Pope Gregory XI returned the papal capital to Rome. The Avignon papacy marked the beginning of the Great Schism as the Sacred College of Cardinals remained in France, naming a second pope. Until 1417, when the Great Schism ended, the Avignon papacy appointed a series of antipopes. For information on the Avignon papacy, see Norman Housley, *The Avignon Papacy and the Crusades 1305–1378* (Oxford: Oxford University Press, 1986); Joëlle Rollo-Koster, *Avignon and Its Papacy, 1309–1417: Popes, Institutions, and Society* (New York: Rowman & Littlefield Publishers, 2015).

20. For information on the location of the papacy and its reunification under Pope Martin V, see Walter Ullmann, *A Short History of the Papacy in the Middle Ages* (London: Methuen & Co, 1972), 301–5.

21. Teresa de Lauretis, "Gaudy Rose: Eco and Narcissism," *Substance* 14, no. 2 (1985): 26.

22. Louis MacKey, "The Name of the Book," *Substance* 14, no. 2 (1985): 37.

23. Leonard G. Schulze, "An Ethics of Significance," *Substance* 14, no. 2 (1985): 88.

24. Victoria V. Vernon, "The Demonics of (True) Belief: Treacherous Texts, Blasphemous Interpretations and Murderous Readers," *MLN* 107, no. 5 (1992): 841.

25. Robert F. Yeager, "Fear of Writing, or Adso and the Poisoned Text," *Substance* 14, no. 2 (1985): 52.

26. Carl A. Rubino, "The Invisible Worm: Ancients and Moderns in *The Name of the Rose*," *Substance* 14, no. 2 (1985): 60.

27. Robert Artigiani, "The 'Model Reader' and the Thermodynamic Model," *Substance* 14, no. 2 (1985): 71.

28. Douglass Parker, "The Curious Case of Pharaoh's Polyp, and Related Matters," *Substance* 14, no. 2 (1985): 83.

29. W. Cary McMullen, "Villainy, Humor, and Heresy," *Theology Today* 46, no. 3 (1989): 285.

30. Leticia Reyes-Tatinclaux, "The Face of Evil: Devilish Borges in Eco's *The Name of the Rose*," *Chasqui* 18, no. 1 (1989): 8.

31. David G. Baxter, "Murder and Mayhem in a Medieval Abbey: The Philosophy of *The Name of the Rose*," *The Journal of Speculative Philosophy* 3, no. 3 (1989): 186.

32. Deborah Parker, "The Literature of Appropriation: Eco's Use of Borges in *Il Nome Della Rosa*," *The Modern Language Review* 85, no. 4 (1990): 849.

33. Leo Corry and Renato Giovanolli, "Jorge Borges, Author of the *Name of the Rose*," *Poetics Today* 13, no. 3 (1992): 425–45.

34. Margaret Hallissy, "Reading the Plans: The Architectural Drawings in Umberto Eco's *The Name of the Rose*," *Critique: Studies in Contemporary Fiction* 42, no. 3 (2001): 284.

35. Jeffrey Garrett, "Missing Eco: On Reading *The Name of the Rose* as Library Criticism," *Library Quarterly: Information, Community, Policy* 61, no. 4 (1991): 386.

36. Lynn Christine Miller, "*The Name of the Rose*: Adaptation as Palimpsest," *Literature and Performance* 7, no. 2 (1987): 77.

37. See Edmund Husserl, *Phenomenology and the Foundations of the Sciences*, trans. Ted E. Klein and William E. Pohl (Dordrecht, Netherlands: Martinus Nijhoff Publishers, 1980).

38. Thomas Mann, *Doctor Faustus: The Life of the German Composer Adrian Leverkühn as Told by a Friend*, trans. John E. Woods (New York: Vintage Books, 1999). Also see Osman Durrani, "The Tearful Teacher: The Role of Serenus Zeitblom in Thomas Mann's *Doktor Faustus*," *Modern Language Review* 80, no. 3 (1985): 652–58.

39. Evelyn Cobley, "Closure and Infinite Semiosis in Mann's *Doctor Faustus* and Eco's *The Name of the Rose*," *Comparative Literature Series* 26, no. 4 (1989): 342.

40. Steven Sallis, "Naming the Rose: Readers and Codes in Umberto Eco's Novel," *Journal of the Midwest Modern Language Association* 19, no. 2 (1986): 3.

41. Cinzia Donatelli Noble, "A Labyrinth of Human Knowledge: Umberto Eco's *Foucault's Pendulum*," *Rocky Mountain Review of Language and Literature* 49, no. 2 (1995): 146.

42. Philip Bell, "Subjectivity and Identity: Semiotics as Psychological Explanation," *Social Semiotics*, 12, no. 2 (2002): 215.

43. Semiotic idealism, rooted in the work of Peirce, refers to the view of objects as dependent upon a person's opinion. This position stands in contrast to William of Ockham's epistemology of "direct realism" and the role of particulars in understanding. It also differs from Reid's

commonsense epistemology based on the perception of items as they are. See Nathan Houser, introduction to *The Essential Peirce: Selected Philosophical Writings, Vol. 1 (1867–1893)*, by Charles Sanders Peirce, ed. Nathan Houser and Christian Kloesel (Bloomington: Indiana University Press, 1992), xxxv; Adams, *William Ockham*, 71–107; and Ryan Nichols, "Visible Figure and Reid's Theory of Visual Perception," *Hume Studies* 28, no. 1 (2002): 49–82.

44. Rocco Capozzi, "Palimpsests and Laughter: The Dialogical Pleasure of Unlimited Intertextuality in *The Name of the Rose*," *Italica* 66, no. 4 (1989): 413.

44. Diego Fasolini, "The Intrusion of Laughter into the Abbey of Umberto Eco's *The Name of the Rose*: The Christian Paradox of Joy Mingling with Sorrow," *Romance Notes* 46, no. 2 (2006): 126.

46. Peter P. Trifonas, "The Aesthetics of Textual Production: Reading and Writing with Umberto Eco," *Studies in Philosophy and Education* 26, no. 3 (2007): 277.

47. Emmanuel Levinas, *In the Time of Nations*, trans. Michael Smith (1994; repr., London: Continuum, 2007), 159.

48. Levinas, *Of God Who Comes to Mind*.

49. Levinas, *Proper Names*, 119.

50. Levinas, *Totality and Infinity*, 85.

51. Levinas, *Entre Nous*, 101.

52. Emmanuel Levinas, *Nine Talmudic Readings*, trans. Annette Aronowicz (1968; repr., Bloomington: Indiana University Press, 1990), 50.

53. Gehrke, "Being for the Other-to-the-Other," 5–19.

54. Richard A. Cohen, introduction to *Humanism of the Other*, by Emmanuel Levinas, trans. Nidra Poller (1976, repr., Champaign: University of Illinois Press, 2003), xix.

55. Levinas cites the prophet Ezekiel as being critical of those who are self-righteous for the sake of "their own salvation," like the hypocritical Pharisees. They ironically witness injustice when they present themselves as righteous in a way that separates them from the "evil" standing next to them. Levinas, *Nine Talmudic Readings*, 188.

56. Seyla Benhabib, *Situating the Self: Gender, Community, and Postmodernism in Contemporary Ethics* (Malden, MA: Polity Press, 1992).

57. Levinas, *Basic Philosophical Writings* (Bloomington: Indiana University Press, 1996), 126.

58. Levinas, *Otherwise than Being*, 157.

59. Emmanuel Levinas, *Outside the Subject*, trans. Michael B. Smith (Stanford, CA: Stanford University Press, 1993), 45.

60. Levinas, *Collected Philosophical Papers*, 44.

61. Levinas, *God, Death, and Time*, 183.

62. Levinas, *Difficult Freedom*, 21.

63. Levinas, *Alterity and Transcendence*, 144.

64. Levinas, *Ethics and Infinity*, 113.

65. Kenneth Burke, *On Symbols and Society*, ed. Joseph R. Gusfield (Chicago: University of Chicago Press, 1989), 70–72.

66. Levinas, *Discovering Existence*, 196.

67. Levinas, *Time and the Other*, 118.

68. Cohen, introduction to *Humanism of the Other*, xxxviii.

69. Levinas asserts that ethical interactions with an Other never ignore "the third, and along with him all others" who are outside our face-to-face communication and our communities of comfort. Levinas, *Entre Nous*, 202–3.

70. Referencing Ezekiel, Levinas argues that religious communities focusing on harmony only within themselves and not outside of themselves risk "punishment"—synagogue and church alike. Levinas, *Nine Talmudic Readings*, 188.

71. "Justice through knowledge" is inseparable from the "extravagant generosity of the for-the-other." Levinas, *Alterity and Transcendence*, 144.

7. POSSESSION AND BURDEN: OTHERWISE THAN MURDOCH'S INFORMATION ACQUISITION

1. Jacques Ellul, *The Technological Society*, trans. John Wilkinson (New York: Alfred A. Knopf, 1964).

2. Tolkien, *The Two Towers*, 260–67.

3. Hannah Arendt, *Men in Dark Times* (1955; repr., San Diego: Harcourt Brace & Company, 1995), 31; Hannah Arendt, *Lectures on Kant's Political Philosophy*, ed. Ronald Beiner (1977; repr., Chicago: University of Chicago Press, 1992).

4. Nick Davies, "Murdoch Papers Paid £1m to Gag Phone-Hacking Victims," *Guardian*, July 8, 2009, https://www.theguardian.com/media/2009/jul/08/murdoch-papers-phone-hacking.

5. Andy Coulson was editor of the *News of the World* from 2003 until 2007. Amelia Hill, "Andy Coulson to Be Arrested over Phone Hacking," *Guardian*, July 7, 2011, https://www.theguardian.com/media/2011/jul/07/andy-coulson-arrest-phone-hacking.

6. After Cameron's appointment to prime minister in 2010, Coulson remained head of communications for his administration. Coulson eventually resigned on January 21, 2011. At a press conference held the day

of Coulson's arrest, six months after his resignation, "no apology was forthcoming" from Cameron for hiring Coulson in the wake of the first scandal; Cameron had decided to give him a "second chance." See Lisa O'Carroll, "Phone-Hacking Scandal: Timeline," *Guardian*, January 21, 2011, https://www.theguardian.com/uk-news/2014/jun/24/phone-hacking-scandal-timeline-trial; and "News of the World Phone-Hacking Scandal—Friday 8 July 2011," *Guardian.com News Blog*, http://www.theguardian.com/media/blog/2011/jul/08/news-of-the-world-phone-hacking-scandal.

7. Glenn Mulcaire was a contracted private investigator for the *News of the World*. He, along with *News of the World* royal editor, Clive Goodman, confessed to phone hacking in November 2006, one year after printing a story about Prince William's knee injury, prompting a phone-hacking complaint from the royals. Mulcaire sued for wrongful termination after his 2007 conviction and received an undisclosed settlement; he was a named defendant in several other lawsuits regarding the hacking. See Roy Greenslade, "Peter Wright Was Wrong to Have Stayed Silent about His Staff Being Hacked," *Guardian*, August 12, 2014, para. 4, http://www.theguardian.com/media/greenslade/2014/aug/12/peterwright-mailonsunday; and James Robinson, "Phone Hacking: Glenn Mulcaire Sues News of the World Publisher," *Guardian*, August 18, 2011, http://www.theguardian.com/media/2011/aug/18/phone-hacking-glenn-mulcaire.

8. James Robinson, "News of the World Phone-Hacking Saga: How the Story Unfolded," *Guardian*, July 8, 2009, para. 4, https://www.theguardian.com/media/2009/jul/08/news-world-phone-tapping-timeline.

9. Les Hinton worked for Rupert Murdoch for fifty-two years before resigning as chief executive officer of Dow Jones & Company and publisher of the *Wall Street Journal*. On July 15, 2011, Hinton resigned in response to the phone-hacking issues.

10. The *Guardian* first reported the hacking on July 4, 2011, although the Dowler family learned of the possible hacking three months prior, before the start of the trial against Levi Bellfield. See James Robinson, "Milly Dowler Phone Hacking: Family Shocked by NoW Revelations," *Guardian*, July 4, 2011, https://www.theguardian.com/uk/2011/jul/04/milly-dowler-family-phone-hacking.

11. Rebekah Brooks served as the chief executive of News International (2009–2011), *News of the World* (2000–2003), and editor of the *Sun* (2000–2003). Brooks resigned on July 15, 2011, after allegations had emerged that she knew about the hacking of Dowler's voice mails. As of March 2014, Brooks

faced four charges in relation to the phone-hacking controversy—one count of conspiracy to hack phones, one count of conspiracy to commit misconduct in public office, and two counts of perverting the course of justice. Adam Withnall, "Hacking Trial: Rebekah Brooks Cleared of One Charge over Prince William Bikini Photo," *Independent*, February 20, 2014, http://www.independent.co.uk/news/uk/crime/hacking-trial -rebekah-brooks-cleared-of-one-charge-over-prince-william-bikini -photo-9140733.html. James Murdoch, son of Rupert Murdoch, is chair- man and chief executive to the Murdoch-owned News Corporation. In response to the phone-hacking scandal, James Murdoch resigned from his position on the board of News Group International, which over- sees the *Sun* and the *Times*. Dan Sabbagh, "James Murdoch Resigns from Sun and Times Boards," *Guardian*, November 23, 2011, https://www .theguardian.com/media/2011/nov/23/james-murdoch-sun-times -boards. As of November 2013, James Murdoch was reappointed as di- rector of BSkyB. Mark Sweney, "James Murdoch Reappointed as BSkyB Director," *Guardian*, November 22, 2013, https://www.theguardian.com /media/2013/nov/22/james-murdoch-bskyb-agm.

12. Dan Sabbagh, "*News of the World*: Murdoch Takes the Initiative, but Will It End the Crisis?," *Guardian*, July 7, 2011.

13. After the *Guardian* reported as fact that Dowler's voice mails were deleted by *News of the World* journalists, new information indicated inconclusive evidence about the deleted voice mails, as they could have been automatically deleted after seventy-two hours. The lack of certainty over the deletions emerged from the Surrey police failing to investigate the hacking until the information went public in 2011.

14. Sweney, "James Murdoch."

15. Hill, "Andy Coulson," para. 4.

16. See "News of the World Phone-Hacking Scandal—Sunday 10 July 2011," *Guardian.com News Blog*, https://www.theguardian.com/media/blog /2011/jul/10/news-world-hacking-scandal-live.

17. According to the British group the Audit Bureau of Circulations, average circulation in the period measured right before the closure of the *News of the World* was just over 2.6 million per issue. See the June 2011 Circula- tion Certificate, http://www.abc.org.uk/Certificates/17216429.pdf.

18. See John Plunkett, "Rupert Murdoch Says 'Sorry' in Ad Campaign," *Guardian*, July 15, 2011, http://www.theguardian.com/media/2011/jul /15/rupert-murdoch-sorry-ad-campaign.

19. Lisa O'Carroll, "James Murdoch 'Was Told of Phone-Hacking Email,'" *Guardian*, September 6, 2011.

20. While Coulson was convicted of phone hacking and served five months in prison of an eighteen-month sentence (being confined to house arrest with an ankle monitor after his release), he faced trial in June 2015 for alleged payments for royal directories after his first prosecution ended in a mistrial. See Lisa O'Carroll, "Andy Coulson Faces Retrial over Alleged Purchase of Royal Phone Directories," *Guardian*, January 22, 2015, http://www.theguardian.com/uk-news/2015/jan/22/andy -coulson-retrial-royal-phone-directories. In July 2015 Justice Saunders ordered Coulson to pay £150,000 toward the cost of the trial. See "Andy Coulson Ordered to Pay £150,000 toward Hacking Trial Costs," *Guardian*, July 22, 2015, http://www.theguardian.com/uk-news/2015/jul/22/ andy-coulson-ordered-to-pay-150000-towards-hacking-trial-costs.

21. Suspicion continues around phone tapping at Murdoch-owned media outlets. Operation Elveden was a follow-up to police bribery revelations from the *News of the World* scandal, leading to at least twenty-one arrests in 2012 at another Murdoch-owned media property, the *Sun*. See Lisa O' Carroll, "Sun Journalists Avoiding Investigative Stories Due to Fear of Arrest," *Guardian*, November 13, 2012, https://www .theguardian.com/media/2012/nov/13/sun-journalists-fear-arrest -whistleblowers. Rupert Murdoch formally denied wrongdoing in a letter to member of Parliament John Whittingdale in a letter dated July 17, 2013. The letter references a March 2013 *Sun* meeting after the arrests at which Murdoch commented that police payoffs had been part of Fleet Street culture for years, making a full denial of admitting to payoffs and arguing that his comments should not be taken out of context. See "Rupert Murdoch's Letter to John Whittingdale," *Guardian*, July 18, 2013, http://www.theguardian.com/media/interactive/2013 /jul/18/rupert-murdoch-letter-john-whittingdale-full-text.

22. Levinas, *Totality and Infinity*, 153.

23. Pierre Hayat, preface to *Alterity and Transcendence*, by Emmanuel Levinas, trans. Michael B. Smith (New York: Columbia University Press, 1999), xviii.

24. Levinas, *Collected Philosophical Papers*, 58.

25. Levinas, *God, Death, and Time*, 84.

26. Levinas, *Basic Philosophical Writings*, 7.

27. Levinas, *Of God Who Comes to Mind*, 92.

28. Emmanuel Levinas, *On Escape: De L'évasion*, trans. Bettina Bergo (Stanford, CA: Stanford University Press, 2003), 50.

29. Levinas, *Outside the Subject*, 60.

30. Levinas, *Proper Names*, 140.

31. Levinas, *Difficult Freedom*, 8–11.
32. Levinas, *Entre Nous*, 6.
33. Emmanuel Levinas, *Existence and Existents*, trans. Alphonso Lingis (Norwell, MA: Kluwer Academic Publishers, 1978), 71.
34. Kant, *Critique of Pure Reason*.
35. Levinas, *Is It Righteous to Be?*, 250.
36. Levinas, *Otherwise than Being*, 82.
37. Levinas, *Theory of Intuition in Husserl's Phenomenology*, 67.
38. Levinas, *Discovering Existence with Husserl*.
39. Ronald C. Arnett, "The Responsive "I": Levinas's Derivative Argument," *Argumentation & Advocacy* 40, no. 1 (2003): 315–38.
40. Levinas, *Nine Talmudic Readings*, 133.
41. Levinas, *In the Time of Nations*, 80.
42. Levinas, *Alterity and Transcendence*, 3.
43. Levinas, *Ethics and Infinity*.
44. Aristotle, *Eudemian Ethics*, trans. Anthony Kenny (Oxford: Oxford University Press, 2011).

8. THE ETHICAL PARVENU: UNREMITTING ACCOUNTABILITY

1. Peter E. Gordon, *Continental Divide: Heidegger, Cassirer, Davos* (Cambridge, MA: Harvard University Press, 2010), 91–93.
2. Ernst Cassirer and Martin Heidegger, "A Discussion between Ernst Cassirer and Martin Heidegger," trans. Francis Slade, ed. Nino Langiulli, in *The Existential Tradition: Selected Writings* (New York: Doubleday, 1971), 193.
3. Kant defines *schematism* as "making sensible the pure concept" through "transposing the priority normally ascribed to thought and to the concept, and recovering its unifying role in its codependency with receptivity or intuition." Frank Schalow, *The Renewal of the Heidegger-Kant Dialogue: Action, Thought, and Responsibility* (Albany: State University of New York Press, 1992), 179.
4. See Michael Friedman, *A Parting of Ways: Carnap, Cassirer, and Heidegger* (Peru, IL: Open Court Publishing, 2000); Deniz Coskun, ed., *Law as Symbolic Form: Ernst Cassirer and the Anthropocentric View of Law* (Dordrecht, Netherlands: Springer, 2007); Gordon, *Continental Divide*; Frank Schalow, "Revisiting the Heidegger-Cassirer Debate," *Comparative and Continental Philosophy* 4, no. 2 (2013): 307–15; Hans-Jörg Rheinberger, "Heidegger and Cassirer on Science after the Cassirer and Heidegger of Davos," *History of European Ideas* 41, no. 4 (2015): 440–46; Thomas A. Discenna, "Rhetoric's Ghost at Davos: Reading Cassirer in

the Rhetorical Tradition," *Rhetorica: A Journal of the History of Rhetoric* 32, no. 3 (2014): 245–66.

5. Levinas, *Is It Righteous to Be?*, 35–36.

6. Cohen, introduction to *Humanism of the Other*, xv.

7. Levinas, *Otherwise than Being*.

8. Cassirer edited volumes 4 and 6 of *Werke: Gesamtausgabe in 10 Bänden und einen Ergänzungsband*, by Immanuel Kant. Also see Ernst Cassirer, *Kant's Life and Thoughts*, trans. James Haden (New Haven, CT: Yale University Press, 1981).

9. Martin Heidegger, Karsten Harries, and Hermann Heidegger, "The Self-Assertion of the German University: Address, Delivered on the Solemn Assumption of the Rectorate of the University Freiburg the Rectorate 1933/34: Facts and Thoughts," *Review of Metaphysics* 38, no. 3 (1985): 467–502.

10. Arnett, *Communication Ethics in Dark Times*, chap. 1.

11. Emmanuel Levinas, *Humanism of the Other*, trans. Nidra Poller (1976; repr., Champaign: University of Illinois Press, 2003), 8.

12. Geoffrey Waite, "On Esotericism: Heidegger and/or Cassirer at Davos," *Political Theory* 26, no. 5 (1998): 603.

13. Waite writes that it is the intention of modern exo/esotericism to render capitalism "like God, ideology, and absolute truth." Exo/esotericism work as a "critique" to "overcome" opposition to ideologies. Exotericism examines the external level of understanding a subject while esotericism is the inner, symbolic level of understanding. Waite explains that the paradox of exo/esotericism hinders our ability to know something in total.

14. Arnett, *Communication Ethics in Dark Times*, chap. 2.

9. HEIDEGGER'S RECTORATE ADDRESS: BEING AS MISTAKEN DIRECTION

1. Richard L. Rubenstein, "The Philosopher and the Jews: The Case of Martin Heidegger," *Modern Judaism* 9, no. 2 (1989): 184.

2. Heidegger's rectorship began only months after Hitler's appointment as chancellor of Germany and the Reichstag fire, which led to the suspension of civil liberties. While Heidegger asserted that he followed the developments in German government and discussed them with colleagues, his own work focused on pre-Socratic thought. See Martin Heidegger, "'Only a God Can Save Us': The *Spiegel* Interview," trans. W. Richardson, in *Heidegger: The Man and the Thinker*, ed. T. Sheehan (Chicago: Precedent Publishing, 1981), 46.

3. Richard Wolin, ed., *The Heidegger Controversy: A Critical Reader* (Cambridge, MA: MIT Press, 1993).

4. Möllendorf was also a Social Democrat, a party that suffered "vicious persecution" at that time under the Baden Reich commissioner Robert Wagner. The ministry intended to install scholars that reflected the Reich's values. See Rüdiger Safranski, *Martin Heidegger: Between Good and Evil*, trans. Ewald Osers (Cambridge, MA: Harvard University Press, 1998), 239–40.

5. While labor and arms were more related to Nazi ideas of work as a unified effort of a people (race), knowledge refers to a more spiritual component of student life, which would appear third in order of importance, despite Heidegger's assertion that it was first. Faye asserts that this third pillar closely connected to racial politics of "blood and earth" and that the form of these three pillars reflected the common rhetorical device of the triad in early Nazi Germany. See Heidegger, "'Only a God Can Save Us,'" 49; and Emmanuel Faye, *Heidegger: The Introduction of Nazism into Philosophy in Light of the Unpublished Seminars of 1933–1935*, trans. Michael B. Smith (New Haven, CT: Yale University Press, 2009), 63–64.

6. The acknowledgment read, "If the following investigation has taken any steps forward in disclosing the 'things themselves,' the author must first of all thank E. Husserl, who, by providing his own incisive personal guidance and by freely turning over his unpublished investigations, familiarized the author with the most diverse areas of phenomenological research during his student years in Freiburg." See Heidegger, "'Only a God Can Save Us.'"

7. Throughout the interview, Heidegger claimed his hope for Germany that required necessary compromises. He resigned as rector in 1934, four years before Husserl's death.

8. Hölderlin replaced Goethe as the poet who best expressed the "destiny" of Germany. Heidegger used his work to "embed [Heidegger's] teaching more than ever in the opaqueness of the occult underpinnings of Hitlerism and Nazism." See Faye, *Heidegger*, 103–5.

9. Martin Heidegger, *What Is Called Thinking*, trans. J. Glenn Gray (New York: Harper & Row Publishers, 1968); Martin Heidegger, *Identity and Difference*, trans. Joan Stambaugh (Chicago: University of Chicago Press, 1969).

10. Faye, *Heidegger*, 39, 174–86.

11. Works addressing the controversy of the rector speech include Bernhard Radloff, *Heidegger and the Question of National Socialism: Disclosure and Gestalt* (Toronto: University of Toronto Press, 2007); Charles R. Bambach, *Heidegger's Roots: Nietzsche, National Socialism, and the Greeks* (Ithaca, NY: Cornell University Press, 2003).

12. Heidegger, Harries, and Heidegger, "The Self-Assertion of the German University," 467.
13. Heidegger identified Heraclitus as the original expression of mythic German power. See Faye, *Heidegger*, 110.
14. Emmanuel Faye, "Nazi Foundations in Heidegger's Work," trans. Alexis Watson and Richard Joseph Golsan, *South Central Review* 23, no. 1 (2006): 66.
15. Fred Dallmayr, "Postmetaphysics and Democracy," *Political Theory* 21, no. 1 (1993): 115, 118.
16. Tom Rockmore, "Philosophy, Literature, and Intellectual Responsibility," *American Philosophical Quarterly* 30, no. 2 (1993): 109–21.
17. Tom Rockmore, "Heidegger after Farías," *History of Philosophy Quarterly* 8, no. 1 (1991): 82.
18. Joseph Grange, "Heidegger as Nazi: A Postmodern Scandal," *Philosophy East and West* 41, no. 4 (1991): 516.
19. Fred Dallmayr, "Rethinking the Political: Some Heideggerian Contributions," *Review of Politics* 52, no. 4 (1990): 524.
20. Richard Wolin, "The French Heidegger Debate," *New German Critique* 45, (1988): 160.
21. Steven Ungar, "Aftereffect and Scandal: Martin Heidegger in France," *South Central Review* 6, no. 2 (1989): 25.
22. Jacques Derrida, "Of Spirit," *Critical Inquiry* 15, no. 2 (1989): 469.
23. Jacques Derrida, "The Principle of Reason: The University in the Eyes of its Pupils," *Diacritics* 13, no. 3 (1983): 18.
24. Samuel Moyn, "Judaism against Paganism: Emmanuel Levinas's Response to Heidegger and Nazism in the 1930s," *History and Memory* 10, no. 1 (1998): 25–58.
25. See Jeff Fort, introduction to *Heidegger and the Politics of Poetry*, by Philippe Lacoue-Labarthe, trans. and ed. Jeff Fort (Urbana: University of Illinois Press, 2007), xi–xii. The 1980s saw a renewed discussion of the political significance of Heidegger's work and its connection to Nazism. Lacoue-Labarthe noted that this discussion has been ongoing.
26. Emmanuel Levinas, "As If Consenting to Horror," trans. Paula Wissing, *Critical Inquiry* 15, no. 2 (1989): 485.
27. Gordon, *Continental Divide*, 1.
28. Krzysztof Ziarek, "Which Other, Whose Alterity? The Human after Humanism," in *Between Levinas and Heidegger*, ed. John E. Drabinski and Eric S. Nelson (Albany: State University of New York Press, 2014), 232.
29. Henry McDonald, "Levinas, Heidegger, and Hitlerism's Ontological Racism," *European Legacy* 15, no. 7 (2011): 896.

30. Emmanuel Levinas, "Some Reflections on the Philosophy of Hitlerism," trans. Seán Hand, *Critical Inquiry* 17, no. 1 (1990): 63.

31. Debate refers to the work of Robert Faurisson, who denied the existence of the Holocaust; the trial of Klaus Barbi, a Nazi officer accused of torturing prisoners; and Victor Farías's text on Heidegger. Mark M. Anderson, "The 'Impossibility of Poetry': Celan and Heidegger in France," *New German Critique* 53 (1991): 5.

32. Levinas, *Totality and Infinity*, 68.

33. Katrin Froese, *Nietzsche, Heidegger and Daoist Thought: Crossing Paths In-Between* (Albany: State University of New York Press, 2006), 92. Heidegger identifies "herd," like Nietzsche, as a desert or a landscape barren of individuality.

34. Adriaan Peperzak, "Phenomenology—Ontology—Metaphysics: Levinas's Perspective on Husserl and Heidegger," *Man and World* 16, no. 2 (1983): 125.

35. C. D. Keyes, "An Evaluation of Levinas' Critique of Heidegger," *Research in Phenomenology* 2, no. 1 (1972): 141.

36. Levinas, *Time and the Other*, 63.

37. Richard A. Cohen, "Levinas, Rosenzweig, and the Phenomenologies of Husserl and Heidegger," *Philosophy Today* 32, no. 2 (1988): 175.

38. Robert Bernasconi, "Race and Earth in Heidegger's Thinking during the Late 1930s," *Southern Journal of Philosophy* 48, no. 1 (2010): 66.

39. Cem Zeytinoglu, "Appositional (Communication): Ethics: Listening to Heidegger and Levinas in Chorus," *Review of Communication* 11, no. 4 (2011): 281.

40. Sheldon Hanlon, "From Existence to Responsibility: Restlessness and Subjectivity in the Early and Late Levinas," *Philosophy Today* 55, no. 3 (2011): 290.

41. Wim Dekkers, "Dwelling, House, and Home: Towards a Home-Led Perspective on Dementia Care," *Medical Health Care and Philosophy* 14, no. 3 (2011): 297, 299.

42. Levinas, *Existence and Existents*, 69. Also see Pieter Tijmes, "Home and Homelessness: Heidegger and Levinas on Dwelling," *Worldviews* 2, no. 3 (1998): 211.

43. Richard A. Cohen, "Levinas: Thinking Least about Death—Contra Heidegger," *International Journal for Philosophy of Religion* 60, no. 1/3 (2006): 21–39.

44. Graham Harman, "Levinas and the Triple Critique of Heidegger," *Philosophy Today* 53, no. 4 (2009): 410.

10. ADIEU TO LEVINAS: THE UNENDING RHETORIC OF THE FACE

1. Derrida, *Adieu to Emmanuel Levinas*. Derrida's work is situated in two sections—an adieu and "A Word of Welcome."

2. Adieu as a greeting or welcome can be traced to the fourteenth-century French language of Languedoc, Provence, and Gascogne. Ronald C. Arnett, "Philosophy of Communication as Carrier of Meaning: Adieu to W. Barnett Pearce," *Qualitative Research Reports in Communication* 14, no. 1 (2013): 7.

3. Levinas, *Otherwise than Being*, 3. Drawn from Hamlet's soliloquy, 3.1.56–90.

4. Derrida offers Sinai as a place that embodies the disruption of the self and the unveiling of the face, drawing from Levinas. He offers geopolitical and theological reflection on this theme, with Sinai representing, in both cases, a border (between Israel and other nations and between God and humanity).

5. John Llewelyn, *Appositions to Jacques Derrida and Emmanuel Levinas* (Bloomington: Indiana University Press, 2002), 75–78. Levinas's concept of disinterestedness was onto-theological. Our relation in love to the Other reflects God's love for us that is beyond interestedness. See also Levinas, *God, Death, and Time*, 219–24.

6. Immanuel Kant, *Perpetual Peace: A Philosophical Essay* (New York: Cosimo, 2010).

7. Jacques Rolland, foreword to *God, Death, and Time*, by Emmanuel Levinas (Stanford, CA: Stanford University Press, 2000), 1.

8. This title refers to Hegel's *Science of Logic* and *The Phenomenology of the Spirit*.

Bibliography

Aboulafia, Mitchell, ed. *Philosophy, Social Theory, and the Thought of George Herbert Mead*. Albany: State University of New York Press, 1991.

Adams, Marilyn McCord. *William Ockham*, vols. 1 and 2. Notre Dame, IN: University of Notre Dame Press, 1987.

Alter, Robert. "The Genius of S. Y. Agnon." *Commentary* 32 (1961): 105–13.

Anderson, Mark M. "The 'Impossibility of Poetry': Celan and Heidegger in France." *New German Critique* 53 (1991): 3–18.

Arendt, Hannah. *Lectures on Kant's Political Philosophy*. Edited by Ronald Beiner. Chicago: University of Chicago Press, 1992. First published 1977.

———. *Men in Dark Times*. San Diego: Harcourt Brace & Company, 1995. First published 1955.

———. *The Origins of Totalitarianism*. New York: Harcourt, 1968.

———. *Responsibility and Judgment*. Edited by Jerome John. New York: Schocken Books, 2003.

Aristotle. *Eudemian Ethics*. Translated by Anthony Kenny. Oxford: Oxford University Press, 2011.

———. *Rhetoric*. Translated by W. Rhys Roberts. Mineola, NY: Dover Publications, 2004.

Arneson, Pat. *Communicative Engagement and Social Liberation: Justice Will Be Made*. Lanham, MD: Fairleigh Dickinson University Press, 2014.

Arnett, Ronald C. "Beyond Dialogue: Beyond Levinas and Otherwise than the I-Thou." *Language and Dialogue* 2, no. 1 (2012): 140–55.

———. *Communication Ethics in Dark Times: Hannah Arendt's Rhetoric of Warning and Hope*. Carbondale: Southern Illinois University Press, 2013.

———. "Communicative Meaning: From Pangloss to Tenacious Hope." In *A Century of Communication Studies: The Unfinished Conversation*, edited by Pat J. Gehrke and William M. Keith, 261–85. New York: Routledge, 2015.

———. "A Dialogic Ethic 'Between' Buber and Levinas: A Responsive Ethical 'I.'" In *Dialogue: Theorizing Differences in Communication Studies*, edited by Rob Anderson, Leslie A. Baxter, and Kenneth N. Cissna, 75–90. Thousand Oaks, CA: Sage, 2004.

———. "Emmanuel Levinas: Priority of the Other." In *Ethical Communication: Moral Stances in Human Dialogue*, edited by Clifford G. Christians and John Merrill, 200–206. Columbia: University of Missouri Press, 2009.

———. "Philosophy of Communication as Carrier of Meaning: Adieu to W. Barnett Pearce." *Qualitative Research Reports in Communication* 14, no. 1 (2013): 1–9.

———. "The Responsive "I": Levinas's Derivative Argument." *Argumentation & Advocacy* 40, no. 1 (2003): 315–38.

———. "A Rhetoric of Sentiment: The House the Scots Built." In *Philosophy of Communication Ethics: Alterity and the Other,* edited by Ronald C. Arnett and Pat Arneson, 25–54. Lanham, MD: Fairleigh Dickinson University Press, 2014.

Arnett, Ronald C., Janie Harden Fritz, and Leeanne M. Bell. *Communication Ethics Literacy: Dialogue and Difference.* Thousand Oaks, CA: Sage, 2009.

Arnett, Ronald C., Janie Harden Fritz, and Annette M. Holba. "The Rhetorical Turn to Otherness: Otherwise than Humanism." *Cosmos and History: Journal of Natural and Social Philosophy* 3, no. 1 (2007): 115–33.

Aronowicz, Annette. "Introducing 'The Temptation of Temptation': Levinas and Europe." *Journal of Scriptural Reasoning* 11, no. 2 (2012), http://jsr.shanti.virginia.edu/back-issues/volume-11-no-2-december-2012-levinas-and-philosophy/introducing-the-temptation-of-temptation-levinas-and-europe/.

Artigiani, Robert. "The 'Model Reader' and the Thermodynamic Model." *Substance* 14, no. 2 (1985): 64–73.

Balducci, Gioacchino. "Umberto Eco in New York: An Interview." *Communication Quarterly* 24, no. 2 (1976): 35–38.

Bambach, Charles R. *Heidegger's Roots: Nietzsche, National Socialism, and the Greeks.* Ithaca, NY: Cornell University Press, 2003.

Band, Arnold J. *Nostalgia and Nightmare: A Study in the Fiction of S. Y. Agnon.* Berkeley: University of California Press, 1968.

Bateson, Gregory, and Mary Catherine Bateson. *Angels Fear: Towards an Epistemology of the Sacred.* Creskill, NJ: Hampton Press, 2005. First published 1987.

Baxter, David G. "Murder and Mayhem in a Medieval Abbey: The Philosophy of *The Name of the Rose.*" *Journal of Speculative Philosophy* 3, no. 3 (1989): 170–89.

Bell, Philip. "Subjectivity and Identity: Semiotics as Psychological Explanation." *Social Semiotics* 12, no. 2 (2002): 201–17.

Benhabib, Seyla. *Situating the Self: Gender, Community, and Postmodernism in Contemporary Ethics.* Malden, MA: Polity Press, 1992.

Bergo, Bettina. *Levinas between Ethics and Politics: For the Beauty That Adorns the Earth.* Pittsburgh: Duquesne University Press, 2003.

———. "What Is Levinas Doing? Phenomenology and the Rhetoric of an Ethical Un-Conscious." *Philosophy & Rhetoric* 38, no. 2 (2005): 122–44.

Bernasconi, Robert. "Race and Earth in Heidegger's Thinking during the Late 1930s." *Southern Journal of Philosophy* 48, no. 1 (2010): 49–66.

Bernstein, Richard J. *The New Constellation: The Ethical-Political Horizons of Modernity/Postmodernity.* Cambridge, MA: MIT Press, 1991.

Birdwhistell, Ray L. *Introduction to Kinesics: An Annotation System for Analysis of Body Motion and Gesture.* Louisville, KY: University of Louisville, 1952.

Blanchot, Maurice, ed. *Textes pour Emmanuel Levinas.* Paris: Jean-Michel Place, 1980.

Bonhoeffer, Dietrich. *Life Together: The Classic Exploration of Christian Community.* New York: Harper & Row, 1954.

Boyarin, Daniel. *Intertextuality and the Reading of Midrash.* Bloomington: Indiana University Press, 1994.

Bruns, Gerald L. *Maurice Blanchot: The Refusal of Philosophy.* Baltimore: Johns Hopkins University Press, 1997.

Buber, Martin. "Guilt and Guilt Feelings." *Psychiatry* 20, no. 2 (1957): 114–29.

———. *I and Thou.* Trans. Ronald Gregor Smith. Edinburgh: T. & T. Clark, 1937.

———. *The Knowledge of Man: A Philosophy of the Interhuman.* Edited by Maurice Friedman. Translated by Maurice Friedman and Ronald Gregor Smith. Atlantic Highlands, NJ: Humanities Press International, 1988. First published 1965.

———. *The Way of Response.* New York: Schocken Books, 1966.

Burke, Kenneth. *On Symbols and Society.* Edited by Joseph R. Gusfield. Chicago: University of Chicago Press, 1989.

Caesar, Michael. *Umberto Eco: Philosophy, Semiotics, and the Work of Fiction.* Malden, MA: Blackwell Publishers, 1999.

Capozzi, Rocco. "Palimpsests and Laughter: The Dialogical Pleasure of Unlimited Intertextuality in *The Name of the Rose.*" *Italica* 66, no. 4 (1989): 412–28.

Cassirer, Ernst. *Kant's Life and Thoughts.* Translated by James Haden. New Haven, CT: Yale University Press, 1981.

Cassirer, Ernst, and Martin Heidegger. "A Discussion between Ernst Cassirer and Martin Heidegger." Translated by Francis Slade. In *The Existential Tradition: Selected Writings,* edited by Nino Langiulli, 192–203. New York: Doubleday, 1971.

Chalier, Catherine. *What Ought I to Do? Morality in Kant and Levinas.* Translated by Jane Marie Todd. Ithaca, NY: Cornell University Press, 2002.

Char, René, ed. *L'Endurance de la pensée, pour saluer Jean Beaufret.* Paris: Plon, 1968.

Cloud, Dana L. *Control and Consolation in American Culture and Politics: Rhetorics of Therapy.* Thousand Oaks, CA: Sage, 1998.

Cmiel, Kenneth. "On Cynicism, Evil, and the Discovery of Communication in the 1940s." *Journal of Communication* 46, no. 3 (1996): 88–107.

Cobley, Evelyn. "Closure and Infinite Semiosis in Mann's *Doctor Faustus* and Eco's *The Name of the Rose.*" *Comparative Literature Series* 26, no. 4 (1989): 341–60.

Coetsier, Meins G. S. *The Existential Philosophy of Etty Hillesum: An Analysis of Her Diaries and Letters.* Leiden, Netherlands: Brill Publishing, 2014.

Cohen, Richard A. Foreword to *Otherwise than Being or Beyond Essence*, by Emmanuel Levinas. Translated by Alphonso Lingis. Pittsburgh: Duquesne University Press, 1998.

———. Introduction to *Ethics and Infinity: Conversations with Philippe Nemo*, by Emmanuel Levinas. Pittsburgh: Duquesne University Press, 1985.

———. Introduction to *Humanism of the Other*, by Emmanuel Levinas. Translated by Nidra Poller. Champaign: University of Illinois Press, 2003.

———. "Levinas, Rosenzweig, and the Phenomenologies of Husserl and Heidegger." *Philosophy Today* 32, no. 2 (1988): 165–78.

———. "Levinas: Thinking Least about Death—Contra Heidegger." *International Journal for Philosophy of Religion* 60, no. 1/3 (2006): 21–39.

Coleman, Stephen. "New Mediation and Direct Representation: Reconceptualizing Representation in the Digital Age." *New Media & Society* 7, no. 2 (2005): 177–98.

Collin, Françoise. *Maurice Blanchot et la question de l'écriture.* Paris: Gallimard, 1971.

Collins, Jeff. *Heidegger and the Nazis.* London: Icon Books, 2000.

Cooke-Jackson, Angela, and Elizabeth K. Hansen. "Appalachian Culture and Reality TV: The Ethical Dilemma of Stereotyping Others." *Journal of Mass Media Ethics* 23, no. 3 (2008): 183–200.

Cooren, François. *Action and Agency in Dialogue: Passion, Incarnation and Ventriloquism.* Philadelphia: John Benjamins Publishing, 2010.

Corry, Leo, and Renato Giovanolli. "Jorge Borges, Author of *The Name of the Rose.*" *Poetics Today* 13, no. 3 (1992): 425–45.

Coskun, Deniz, ed. *Law as Symbolic Form: Ernst Cassirer and the Anthropocentric View of Law.* Dordrecht, Netherlands: Springer, 2007.

Critchley, Simon, and Robert Bernasconi. *The Cambridge Companion to Emmanuel Levinas.* New York: Cambridge University Press, 2002.

Cubitt, Sean. "Immersed in Time." *Visual Communication* 6, no. 2 (2007): 220–29.

Dallmayr, Fred. "Postmetaphysics and Democracy." *Political Theory* 21, no. 1 (1993): 101–27.

———. "Rethinking the Political: Some Heideggerian Contributions." *Review of Politics* 52, no. 4 (1990), 524–52.

Davis, D. Diane. "Finitude's Clamor; Or, Notes toward a Communitarian Literacy." *College Composition and Communication* 53, no. 1 (2001): 119–45.

———. *Inessential Solidarity: Rhetoric and Foreigner Relations.* Pittsburgh: University of Pittsburgh Press, 2010.

Deetz, Stanley. "Reclaiming the Subject Matter as a Guide to Mutual Understanding: Effectiveness and Ethics in Interpersonal Interaction." *Communication Quarterly* 38, no. 3 (1990): 226–43.

Dekkers, Wim. "Dwelling, House, and Home: Towards a Home-Led Perspective on Dementia Care." *Medical Health Care and Philosophy* 14, no. 3 (2011): 291–300.

de Lauretis, Teresa. "Gaudy Rose: Eco and Narcissism." *Substance* 14, no. 2 (1985): 13–29.

Derrida, Jacques. *Adieu to Emmanuel Levinas.* Translated by Pascale Anne Brault and Michael Naas. Stanford, CA: Stanford University Press, 1999.

———. *Of Grammatology.* Baltimore: Johns Hopkins University Press, 1997. First published 1967.

———. "Of Spirit." *Critical Inquiry* 15, no. 2 (1989): 457–74.

———. "The Principle of Reason: The University in the Eyes of Its Pupils." *Diacritics* 13, no. 3 (1983): 2–20.

———. "Violence and Metaphysics: An Essay on the Thought of Emmanuel Levinas." In *Writing and Difference*, edited and translated by Alan Bass, 79–153. Chicago: University of Chicago Press, 1978.

Dershowitz, Alan M. "Elie Wiesel: A Biblical Life." In *Celebrating Elie Wiesel: Stories, Essays, Reflections*, edited by Alan Rosen. Notre Dame, IN: University of Notre Dame Press, 1998.

Discenna, Thomas A. "Rhetoric's Ghost at Davos: Reading Cassirer in the Rhetorical Tradition." *Rhetorica: A Journal of the History of Rhetoric* 32, no. 3 (2014): 245–66.

Doniger, Wendy, ed. *Merriam-Webster's Encyclopedia of World Religions.* Springfield, MA: Merriam-Webster, 1999.

Drucker, Peter F. "The Unfashionable Kierkegaard." *Sewanee Review* 57, no. 4 (1949): 587–602.

Durrani, Osman. "The Tearful Teacher: The Role of Serenus Zeitblom in Thomas Mann's *Doktor Faustus*." *Modern Language Review* 80, no. 3 (1985): 652–58.

Eco, Umberto. "'Casablanca:' Cult Movies and Intertextual Collage." *Substance* 14, no. 2 (1985): 3–12.

———. *The Name of the Rose.* Translated by William Weaver. Orlando, FL: Harcourt, 1983.

———. *The Role of the Reader: Explorations in the Semiotics of Texts.* Bloomington: Indiana University Press, 1979.

Eisenstadt, Oona. "Levinas versus Levinas: Hebrew, Greek, and Linguistic Justice." *Philosophy & Rhetoric* 38, no. 2 (2005): 145–58.

Ellul, Jacques. *The Technological Society.* Translated by John Wilkinson. New York: Alfred A. Knopf, 1964.

———. *Violence: Reflections from a Christian Perspective.* Eugene, OR: Wipf and Stock Publisher, 2007. First published 1969.

Eshel, Amir. "Paul Celan's Other: History, Poetics, and Ethics." *New German Critique* no. 91 (2004): 57–77.

Evdoridou, Elissavet. "Multiscale Textual Semiotic Analysis." *Semiotica* 171, no. 1/4 (2008): 251–64.

Fackenheim, Emil L., and Raphael Jospe, ed. *Jewish Philosophy and the Academy.* Cranbury, NJ: Associated University Presses, 1996.

Farías, Victor. *Heidegger and Nazism.* Philadelphia: Temple University Press, 1989.

Fasolini, Diego. "The Intrusion of Laughter into the Abbey of Umberto Eco's *The Name of the Rose:* The Christian Paradox of Joy Mingling with Sorrow." *Romance Notes* 46, no. 2 (2006): 119–30.

Faye, Emmanuel. *Heidegger: The Introduction of Nazism into Philosophy in Light of the Unpublished Seminars of 1933–1935.* Translated by Michael B. Smith. New Haven, CT: Yale University Press, 2009.

———. "Nazi Foundations in Heidegger's Work." Translated by Alexis Watson and Richard Joseph Golsan. *South Central Review* 23, no. 1 (2006): 55–66.

Fort, Jeff. Introduction to *Heidegger and the Politics of Poetry,* by Philippe Lacoue-Labarthe, ix–xviii. Edited by Jeff Fort. Urbana: University of Illinois Press, 2007.

Frank, David A. "The Jewish Countermodel: Talmudic Argumentation, the New Rhetoric Project, and the Classical Tradition of Rhetoric." *Journal of Communication and Religion* 26, no. 2 (2003): 163–94.

Friedman, Maurice. *Martin Buber's Life and Work.* Detroit, MI: Wayne State University Press, 1988. First published 1981.

Friedman, Michael. *A Parting of Ways: Carnap, Cassirer, and Heidegger.* Peru, IL: Open Court Publishing, 2000.

Froese, Katrin. *Nietzsche, Heidegger and Daoist Thought: Crossing Paths In-Between.* Albany: State University of New York Press, 2006.

Gadamer, Hans-Georg. *Truth and Method*. London: Continuum; New York: Bloomsbury, 2013. First published 1975.

Garrett, Jeffrey. "Missing Eco: On Reading *The Name of the Rose* as Library Criticism." *Library Quarterly: Information, Community, Policy* 61, no. 4 (1991): 373–88.

Gehrke, Pat J. "Before the One and the Other: Ethico-Political Communication and Community." In *Philosophy of Communication Ethics: Alterity and the Other*, edited by Ronald C. Arnett and Pat Arneson, 55–73. Lanham, MD: Fairleigh Dickinson University Press, 2014.

———. "Being for the Other-to-the-Other: Justice and Communication in Levinasian Ethics." *Review of Communication* 10, no. 1 (2010): 5–19.

———. "The Ethical Importance of Being Human: God and Humanism in Levinas's Philosophy." *Philosophy Today* 50, no. 4 (2006): 428–36.

Gelber, Mark. "Theodore Herzl." In *Routledge Encyclopedia of Jewish Writers of the Twentieth Century*, edited by Sorrel Kerbel, 443–44. New York: Taylor and Francis, 2003.

Geroulanos, Stefanos. *An Atheism That Is Not Humanism Emerges in French Thought*. Stanford, CA: Stanford University Press, 2010.

Gordon, Peter E. *Continental Divide: Heidegger, Cassirer, Davos*. Cambridge, MA: Harvard University Press, 2010.

Grange, Joseph. "Heidegger as Nazi: A Postmodern Scandal." *Philosophy East and West* 41, no. 4 (1991), 515–22.

Green, Rochelle M., Bonnie Mann, and Amy E. Story. "Care, Domination, and Representation." *Journal of Mass Media Ethics* 21, no. 2/3 (2006): 177–95.

Gubman, Boris. "Jacques Derrida on Philosophy, Language, and Power in the Age of Globalization." *American Journal of Semiotics* 18, no. 1–4 (2002): 281–88.

Hall, Edward T. *The Silent Language*. New York: Anchor, 1973.

Hallissy, Margaret. "Reading the Plans: The Architectural Drawings in Umberto Eco's *The Name of the Rose*." *Critique: Studies in Contemporary Fiction* 42, no. 3 (2001): 271–86.

Hanlon, Sheldon. "From Existence to Responsibility: Restlessness and Subjectivity in the Early and Late Levinas." *Philosophy Today* 55, no. 3 (2011): 282–97.

Hansel, Joëlle. "Ethics as Teaching: The Figure of the Master in *Totality and Infinity*." Translated by Scott Davidson. In *Totality and Infinity at 50*, edited by Scott Davidson and Diane Perpich, 189–208. Pittsburgh: Duquesne University Press, 2012.

———. *Levinas in Jerusalem: Phenomenology, Ethics, Politics, Aesthetics*. Dordrecht, Netherlands: Springer, 2009.

Hansson, Jonas, and Svante Nordin. *Ernst Cassirer: The Swedish Years.* Bern, Switzerland: Peter Lang, 2006.

Harman, Graham. "Levinas and the Triple Critique of Heidegger." *Philosophy Today* 53, no. 4 (2009): 407–13.

Hatfield, Gary. Introduction to *Prolegomena to Any Future Metaphysics with Selections from the* Critique of Pure Reason, by Immanuel Kant. New York: Cambridge University Press, 2004. First published 1997.

Hatley, James. "Generations: Levinas in the Jewish Context." *Philosophy & Rhetoric* 38, no. 2 (2005): 173–89.

Hawkins, Beth. *Reluctant Theologians: Franz Kafka, Paul Celan, Edmond Jabès.* Bronx, NY: Fordham University Press, 2003.

Hayat, Pierre. Preface to *Alterity and Transcendence* by Emmanuel Levinas, ix–xxiv. Translated by Michael B. Smith. New York: Columbia University Press, 1999.

Heidegger, Martin. *Being and Time.* Translated by Joan Stambaugh. Albany: State University of New York Press, 2010.

———. *Identity and Difference.* Translated by Joan Stambaugh. Chicago: University of Chicago Press, 1969.

———. *Introduction to Metaphysics.* Translated by Gregory Fried and Richard Polt. New Haven, CT: Yale University Press, 2000.

———. "Letter on 'Humanism.'" In *Pathways*, edited by William McNeill, 239–76. Cambridge: Cambridge University Press, 1998.

———. "'Only a God Can Save Us': The *Spiegel* Interview." Translated by W. Richardson. In *Heidegger: The Man and the Thinker*, edited by T. Sheehan, 45–68. Chicago: Precedent Publishing, 1981.

———. *What Is Called Thinking.* Translated by J. Glenn Gray. New York: Harper & Row Publishers, 1968.

Heidegger, Martin, Karsten Harries, and Hermann Heidegger. "The Self-Assertion of the German University: Address, Delivered on the Solemn Assumption of the Rectorate of the University Freiburg the Rectorate 1933/34: Facts and Thoughts." *Review of Metaphysics* 38, no. 3 (1985): 467–502.

Heller, Agnes. "The Contemporary Historical Novel." *Thesis Eleven* 106, no. 1 (2011): 88–97.

Hellman, John. "Jacques Chavalier, Bergsonism, and Modern French Catholic Intellectuals." *Biography* 4, no. 2 (1982): 138–53.

Hilberg, Raul. *The Destruction of the European Jews*, vol. 3, 3rd ed. New Haven, CT: Yale University Press, 2003.

Hochman, Baruch. *The Fiction of S. Y. Agnon.* Ithaca, NY: Cornell University Press, 1970.

Holba, Annette M. *Philosophical Leisure: Recuperative Praxis for Human Communication*. Milwaukee, WI: Marquette University Press, 2007.

———. *Transformative Leisure: A Philosophy of Communication*. Milwaukee, WI: Marquette University Press, 2013.

Houser, Nathan. Introduction to *The Essential Peirce: Selected Philosophical Writings, Vol. 1 (1867–1893)*, by Charles Sanders Peirce, edited by Nathan Houser and Christian Kloesel, xix–xli. Bloomington: Indiana University Press, 1992.

Housley, Norman. *The Avignon Papacy and the Crusades 1305–1378*. Oxford: Oxford University Press, 1986.

Houston Grey, Stephanie. "Exhibitions in Life and Death: The Photography of Lucinda Devlin, Gunther von Hagens' *Body Worlds*, and the Disassembly of Scientific Progress." *American Communication Journal* 10, special edition (2008), http://ac-journal.org/journal/pubs/2008/Special%20Edition%2008%20-%20Aesthetics/Article_7.pdf.

Hunt, Lynn, ed. *The French Revolution and Human Rights: A Brief Documentary History*. Boston: Bedford, 1996.

Husserl, Edmund. *The Crisis of European Sciences and Transcendental Phenomenology: An Introduction to Phenomenological Philosophy*. Translated by David Carr. Evanston, IL: Northwestern University Press, 1970.

———. *Experience and Judgment*. Edited by Ludwig Landgrebe. Translated by James S. Churchill and Karl Ameriks. Evanston, IL: Northwestern University Press, 1973. First published 1948.

———. *Phenomenology and the Foundations of the Sciences*. Translated by Ted E. Klein and William E. Pohl. Dordrecht, Netherlands: Martinus Nijhoff Publishers, 1980.

Hyde, Michael J. *The Call of Conscience: Heidegger and Levinas, Rhetoric and the Euthanasia Debate*. Columbia: University of South Carolina Press, 2001.

———. *The Life-Giving Gift of Acknowledgment*. West Lafayette, IN: Purdue University Press, 2005.

Hyde, Michael J., and Kenneth Rufo. "The Call of Conscience, Rhetorical Interruptions, and the Euthanasia Controversy." *Journal of Applied Communication Research* 28, no. 1 (2000): 1–23.

Johnson, Laurie. "Face-Interface or the Prospect of a Virtual Ethics." *Ethical Space: The International Journal of Communication Ethics* 4, no. 1/2 (2007): 49–56.

Jovanovic, Spoma. "Difficult Conversations as Moral Imperatives: Negotiating Ethnic Identities during War." *Communication Quarterly* 51, no. 1 (2003): 57–72.

Jovanovic, Spoma, and Roy V. Wood. "Speaking from the Bedrock of Ethics." *Philosophy & Rhetoric* 37, no. 4 (2004): 317–34.

Kant, Immanuel. *Critique of Judgment*. Translated by J. H. Bernard. New York: Hafner Press, 1951.

———. *Critique of Pure Reason.* Translated by Werner S. Pluhar. Indianapolis, IN: Hackett Publishing Company, 1996. First published 1781.

———. *Perpetual Peace: A Philosophical Essay.* New York: Cosimo, 2010.

———. *Prolegomena to Any Future Metaphysics with Selections from the* Critique of Pure Reason. Edited by Gary Hatfield. New York: Cambridge University Press, 2004. First published 1997.

Katz, Claire Elise. "Emmanuel Levinas: The Rhetoric of Ethics." *Philosophy & Rhetoric* 38, no. 2 (2005): 99–102.

———. "Levinas—Between Philosophy and Rhetoric: The 'Teaching' of Levinas's Scriptural References." *Philosophy & Rhetoric* 38, no. 2 (2005): 159–72.

Kelly, Michael. "Jean Lacroix." In *The New Oxford Companion to Literature in French*, edited by Peter France, 431. Oxford: Clarendon Press, 1995.

Kemp, Peter. "Ricoeur between Heidegger and Levinas: Original Affirmation between Ontological Attestation and Ethical Injunction." In *Paul Ricoeur: The Hermeneutics of Action*, edited by Paul Kearney, 41–62. Thousand Oaks, CA: Sage, 1996.

Kendon, Adam. *Gesture: Visible Action as Utterance.* Cambridge: Cambridge University Press, 2004.

Keyes, C. D. "An Evaluation of Levinas' Critique of Heidegger." *Research in Phenomenology* 2, no. 1 (1972): 121–42.

Kigel, Michael. Translator's notes to *Emmanuel Levinas: His Life and Legacy*, by Salomon Malka, xiii–xxvi. Pittsburgh: Duquesne University Press, 2006.

Klein, Richard. "Prolegomenon to Derrida." *Diacritics* 2, no. 4 (1972): 29–34.

Kleinberg, Ethan. *Generation Existential: Heidegger's Philosophy in France, 1927–1961.* Ithaca, NY: Cornell University Press, 2005.

Laub, Thomas J. *After the Fall: German Policy in Occupied France, 1940–1944.* Oxford: Oxford University Press, 2010.

Lee, Harper. *To Kill a Mockingbird.* New York: HarperCollins Publishers, 2010. First published 1960.

Levinas, Emmanuel. *Alterity and Transcendence.* Translated by Michael B. Smith. New York: Columbia University Press, 1999.

———. "As If Consenting to Horror." Translated by Paula Wissing. *Critical Inquiry* 15, no. 2 (1989): 485–88.

———. *Basic Philosophical Writings.* Edited by Adriaan T. Peperzak, Simon Critchley, and Robert Bernasconi. Bloomington: Indiana University Press, 1996.

———. *Collected Philosophical Papers*. Translated by Alphonso Lingis. Dordrecht, Netherlands: Martinus Nijhoff Publishers, 1987.

———. *Difficult Freedom: Essays on Judaism*. Translated by Seán Hand. Baltimore: Johns Hopkins University Press, 1997. First published 1990.

———. *Discovering Existence with Husserl*. Translated by Richard A. Cohen and Michael B. Smith. Evanston, IL: Northwestern University Press, 1998.

———. *Entre Nous: Thinking-of-the-Other*. Translated by Michael B. Smith and Barbara Harshav. New York: Columbia University Press, 1998.

———. *Ethics and Infinity: Conversations with Philippe Nemo*. Translated by Richard A. Cohen. Pittsburgh: Duquesne University Press, 1985.

———. "Ethics as First Philosophy." In *The Levinas Reader*, edited by Seán Hand, 75–85. Malden, MA: Blackwell Publishers, 1989.

———. *Existence and Existents*. Translated by Alphonso Lingis. Norwell, MA: Kluwer Academic Publishers, 1978.

———. *God, Death, and Time*. Translated by Bettina Bergo. Stanford, CA: Stanford University Press, 2000. First published 1993.

———. *Humanism of the Other*. Translated by Nidra Poller. Champaign: University of Illinois Press, 2003. First published 1976.

———. *In the Time of Nations*. Translated by Michael Smith. London: Continuum, 2007. First published in 1994.

———. *Is It Righteous to Be? Interviews with Emmanuel Levinas*. Edited by Jill Robbins. Stanford, CA: Stanford University Press, 2001.

———. *Nine Talmudic Readings*. Translated by Annette Aronowicz. Bloomington: Indiana University Press, 1990. First published 1968.

———. *Of God Who Comes to Mind*. Translated by Bettina Bergo. Stanford, CA: Stanford University Press, 1998.

———. *On Escape: De L'évasion*. Translated by Bettina Bergo. Stanford, CA: Stanford University Press, 2003.

———. *Otherwise than Being or Beyond Essence*. Translated by Alphonso Lingis. Pittsburgh: Duquesne University Press, 1998. First published 1981.

———. *Outside the Subject*. Translated by Michael B. Smith. Stanford, CA: Stanford University Press, 1993.

———. *Proper Names*. Translated by Michael B. Smith. Stanford, CA: Stanford University Press, 1996. First published 1975.

———. "Some Reflections on the Philosophy of Hitlerism." Translated by Seán Hand. *Critical Inquiry* 17, no. 1 (1990): 62–71.

———. *The Theory of Intuition in Husserl's Phenomenology*, 2nd ed. Translated by André Orianne. Evanston, IL: Northwestern University Press, 1995. First published 1973.

———. *Time and the Other.* Translated by Richard. A. Cohen. Pittsburgh: Duquesne University Press, 1987. First published 1979.

———. *Totality and Infinity: An Essay on Exteriority.* Translated by Alphonso Lingis. Pittsburgh: Duquesne University Press, 1969. First published 1961.

———. "The Trace of the Other." Translated by Alphonso Lingis. In *Deconstruction in Context,* edited by Mark C. Taylor, 348–59. Chicago: University of Chicago Press, 1986.

———. *Unforeseen History.* Translated by Nidra Poller. Urbana: University of Illinois Press, 1994.

Levinas, Michael. "The Final Meeting between Emmanuel Levinas and Maurice Blanchot." *Critical Inquiry* 36, no. 4 (2010): 649–51.

Lipari, Lisbeth. "Listening for the Other: Ethical Implications of the Buber-Levinas Encounter." *Communication Theory* 14, no. 2 (2004): 122–41.

———. *Listening, Thinking, Being: Toward an Ethics of Attunement.* University Park: Pennsylvania State University Press, 2014.

———. "Rhetoric's Other: Levinas, Listening and the Ethical Response." *Philosophy & Rhetoric* 45, no. 3 (2012): 227–45.

Llewelyn, John. *Appositions to Jacques Derrida and Emmanuel Levinas.* Bloomington: Indiana University Press, 2002.

Louch, A. R. Review of *Lectures on Philosophy,* by G. E. Moore. *Journal of the History of Philosophy* 6, no. 2 (1986): 182–83.

Lyne, John. Review of *The Name of the Rose,* by Umberto Eco. *Quarterly Journal of Speech* 71, no. 4 (1985): 489–91.

MacIntyre, Alasdair C. *After Virtue: A Study in Moral Theory.* Notre Dame, IN: University of Notre Dame Press, 1984. First published 1981.

MacKey, Louis. "The Name of the Book." *Substance* 14, no. 2 (1985): 30–39.

Malka, Salomon. *Emmanuel Levinas: His Life and Legacy.* Translated by Michael Kigel and Sonja M. Embree. Pittsburgh: Duquesne University Press, 2006.

———. *Monsieur Chouchani: L'énigme d'un maître du XXe siècle.* Paris: J.C. Lattes, 1994.

Mann, Thomas. *Doctor Faustus: The Life of the German Composer Adrian Leverkühn as Told by a Friend.* Translated by John E. Woods. New York: Vintage Books, 1999.

Manning, Robert John Sheffler. *Interpreting Otherwise than Heidegger: Emmanuel Levinas's Ethics as First Philosophy.* Pittsburgh: Duquesne University Press, 1993.

Marcel, Gabriel. "Max Picard." In *In the Flight from God,* edited by J. M. Cameron. Translated by Marianne Kuschnitzky. Chicago: Henry Regnery Company, 1951. First published 1934.

Marie, Pierre-Antoine. "Sens et opinion selon Jeanne Delhomme." *Revue de Métaphysique et de Morale* 73, no. 4 (1968): 492–506.

McCarron, Gary. "Undecided Stories: Alfred Hitchcock's *Blackmail* and the Problem of Moral Agency." *Canadian Journal of Communication* 33, no. 1 (2008): 65–80.

McDonald, Henry. "Levinas, Heidegger, and Hitlerism's Ontological Racism." *European Legacy* 15, no. 7 (2011): 891–96.

McMullen, W. Cary. "Villainy, Humor, and Heresy." *Theology Today* 46, no. 3 (1989): 283–87.

Mead, George Herbert. *Mind, Self, and Society: From the Standpoint of a Social Behaviorist.* Edited by Charles W. Morris. Chicago: University of Chicago Press, 1962. First published 1934.

Merleau-Ponty, Maurice. *Phenomenology of Perception.* Translated by Colin Smith. London: Routledge, 1962.

Merton, Thomas. *Seven Storey Mountain.* New York: Mariner Books, 1999.

Miller, Lynn Christine. "*The Name of the Rose*: Adaptation as Palimpsest." *Literature and Performance* 7, no. 2 (1987): 77–78.

Motte, Warren F. "Questioning Jabès." *French Forum* 11, no. 1 (1986): 83–94.

Moyn, Samuel. "Judaism against Paganism: Emmanuel Levinas's Response to Heidegger and Nazism in the 1930s." *History and Memory* 10, no. 1 (1998): 25–58.

———. *Origins of the Other: Emmanuel Levinas between Revelation and Ethics.* Ithaca, NY: Cornell University Press, 2005.

Murphy, Mary McDonagh. *Scout, Atticus, and Boo: A Celebration of Fifty Years of* To Kill a Mockingbird. New York: HarperCollins Publishers, 2010.

Murray, J. "Marcel Proust." *Modern Language Review* 21, no. 1 (1926): 34–43.

Murray, Jeffrey W. "The Dialogical Prioritization of Calls: Toward a Communicative Model of Justice." *New Jersey Journal of Communication* 11, no. 1 (2003): 2–23.

———. "Kenneth Burke: A Dialogue of Motives." *Philosophy & Rhetoric* 35, no. 1 (2002): 22–49.

———. "An Other Ethics for Kenneth Burke." *Communication Studies* 49, no. 1 (1998): 29–48.

———. "The Paradox of Emmanuel Levinas: Knowledge of the Absolute Other." *Qualitative Research Reports in Communication* 3, no. 2 (2002): 39–46.

———. "Toward a Post-Habermasian Discourse Ethics: The Acknowledgment of the Other." *New Jersey Journal of Communication* 9, no. 1 (2001): 1–19.

Nemo, Philippe. Foreword to *Emmanuel Levinas: His Life and Legacy*, by Salomon Malka, vii–xii. Translated by Michael Kigel and Sonja E. Embree. Pittsburgh: Duquesne University Press, 2006.

———. Preface to *Ethics and Infinity: Conversations with Philippe Nemo*, by Emmanuel Levinas. Pittsburgh: Duquesne University Press, 1985.

Nichols, Ryan. "Visible Figure and Reid's Theory of Visual Perception." *Hume Studies* 28, no. 1 (2002): 49–82.

Noble, Cinzia Donatelli. "A Labyrinth of Human Knowledge: Umberto Eco's *Foucault's Pendulum*." *Rocky Mountain Review of Language and Literature* 49, no. 2 (1995): 141–52.

Olson, Lester C. "On the Margins of Rhetoric: Audre Lorde Transforming Silence into Language and Action." *Quarterly Journal of Speech* 83, no. 1 (1997): 49–70.

Ong, Jonathan Corpus. "The Cosmopolitan Continuum: Locating Cosmopolitanism in Media and Cultural Studies." *Media, Culture & Society* 31, no. 3 (2009): 449–66.

Parker, Deborah. "The Literature of Appropriation: Eco's Use of Borges in *Il Nome Della Rosa*." *Modern Language Review* 85, no. 4 (1990): 842–49.

Parker, Douglass. "The Curious Case of Pharaoh's Polyp, and Related Matters." *Substance* 14, no. 2 (1985): 74–86.

Pascal, Blaise. *Thoughts, Letters, and Minor Works*. New York: P. F. Collier & Son Company, 1910.

Peperzak, Adriaan T. *Ethics as First Philosophy: The Significance of Emmanuel Levinas for Philosophy, Literature, and Religion*. New York: Routledge, 1995.

———. "Phenomenology—Ontology—Metaphysics: Levinas's Perspective on Husserl and Heidegger." *Man and World* 16, no. 2 (1983): 113–27.

Perpich, Diane. "Figurative Language and the 'Face' in Levinas's Philosophy." *Philosophy & Rhetoric* 38, no. 2 (2005): 103–21.

Petrilli, Susan. "Iconicity in Translation: On Similarity, Alterity, and Dialogism in the Relation among Signs." *American Journal of Semiotics* 24, no. 4 (2008): 237–302.

———. "On Communication: Contributions to the Human Sciences and to Humanism from Semiotics Understood as Semioethics." *American Journal of Semiotics* 24, no. 4 (2008): 193–236.

———. "Semiotic Phenomenology of Predicative Judgment." *American Journal of Semiotics* 24, no. 4 (2008): 159–92.

———. "Working with Interpreters of the 'Meaning of Meaning': International Trends among 20th-Century Sign Theorists." *American Journal of Semiotics* 24, no. 4 (2008): 49–88.

Pinchevski, Amit. *By Way of Interruption: Levinas and the Ethics of Communication.* Pittsburgh: Duquesne University Press, 2005.

———. "Emmanuel Levinas: Contact and Interruption." In *Philosophical Profiles in the Theory of Communication,* edited by Jason Hannan, 343–66. New York: Peter Lang Publishing, 2012.

———. "Ethics on the Line." *Southern Communication Journal* 68, no. 2 (2003): 152–66.

———. "Levinas as a Media Theorist: Toward an Ethics of Mediation." *Philosophy & Rhetoric* 47, no. 1 (2014): 48–72.

Poulos, Christopher N. "Accidental Dialogue." *Communication Theory* 18, no. 1 (2008): 117–38.

Puknat, Siegfried B. "Max Picard." *Books Abroad* 25, no. 4 (1951), 340–43.

Radford, Gary. *On Eco.* Belmont, CA: Wadsworth Publishing, 2002.

Radloff, Bernhard. *Heidegger and the Question of National Socialism: Disclosure and Gestalt.* Toronto: University of Toronto Press, 2007.

Reyes-Tatinclaux, Leticia. "The Face of Evil: Devilish Borges in Eco's *The Name of the Rose.*" *Chasqui* 18, no. 1 (1989): 3–9.

Rheinberger, Hans-Jörg. "Heidegger and Cassirer on Science after the Cassirer and Heidegger of Davos." *History of European Ideas* 41, no. 4 (2015): 440–46.

Richardson, William J. *Heidegger: The Man and the Thinker.* Edited by T. Sheehan. Chicago: Precedent Publishing, 1981.

———. *Heidegger: Through Phenomenology to Thought.* Dordrecht, Netherlands: Martinus Nijhoff, 1963.

Rickey, Christopher. *Revolutionary Saints: Heidegger, National Socialism, and Antinomian Politics.* University Park: Pennsylvania University Press, 2002.

Ricoeur, Paul. "In Memoriam: Emmanuel Levinas." *Philosophy Today* 40, no. 3 (1996): 331–33.

———. *Time and Narrative.* Translated by Kathleen McLaughlin and David Pellauer. Chicago: University of Chicago Press, 1985. First published 1983 by Éditions du Seuil.

Rockmore, Tom. "Heidegger after Farías." *History of Philosophy Quarterly* 8, no. 1 (1991), 81–102.

———. *On Heidegger's Nazism and Philosophy.* Berkeley: University of California Press, 1992.

———. "Philosophy, Literature, and Intellectual Responsibility." *American Philosophical Quarterly* 30, no. 2 (1993), 109–21.

Rockmore, Tom, and Joseph Margolis, eds. *The Heidegger Case: On Philosophy and Politics.* Philadelphia: Temple University Press, 1992.

Rolland, Jacques. Foreword to *God, Death, and Time,* by Emmanuel Levinas, 1–6. Stanford, CA: Stanford University Press, 2000.

Rollo-Koster, Joëlle. *Avignon and Its Papacy, 1309–1417: Popes, Institutions, and Society.* New York: Rowman & Littlefield Publishers, 2015.

Rosenzweig, Franz. *The Star of Redemption.* Translated by William W. Hallo. Notre Dame, IN: University of Notre Dame Press, 2005.

Rubenstein, Richard L. "The Philosopher and the Jews: The Case of Martin Heidegger." *Modern Judaism* 9, no. 2, (1989): 179–96.

Rubino, Carl A. "The Invisible Worm: Ancients and Moderns in *The Name of the Rose.*" *Substance* 14, no. 2 (1985): 54–63.

Rushing, Robert A. "From Monk to Monks: The End of Enjoyment in Umberto Eco's *The Name of the Rose.*" *Symposium* 59, no. 2 (2005): 116–28.

Rutkoff, Peter M., and William B. Scott. "The French in New York: Resistance and Structure." *Social Research* 50, no. 1 (1983): 185–214.

Safranski, Rüdiger. *Martin Heidegger: Between Good and Evil.* Translated by Ewald Osers. Cambridge, MA: Harvard University Press, 1998.

Sallis, Steven. "Naming the Rose: Readers and Codes in Umberto Eco's Novel." *Journal of the Midwest Modern Language Association* 19, no. 2 (1986): 3–12.

Salvo, Michael J. "Ethics of Engagement: User-Centered Design and Rhetorical Methodology." *Technical Communication Quarterly* 10, no. 3 (2001): 273–90.

Schalow, Frank. *The Renewal of the Heidegger-Kant Dialogue: Action, Thought, and Responsibility.* Albany: State University of New York Press, 1992.

———. "Revisiting the Heidegger-Cassirer Debate." *Comparative and Continental Philosophy* 4, no. 2 (2013): 307–15.

Scheindlin, Raymond P. *A Short History of the Jewish People: From Legendary Times to Modern Statehood.* New York: Oxford University Press, 1998.

Scholl, Inge. *The White Rose: Munich, 1942–1943.* Translated by Arthur R. Schultz. Hanover, NH: Wesleyan University Press, 1983.

Schrag, Calvin O. *Communicative Praxis and the Space of Subjectivity.* West Lafayette, IN: Purdue University Press, 2003. First published 1986.

———. *The Self after Postmodernity.* New Haven, CT: Yale University Press, 1997.

Schulze, Leonard G. "An Ethics of Significance." *Substance* 14, no. 2 (1985): 87–101.

Schuster, Marc-Oliver. "Bi-Paradigmatic Irony as a Postmodern Sign." *Semiotica* 183, no. 1/4 (2011): 359–77.

Scolari, Carlos. "Digital Eco_logy: Umberto Eco and a Semiotic Approach to Digital Communication." *Information, Communication & Society* 12, no. 1 (2009): 129–48.

Sheringham, Michael. "French Autobiography: Texts, Contexts, Poetics." *Journal of European Studies* 16, no. 1 (1986): 59–71.

Sluga, Hans. *Heidegger's Crisis: Philosophy and Politics in Nazi Germany.* Cambridge, MA: Harvard College, 1993.

Snyman, Gerrie. "Rhetoric and Ethics: Looking at the Marks of Our Reading/Speaking in Society." *Communicatio* 28, no. 1 (2002): 39–48.

Stone, Ira F. *Reading Levinas/Reading Talmud: An Introduction.* Philadelphia: Jewish Publication Society, 1998.

Tancheva, Kornelia. "Recasting the Debate: The Sign of the Library in Popular Culture." *Libraries & Culture* 40, no. 4 (2005): 530–46.

Taylor, Charles. *Sources of the Self: The Making of the Modern Mind.* Cambridge: Cambridge University Press, 2006. First published 1989.

Tijmes, Pieter. "Home and Homelessness: Heidegger and Levinas on Dwelling." *Worldviews* 2, no. 3 (1998): 201–13.

Tolkien, J. R. R. *The Two Towers: Being the Second Part of* The Lord of the Rings. New York: Ballantine Books, 1954.

Tresidder, Jack. *The Complete Dictionary of Symbols.* San Francisco: Chronicle Books, 2005.

Trezise, Thomas. Review of *Proper Names*, by Emmanuel Levinas. *Comparative Literature Studies* 37, no. 3 (2000): 352–60.

Trifonas, Peter P. "The Aesthetics of Textual Production: Reading and Writing with Umberto Eco." *Studies in Philosophy and Education* 26, no. 3 (2007): 267–77.

Ullmann, Walter. *A Short History of the Papacy in the Middle Ages.* London: Methuen & Company, 1972.

Ungar, Steven. "Aftereffect and Scandal: Martin Heidegger in France." *South Central Review* 6, no. 2 (1989): 19–31.

Vernon, Victoria V. "The Demonics of (True) Belief: Treacherous Texts, Blasphemous Interpretations and Murderous Readers." *MLN* 107, no. 5 (1992): 840–54.

Waite, Geoffrey. "On Esotericism: Heidegger and/or Cassirer at Davos." *Political Theory* 26, no. 5 (1998): 603–51.

Wald, Henri. *Introduction to Dialectical Logic.* Romania: Academieie Republicii Socialiste Romania, 1975.

Wiesel, Elie. *All Rivers Run to the Sea: Memoirs of Elie Wiesel.* New York: Alfred A. Knopf, 1995.

———. *Legends of Our Time.* New York: Schocken Books, 1968.

Wolin, Richard. "The French Heidegger Debate." *New German Critique* no. 45 (1988): 135–61.

———, ed. *The Heidegger Controversy: A Critical Reader*. Cambridge, MA: MIT Press, 1993.

Wood, Julia T. *Interpersonal Communication: Everyday Encounters*, 4th ed. Belmont, CA: Wadsworth/Thompson, 2004.

———. *Spinning the Symbolic Web: Human Communication as Symbolic Interaction*. Norwood, NJ: Ablex, 1992.

Yeager, Robert F. "Fear of Writing, or Adso and the Poisoned Text." *Substance* 14, no. 2 (1985): 40–53.

Young, Julian. *Heidegger, Philosophy, Nazism*. New York: Cambridge University Press, 1997.

Zeytinoglu, Cem. "Appositional (Communication): Ethics: Listening to Heidegger and Levinas in Chorus." *Review of Communication* 11, no. 4 (2011): 272–85.

Ziarek, Krzysztof. "Which Other, Whose Alterity? The Human after Humanism." In *Between Levinas and Heidegger*, edited by John E. Drabinski and Eric S. Nelson, 227–44. Albany: State University of New York Press, 2014.

Index

RONALD C. ARNETT is the chair and a professor of the Department of Communication & Rhetorical Studies at Duquesne University and the Patricia Doherty Yoder and Ronald Wolfe Endowed Chair in Communication Ethics. He is the author, coauthor, or coeditor of fourteen books and the recipient of five book awards, including the 2013 Top Book Award for *Communication Ethics in Dark Times: Hannah Arendt's Rhetoric of Warning and Hope* from the Communication Ethics Division of the National Communication Association. Arnett is the recipient of a number of other awards, including the 2005 Scholar of the Year Award from the Religious Communication Association, the 2013 Presidential Award for Excellence in Scholarship from Duquesne University, and the 2016 Paul Boase Prize for Scholarship, and was named the 2009 Centennial Scholar of Communication and Centennial Scholar of Philosophy of Communication by the Eastern Communication Association.